THE PAPER OFFICE, 2ND EDITION

THE CLINICIAN'S TOOLBOX™

A Guilford Series

Edward L. Zuckerman, Series Editor

CLINICIAN'S THESAURUS, 4th Edition
The Guidebook for Writing Psychological Reports
Edward L. Zuckerman

CLINICIAN'S THESAURUS
Electronic Edition, Version 4.0
Edward L. Zuckerman

BREAKING FREE OF MANAGED CARE
A Step-by-Step Guide to Regaining Control of Your Practice
Dana C. Ackley

THE PAPER OFFICE, 2nd Edition
Forms, Guidelines, and Resources
Edward L. Zuckerman

The Paper Office

2ND EDITION

FORMS, GUIDELINES, AND RESOURCES

Edward L. Zuckerman, PhD

THE GUILFORD PRESS

New York London

© 1997 Edward L. Zuckerman

Published by The Guilford Press
A Division of Guilford Publications, Inc.
72 Spring Street, New York, NY 10012

Printed in the United States of America

This book is printed on acid-free paper.

Last digit is print number: 9 8 7 6 5 4

Library of Congress Cataloging-in-Publication Data

Zuckerman, Edward L.
  The paper office : forms, guidelines, and resources / Edward L.
Zuckerman. — 2nd ed.
    p. cm. — (The Clinician's toolbox)
  Includes bibliographical references and index.
  ISBN 1-57230-104-X
  1. Psychiatric records—Forms. 2. Psychiatric records—Handbooks,
manuals, etc. 3. Psychotherapy—Practice—Handbooks, manuals, etc.
I. Title. II. Series: Zuckerman, Edward L. Clinician's toolbox.
  [DNLM: 1. Psychotherapy—organization & administration—United
States. 2. Records. 3. Jurisprudence—United States. 4. Private
Practice—organization & administration—United States. WM 420
Z935p 1997]
RC455.2.M38Z828   1997
616.89'14'068—dc20
DNLM/DLC
for Library of Congress   96-27737
                                                             CIP

To my beloved daughter, Lilly Charlotte Lawrence Zuckerman.

This book is for the education you richly deserve.

Acknowledgments

Many of my professional colleagues have generously taken the time to offer their advice, suggestions, and creations (and I hope that you, the present reader, will do the same; see below). In most cases their names appear next to their contributions throughout this book, and I must restate my gratitude for their assistance in making this book as useful to our professions as it has become. Thank you all.

Joan Anderson
Marc Andrews, ACSW, Pittsburgh, PA
Mitchell Berk, CSW, MA, Island Park, NY
Pearl Brostoff, PhD, Pittsburgh, PA
Margaret Burton, EdD, Pittsburgh, PA
Carol A. Carver, PhD, Corvallis, OR
David Clovard, MD, Raleigh, NC
Harry Corsover, PhD, Evergreen, CO
Estelle Disch, PhD, Boston, MA
Constance Fisher, PhD, Pittsburgh, PA
Roger Glover, PhD, Pittsburgh, PA
Sanford Golin, PhD, Pittsburgh, PA
Irvin P. R. Guyett, PhD, Pittsburgh, PA
Ronnie M. Hirsch, PhD, New York, NY
Glenn W. Humphrey, OFM, PhD, New York, NY
Susan Hutchinson, DSW, LCSW, Irvine, CA
Richard E. Jensen, PhD, St. Charles, IL
Herbert Klein, PhD, Jupiter, FL
Sam Knapp, EdD, Harrisburg, PA
Mark Leach, PhD, Hattiesburg, MS
Don-David Lusterman, PhD, Baldwin, NY
Robert E. McCarthy, PhD, Myrtle Beach, SC
Ray Milke, PhD, Pittsburgh, PA

David A. Miller, PhD, Kansas City, MO
Rita Pellow, PhD, Pittsburgh, PA
Joseph Rosenfeld, PhD, Southampton, PA
Mason B. Scott, EdD, Pittsburgh, PA
John M. Smothers, PhD, ABPP, Kensington, MD
Eugene Snellings, CSW, ACP, Baton Rouge, LA
Ruth H. Sosis, PhD, Cincinnati, OH

I also wish to express my appreciation to Bob Matloff and Seymour Weingarten of The Guilford Press for their continuing support and trust in the value of this project, as well as for their honesty and openness as friends and associates. The best thing they did for me was to provide me with an ideal editor, Barbara Watkins. She has been consistently smart, articulate, patient, enthusiastic, and a damn quick learner. I must also express my great appreciation for the tireless efforts of production editor Anna Brackett, whose superb sense of style, proportion, and language have greatly increased this book's readability, clarity, and value.

Contents

Note. All figures, forms, and handouts are shown in *italic.*

5. INTAKE AND ASSESSMENT FORMS AND PROCEDURES   185

List of Figures, Forms and Handouts

Introduction

Ways This Book Can Help You

This book is designed for both the novice independent therapist and the experienced practitioner.

If you are a clinician just entering independent practice, who wishes to start up a practice properly, this book will help you get organized and develop good professional habits. It will make you

- less vulnerable (and therefore less anxious) when doing clinical work,

- more efficient, and

- more profitable and stable as a business.

All of this should result in giving you more satisfaction with the career of therapist. This book cannot contain everything you should know to be in independent practice; it does contain all you need to make the correct initial decisions about office practices and paperwork, and so it will help you start out right.

If you have been in private practice for a few years, this book offers the means to update your practice to conform to current legal and ethical developments. We live in a world that has become more litigious. Standards of professional practice and conduct have evolved rapidly, becoming ever more complex and subtle. Private practice has become more difficult because of the anxieties raised by malpractice cases and ethics complaints. For all of us, the remedies for this anxiety lie in increasing our coping skills (such as by acquiring particular expertise), developing fuller and more realistic understanding of the issues, and taking preventative actions. As therapists, our best defenses against malpractice are to offer high-quality and thoughtful care, use rational and effective procedures, and document our reasons and decisions thoroughly.

The resources in this book are specifically and carefully tailored to meet each of these needs. *The Paper Office* provides the basic operational "tools" needed by psychotherapists of any orientation, training level, or discipline. It should be emphasized that they are designed for the solo practitioner and the small-group practice, and may not meet the needs of a large or diverse group, agency, prison, school, or military practice. In addition, *The Paper Office*'s forms and other materials are designed only for outpatient settings—not hospitals of any kind, and not university or teaching settings. However, I may be developing versions for some of these settings, and would be very interested in hearing from you if you have materials like this.

What This Book Contains

This book provides both practical information and ready-to-use resources:

- Brief, highly informative guidelines and checklists provide the facts needed to alert you to the most important legal and ethical issues, and to direct you in developing solid working procedures.

- Paper resources—sample documents and photocopiable forms—offer effective ways to meet specific challenges to your practice.

- This book is designed to function as "a malpractice risk reduction kit."

The forms and other materials offered are administrative and procedural. They organize information to support the delivery of clinical services and to protect both clients and therapists. These materials will enable you to do the following:

- Collect identifying and personal data.

- Guide the taking of relevant histories.

- Clarify a client's financial and insurance resources.

- Document the client's mental status and suicide risk.

- Organize the results of the intake evaluations (e.g., diagnoses, prognoses, treatment plans).

- Assure informed consent (to evaluation, treatment, release of records, etc.).

- Partially socialize clients into the way therapy unfolds.

This book assumes that you, the reader, are already a trained, practicing clinician. It assumes that you know how to do evaluations and therapy, and that you deal with clients and families. Therefore, the forms offered in this book are not forms for collecting data on symptoms or dynamics. For example, although you are offered a way of summarizing a client's mental status (Form 35), you are not given any tests or protocol of questions to collect the data the form summarizes.

Unique Features

The professions' ethical standards, principles, and guidelines have been incorporated into each form and sample document. This avoids the remoteness of reading about abstract principles, the narrowness of individual case studies, and the possibility of overlooking the necessary application of an important principle in your practice's procedures and paperwork. Jerome S. Bruner refers to this kind of educational design as "scaffolding." After the principles are learned through these applications, they can be more easily applied to new situations through your sensitized and enhanced ethical reasoning.

The forms and other materials have been designed and updated to meet current legal and ethical standards for the practice of psychotherapy by the several disciplines. As you know, there are significant differences in these standards by state, discipline, and population. To be comprehensive, this book tries to include any point or issue raised in any jurisdiction. It is very likely that concerns now raised in only a few places will eventually be applied in every location, and so these should be addressed now. The courts, the mass media, and the public have generally not paid attention to the differences among the professions, and so the book is inclusive in this respect as well.

However, you must know your local rules. Although I have made sincere and extensive efforts to be inclusive, I cannot guarantee that these materials will meet *all* the ethical and legal rules of *all* professions and jurisdictions. Your best sources of current and localized information are your state's and discipline's organizations. Join them, contribute to them, and participate in them; doing so will make you more aware and sophisticated, and will keep your practice up to date. This knowledge is necessary for continuing to use the best practices and for reducing your risks.

In a similar vein, some readers have asked whether this book has been read and reviewed by lawyers. It has not, both because of the problem stated above of local and discipline differences, and because there would be some conflicting opinions that could not be resolved. Instead, I have relied heavily on published articles that have had the benefit of peer review, and on books by authorities who represent the consensus or vanguard in the field.

How to Use This Book in Your Practice

If you are an experienced clinician, read the table of contents for the forms and other materials you think are most important to the way you currently practice. Some will be ones you know you should implement to meet ethical and legal standards; others will make you more efficient and help you be better organized.

If you are a beginning practitioner, I recommend that you start with the materials offered in "Quick Start," below.

The sections of this book are generally organized as follows:

- The background you need to make use of the forms or other materials is offered first. Much of this information is displayed for rapid learning in the form of guidelines and checklists.

- The legal and ethical aspects and options for each element of the forms or sample documents, and any areas where these can be modified for your own practice, are described next.

- The model forms or other materials are then presented. (Note that the in-text discussion of each form or handout is indicated in the left margin with the form or handout number itself in a box; e.g., FORM 1 .)

Quick Start: Recommended Basic Materials

Form 18   First-contact record
Form 22   Client demographic information form
Form 23   Client clinical information form
Form 24   Brief health information form
Form 25   Chemical use survey
Form 26   Financial information form
Form 28   Adult checklist of concerns
Form 29   Child checklist of characteristics
Form 31   Intake interview questions and guide
Form 32   Mental status evaluation and report
Form 34   Suicide risk assessment summary and recommendations
Form 35   Intake summary and case formulation
Form 36   Individualized treatment plan for managed care organizations
Form 39   Structured progress note form
Form 42   Briefer form for requesting/releasing confidential records and information
Form 44   Release-of-records form letter

This collection of materials can be produced for your practice in just a few minutes for a few cents, and more can be made as needed. The forms will photocopy clearly and look quite professional. On these forms, a 2-inch space at the top is allowed for your own letterhead. If you want to modify them or use ones that must be tailored to your practice, you can use the CD-ROM that contains the text of all the forms and sample documents you will need (see below), or you can retype the wording for yourself.

Use the forms for 3 months with every new (and some old) clients. Mark the end of the 3-month period in your appointment book when you start. Then relax and focus on doing a fine job as a therapist. After 3 months, review how the forms are working for you. Decide which additional forms you want to incorporate into your practice or what changes you need to make to fit them better into your practice. Make any modifications or additions, and write to me with your suggestions and criticisms. If you make changes, please see the section below on sharing your changes.

Availability of Materials on CD-ROM

To save you time and effort, a CD-ROM is included here (in a pocket inside the back cover) that contains the text of all the forms and other materials you might use in your practice. **You can copy these materials onto your computer's hard disk and open them as simple word-processing documents.** Then add your letterhead and make any changes to customize them to your setting, style, and local rules.

Windows users: The CD enclosed has a folder named Windows containing files in three formats: Microsoft Word 6.0, Rich Text Format (RTF), and ASCII. If you do not use Word, almost any other kind of Windows-based word processor can open Word or RTF files. (You may need to adjust some of the formatting to your specifications.)

Mac users: The CD-ROM enclosed has a folder named Mac containing files in two MacIntosh formats: RTF and ASCII. ASCII is the "lowest common denominator" or default format in which text is stored on computers. The ASCII version will give you all of the words but none of the formatting for the forms in the book. Therefore, you will have to spend some time inputting, on your computer, the boldface, underlining, fonts, margins, and other formatting that you desire. Instructions for installing and using the CD are on the last page of this book.

Continuing Education Credits

Psychologists may earn five continuing education (CE) credits for mastering the material covered in *The Paper Office*. A CE test in Microsoft Word, RTF, and ASCII formats is provided on the enclosed CD-ROM (see the last page of this book for details on retrieving it). The test should be printed out, completed, and mailed to The Guilford Press according to the instructions that appear on it. A processing fee of $45.00 is due upon submittal of the completed test. Additional test forms may be requested free of charge from Guilford, if needed. Guilford Publications is approved by the American Psychological Association to offer CE credits for psychologists and maintains full responsibility for the program.

A Cautionary Note and Disclaimer

Although the publisher and I have made reasonable efforts to assure that the contents of this book are both accurate and up to date, we cannot be responsible for matters beyond its scope or level of detail, local variations, or future developments. For example, the laws and regulations that apply to your work as a clinician may be federal, state, or local, or they may pertain specifically to drug and alcohol clients, clients of mental health/mental retardation programs, clients of specific government programs, or AIDS patients. In addition, special rules may govern practitioners working in schools, health facilities, outpatient clinics, or the like. Your local professional societies and experts on the scene are the best sources for information about current and applicable rules, both ethical and legal.

Neither the publisher nor I assume responsibility for any loss incurred as a result of the application of any of the information contained in this book, or for any incidental or consequential damages in connection with or arising out of the furnishing of the materials in this book. No representation is made that they are the only or best ways to practice as a professional psychotherapist. This book is intended to assist an informed intermediary in the treatment of clients and patients, that is, the professional psychotherapist. It is neither recommended nor appropriate for use by amateurs or for self-help.

This book is sold with the understanding that the publisher, distributors, and I are not attorneys, accountants, or ethicists, nor are we engaged in rendering legal, financial, ethical, or other professional consulting services. If materials other than those presented here are needed to manage the purchaser's professional practice or a specific clinical case in any respect, we advise you to engage the services of a competent professional. Any forms that create a contract between the practitioner and the client should be reviewed by your legal counsel and should be modified to conform to local law and practice.

No warranty is expressed or implied and in no event shall the publisher, author, or any reseller be liable for consequential or incidental damages.

About Reproducing Materials in This Book

One of the main advantages of this book over other books on ethics or practice is the high quality of the materials—the forms, checklists, patient education handouts, and so forth—and it was probably for these materials that you purchased it. However, before you begin using these materials to enhance your practice, I must remind you of the legal context of copyright in which they exist. **I have legal copyright to many of the forms and handouts in this book,** but I want you to be able to use them in your practice. Thus, I ask the following:

1. You, the individual professional who purchased this book, may photocopy or print from CD-ROM any of the forms and handouts in the book for which photocopying rights are expressly granted in the form's or handout's caption, but only for use in your individual clinical practice and with your own patients.

   This means you cannot give copies to your associates, supervisees, friends, or other professionals for their own use. A professional should not use these forms without understanding fully their ethical and legal underpinnings, context, and implications, and not owning the book will significantly limit that understanding and expose him or her to increased malpractice risk. If others want to use these materials they must purchase a copy of *The Paper Office* themselves.

2. You may modify the reproducible forms and figures to suit your practice or your needs. In fact, **you should modify them** for the specific legal or other conditions that apply to your practice, and in any way that will further your clients' understanding. However, modification does not invalidate my copyright.

- Again, the modified version can only be used in your individual clinical practice with your own patients.

- If you do modify them and feel that you've made a significant improvement, please send me a copy so that I can see if your changes should be incorporated into the next edition of *The Paper Office*. If they are, you will receive full credit in that edition and a free copy of it.

3. If you work in a clinic or group practice and want to use these materials in that setting; you must buy a copy of this book for each individual who will use the materials. Multiple-copy discounts are available.

4. If you are leading a class, workshop, or other educational program and want to distribute copies of some of these materials you should do the following:

   - Review the law regarding copyright restrictions on what is and is not "fair use." For example, decide whether providing copies of the materials in this book would in any way reduce the sales of the book, which would then make your distribution illegal.

   - Consider requiring students to purchase copies of this book, because the use of these materials without the legal and ethical guidance contained in this book may get them into trouble.

5. Some materials in this book are copyrighted by individuals who did not grant reproduction rights beyond their publication in *The Paper Office*. Therefore, such materials may not be reproduced without the written permission of the copyright holder indicated on the form itself.

6. In addition, all materials for which photocopying rights are not given in a caption, and that are not copyrighted by other individuals, are copyrighted by Edward L. Zuckerman. Their reproduction is forbidden without prior written permission from Guilford Publications.

Your Forms and Other Contributions: A Nice Offer

- If you're disappointed with any part of this book, send in your criticisms and improvements.

- If you need forms or materials not offered here, let me know.

- If you design or find better or additional forms that you think should be included here, please send them to me for the next revision of this book or for specialized versions of *The Paper Office*. You will receive full credit for your contributions and comments if they are used, and you will receive **a free copy of the next version or edition** if your valuable contributions have been included.

Send your contributions to me at this address:

Edward L. Zuckerman, PhD
P.O. Box 222
Armbrust, PA 15616
(e-mail: edzucker@westol.com)

Future Developments

As this field develops, this book will be revised to meet the needs of practicing clinicians. The publishers and I will be very grateful for your comments, suggestions, and criticisms. There is a feedback form at the back of the book to make your contributing easier. If you bought this book directly from the publisher, your name will be put on a mailing list, and you will be advised when new editions become available. If you bought it from another source (a bookstore, etc.), please complete and return the feedback form to receive notices of updates.

It is my hope that by sharing the best efforts and ideas I have been able to borrow, modify, and devise, this book will make your professional life easier and more productive, and will further the professional development of all the practitioners of the craft of therapy.

CHAPTER 1

Basic Paperwork and Communication Tools

1.1   Basic Paperwork Tools: An Overview

> *I must create a System or be enslaved by another man's.*
> —WILLIAM BLAKE

Your psychotherapeutic skills and personal resources are the basis of your effectiveness as a therapist. But practice also requires the effective operation of your professional office, and this is based on specialized paperwork. This book presents the essential paperwork tools to help you operate a solo or small-group psychotherapy practice ethically, legally, and profitably.

First, therapeutic practice has ethical dimensions. Mental health clinicians have been in the forefront of the development of professional ethical guidelines. Concepts such as confidentiality, informed consent, and boundary issues have been articulated through careful deliberations. Professional ethics safeguard patients, enhance therapists' trustworthiness, and improve the climates of communities.

Therapeutic practice also has legal dimensions. Therapists live and work in a complex and rapidly developing legal context designed to protect the individual and reinforce socially approved behaviors. The United States is a nation under laws, and social policies are incorporated into laws.

Finally, therapeutic practice has financial dimensions. The delivery of U.S. health care services is inescapably intertwined with commerce, and mental health services are no exception. Therapists must be paid for services, and so financial functions such as income, expenses, fees, billing, and taxes must be attended to. Therapists operate in offices and meet for appointments, and so they use standard business resources and office equipment.

Thus, there are four aspects of a psychotherapy practice: the therapeutic, the ethical, the legal, and the financial. These four dimensions interact, intertwine, and may compete with one another. We, as professional therapists, need to take account of all of them. We must also respond effectively to their continually evolving interactions. Sometimes the demands of doing so seem burdensome, but we cannot ignore them. This book is one carefully reasoned response to this burden and obligation.

Each tool in *The Paper Office* has a primary function in one of these four areas, but each tool also has ramifications in the other areas. For example, stationery and business cards are important business tools. But the professions have important legal and ethical rules about how therapists present themselves. Similarly, the making and keeping of financial and treatment records are basic administrative office tasks. But rules of confidentiality mean that treatment records cannot be handled and copied like documents in other kinds of business. Also, ensuring payment for services is essential, but the way this is done can affect treatment in many ways that are unique to the practice of psychotherapy. **This book's photocopiable forms and sample documents, guidelines and checklists, and step-by-step procedures will help you integrate the relevant legal and ethical principles and current practices into your ordinary paperwork, thus lightening your burden.** The adoption of just those tools and procedures appropriate for your practices will reduce your malpractice and ethics violation risks substantially. Review the materials described in the following chapters, and evaluate for yourself how much they will lower your anxiety over your practices.

This first chapter begins (at the beginning) with an overview of some office administration basics: What needs to go on a letterhead and in a resume, and what should not? What records do you need to keep? Where and how should you keep them, and for how long? Chapter 2 takes a detailed look at financial tools and procedures, from tracking income and expenses to procedures for billing and to methods for getting paid. Chapters 3 and 4 explore practical ways to meet the ethical and legal requirements of practice, including methods for reducing malpractice risk, and a range of specific tools for obtaining informed consent. Chapters 5 and 6 offer detailed forms and procedures for recording treatment from intake through termination. Chapter 7 offers methods for ensuring confidentiality and offers many forms and form letters for releasing and obtaining client records. The Appendix is a guide to further resources.

1.2 Presenting Yourself on Paper

Ethical Aspects of Self-Presentation

In choosing the wording that presents you and your practice to the public, it is important to recognize that there are legal, ethical, and rational differences between competence, credentials, and titles. The American Psychological Association (APA, 1992a) code of ethics states that the psychologist must not misrepresent himself or herself in regard to training, skills, or credentials. Furthermore, it is solely the professional's responsibility to assure the absence of confusion, ambiguity, or falsity. **Be certain that your credentials are stated accurately and precisely every time.**

Guidelines for Clear and Accurate Self-Presentations

- Always use your highest degree. Earlier ones are unnecessary, and their use suggests pomposity (always inappropriate in a therapist) rather than extra training. However, it *is* appropriate to use two degrees if the degrees are in different but relevant fields (e.g., a forensic psychologist's possession of a PhD and a JD). Use the exact degree's abbreviation rather than "Dr."; this lessens confusion. Do not use both "Dr." and "PhD" or "EdD"; this is redundant. "Ph.D." and "PhD" are both acceptable styles because they do not mislead. "PhD" is a more modern style.

- The use of "Doctor" for nonphysicians is acceptable in casual conversations and nonmedical settings, where it is not misleading. Leading-edge thinking also suggests that those having a doctorate from a nonpsychological program (such as biochemistry) should not use "Doctor" in psychological settings.

- A professional title is optional but often clarifying. However, depending on the state, some titles have legal definitions. Check your state's definition of the following to ensure legitimacy: "consultant," "evaluator," "clinical psychologist," "counselor," "therapist," "psychoanalyst," and "psychotherapist."

- No one can use the title "psychologist" in any state unless he or she is licensed or similarly credentialed. "Licensed psychologist" (or "certified psychologist") is now considered acceptable, but this was not always the case. Using both words together was seen as redundant. It was also seen as misleading, in that it seemed to suggest that a *"licensed* psychologist" was somehow better than just a "psychologist," or even that there were *unlicensed* psychologists. "Licensed psychologist" is currently permissible, however, and you can include your license number for clarity.

- Specialties of practice (e.g., "practice confined to children" or "forensic evaluations," or perhaps someday "pediatric forensic evaluations") are useful to introduce yourself to other professionals or possible referrers, and to convey your areas of competence. However, beware of creating false impressions, because you will have to deliver what you advertise at a high level of expertise. When clinicians present themselves to clients as having certain areas of competence, the courts have generally held them to the standards that professional organizations set, even if the clinician is not a member of such organizations or qualified for membership. Evidence of competence differs by specialty (e.g., by the Academy of Certified Social Workers, National Register of Health Service Providers in Psychology, board certification), so know and use only the ones appropriate for your profession, and be scrupulous about your qualifications. There are "boards" whose only requirement for membership is paying a fee. Do not bother to join such boards, because other professionals know which are real credentials and which aren't. They will think less of you and your real credentials if you indicate membership in such "junk boards."

- "Member/Fellow [as appropriate] of the American Psychological Association" is now acceptable. For years it was frowned on because it suggested a credential where there was none; there is no special training or particular skill required for APA membership. However, it does represent conformance to the APA's ethical code, and so is quite important.

The Name of Your Practice

Your practice's name is up to you. The simplest option is to be yourself: "First name Last name, Degree," or, more traditionally, "John Doe, PhD."

You may also create a name for your practice, such as the professional-sounding "Associated Associates" or the grandiose "The American Research Foundation for Interpersonal Therapeutics." This is called "doing business as" (D/B/A). Descriptive terms such as "Therapy" or "Counseling" may be useful pegs to keep you in others' memories, but some have been used so often that they offer no identity. Check the phone book for examples, and try for some uniqueness. Location names are assumed to stick in memory (e.g., Allegheny, Gateway, and Three Rivers are popular in Pittsburgh), and they may be helpful, as patients (or at least referrers) seem to prefer a local therapist.

If you are going to operate your practice under anything other than your real name, you need to register this D/B/A name with your state government for legal reasons. Usually the appropriate government office is called something like the Corporation Bureau of the Department of State. You can call your practice anything except a name someone else has already taken or something a government official finds improper. You will need to fill out a simple form that identifies you as the person behind the facade, pay a small fee, and publish the name in your local newspaper of record. The newspaper's classified ad department will help you with the procedure, and the fee for this is modest.

Your Stationery and Cards

Checklist for Necessary Information for Letterheads

❏ Use your legal name without nicknames (unless you live in the South, in a small community, or in some other locality where nicknames are acceptable). If there is a similarly named professional in your area, add initials or, better yet, a distinguishing subtitle or practice name.

❏ Include your highest degree, specializations, and credentials.

❏ Include your complete address with zip codes. Use all nine digits these days. (Remember, the referral or check lost in the mail is worse than worthless; it's a hassle.) If you have multiple addresses, indicate them, but make it clear to which address mail (especially payments to you) is to be sent. Do not use abbreviations (e.g., Bldg.), as they are tacky and do not save space on a letterhead. In particular, avoid using erroneous or outmoded abbreviations (e.g., Penna. is archaic for Pennsylvania).

❏ An e-mail address on all your forms is no longer an affectation. I recommend its inclusion, both for its convenience and for the image it conveys of someone who is in the *avant garde* or at least *au courant*.

❏ Your telephone number should always include your area code. You can add a note like "24-Hour Answering Service," if it's true and you want to encourage after-hours calls. If you will be getting a separate fax line, and are getting new phone numbers, order both numbers at the same time and you can get them in sequence for simplicity.

❏ List your Social Security or tax identification number and license number (with type and state) on anything that will become a bill or accompany a bill, because insurers need these to pay you.

❏ Check and recheck the accuracy of *every word and number* before you print hundreds of any card or paper. I once had to rewrite my area code on 1,000 cards.

Logos

Logos are popular but not yet standardized. Orthopedists are using a braced-tree design, podiatrists a foot in a winged serpent (Aesculapius) design, and psychologists and psychotherapists the Greek letter "psi" (Ψ), but these devices have no meaning for the uninitiated. Most stationery printers offer at least one other logo you might consider, or you could use a simple letter monogram. You may want to design a logo suitable for the name of your practice (tree motifs are non-threatening). You could have the printer do it for a small charge, or actually hire a professional who has done this before and have a really good job done. (Therapists are notorious for their resistance to using other professionals.) If you can't find an experienced artist, call the owners of a funeral home that has a nice text/logo and ask who did theirs. (This is a good tip—really!)

Phrases such as "We care for you" are tacky. You don't really care for the people who may see your card until they become patients, and we should presume that all therapists care for their patients (as noted by Constance Fisher, PhD, of Pittsburgh, PA).

Type Style and Size

You cannot go wrong with a typeface from one of the large medical stationery printers. Roman is preferable to *italic*. **Bold** in small sizes is not sharp and uses more space. Serif and sans serif faces are equally acceptable these days for professionals. Larger type is easier to read for seniors (over 40 and also your likely referrers) and for anyone struggling with a seventh-generation photocopy: This is 10 point, this is 12 point, this is 14 point.

Paper and Envelopes

When I receive it, I always notice crisp, heavy, linen-textured, laid, 100% cotton rag, watermarked, ivory-colored bond paper. I fiddle with it and admire it, but am not impressed by the professional behind it—only curious about how much extra this person has to charge me or my clients for this affectation. Are there any documents created by therapists that deserve or need anything but ordinary 20-pound white paper? If the client's records are to be destroyed in a few years to prevent misinterpretation, why use archival acid-free paper that will last 200 years?

If you use a word processor, you may not need printed stationery at all. You can print the letterhead on each page as it comes out of your laser or inkjet printer (minimum 300-dot-per-inch resolution) or your letter-quality (24-pin) impact printer. Near-letter quality (9-pin) printers are no longer acceptable for business correspondence in this country. You can buy heavier or preprinted stationery in sheets designed to feed continuously into your printer, or you can buy a printer that takes cut sheets of your printed stationery if you prefer.

You need envelopes with your name and address, because if a letter is undeliverable it will be returned to you only if the return address is on the envelope. Your computer's printer may be able to print a return address on blank envelopes. Although this is not cheaper, it allows you to select a format to suit each letter and addressee.

For sending out bills, you will need envelopes imprinted with your name and address, or you can use a "two-window envelope" that shows your address through the upper window and the patient's address through the lower window. Save a tree: If you decide on imprinted envelopes, you need buy only a year's supply of #10 window envelopes for billing and regular imprinted envelopes for correspondence (a box of each, usually 500). No business occasion requires fancier stationery, so spend your money on your well-earned pleasures.

Business Cards

Business cards are essential. Carry a few in your wallet and in your datebook, because they have many purposes. You can offer a card to introduce yourself tactfully; the recipient can easily make conversation by inquiring about your location or what you have listed as your specialties. Since the cards have your address, give them when asking someone to send you something or to call you later. When you make presentations, always bring some cards to give to audience members so that they may call on you for professional services. You can also use them for small notes to others, or can use others' cards to note your promises to call or send something to them.

Plain black ink, slightly raised, roman lettering on a firm (but not too stiff), very white card is always acceptable. The catalogs of the major medical printers (see the Appendix, Section A.3b) offer dozens of designs, typefaces, and colors. After you have made some contacts in your practice area, you can discover the local standards of good taste by examining the cards for which you have traded and then follow these examples. Even so, wait until you have been in practice a few years before ordering 5,000, baby blue, translucent smoky plastic, gold-foil-lettered cards with a logo of doughboy figures hugging each other. (Yes, I received these from a therapist.) Remember the old rule about dressing for a party: You can always dress down from formal attire, but you can't dress up from jeans.

Some business cards incorporate an appointment card on the back. These can provide for single or multiple appointments and different formats; these features make the card even more useful and not much more expensive. Medical Arts Press offers a card that has "Questions to ask my doctor" or "Special instructions" printed on the back. Local printers could do the same for you if this makes sense for your way of practicing. If you have two related positions (e.g., a clinic staff job and a private practice), you can have each printed on one side of a card. If you do business in another language or country, you can have cards printed with translations or addresses on each side.

Announcement Cards

Announcement cards are usually heavy cardboard ("pasteboard"), paneled cards about 4" high and 5" wide, which you are supposed to send to anyone who might conceivably refer a patient to you. They simply announce the opening of your office, your specialties, and your location, or the fact that you have taken on a partner or moved. All the medical stationers' catalogs show sample designs from which to choose. I have 2,000 of them that I never sent. I don't keep the ones I receive because they do not fit into any filing system. The addresses are more easily found in the phone book, anyway. A better method might be to send a letter, which allows a fuller description of your work with some personalized elements, and include a few business cards (which *can* be filed) or perhaps a preprinted Rolodex™ card (see your local printer or run them off on your photocopier).

Sources

For sources of good-quality and inexpensive cards, stationery, office forms, and other products for health care professionals, again see the list of suppliers in the Appendix (Section A.3b).

Your Resume and Curriculum Vitae

A resume usually presents your current job functions or future goals, the strongest of your educational and vocational accomplishments, or other relevant experiences. It is generally required if you are seeking to change jobs. Two pages is the maximum length, and one page is often all that others expect to read. A curriculum vitae (Latin for "course of life," usually abbreviated as CV) is more formal and professional in orientation. It is usually sequential and emphasizes any activities that bear on your career development (education, honors, scholarships, professional experiences, grants received, publications, memberships, licenses, etc.). The distinctions between a resume and a CV are often blurred these days, however.

Any bookstore will provide several books of samples and guidelines for writing a resume or CV and for phrasing one's accomplishments attractively. There are several from a small publisher called Ten Speed Press, which I like for their simplicity and efficiency, but which are not as polished and professional as some others.

Keeping your resume or CV on a word processor permits you to add new information easily and to reorganize and tailor information to the recipient's needs. For example, you might emphasize your teaching experience for a school consulting job, your clinical work and training for a hospital, or your publications for a research position. Always date it currently. As an effective alternative that will get more attention when many people apply to the same job, you can write up your resume as a letter, describing your skills and history together.

Many professionals keep a file folder labeled "Resume" (or "CV" or "Professional Development") in which they place any paper that documents activities to be added to the resume or CV, such as presentations made, publications, training received, continuing education unit credits, or anything that mentions them by name. Periodically, they then update the resume or CV from this folder.

Keep copies of your resume or CV available and up to date, so you can give it to potential consultees, other professionals, referrers, credentialing groups, hospital medical staffs, and potential employers. It should function as an expanded business card. In particular, if you do any public speaking, bring a full resume or CV (as a resource for those who hired you) and a one-paragraph narrative presentation of your relevant credentials and experiences, printed or typed in large letters. Ask the person introducing you to read it to the group. Remember, your peers (and an ethics committee) will hold you alone fully responsible for assuring that the media present you correctly.

Checklist for Your Resume or CV

❏ Plain white paper is sufficient unless you are applying for a job where your sense of style matters.

❏ Use one typeface, and only a few **boldfaced** words. Use underlining instead of italics only if you are typewriting. Using ALL CAPITALS is like shouting, so be judicious. Boldface is a tasteful emphasizer if used with discretion. Do not use fancy layout or display typefaces.

❏ Your resume or CV must be scrupulously accurate—no lies, distortions, exaggerations, or other misrepresentations. These are ethical violations and reportable as such, which might cut short your promising career. Careful readers who find inappropriate statements will lose faith in your competence.

❏ Both resumes and CVs are business forms, and so there is no room for your sex, marital status, age, children, hobbies, musical interests, charitable or religious activities, or the like. If in doubt, leave it out. However, many people offer both a work and home address and phone, because professional contacts are often blended into social ones.

Creating a Different Version of Your Resume or CV

It is helpful to have at least two versions of your resume or CV. The "maximum version" should have every heading and entry, name and date. New material can be added, and selections from it can be tailored to specific audiences. A single-page "synoptic version" can be used for others less fascinated with *all* of your accomplishments.

Figure 1 shows a partially filled-in sample CV, to illustrate the headings and layout for a maximum version.

1.3 Your Appointment Book

We all need a simple way to keep track of our obligations. Call it an "appointment book," "datebook," "calendar," "schedule," "little black book," or "*vade mecum*," but it is a necessity of every practitioner. I have found it practical to operate by the rule "If it is not in my book, it does not exist," and so I write down all plans and appointments, both personal and professional. However, it appears to be a universal law that anything written in your datebook in ink will have to be changed.

Your appointment book is a record of your business; thus, it should be kept indefinitely. It not only documents your activities, but also records the services you rendered. It can be

SIGMUND J. THERAPIST
1001 Spectacular View Lane
Terrific City, Supreme State 12345
(900) 555-1212

January 15, 1997

EDUCATION

1975   PhD in Clinical Psychology—Distinguished University, Sovereign State
1971–1972   Internship in Clinical Psychology (American Psychological Association-approved)—Psychology
            Department, Splendid Health Center, Altered State University, Altered State

ADDITIONAL EDUCATIONAL EXPERIENCES

HONORS

CREDENTIALS

1975   Licensed as a Psychologist in Supreme State, Number 12345
1977   National Register of Health Service Providers in Psychology, Number 12345
1977   Fellow, American Psychological Association, Number 1234-5678

TEACHING EXPERIENCE

1986–1997   Superb University, Department of Psychology, Terrific City, Supreme State 12345
            Adjunct Associate Professor since 1988

CLINICAL PRACTICE

1978–1997   Independent Practice of General Clinical Psychology at Excellent Hospital, Terrific City,
            Supreme State 12345

RESEARCH/CONSULTATION EXPERIENCE

1968–1970   Research Assistant (half-time)—Project Champion, Psychology Department, Magnificent University,
            Marvelous City, Ecstatic State 12345

PUBLICATIONS

TRAINING PROGRAMS PRESENTED

RECOMMENDATIONS

            Professional, business, and personal recommendations are available.

REFERENCES

FIGURE 1. Sample curriculum vitae, partially filled in.

of value with the tax people or in court, and can be used to reconstruct your day even years later, so keep your old ones.

What an Appointment Book Should Include

Because most diaries do not cover time beyond 5 P.M. and have no other features, they are unsuitable for many private practitioners. Look for a book that covers an 8 A.M. to 9 P.M. schedule. The diary should also include a phone/address book (removable for transfer to the next year's book), an area code map, and spaces for daily notes. With all this, it should nevertheless be small enough to fit into a shirt pocket or purse.

The Ohio Psychological Publishing Company sells an appointment calendar that has a 13-hour-per-day, 6-day-per-week schedule, with 15-minute intervals to meet the needs of even the most "workaholic" clinician. It also includes DSM and ICD codes, a listing of psychotropic medications, mental health law terms, and other useful sections. It is 8½" × 11" and lies flat when open. If you write, ask for the company's catalog, as it has many excellent publications. See the Appendix, Section A.4, for their address.

Computerized Datebooks and Schedulers

They say that computerized datebooks are the wave of the future, but for a small practitioner these can seem like using a howitzer to kill a hamster. You may not have the computer when or where you want to record an appointment. You have to turn the computer on just to change an entry. Finally, these software programs change so frequently that I cannot recommend any.

The "palm-top" computers and electronic datebooks must communicate well with your larger computers, so that the calendars on each can be integrated. Again, this hardware changes so fast that I cannot recommend any, but if you are curious you might look into the Apple Newton, Psion, Zarus, and Sony Magic Cap.

1.4 Basics of Record Keeping

One of the attractions of private practice is the freedom from agency-imposed requirements, and one of those most eagerly dispensed with is elaborate record keeping. Although you cannot escape the need for records, you can adopt record-keeping methods that are simpler and more closely tailored to your needs. Kagle (1991, p. 148) has an excellent discussion of the benefits of record keeping for the clinician.

You will need to keep both business or financial records and case or clinical records. Keeping them separately is simpler. Business records consist of your income and expense records, checkbook, payrolls, tax forms, business and professional licenses, billing forms, and so forth. Your accountant can help you set these up efficiently. (Get an accountant; it's a good investment.) For a detailed discussion of financial record keeping, see Chapter 2.

Clinical records (whose confidentiality must be protected) include your datebook or schedule, case records (including intake forms, treatment plans, progress notes, referral notes, periodic summaries, discharge plans, etc.), correspondence with clients and with others about clients, and the like.

For guidance in recording the intake and initial evaluation of a case, see the forms in Chapter 5. Chapter 6 covers treatment plans and what and how to record the progress of treatment. For a full discussion of confidentiality concerns, see Chapter 7.

The remainder of this chapter provides an overview of clinical records, including the reasons to keep them, the nature of their contents, and their physical structure and organization. It also includes a discussion of how to maintain the security of your records, and how long to retain them.

Why Keep Records?

First, records must be kept to comply with your profession's ethical expectations. For example, "Psychologists appropriately document their professional and scientific work in order to facilitate provision of services later by them or by other professionals, to ensure accountability, and to meet other requirements of institutions or the law" (APA, 1992a, Standard 1.23). A more recent set of record-keeping guidelines is provided by the APA's Committee on Professional Practice and Standards (1993). On the basis of these guidelines, many states (e.g., Pennsylvania) are *requiring* licensed mental health practitioners to keep records. You cannot disregard these requirements on the basis of expediency, concern for confidentiality, or a feeling that "My notes are only about process and are illegible, so they would be of no use to anyone else." If challenged by an ethics committee or in court, you will be held to your profession's standards, simply because you present yourself as a practitioner. **Not keeping records is now grounds for a malpractice claim.** Having no records is illegal and unprofessional, thus demonstrating poor care (Slovenko, 1973). "An inadequate record will itself be seen as evidence of sub-standard care, no matter what care was actually provided" (Weiner & Wettstein, 1993, p. 179).

Adequate record keeping allows you to defend yourself. Records will be your basic defense in the event of a malpractice or ethics complaint or other litigation. See Soisson et al. (1987) for the specific advantages of having good records in defending a malpractice claim.

In additon, your records document your provision of services. This is a legal obligation and is necessary to receive payment from anyone. "Courts and external review bodies view the absence of documentation in the record about an event as evidence that it never occurred, no matter what the subsequent claims of the clinicians" (Weiner & Wettstein, 1993, p. 179).

Records document the thoroughness of your assessment. They help you to organize your thoughts about a patient and case. Your records establish a baseline of current functioning for structuring treatment or for evaluating progress and the impact of providing services.

Records have many additional uses. Your records show whether a client meets an eligibility requirement (e.g., disability). They may be useful for some presently unknown hindsight evaluation (perhaps a psychological autopsy or the establishment of disability's onset) or for the patient's own use. They are needed for supervisory review, consultation, peer review, quality control, and statistical reporting. They may be needed to maintain the client's continuity of care in future therapy or with other therapists. They provide clues as to which treatments have been successful and which are to be avoided. They offer crucial information for interdisciplinary communication. They allow you to review past successes at a future time. They replace memory, which is often inaccurate. Records are useful for self-education and student education, or for research. Lastly, you need to keep records because you are being paid to.

To summarize, **keeping records is not optional.** If you currently do not take notes or take insufficient ones, you are not alone: 7.6% of the psychologists responding to one survey (Fulero & Wilbert, 1988) did not keep sufficient records or kept none. If you are among this group, you are playing with fire as well as doing your clients a disservice. Change now; set up your record-keeping practices before the sun goes down again.

What Should Be in the Records?

The minimum contents of clinical records are specified for psychologists (APA, Committee on Professional Practice and Standards, 1993). The following information must be provided in sufficient detail to allow another therapist to take over the case and to allow regulatory and administrative review of service delivery:

- Client identifying data

- Dates of service, types of service, fees

- Assessment

- Plan for intervention

- Other materials (e.g., consultations, summary reports, testing reports, supporting data, releases)

This is a very minimal list and does not cover all the reasons for record keeping as described above. *The Paper Office*'s content and forms are designed to meet and exceed these guidelines.

I agree with Knapp (1992a) that records should be the following:

- **Comprehensive.** All the relevant data should be included: names and addresses, fee arrangements, dates and kinds of services rendered, results of consultations and testing, correspondence, releases, reports prepared, notes of phone calls and meetings, progress notes, and discharge summary.

- **Objective.** Facts need to be separated from opinion; observable behaviors need to be included.

- **Substantive.** The diagnosis, presenting problem, treatment plans, and your rationale for each of these should be contained in the records.

- **Consistent.** Your behavior should match your treatment plan and diagnosis, or you should document the reasons for any inconsistencies.

- **Retrievable.** Your notes need to be readable, your records findable, and your charts organized.

- **Current.** You should make your notes in a timely fashion.

- **Secure.** You must make certain that your records are inaccessible to unauthorized others.

All of these characteristics are discussed below.

The Physical Structure for Organizing Your Case Records

As indicated above, each client must have a range of specific information in his or her record. It is a challenge to keep all of this information logically separated and yet easily accessible. Here are some possibilities. The first two methods are variations on using the traditional manila folder and the third uses a three-ring binder. I also briefly discuss computerized record keeping.

The Basic Manila Folder Method

FORM 1

You can use an ordinary manila folder for each client. Although this format is simple and cheap, it has liabilities: Loose pages can get lost or misplaced; also, pages and entries are kept in the sequence in which they were created, and so information is not organized by topic or relevance. This traditional, even classic approach to record keeping can be improved by developing a checklist of the contents (see Form 1) which can be printed on the outside of each manila folder. There is no indication of the client's name on the outside, for privacy reasons. You should tailor Form 1 to your own office procedures and forms.

Checklist for Client Records

Client # _____   **Intake date** _____

1. Informed consent materials

		Date	By whom

- ☐ Information brochure for clients given and signed
- ☐ Risks, benefits, outcome, alternatives of treatment discussed and noted
- ☐ Handout on limits of confidentiality given and signed*
- ☐ Duty to warn, danger to self/others discussed and noted
- ☐ Requests for records from others signed and sent*
- ☐ Payment policy discussed, agreement to pay signed*
- ☐ Consent/contract to treatment given and signed*
- ☐ Consent for follow-up given and signed*
- ☐ Consent to evaluate without commitment to treat discussed and noted
- ☐ Other consents discussed and noted (research, recordings, etc.)

2. Further evaluations or consultations needed—indicate questions to be addressed

- ☐ Medical: _____   ☐ Psychiatric: _____
- ☐ Vocational/educational: _____   ☐ Other: _____

3. Case management information

a. Referral received: Date _____ By whom? _____

b. First contact: Date _____ By whom? _____

c. Intake completed: Date _____ By whom? _____

d. Initial treatment plan sent to MCO: Date _____ By whom? _____

   Consultation with MCO reviewer named: _____ Authorization number: _____

   Number of sessions authorized: _____ Review schedule for: _____

e. Reauthorization request: Date _____ By whom? _____

   Consultation with MCO reviewer named: _____ Authorization number: _____

   Number of sessions authorized: _____ Review schedule for: _____

   Reauthorization request: Date _____ By whom? _____

   Consultation with MCO reviewer named: _____ Authorization number: _____

   Number of sessions authorized: _____ Review schedule for: _____

   Reauthorization request: Date _____ By whom? _____

   Consultation with MCO reviewer named: _____ Authorization number: _____

   Number of sessions authorized: _____ Review schedule for: _____

f. Forms and records requested and released

Req. date	Form/record	Sent to	On date	By

The Folder with Sections

The major medical publishers (see the Appendix, Section A.4, for names and addresses) have catalogs of systems specifically designed for recording of patient care efforts. For example, these may have dividers preprinted with various headings ("Intake," "Treatment Plan," "Legal Stuff," etc.) in a standard hospital or medical office chart. Different colors of paper can be used for each section, with the most frequently used pages in ordinary white. Look at all the options before you decide. Even if it costs more, an easier and more usable record-making system will pay for itself very soon. How much do you charge other people for your time? How much of it do *you* waste each month searching in your folders?

The Three-Ring Binder Method

Allow me to introduce Zuckerman's Unpretentious Clinical Keeping-of-Records System (ZUCKRS). It is a simple three-ring binder that holds all the materials about each active patient in a separate section and can be carried to the office each day. Although this system is almost embarrassingly low tech, it has been adopted by many of the therapists who have seen it.

The Binder. A plain vinyl-over-board binder without lettering or logo, in a dark color (like a dark blue suit), is always acceptable. Taste enters here: Neon pink will probably assure that you do not leave your book behind, but it may (or should?) clash with your office decor. You can express your taste, but inconspicuousness may be prudent. If your ego decides the binder is a good idea, use your therapy talents to overcome your feeling that binders are not for adults, or to curb your grandiose inclination to buy the alligator leather version. Different colors for different settings or offices do make sense. If your accountant encourages you to make capital investments, there are heavy-duty designs with piano-hinged covers and other features for tech lovers. The "D-ring" design is not necessary but may be easier on the pages. Buy the best quality, because the rings will meet evenly and the pages will not get caught. Use a binder sized for your current practice, and replace it with larger ones as your practice grows, but keep it underfilled for convenience.

Paper. You need filler paper designed for three-ring binders. This is discounted in August during back-to-school sales. It tears less when there is at least ¼" of paper next to the holes. When marked "college-ruled," it has lines a little less than ¼" apart. Cheaper filler paper is 8" × 10½", slightly smaller than a regular 8½" × 11" page, such as you would use for a form. Forms will then show at the outside margin or edge of the page, and this may be useful. Whatever kind of paper you choose, make it your standard. Use it for writing all your professional work, and always keep a supply of it everywhere you write. You will save great effort and time. This method allows you to keep all your professional work (teaching notes, consultations, bestseller-in-progress, etc.) in separate three-ring binders cleanly and efficiently. Using colored paper for different parts of the client's record is trendy, but, except for yellow, it won't photocopy as well as white. You will also need a three-ring punch for your forms and paperwork received.

Dividers. The common Mylar-reinforced dividers, especially with colored tabs, are usable. But better are the very wide dividers (9" × 11") made of the heaviest paper material or solid plastic, which are available at real stationers. These will last much longer and be neater. It is probably best not to write patients' names on the tabs or the edges of your forms for security reasons. Many people can easily read upside down. If you use alphabetical tabs you will be able to find a client's section quickly, but you will have to separate Smith and Smythe somehow. It may be easier simply to place clients in alphabetical order but to use unnamed dividers. The few seconds spent searching for the record can be a way for both the patient and therapist to focus mentally on what is going to be their work in the hour.

Checklist for the Contents of Each Client's Section. The following are listed in sequential order, not in order of importance. These contents are discussed and specific forms or sample documents are provided later in *The Paper Office* as indicated.

- ❏ A billing form (Form 5).

- ❏ First-contact record (Form 21) and similar records (see Section 5.2).

- ❏ Progress or session notes, and homework done by the client (see Section 6.2).

- ❏ Some blank paper for recording the session notes.

- ❏ Documentation of informed consent—for example, a signed copy of the client information brochure (se Section 4.2), and other forms and materials regarding treatment and consent to evaluation that appear in Chapter 4.

- ❏ Psychological testing done by you.

- ❏ Previous records (medical, psychological, educational, etc.) that you obtain (see Section 7.4). These would include copies of release forms you have used.

- ❏ Correspondence from, to, and about the client.

- ❏ Newspaper or other clippings about the client, or clippings that the client brings in.

- ❏ Anything else you think is relevant at present or in the future.

Computerized Client Records

The easiest way to keep clinical records on a computer is simply to create a folder or directory for each client, and to add a file or page for each visit. You can do this by creating a blank progress note (see Forms 42 and 43 for formats you can adopt) as a template (or "stationery"), and opening it each time you want to make a record. Fill in the current information, save it to the client's folder or directory, and entitle it with the client's initials and today's date. If you don't want to write so much, you can just open a file in each client's folder or directory called "Progress Notes" and add to what you have written before. Many of the computerized billing programs also now offer some way to incorporate progress notes. Keep in mind, however, that there are security considerations with all computer records; these are discussed in the next section.

When a Case Is Closed

After termination, or if the records become too bulky, a client's pages can be transferred from other formats to a manila folder and filed for "permanent" storage in a locked cabinet. If you indicate the dates of service provision on the outside, it will make it easier to prune your records after 15 years or whatever number of years you select as a disposal date (as suggested by Constance Fisher, PhD, of Pittsburgh, PA). See Section 1.6, below, on retention of records and their disposal.

1.5 Record Security

Keep all your case records, including the identifying data in your billing system, in a locked and secure place (APA, 1981). But remember Daniel Ellsberg's psychiatrist and the Nixon "plumbers"; no place is totally secure. A three-ring binder (see above) can be kept in your personal possession, which is sometimes better.

Computerized records, even billing information, must be secured as well. Many therapists quaintly insist on a paper "hard copy" backup of computerized records, without realizing that by printing out their records they have increased the risk of disclosure from almost zero to fairly high, because many more people can read paper than can use a computer. Some word processors include encryption programs like DES (Data Encryption Software, available on the internet from, among other sources, http://members.aol.com/aseone/index.html), but if yours does not, buy and *use* an encryption program such as Norton Utilities or Zimmerman's Pretty Good Privacy, which is unbreakable and free. You can get information about it at http://www.mit.edu/network/pgp.html (the commercial version is called ViaCrypt). The site http://www.epic.org/privacy/tools.html offers tools for encrypting telephone calls, e-mail, your hard drive, and anonymous e-mailers. However, if these sites are no longer working, try a search of the 'net under PGP and Zimmerman.

Secure your computerized records from disasters as well as prying eyes. Design a simple-to-use and practical-to-implement regular backup program for your computer records. Many computer programs' manuals will teach you how to set up one. (Yes, I know we all say we do this, and most of us still don't. I do now, but only after a painful disaster.) The simplest backup method is to make a copy each week of your clinical files to a floppy disk and store it off-site in a secure place. More sophisticated programs like Retrospect allow this to be done automatically on a schedule and only for those files that have changed.

If your computer ever needs service, anyone at the repair facility can read your clinical files, if you have not password-protected them, so this is a must. Finally, when you sell or give away your old computer, you should erase the files on your hard disk. Deleting the files or putting them in the Trash/Recycle Bin is not enough; when you do this, only their addresses are removed. You need to use a program like Norton Utilities to make them truly unrecoverable.

1.6 Retention of Records

When therapy ends and the case is closed, the records need to be preserved so that you can do the following:

- Comply with laws and ethics.

- Assure continuity of care (such as patient transfer).

- Defend yourself from some belated accusation. Despite statutes of limitations, the laws are in flux, and court decisions have extended the client's time to sue.

- Qualify the client for some services in the future (e.g., Social Security disability, a special college program for a person with a learning disability).

- Restart a case because a patient returns for treatment.

- Cope with some other situation that is presently unforeseeable.

How Long Should Records Be Kept?

When deciding what records to keep and for how long, you should consider your state's "statute of limitations" and the common rules of "5 years or more after a minor reaches majority" and "5 years after the end of treatment." The Internal Revenue Service requires you to keep business, not clinical, records of your income for 7 years. The APA's guidelines for clinical psychologists (APA, Committee on Professional Practice and Standards, 1993) mirror the federal policy: the full record for 3 years (after last contact or completion of services), and the full record or a summary for 12 more years for client welfare. (For example, Social Security disability, Title II, can entitle a client to payments if he or she was disabled within 5 years of last working/paying FICA taxes.) State laws vary. Different areas of law have different rules; malpractice may have a 3-year time limit, whereas the limit for breach of contract may be 6 years. Note that generally there is no statute of limitations on filing a complaint before a licensing board, and that records may be your best defense. On the other hand, records can become outdated and therefore invalid or of limited utility. If you have to release such records, make sure to inform the recipient of these limitations. When you are asked for a record, see Section 7.3 on releasing records.

Suggestions on Retaining Records

- If you have a secure space, keep the whole record for your own protection.

- Children's records should be retained until 5 years after they reach their majority, even though their findings may become out of date. Write that "discard date" on the outside of the folder when you close the case and store the record.

- Keep adults' records for 12 years, or keep a summary forever. Write the 12-year "discard date" on the outside of the folder when you store the record.

- At your established "discard date," destroy the records or offer to give them to another professional caring for the client. Design a mechanism to find a current address at some specified future time, and to send each patient a letter giving him or her the choice of having records transferred to a successor therapist whom they have seen or are seeing, or another practitioner (or anyone who would understand the issues) chosen by the patient. Do not offer clients the choices of receiving the records directly or of destroying the records, because (1) they cannot anticipate the needs for the records; (2) they do not own the records; (3) they do not have the training to understand the records; and (4) the records may be needed by you.

- Whatever procedures you choose, be sure to document it in sufficient detail, and keep copies of your plan where your attorney, your family, or another therapist can find it. Also, be absolutely consistent in using your procedures, because any exceptions would suggest to a malpractice attorney that you have something to hide.

Preserving Records When You Retire or Die

Your ethical responsibility for your records does not end with your retirement or death (Stromberg et al., 1988, p. 404). You are ethically required to protect the confidentiality of and access to your records if you should become unable to care for them. I suggest making a reciprocal, written arrangement with a therapist peer about availability and disposal. If you do not arrange it *this week*, you will forget.

If you are in a group practice, make this responsibility part of the group's agreement. For other situations, you need to consider the selection and motivation of a guardian of your records. It is best to have a fellow professional become the guardian. He or she will understand current confidentiality concerns and the applicable laws, and will be able to release records appropriately. The guardian should not be the executor of your will or your attorney. Decide how your ex-clients should be notified when you die, become disabled, or retire. They need to be informed of your record-maintaining policy, and of who will be the guardian of the records. Decide how accounts receivable are to be handled.

Disposal of Your Records

Even when destroying records, you have to maintain their confidentiality. You can't just throw them in the trash. A simple shredder isn't expensive but takes time. You might organize a group of your peers with old records to take them all to a professional disposal firm (look in the Yellow Pages under "Records"). A more thorough discussion of this topic and guidelines can be found in Hall (1987/1988).

CHAPTER 2

Financial Tools and Procedures

2.1 Setting Financial Policies for Your Practice

> Money matters will be treated by cultured people in the same manner as sexual matters, with the same inconsistency, prudishness, and hypocrisy. The therapist must be determined not to concur in this attitude, and in his [sic] dealings with patients to treat money matters with the same matter-of-course frankness that he wishes to induce in them in matters relating to sexual life.
> —SIGMUND FREUD (1913/1958, p. 131)

The provision of therapy is both a business and a profession. As a business, it involves un-avoidable dealings with money, and this is often problematic for therapists. They enter the field with a commitment to human service. Many have been trained at public expense or have worked in a public service setting; they may believe that making a profit from the misery in others' lives is unjust. However, the simple truth is that a therapist who does not succeed as a businessperson will not be able to work independently.

As a therapist, you *must* make decisions about many aspects of the business relationship with your clients. Choose options that seem fair, protective of both parties, and enforceable; then communicate them clearly, both orally and in writing. You will need policies to answer the following questions:

- When will you discuss money with the client?

28

- How much will you charge?

    Will you have different charges for different activities, or a per-hour charge for everything you do?

    Will you give discounts, do free therapy, or use a sliding scale of charges based on income?

    Will you charge for broken appointments, and if so how much?

- How will you handle insurance coverage?

    Will you accept only what the client's insurance will pay, and not collect anything from the client? (The insurers view this as potential fraud; see below.)

    Will you require "assignment of benefits" (be paid directly by the insurance company), or trust the client to pay you?

    Will you prepare insurance claim forms for patients, or simply supply a bill they can submit?

    Will you join managed care organizations' (MCOs') "panels" of providers and "participate" (i.e., agree to provide services at the rates set by third-party payers)?

- How will you handle delinquent accounts and when?

    Will you only send reminders and rebill, or use collection letters?

    At what point will you use collection agencies? Lawyers? Small-claims court? At what point will you write off bad debts?

    When will you discontinue seeing a patient for not paying your fees?

When you have made these decisions, incorporate them into your means of gaining informed consent (see Section 4.2, the client information brochure).

About Fees

Because few professional training programs teach about fees, some basics are covered here.

One of the "professional pleasures" offered by private practice is the freedom to take on a case that interests you without regard to the client's ability to pay. Do not let greed or fear take away this freedom. As you might guess, the belief that "paying for therapy is therapeutic" is endorsed most strongly by psychoanalysts and least strongly by social workers. It has repeatedly not been scientifically supported, and its popularity is generally declining (Pope, 1988c). A review of the literature found no clear relationship between fee paying and outcome (Herron & Sitkowski, 1986). Ethically, free therapy cannot be of a lesser quality than paid therapy, so do not try to cut corners; learn to live with this, or do not do *pro bono* (unpaid) work at all. The American Psychological Association (APA) strongly recommends that all psychologists do some unpaid work. The amount of such work is left to the conscience of the individual clinician. If a client has an unexpected and long-lasting loss of income, and neither termination nor transfer is desirable, you might consider your work *pro bono* and bite the bullet.

"Professional courtesy" (discounts to peers, health care providers, students, clergy, etc.) is rapidly disappearing because of social changes and the prevalence of health insurance. If a client who might be entitled to professional courtesy asks for it, you could probably offer a discount of 10% without too much pain.

Most therapists do not raise a private client's fee during the course of treatment, unless treatment lasts many years and inflation erodes the therapist's income. Clients and third-party payers seem not to mind some raises over time. I suggest that you change your fees yearly and indicate this in your client information brochure.

Finally, if you are terminating a client for lack of payment, be cautious and thorough, and try to get a payment plan agreed to. If it appears that it will be a sticky situation, consult with a colleague about issues of abandonment, client welfare, and the like, and note the consultation in your records. See also Section 6.3 on termination.

Ethical Guidelines on Fees

Pope (1988c) has examined the laws and ethics pertaining to fee policies and procedures. The following discussion is based on his suggestions for avoiding common pitfalls.

Ethically, you should make financial arrangements in advance of treatment, so that consent to treatment is fully informed. It is best to have clients know your charges before you even meet for the first time, so that they are not seduced by your interview into forming a relationship that then imposes financial hardship or is even exploitative. Tell the client your policies on raising fees during the course of treatment, charging for missed appointments, the maximum balance due you will tolerate, your use of a collection agency, and so forth. Make certain that the financial arrangements are fully understood by the client. For this a written fee policy is essential, and this policy should be stated in the client information brochure.

You should know by the end of the first evaluation hour, from the social history information you have obtained, whether a client is able to pay you. Therefore, **give no "free initial consultations,"** because the client is by then committed to you, having revealed his or her personal issues. (This is called "undue influence" by lawyers.)

Fee-splitting, that is, taking a fee or paying fees for making a referral, is still open to interpretation. The rules in psychology (APA, 1992a, Standard 1.27) allow fee-splitting when the client is fully informed in advance and the dividing of payment is based on the services provided and not payment for simply making the referral. However, this is too vague to enforce, local rules differ, and arrangements are often complex. In its later agreement with the Federal Trade Commission (APA, 1992b), the APA agreed not to prohibit paying for referrals.

Accepting payment for your services in anything but money is "barter." Barter is an ancient, flexible, and honorable method, and gives more people access to your services. The new APA code of ethics (APA, 1992a, Section 1.18) allows barter and offers some minimal standards and guidelines. However, barter presents great potential for abuse, exploitation, conflicts, and distortion of the professional relationship. I strongly recommend that you **do not barter** or exchange therapy for either goods (whose value can be questioned) or services (as this creates a dual relationship—i.e., that of employer–employee). Barter is a frequent source of ethics complaints. If a client has no money and you wish to help, offer your services *pro bono.*

Lastly, do not take contingency fees for forensic cases. Doing so appears to compromise your professional independence.

Setting Your Fee

Your "fee" is the amount you are willing to sell your services for. This should be the same as the amount you actually charge every client. Routinely accepting a lower fee by waiving insurance copayments is seen as fraud by third-party payers; when you do this, your actual, collected fee is not the stated fee you are charging the insurers. If you decide to accept a lower payment from a client in financial distress or for any other reason, do so only occasionally, with good reasons, and document your rationale in detail in your notes. Make sure you can justify the fee you set for each client; you may have to.

There is no standard method for setting fees, but here are some options:

- **Cost-plus pricing** is determining your fee by adding together your fixed and variable costs plus a profit. This is the traditional pricing method in many businesses, although not in private practice. But if you take the time to compute your costs (your "nut"), it will allow you to know whether you are really making a go of your practice.

- **Competitive pricing** is setting your prices to match, exceed, or underprice your competition, depending on whom you see as your competitors. Psychiatrists charge the most, with psychologists charging 80–90% of that, and social workers charging 70% or less. Counselors and psychiatric nurses charge about 50%. The newsletter *Psychotherapy Finances* (see the Appendix, Section A.1f) publishes a fee survey each year, with enlightening information and comparisons. Setting your fee at 90% of the UCR (usual, customary, and reasonable) fee of your peers in the area will prevent difficulty with the insurance company, but 100% is quite reasonable.

- **Pricing by negotiation** is accepting a price that is arranged in the marketplace of buyers and sellers. With private-pay patients, be mindful that they are needy and therefore not your equals in negotiating a fee. The negotiation process requires self-esteem and autonomy, which patients often lack. They also usually lack an appreciation of your (quite high) costs in providing your services. As you know, the actual buyers of mental health services for many clients are their employers or their employers' delegates—the whole panoply of MCO contractors. They do not appear to lack autonomy and negotiation resources. Although there are alternatives to managed care (see especially Ackley, 1997) developing a knowledge base in this area will be essential for most therapists (see the Appendix, Section A.1f).

- **Pricing by time** is charging for time, not for the services provided. This means charging everyone the same rate for any kind of service (therapy, consulting, teaching, supervising, etc.). Because it is rarely possible to charge for preparation, teaching and lecturing tend to be underbilled. You can try to reduce these costs by specializing in only a few topics at a time and by selling these preparations to several audiences.

- **Pricing by setting an income goal** is setting a yearly income goal, dividing it by the number of hours you want to work, and calculating your hourly charge. This is worth considering for life or financial planning. Is this a self-esteem test? Is this a test of how role-socialized you are? Did you pass?

Three further points: In the end, your services are only worth what someone will pay for them. Guilds (such as disciplines' organizations) may try to raise wages by reducing supply, legislation, negotiation, or other less open means. Also, by redesigning how to apply your knowledge, you can greatly change your income.

Discussing Fees

The resistance to setting up a fee arrangement in the first session comes almost completely from the therapist. If you say, "We can worry about the money later," you are increasing your uncollectable fees by 20%. It is also unethical because it prevents informed consent. One simple way of discussing fees is to raise the issue toward the end of the first session, after you have discussed the length of treatment. You can use phrasing like this:

> "There is one more issue we must talk about, and that is fees. My regular fee is $____ per session. Take a minute and consider what I have said about how long your treatment should take, and weigh your income and expenses, and tell me if you can afford that."

I find that most clients agree to pay this amount. If they say they cannot or appear very reluctant, I usually say, "Well, in light of your situation, tell me what you can afford and I will accept that."

I have used this policy for years with few abuses or regrets. However, it is a sliding scale and leaves you open to accusations of fraud by any insurers you deal with. If you adopt it, therefore, be aware that you are at risk even if you do not put anything like this in your client information brochure, because a patient may complain. It may be better to develop a credit policy for all patients. This is also a good time to introduce or reinforce paying for each session at its end. Note that these policies do not apply to those who have you bill their insurers or use MCOs.

If someone other than the client pays the fee, make that responsibility clear to the payer with a formal agreement (see Form 27). Also make it clear that this arrangement does not entitle the payer to confidential information. When the client is a child, however, parents do have the right to general information on progress. This should be spelled out in detail in your client information brochure (see Section 4.2).

Tips on Collecting Fees

- **Simply do not allow clients to run up large unpaid bills.** You should allow no more than two sessions without payment to elapse before you raise the issue with a patient, because unless you raise the possibility of legal or ethical consequences, you cannot terminate a client in great psychological need just for financial problems. If you extend credit, you should set a dollar limit, such as $1,000, on a maximum balance.

- Big balances may tempt patients to devise malpractice suits or ethics complaints to escape them. This is a major source of such complaints.

- The longer the delay, the smaller the collection. The established wisdom of collection agents is that if a payment is over 90 days late, you will collect 50% or less.

- If you allow a patient not to pay, you will both feel rotten. It sets a poor example by not handling disagreeable and important issues or delaying their handling. The patient may come to believe that you are not a good therapist.

- You may need a simple book of two-part receipts for the few patients who pay cash. Don't waste your money on custom-printed receipts unless you use the form for other purposes (see Form 4).

- If a client gives you a check that makes you suspicious, cash it *immediately* at the client's bank. If the account does not have sufficient funds, don't try again until you know the check will clear—you can call the bank every day or two and ask if the funds are there. When the account has the funds, cash the check immediately.

2.2 The Income Record

A record of your income is essential and can be as simple as a single page of inexpensive, ruled, 8½" × 11" accounting paper for each month with appropriate headings written. Figure 2 shows the type of income record I use, shortened here for space reasons, but you should adapt it to your style and needs.

For each month, I use a fresh sheet with eight columns, as shown in the figure. The date each check is received is recorded in the first column. I write the number of the check in the next column. This will assist in clarifications with a client should confusion arise, but this column is optional. The last name of the person who gave me the check is recorded in the third column. I add initials if the name is common and if I might take on another patient by that name.

The next three columns, "Office 1," "Office 2," and "Paychecks," correspond to categories I need to keep separate for tax purposes or for evaluating programs. I have two offices in different communities, so taxes are paid to two municipalities accordingly. Paychecks, from which taxes have already been deducted, are recorded in the third column. The "Other" column is reserved for special income that does not fit these labels.

Income Record

For: July 1999

Date	Check #	Source of income	Office 1	Office 2	Paychecks	Other	Deposits
4	207	Lenin	100				
	456	Nixon	75				
6	129	Stalin		100			575.00 (7/10)
8	567	Hoover, J. E.		200(I)[1]			
	130	Stalin		100			
11	—	Lenin	100($)[2]				
	459	Nixon	75				
12	938	Bonaparte		68			
14	004	Lecture to MIT				100	1,064.33 (7/17)
15	888	Lecture to KGB				100	
15	996				621.33		
Subtotals			350	468	621.33	200	
Grand total							1,639.33

[1] If it was an insurance payment, a letter "I" can be inserted to clarify the source.
[2] If a client pays you in cash, you can insert "$" to keep your records clear.

FIGURE 2. Sample income record.

I make deposits to my practice's checking account weekly. I cluster the checks in each deposit with a large bracket, and write the total amount and date of deposit in the last column. At the end of the month, the totals are recorded at the bottom of the page for each column and a grand total is computed. I use the monthly totals for estimating quarterly taxes to be paid. As your practice grows, actually endorsing each check with your signature and account number becomes tiring. Instead, you can obtain a stamp that says "For Deposit Only" with your account number and name. Your bank can usually provide the stamp more cheaply than stationery suppliers can. The stamp also allows your secretary to make up your deposits.

2.3 The Expense Record I: Your Checkbook

There are two components to recording your professional expenses. The first is your business checkbook, and the second is an expense summary, completed on a monthly or quarterly basis. Remember that every legitimate and necessary business expense (because it is deductible against income) is really very valuable to you. The true cost of purchases for your business is about 50% of what you pay, because they are tax-deductible, and you are probably in the 50% tax bracket (federal income tax of 28%, state and perhaps local income taxes,

FICA of 13%, sales tax of about 6%, etc.). This is the way the U.S. Congress, in its wisdom, has set up the country. Enjoy it. Buy whatever will make your business easier and more efficient.

Choosing a Checking Account

A checking account used exclusively for your practice is crucial in business record keeping. Accurate and full documentation of business expenses is a source of self-direction, as well as a safeguard against the anxieties of an audit. A checking account is also essential for paying your business-related obligations.

Try to avoid getting a business account, which has all kinds of fancy expenses associated with it. A personal account may also make it easier to get a card to use automatic teller machines for night and weekend deposits. Choose the least expensive account possible. Each bank has marginally different offerings, so investigate the various features. Basically, you want the highest interest and lowest bank fees for your lowest minimum balance. Consider the following (in order of cost importance): (1) the costs of services such as informing you of an incorrect deposit calculation, stop-payment orders, overdraft protection/loans, and especially the handling of "bounced" checks you deposit; (2) the lowest cost of monthly service charges for the size of your practice; (3) interest-bearing checking accounts and their minimum balance requirements for paying interest; (4) the lowest minimum balance required to prevent a service charge; and (5) the cost of blank checks. (Note that you do not have to buy your checks from your bank. Medical printers and several "checks by mail" companies are cheaper, and checks are a major expense.)

Guidelines for a Business Checkbook

- The smallest size of checks is perfectly acceptable, cheaper, and easier to store both at home and in your wallet. Plain blue or yellow checks are fine. Never let your 3-year-old select the balloons-floating-in-the-sky design (as I did once).

- Buy the smallest number of checks at a time (200 or fewer), as larger quantities aren't usually cheaper and the check printer can get them to you in less than a week.

- Many prefer the three-checks-to-a-page format with a 6" × 8" check register, because both fit into a 7" × 9" loose-leaf binder that will stand up neatly in a bookcase or on the desk with other books.

- Many businesses use "one-write" checkbooks, in which the writing of a check automatically (with carbon on the back of the check) creates a ledger on the page behind it. The amounts are assigned to columns that correspond to tax or other financial purposes. For example, some column headings could be "Auto Expenses," "Rents," "Professional Library," and "Office Expenses." This simplifies bookkeeping by allowing the column totals to be used for tax accounting. This system, however, has several limitations for a small practice: The book is cumbersome; if you take a check with you and fill it out at the store, you will have to enter it into the checkbook the old-fashioned way; the checks are large, have to be specially ordered from a commercial printer, and cost more; finally, the time saved is minimal for the small number of checks most therapists write each year.

■ If your practice is large, or if you only deposit checks monthly, get the deposit slips that allow you to list 16 or 19 checks on the back, and not the smaller deposit tickets (which sometimes will require you to use several).

■ You may want to balance your account monthly, or you may prefer to let it go if it is in the ballpark, to save time. Some people round up the amounts of all checks and thus ensure that they will have a surplus cushion.

■ Start a new check register each tax or calendar year, even if it is not used up, for simplicity of record keeping.

Choosing a Credit Card

Although the issue of a business credit card is not directly connected with that of a business checking account, I'd like to mention it briefly in passing. It makes sense to get a separate credit card for your business and avoid using it for personal purchases. If you have more than one business, get a card for each. Write a note on an adhesive slip on each card to keep each card's use clear. Get bank cards (Visa or MasterCard) for all your accounts to save costs. The "Gold" versions are as good as the private cards in terms of offered services you really can use, such as rental car insurance coverage. If they are both or all from the same bank and all come due at the same time, you will save on postage when paying your bills. If you maintain a large balance each month, look for the lowest interest rates; if you pay off your balance, look for no yearly fees, and lowest costs for advances and other fees.

2.4 The Expense Record II: Monthly/Quarterly Expense Summary

FORM 2

The second step in systematic recording of expenses is having a running summary of your expenses. Form 2 offers a list of headings in standard accounting format that match the categories on business and personal income tax forms. You need enter only each expense's date and amount, and so you can place many checks, receipts, bills, and so forth on the same horizontal line. The line and section totals (e.g., auto expenses) can be entered into your federal and state quarterly estimated income tax forms, so that you do not overpay or underpay your taxes. When you have completed a year's worth of these, you will also have a good sense of where your money is going, feel more comfortable with the business side of your practice, and be able to plan better.

Business Expenses

Month: _____ or Quarter: 1 2 3 4 of Year: _____

	1	2	3	4	Total
Prof. services: Accounting					
Legal expenses					
Secretarial					
Supervision/consultation					
Professional liability insurance					
Professional licenses					
Professional library					
Professional dues					
Advertising					
Auto expenses: Loan					
Fuel					
Insurance					
Repairs					
Supplies					
Registration fees					
Other					
Bank fees, checks					
Business entertainment					
Business gifts					
Office expenses: Supplies					
Supplies					
Equipment					
Subscriptions					
Rent(s)					
Telephone					
Answering service					
Utilities					
Repairs					
Postage					
Printing					
Refunds given					
Taxes paid (on business):					
Business privilege					
Property					
Sales					
Training/Prof. development					
Travel, meals					
Miscellaneous (small amounts):					
Other (specify reason & payee):					
Cash expenses (total and staple receipts on back):					

FORM 2. Monthly/quarterly expense summary. From *The Paper Office,* p. 37. Copyright 1997 by Edward L. Zuckerman. Permission to photocopy this form is granted to purchasers of *The Paper Office* for personal use only (see copyright page for details).

2.5 Methods of Billing

The simplest and cheapest method of billing is *not* having to bill: Have clients pay at the time of each session.

Credit Cards

The second simplest method of billing is to accept credit card payments. This ensures full payment, avoids the delay of billing, and makes payment certain; but they cost about 4% of the amount of each transaction plus a yearly fee of $50 or so. There is also some additional bookkeeping and mailing involved. The Maryland Bank, N.A. banking organization seems quite interested in recruiting APA members as "vendors," and offers a low-cost, small-scale program (see the Appendix, Section A.3c).

Most clients, however, still need records of the services received and of their payments to you, for tax purposes or for reimbursement from health insurance. To save yourself grief, find a billing method that works for you in terms of your resources (time, secretarial help, computer access, size of your practice), and use it until something *markedly* better comes along. The various options are covered below.

Whichever of the following options you choose, **you should bill often.** I know this is a burden, but you will collect more money in the long run. Monthly billing is too slow; billing every 2 weeks is best.

Statements

If your office help is cheap and reliable, sending out statements could work for you. However, putting together traditional, typed, letter-like statements is time-consuming, because so much writing is needed each month.

Statement Cards

Many therapists use a statement card, writing in each month's contacts, charges, and payments, and then computing a balance due. They then send out a photocopy of this 5¾" × 8½" card each month in a #9 window envelope. Medical printers offer the materials needed.

SuperΨbills

Some therapists have adopted the SuperΨbill approach. It has a three-part "no-carbon-required" form with diagnostic codes, patient insurance submission instructions, service codes, and your practice's identification imprinted on it. You only have to make checkoffs and mail it out. It is available from The Overheadshrinkers and from SYCOM (see the list of suppliers in the Appendix, Section A.3b). Also, some computerized billing programs will print a kind of "superbill."

Computerized Billing Programs

Mental health billing is the most complex area of medical billing. To meet the needs of practitioners, there are about 100 computerized billing programs publicly available. The simpler and cheaper ones serve those in solo practice, and the more complex and expensive ones serve large groups or health care organizations. There are programs that simply construct a bill to give to clients, and ones that track MCOs' session limits, bill multiple payers separately, keep progress notes, send out reminders, and help with treatment planning. The evaluation of these programs is beyond the scope of this chapter, but if you bill more than 25 clients a month and do not have an ace billing person working for you, you should investigate them. Most are advertised in your professional newsletters.

Billing Services

There are companies that will do your billing for you. Look under "Billing Services" in the Yellow Pages or ask around. One that has advertised widely is ABS, Inc. (see the Appendix, Section A.3c).

Billing services will provide a variety of valuable services, including allowing you to accept credit card payments, as well as electronic claim submission (ECS). They can bill all kind of insurers and third parties, using these parties' current forms, procedures, and policies, and with faster turnaround on your accounts receivable. They offer help with audits by payers, verification of benefits, and toll-free assistance, and they can save you postage (although your telephone bill for faxes may go up a little). They send nicely printed bills to the client, bills to third parties with all the needed information, and monthly reports on the status of your accounts receivable. The cost to therapists is based on a percentage of the amount collected.

Itemized Billing: A Detailed Example

Describing the detailed process and procedures of treatment is always a challenge, and yet the current pressures from third-party payers to do so are intense. Figure 3 is a painfully well worked out example we can all learn from.

A Weekly Summary for Billing

FORM 3

If you have someone else make up and send out your bills, you will need to specify whom to bill and for what services; Form 3 will do that. The format is slightly modified from one designed by Mason B. Scott, EdD, of Pittsburgh, PA, and is especially useful if clients are seen several times a week. It is also suitable for billing consultation hours and other indirect or non-client-related services. This form is filled out by the therapist from (or instead of) an appointment book. Make all entries in pencil, and select appropriate service codes for your practice.

When a client comes in, the billing code (BC) box is marked with a slash ("/") to show that the client was seen and should be billed; when the client is actually billed, a backslash ("\")

Itemized Billing: A Detailed Example

CALVIN L. SKOLNIK, MD, INC.
A Psychiatry Corporation

January 5, 1978

Mr. Sheldon Rosenberg
492 West Maple Dr.
East Orange, NJ

Dear Mr. Rosenberg:

In response to the request by your insurer, Great Lakes Casualty and Surety Co., for more precise documentation of professional services rendered, I have prepared the enclosed itemization for the month of December. I trust that this will clarify the situation sufficiently for your benefit payments to be resumed.

Until next Tuesday at 11:00, I remain

Cordially,
CALVIN L. SKOLNIK, MD

Charges

140	clarifications	@ .25	$35.00
157	restatements	@ .25	39.25
17	broad-focus questions	@ .35	5.95
42	narrow-focus questions	@ .30	12.60
86	reflections of dominant emotional theme	@ .35	30.10
38	resolutions of inconsistencies	@ .45	17.10
22	pointings out of nonverbal communications	@ .40	8.80
187	encouragements to say more	@ .15	28.05
371	sympathetic nods with furrowed brow	@ .10	37.10
517	acknowledgements of information reception (Uh-huhs, Um-hmmms, etc.)	@ .08	41.36
24	interpretations of unconscious defense configurations	@ .30	7.20
16	absolutions for evil deeds	@ .50	8.00
2	pieces of advice	@ .75	1.50
6	expressions of personal feelings	@ .50	3.00
2	personal reminiscences	@ .65	1.30
35	misc. responses (sighs, grunts, belches, etc.)	@ .20	7.00
7	listening to remarks disparaging therapist's appearance, personal habits, or technique	@ 1.75	12.25
12	listening to sarcastic remarks about psychiatry	@ 1.00	12.00
3	listening to psychiatrist jokes	@ .80	2.40
3	telephone calls to therapist	@ .15	.45
1	telephone call to therapist at especially inopportune moment	@10.50	10.50
22	Kleenex tissues	@ .005	.11
1	ashtray	@ 3.50	3.50
1	filling and repainting of one ashtray-size dent in wall	@27.50	27.50
1	shampooing of soft drink stain on csarpet	@15.00	15.00
1	letter of excuse from work	@ 2.50	2.50
2	surcharges for especially boring or difficult sessions	@35.00	70.00
	Subtotal: charges		$438.52

Credits

4	unusually interesting anecdotes	@ .45	1.80
3	good jokes	@ .50	1.50
1	item of gossip about another patient which was found useful in her therapy	@ 3.50	3.50
1	apology for sarcastic remark	@ 1.00	1.00
1	use of case history at American Psychiatric Association Convention	@10.00	10.00
½	chicken salad sandwich on whole wheat w/mayo	@ 1.75	.88
7	bummed cigarettes (65¢)		.23
1	damaged Librium tablet, returned unused		.10
	Subtotal: credits		$18.99
	Total: PLEASE REMIT—		$419.53

FIGURE 3. Itemized billing: A detailed example. Reprinted from Hoffman (1980). Copyright 1980 by the *Journal of Irreproducible Results*. Reprinted by permission of the publisher.

is used to form an "×." If the client cancels, // is used to indicate that the client is to be billed. If the therapist cancels or some other unusual circumstance arises and the client is not to be billed, /// is used. The form can also be used for keeping track of phone calls to clients: Each name and number is entered, and when the call is completed, the name is crossed out with a single horizontal line. Calls to be billed are marked with a slash in the BC box, as appointments are. Calls not completed are rewritten to the next week's form. The form is sent weekly to the person doing the billing, who has a list of names and usual charges, and so creates the bills that are sent out each month.

A Record of Services Provided

FORM 4   Some therapists, in lieu of a bill, provide the patient with a form like Form 4 after every visit. Professional billers call it "a walk-out statement." It has the advantages of (1) replacing most cumulative billing; (2) providing a reminder at the end of the session to pay and a receipt for payments made; (3) indicating and reminding the client of the next appointment; and (4) being a record of services provided for insurance claims.

Form 4 also documents each visit with a signature and confirms the client's consent to receiving services. You can use this form when you think a client has some undefined or unarticulated reluctance about treatment; have the client sign the form as soon as he or she comes in. Clients will go along with almost any procedure if you make it seem matter-of-fact and customary. Lastly, the form reinforces the client's assumption of financial responsibility for your fees.

This form is based on one used by Irvin P. R. Guyett, PhD, of Pittsburgh, PA. If you want to print it up by the hundreds, it can be made into a no-carbon-required form, which will create a copy for the client and one for you or your bill-generating person. Under "SS/Fed. EIN #," add your Social Security or federal employer identification number. The latter you need to get if you employ anyone (i.e., give him or her a W-2 form). Insurance companies require one or the other of these numbers to pay you. You can replace "State license" with another indication that you are a credentialed and payable professional, if you so desire. It is often useful to print a number of diagnostic codes and their titles in the "Diagnosis" space, which you can simply circle, to save time. Under "Services performed," you can print appropriate codes and their titles as well, although none are offered here because they change fairly often (for a discussion of *Current Procedures and Terminology* [CPT] codes, see Section 2.7).

Billing Summary

Name of service provider: _____   For the week of _____ to _____

Client's name	Mon.			Tues.			Wed.			Thurs.			Fri.			Sat.		
	BC	Hr	SC	BC	Hr	SC	BC	Hr	SC	BC	Hr	SC	BC	Hr	SC	BC	Hr	SC
_____																		
_____																		
_____																		
_____																		
_____																		
_____																		
_____																		
_____																		
_____																		
_____																		
_____																		
_____																		
_____																		
_____																		
_____																		
_____																		
_____																		
_____																		
_____																		
_____																		
Totals																		

Grand total _____

Billing codes (BC): / = Seen; // = Cancelled but to be billed; /// = Cancelled but not billed; \ = Billed.   **Hr:** Number of hours.
Service codes (SC): C = Consultation; P = Psychological examination; NP = Neuropsychological examination; I = Interpretation; RP = Report preparation; RR = Records review; D = Deposition; T = Testimony; PC = Phone consultation. If no code is indicated, bill for 1 hour of psychotherapy. ExT = 1.5 hours of psychotherapy.

FORM 3. Weekly summary for billing.   Adapted from a form devised by Mason B. Scott, EdD, of Pittsburgh, PA, and used by permission of Dr. Scott.—From *The Paper Office*, p. 42. Permission to photocopy this form is granted to purchasers of *The Paper Office* for personal use only (see copyright page for details).

My Documents / Private Practice / Billing

Record of Services Provided

SS/Fed EIN #: _____   State license #: _____

Client: _____   Date of service: _____

Diagnosis (DSM/ICD code): _____

Services performed (CPT or other codes):   Service location (if different from above):

  1. _____   _____

     _____   _____

  2. _____   _____

     _____   _____

This is session number _____ of a total of _____ visits authorized by your managed care organization on _____.

Fee	Adjustment	Charges	Amount paid	Balance due

Signature of client, which indicates acceptance of services and final responsibility for payment, regardless of any third-party benefits: _____

Therapist's signature: _____

Date of our next appointment: _____, the _____ of _____, at time _____ A.M./P.M.

FORM 4. Record of services provided.   Adapted from a form devised by Irvin P. R. Guyett, PhD, of Pittsburgh, PA, and used by permission of Dr. Guyett.—From *The Paper Office*, p. 43. Permission to photocopy this form is granted to purchasers of *The Paper Office* for personal use only (see copyright page for details).

The Patient Account Ledger Billing Form

FORM 5

For clients who are "self-paying" and those with simple indemnity coverage, the patient account ledger (PAL; Form 5) will maintain a record quite well. Its advantages are that it is:

- More informative than the traditional statement or bill "For professional services rendered."

- Easily kept up to date with pen-and-ink entries.

- Accessible at the front of the chart, to remind you to discuss any delays in payment.

- Photocopiable, to provide the client with a current statement at any time.

The PAL (Form 5) begins with a blank for the patient's account number. If you file records by patients' names, you will not need an account or case number. If you do use numbers, you will need a separate cross-file. The block for name and address is designed to fit into the window of a #10 envelope when folded facing you at the equals (=) sign along the right margin. (Check to see that it does before you make 500 copies, though.) The "Identification #" is important; insurance companies need it to pay you. Use your Social Security or federal employer ID number. On the line for "Diagnosis" are spaces for both a code number and name. The name of the diagnosis is optional here; using only the number may increase privacy. Insurance companies generally want to know both the number and name and usually want the ICD-9 or ICD-10 diagnosis. Some, however, want the DSM-IV format. Make sure you have both available and circle which one you are using on the form.

Under the "Treatment Record" heading, each visit gets it own line, starting with "Date." If the patient is seen over several calendar years, drawing a heavy line under the last service date in the year makes this clearer. It may seem distrustful, but when you photocopy the PAL to send it out, routinely signing or marking it under you last entry will prevent the client's adding sessions to recover additional reimbursement illegally.

Toward the bottom of the form, the friendly reminder (and guilt inducer) about prompt payment is optional. Under it is a line for "Service Codes." Use this space to write in your most frequently used codes. Your services should be described in CPT codes (see Section 2.7) or whatever that particular insurance company accepts. Review the entire current listing to describe accurately and *fully* the services you do, will, and did provide. The "Terms" line is optional. If you choose to add it be certain to include the terms in your client information brochure (see Section 4.2).

To send out bills using the PAL, follow this checklist:

❏ Create a PAL for each client. Go through your case notes and record the date and duration of each occasion of service (therapy session) on each patient's PAL. The PAL can be the first page in each patient's section of your three-ring binder (see Section 1.4). The start of each session's notes can be indicated by a circled number and the date.

❏ Look at your income record (see Section 2.2) to see what payments you have received from this particular client, and enter them on the PAL. As you find a record of a payment received, place a small dot next to the name, so that when you have finished the PALs you can see whether any payments received have not been transferred onto a PAL.

❏ Fill in the rest of the blanks and compute a current balance. If there were special payment arrangements made with the client, these can be noted on the back of the PAL, so that they can be easily reviewed and charges can be adjusted accordingly.

❏ If the balance due is high, write this on a Post-It note and attach it to the PAL. (See Section 2.6 on collecting overdue fees.)

❏ Write today's date on the back of each PAL. This will tell you when you sent out each bill, if there is a need to know this history (e.g., a client wants to know when a bill was sent because it hasn't been received) or to remind you that you need to send out your bills again. Write a note in your datebook on your next billing date.

❏ When all PALs are completed, make a photocopy of each and return the original PALs to the appropriate sections of your binder.

❏ Fold each PAL first on the line indicated by the printed "=" sign in the right margin and once more in the bottom half of the form, so that the client's name and address will fit in a #10 window envelope. Then simply insert it in a window envelope with the patient's address showing.

❏ Stamp and mail the bills. Total time: 1 hour for 30 bills.

Excell- My Doc. IPP / Patient Account Ledger

Patient Account Ledger

Acct. #: _____ Page #: _____ Therapist's SS/Fed EIN#: _____

Name: _____ State license #: _____

Address: _____ Patient's insurance policy #: _____

_____ Patient's employer: _____

Phone: Home: _____ Work: _____ Soc. Sec. #: _____

Diagnosis (ICD/DSM code): _____ _____

Treatment Record:

Date	Service	# of hrs	Charge	Paid	Bal. Due	Date	Service	# of hrs	Charge	Paid	Bal. due

Prompt payment for services already rendered is greatly appreciated.

Service codes: _____

All services were provided in the provider's office unless otherwise indicated.

Terms: Due upon receipt. A service charge of 1.5% per month will be added to all accounts over 30 days late. Any accounts that are turned over to an attorney for collection will include reasonable collection fees and court costs.

This is a strictly confidential patient medical record. Redisclosure or transfer is expressly prohibited by law.

2.6 Collecting Overdue Fees from Clients

Note. Collecting from insurance companies is covered in Section 2.7.

Regular billing gives you a good grasp of your accounts, so that you will know when someone slips from 30 to 45 or even 120 days behind. The later a client is in paying, the less likely it is that you will collect the full sum owed you; the curve is steep and negatively accelerated.

If you are squeamish about dunning your clients for money or think that it negatively affects the intimate therapeutic relationship, find another way to assure that you will be paid, or you will have to leave private practice. You can work it through with your own therapist (more work and more costly), hire someone to dun clients (cheaper and easier), use a paperwork solution such as that described below, or have your secretary (or spouse, calling as Office Manager) call the slow payers.

The following discussion covers the methods of collecting overdue fees, starting with phone calls (the most effective method), and then moving on to various written notes and notices.

Calling the Client

A phone call from you is the best way to assure payment. A second choice is a personal call from a secretary or office manager. This has been shown to be many times more productive than using the mail. Be sure, though, that whoever makes the call understands the limitations on what he or she can do and say. Read up on the federal and state laws and practices in this area before starting. In general, the caller must always be polite, show concern for the client's best interests, listen to explanations, offer to work out a payment schedule, and follow up methodically. Calls may be made only between 8 A.M. and 9 P.M. The caller should carefully note his or her efforts and the client's response on a 3" × 5" "tickler card" (see

FORM 6

Form 6) which can go into your "tickler file" (see below). You can run off copies of this card on your photocopier.

Client: _____

Days past due: 10   20   45   60   90   120   Over 120

Action (call, letter, other): _____

Date of action: _____   Time of action: _____

Results: _____

Follow-up date: _____

Final action (atty., collection agency, other): _____

Amounts collected/written off: _____

FORM 6.   A tickler card.   From *The Paper Office,* p. 48. Copyright 1997 by Edward L. Zuckerman. Permission to photocopy this form is granted to purchasers of *The Paper Office* for personal use only (see copyright page for details).

Client: _____

Days past due: 10   20   45   60   90   120   Over 120

Action (call, letter, other): _____

Date of action: _____   Time of action: _____

Results: _____

Follow-up date: _____

Final action (atty., collection agency, other): _____

Amounts collected/written off: _____

FORM 6.   A tickler card.   From *The Paper Office,* p. 48. Copyright 1997 by Edward L. Zuckerman. Permission to photocopy this form is granted to purchasers of *The Paper Office* for personal use only (see copyright page for details).

The Tickler File

A "tickler file" is a systematic way of reminding yourself of tasks to be done. It is particularly useful for the repeated calls needed for collections. Checking the ticker file must be a daily part of the office routines or it won't work, so consider its implementation carefully.

The usual tickler file is a file card box in which you place index cards indicating what has to be done, by what date, and by whom (if appropriate). Other information can also be noted so that the tasks get done or can be rescheduled to a later date. The cards are filed under day dividers. The standard is 63 dividers—three sets of cards numbered 1 through 31 (one for each day of the next 3 months) in a different color for each month. You also need dividers named for each of the year's months, and perhaps 10 more dividers labeled for the each of next 10 years. If a task is completed, its card can be destroyed or filed for reference. If the task cannot be completed or the client promises payment by a certain day, the card is moved to that new date. You can buy tickler files from SYCOM and other suppliers (see the Appendix, Section A.3b) or make one yourself.

Sending a Note on the Bill

When there is a larger-than-expected unpaid balance, or a payment is more than 30 days late, I attach a yellow Post-It Note (removable so the bill can still be submitted to the insurance company) to the bill. Since such a client's case is usually closed, the note usually says something like "Is there some problem with this account?" or "Are you having a money problem?" or "Is there some trouble with your insurance company?" It then requests or informs the client of action: "Please call/talk to me if there is some difficulty with this," or "Can you pay me something on this account?" or "I will call you next week about this."

The next step can be to include a handwritten note with the next bill. (This note is designed to inspire some guilt; consider carefully whether you want to do this.) Such a note can be phrased as follows:

> Dear H. Rorschach,
>
> My records indicate a significant unpaid balance. Are you having trouble paying this bill?
>
> I have provided my best services and trusted you to keep your part of our contract by paying me as soon as I billed you. However, you still owe me the balance indicated on the enclosed bill. What has happened?
>
> Please call me so we can reestablish our trusting relationship by clearing up this account.
>
> Very truly yours,
> SIGMUND J. THERAPIST

Printers also offer brightly colored labels or stickers to attach to your bill and dunning cards, with phrases such as these:

- "Friendly reminder!" or "Please!"

- "Please pay this bill directly to this office. You are responsible for the entire fee, regardless of any insurance claim."

- "To help you clear up this debt, we are willing to make arrangements for payments that you can meet regularly."

- "Past due. Your prompt attention is courteously requested."

Hundreds more of such items with clear and effective phrasings can be ordered from the suppliers listed in the Appendix, Section A.3b.

Sending Collection Letters

Collection letters seem to work better than stickers. Meek (1987) provides an excellent discussion of such letters in just three pages. For those of you who have never received them, collection letters come in increasing intensity of wording (and often of paper color as well). The "first-level" notes offered below are increasingly demanding in tone, but all indicate a willingness to talk and work out a payment plan. The "second-level" letter informs the client that you will no longer provide services until payment is made. The "third-level" letter threatens legal action.

First-Level Collection Letters

Your brochure for clients, and the bills themselves, should indicate that bills are "due upon receipt and payable immediately." Then, if you haven't received payment after 15 days, the account is overdue, and you can send a reminder:

> Just a reminder
>
> May I call your attention to this unpaid balance? If there is some question or problem, or full payment is not possible for you now, please call my office so we can find a solution, because I do value you as a client.

The next letter, at the end of the second month, is more aggressive:

> You haven't made a payment on this balance. I must hear from you immediately. If you want to work out a payment plan, call me. If not, please pay the balance in full. Your prompt attention to this matter will be greatly appreciated and will prevent further actions.

Second-Level Collection Letter

The second-level letter informs the client that you can no longer provide services.

> Your account is long overdue, and it is your responsibility to pay this bill. Your insurance has paid its share of the bill, leaving this balance, which is your responsibility.
>
> I cannot provide any future professional services to you or your family until this account is paid up. I will not release any records to other health care professionals, therapists, or insurance companies, even with a signed release from you, until this account is paid up.
>
> I recommend that you seek any mental health care you need from your local community mental health center. If you have a dire emergency, go to the nearest hospital emergency room and ask for the psychiatric consultant on call.

Alternatively, you can offer the continuation of services only on a "cash payment at the time of service" basis. The second paragraph of this letter is risky because it is against the stated policy of the APA (1992a, Section 5.11), which concludes that psychologists may not withold records "needed for a patient's or client's treatment solely because payment has not been received." (I am grateful to Carol A. Carver, PhD, of Corvallis, OR, for this clarification.) However, it may be ethically acceptable if you state it in your client information brochure or otherwise warn the client in advance of nonpayment's consequences. Also, there are many situations in which the records are requested and no harm can come to the client if they are not released, or in which a client can pay your bill but has lacked any incentive until now. As always with ethical situations, consider them on a case-by-case basis.

Third-Level Collection Letter

A third-level collection letter is one that threatens "further action":

> Your account is long past due, and you have not responded to our earlier requests for payment.
>
> It is my usual practice to submit such accounts to a collection agency or to take legal action in small-claims court. I would much prefer not to pursue these actions, but will unless I hear from you about the following options in the next *five* business days. Please indicate your preference for the handling of this account.
>
> ❏ I prefer to settle this account now. I enclose payment in full of $_____.
>
> ❏ I wish to make payments of $_____ each week until this account is paid off, and I enclose my first payment. Please contact me about financing this debt.
>
> ❏ I request that you cancel the balance of this account for the following reasons: _____ _____
>
> Failure to indicate one of these options by return mail in the next *five* days will result in my turning this account over to a collection agency or going to court against you simply to protect my interests. In court I will have to seek not only this amount, but also interest, court costs, and lawyers' fees.
>
> THIS IS THE LAST NOTICE YOU WILL RECEIVE FROM ME.

Be careful not to express your anger or frustration. Your letters should avoid sarcasm ("Don't you think you have stalled long enough?") or accusations, which make people hostile and even more resistant.

Other Methods

If a bill is several years old, and you don't want to sue now but might in the future, you can extend the debt's payment time. Try to get an acknowledgment of the debt (by a dated signature on a letter), a small payment, or even a promise to pay. Sometimes people's financial situations change and they will actually pay their debts off. Ask; it's cheap to try.

As the third-level collection letter suggests, you can use small-claims court in your district. It is simple and cheap, and no lawyer or other professional is required. It is almost always successful, but you need to decide the following: (1) Have you tried all other methods first? (2) Is there anything to collect? Does the client have the money? and (3) Do you want to make an enemy for this much money? The journal *Psychotherapy Finances* discusses small-claims court in its binder *Guide to Private Practice* (see the Appendix, Section A.1a, for the address), and Hussey (1986) also provides a good discussion.

The APA has recently allowed the use of collection agencies, so you can threaten to use them to collect an old bill. However, never turn over a debt to a collection agency without first having spoken with the client. Surprising the client with a call from a collection agency may provoke a retaliatory ethics or malpractice complaint. About a dozen state psychological associations have endorsed a national collection agency (I. C. System, Inc.; see the Appendix, Section A.3c), and you can write to inquire about this agency's services and costs. Hussey (1986) has good advice on collection agencies.

Investigate and carefully read your contract with a collection agency, to reduce problems. Some problems I have heard of include being locked into a single agency for collecting your money; being required to pay a fee if you discontinue having an agency collect for you (there are several options with I. C. System, so ask); having collection activities dropped if you or the agency is sued or threatened with a suit by the client (I. C. System includes $1 million errors-and-omissions coverage for its clients); receiving very limited (and often ineffective) investigation to find a client who has "skipped out"; and having to supply a lot of material to support your bill. Overall, some agencies are clearer and fairer than others, so be thorough and ask lots of questions. I. C. System has a booklet, *Credit and Collections Manual*, which is most educational about all aspects of collections and is free to those who sign up with this agency.

As a final word, keep in mind that if patients are not allowed to get behind in their payments to you, sophisticated collection methods will not be needed. Have clients pay upon receipt of services, or bill early and often. **Don't let patients get behind in their payments to you!**

2.7 Billing Third Parties—and Getting Reimbursed

In the old days, you had a professional relationship only with the client (first party) and not with the insurance company (third party). The client paid you and then might recover payment from the indemnity insurer with whom he or she had a contract. These days you are more likely to have a contract with a preferred provider organization or health maintenance organization (HMO), and so you *do* have a professional relationship with a third party. Your contract will stipulate all the billing procedures and limitations.

Advice on Procedures for Clients with Health Insurance

Before you provide any services, you should confirm that the client is indeed covered for your services. This is called "verification of coverage." Forman (1983) has suggested that you, the therapist, assume the responsibility for discovering how much of the fee is covered by the client's insurance; this will create more goodwill, make your practice more accessible, and make your billing contract more correct. (Clients rarely know accurately what their insurance will pay, and are usually not in the best position to learn at the time they contact you. Most clients will be quite grateful to be relieved of this burden.) Besides, the cost of this checking can be factored into the price the patient pays. If this offer is made at the initial phone call, you will need only the patient's name, employer group number, personal identification number (usually a Social Security number), and a phone number for the insurer. Many insurers have special phone numbers for their providers, which are better staffed and quicker to respond to questions than those for the subscribers.

If you expect any interactions with third-party payers, get copies of your state's licensing law and any other laws (such as "freedom of choice" laws) that affect you. Also, have copies of your curriculum vitae or resume, your license, and your professional liability insurance contract's cover page available, as well as copies of the procedures and regulations of any MCO panels to which you belong.

There is a standard form for submitting almost all health insurance claims, called the HCFA-1500. It is revised occasionally and is available from printers, who will place your practice information in the appropriate block. It may also be available from the insurance companies who require you to submit it, and it is available from some of the medical printers listed in Section A.3b of the Appendix.

The HCFA-1500 can be completed in several ways, depending on the size of your practice and wallet:

■ Computer-based billing/office management systems do a superb job. This is their biggest selling point. Most of these programs now can even submit your bill to an insurer over the phone lines with a kind of e-mail called "electronic claims submission."

■ You may be able to set up your computer and printer with a template in a word-processing or data base program to print the essential information onto preprinted or photocopied HCFA-1500 forms.

■ You can fill out one master form (such as the HCFA-1500 or the form from the client's insurance company) for each patient, make several photocopies, and enter (by hand or typewriter) the current billing period's services-provided information. Repeat on another copy of the form each month. This is cheap, simple, and really quick if you have only 10 patients who need this kind of billing.

■ Some insurers have their own forms and require these to be completed. Complete one model copy for each patient, leaving out the dates of service, and make photocopies for each billing cycle.

If you must share more information than patients' names, dates/kinds of services, and diagnoses with the insurance company, another person, or any other third party, be sure to get a release-of-information form signed (see Section 7.5 for various types of these forms).

What You Need to Know for Insurance Processing

If you do not have the following information and skills, learn them from private seminars, other billers, training programs provided by the larger insurers (e.g., Blue Cross/Blue Shield), or national training organizations.

- Know which of your services are reimbursable and for what amounts. *Physicians' Current Procedural Terminology* (CPT; for the most recent edition, see American Medical Association, 1995) is an enormous multivolume publication defining all recognized health treatment practices. You will need CPT code names and numbers to bill for your services. As a therapist you only need to know a few codes, but these must be current, as many change yearly. Also, different insurers accept different codes. Again, consult a local expert.

- Know what forms and terms to use. You will need clinical record forms (the HCFA-1500 or the insurer's own billing form). Be familiar with the jargon of billing (e.g. "duration of session," "place of service," "coinsurer," "coordination of benefits," "verification of benefits," etc.). Small (1994) is an excellent resource and guide to all these aspects and details.

- Understand how to get around companies that deliberately delay payment and devise obstacles, or at least know how to pursue these organizations energetically.

- Understand deductibles, copayments, and percentage coverages, as well as how they are computed.

- Obtain precise information concerning the lifetime and annual deductible or limitations.

- Be sophisticated about how to use time of billing to your advantage. For example, are yearly deductibles based on calendar years or on 365-day periods from diagnosis or initiation of service?

- Make arrangements for the "physician referral" issue.

Billing for Medicare Patients

Billing Medicare is a highly changeable and specialized "art" form. Here are some guidelines:

- Make certain a client's Medicare Part B is actually paid up to date to cover your services; if not, he or she must reenroll. Even if the client does so immediately, the coverage is not retroactive, and so you will not get paid for services provided in the interim.

- Ask and then check to make certain that the client isn't enrolled in an HMO, because such enrollment will cancel his or her Part B Medicare coverage. If the client wishes to use Medicare, he or she must disenroll, *in writing,* from the HMO. Then Medicare, again, if paid up, will start from the date of disenrollment. Medicare authorization and assignment-of-benefits statements may be required. Consult someone knowledgeable in current practices. As noted above, Small (1994) is an excellent guide to all billing issues.

- According to the 1989 Medicare law, you must notify the patient's primary physician (unless of course you are a patient's primary physician) after treatment has begun unless the patient specifically requests that no notice be given. You should discuss the desirability of this notification, carry it out by letter or phone if the patient agrees, and document these steps and this decision in your notes (Knapp, 1992b).

Checklist for Avoiding Illegal and Unethical Billing Procedures

Kovacs (1987) examines billing practices that put you at legal risk. Here is a checklist of ways to avoid such risks:

❏ Bill only for services actually rendered, not for missed appointments. (Collect for these from the patient.)

❏ Bill only in the name of the patient. If you see a couple, do not bill both members as individuals. Generally, a couple cannot be considered a "patient," so make some other payment arrangement besides the partners' health insurance coverage for couple counseling. Billing for only one person when you are doing relationship therapy is incorrect and illegal. Similarly, bill members of a therapy group for group therapy, not as if they were individual therapy patients.

❏ Do not mislead the insurance company into believing that you provided a service when in fact a trainee or assistant did, even if the insurance company will not pay for services provided by others (as it should). This is an issue we should take up with lawmakers.

❏ Charge the insurer only the fees you and the client agree upon. If the patient really cannot afford your fee, (1) lower it or (2) refer him or her to another provider or clinic.

❏ Do not bill for double your usual fee so that the insurance company will pay half and you will then receive your usual fee.

❏ Do not try to collect more than 100% of your fee by billing two insurers when a patient is covered by his or her own and a spouse's plan (Knapp & VandeCreek, 1990, p. 67). However, it is perfectly acceptable to bill the second insurer for the part not paid by the first.

❏ Accepting the actual amount paid by a third party as full payment of your fee when it is not will be considered fraud, submission of a false claim, or violation of the anti-kickback provisions of your contract with the payer. If you have told the third party your fee is x dollars, and now you in effect accept less as full payment and do not collect the patient's part, this is probably illegal. Do not advertise or state in your client information brochure that "Medicare is accepted as payment in full" or "Insurance is accepted as full payment." State in writing your financial policy concerning waiving the copayment only for the indigent, and define your criteria for "indigent." Do not offer the waiver; let the client ask for it. Do not routinely claim to the third party that a patient's financial hardship prevents his or her payment. Investigate and document the client's income and insurance coverage before waiving the copayment. Do not fail to make a good-faith effort to collect the client's part of the fee (the copayment) unless you have documented his or her indigence. Document your collection efforts.

❏ Do not change the diagnosis or the service so that the insurance company will pay for the service. For example, do not call a V-code diagnosis an "Adjustment Disorder," or turn "Adjustment Disorder" into "Dysthymia," or change "biofeedback" into "psychotherapy" if these are not accurate.

❑ Don't "cream and dump." That is, don't see those with insurance until their coverage is exhausted and then refer them away.

❑ Do not pretend you were "too busy with clinical issues to worry about the paperwork," or say that you "trusted your assistant," or use other excuses for fraudulent billing.

Failure to follow these rules can result in your being prosecuted. You may then be convicted of insurance fraud, perjury to commit fraud, or collusion with the patient; you can subsequently be fined and jailed (I have heard that psychologists have served time for insurance fraud). Fraud, perjury, and collusion are all felonies and will usually cost you your license and livelihood. Furthermore, they are not good for the patient to see or to participate in.

Late Payments from Insurers

Insurers must either pay or deny a claim within a limited time period (usually 30 days) after it is submitted. You can threaten to report insurers to the state insurance commissioner if they are too slow. If you can do so, and it is worthwhile to you, monitor the progress of all claims you submit, and keep after the insurers on old claims. Computerized billing programs can often do this automatically.

To assure that the insurance company has gotten the mail he sends, Irvin P. R. Guyett, PhD, of Pittsburgh, PA, includes a self-addressed postcard that the insurance clerk is to sign, date, and return to indicate receipt of the forms. If the postcard is not returned in 10 days, he sends the same materials again with a card and a note. The note clearly indicates that this is a second submission, because the first was apparently lost in the mail or in their office, as he did not receive the return card. If appropriate, a call before the resending may speed things up, because the insurer doesn't want the extra paperwork.

A form letter to the insurance company reminding it of an unpaid claim may be productive. SYCOM (see the Appendix, Section A.3b) offers an "action request memo," or you may use a simple letter like this:

> To: [Insurance company]
>
> Re: Payment not received on insured [name]: _____
>   Insured's identification no.: _____
>   Patient (if other than insured): _____
>
> Dear _____:
>
> In reviewing our files, we find no record of receipt of payment on this claim, and so have enclosed a duplicate copy of the claim we submitted originally on _____.
>
> Please process this claim as soon as possible, as services were rendered in good faith some time ago. We thank you for your immediate attention to this matter.

Usually, insurers will respond to such a letter by indicating that some information is missing on the claim form you submitted. If so, remedy the situation immediately (a fax machine is very handy here). However, if what they ask is confidential, write to them supplying alternative information.

If you find that a particular insurer repeatedly delays payments (some insurers have apparently chosen this method to increase their profits), include stronger language in your letters, and quote or cite your state's rules on timely payment. Also, send carbon copies of all your communications with the insurer to your state's insurance commissioner, and note this policy at the bottom of all future letters to the insurer.

CHAPTER 3
Reducing Malpractice Risk by Operating Ethically

3.1   Ethics and Malpractice

> *Study widely.*
> *Question thoroughly.*
> *Deliberate carefully.*
> *Analyze clearly.*
> *Act conscientiously.*
> —The sage kings Yao and Shun,
>   as described by Yamazaki Ansai

Why Are Ethical and Legal Issues So Complicated?

Abstract ideas of right and wrong can be simple. Unfortunately, the real world can be quite complicated:

- Principles must be stated abstractly to be comprehensive, and yet each case and situation is unique. "Should" and "must" are often too vague to direct specific actions; actions require precise answers (when, how, where, etc.).

- Ethics and laws can sometimes conflict, such as when the client's best interests require confidentiality but the law requires disclosure. Two ethical imperatives can also be in conflict in a particular situation.

- Therapy's goals may conflict with ethical guidelines. For example, full disclosure of a treatment's risks is necessary for informed consent, but may weaken a client's motivation for therapy. Success rates may make him or her disappointed with the therapist or hopeless about therapy's outcome.

58

- There are many ways to view a case and its issues; some views may be in conflict, and we cannot know all of them. Even experts will differ in their interpretations, recommendations, and judgments, as each can have different conceptual bases.

- The field of psychology keeps evolving. Laws and court decisions keep changing. Each state has different laws; departments within a state government can have different rules; and there are gaps and overlaps in the laws and rules.

In addition to the points made above, keep in mind that written standards for ethical behavior can be of two kinds: "minimal standards," which are mandatory, with punishment for violations; and "aspirational standards," which are not mandatory and do not involve punishment for violations, but toward which we are expected to strive. Haas et al. (1986) found that "When psychologists are faced with a variety of ethical dilemmas, they will often make decisions based on their personal value systems and not on the basis of defined ethical principles" (p. 321). Such decisions may "feel right," but how can we be sure that this is good enough to protect us legally and ethically? How can we do better? As professionals committed to empiricism, let's look at the data.

The Major Malpractice Risks for Clinicians

Pope (1989a) reviewed the data on malpractice lawsuits against psychologists from January 16, 1986, to July 1, 1988, and found 27 major causes for successful suits. His findings are summarized in Table 1. The major issues are indicated in boldface, and the causes are ranked by the percentage of claims each represents. Note how few "failure to warn" cases there were (ranked 23rd), although such cases generate a lot of therapist anxiety. Note also how relatively large problems related to fee collection were (ranked 5th), despite which many therapists vigorously pursue monies owed them.

Other data come from a report by the American Psychological Association (APA) Committee on Ethics (1988). This committee reviewed complaints over a 5-year period and found a pattern similar to that found by Pope. The majority of ethics complaints came from the following small number of issues:

- Dual relationships, including sexual intimacies (23%)

- Violations of various APA practice and research standards and guidelines, or of governmental laws and institutional regulations (16%)

- Therapist behavior that violated or diminished the legal or civil rights of others (8%)

- A professional's failure to preserve appropriate confidentiality of patients or students (4%)

More recent experience (Sam Knapp, personal communication, October 2, 1996) suggests two additional areas of concern: First, child custody evaluations, which by their nature leave someone unhappy, have produced a large number of complaints on the issues of breach of confidentiality and violations of the ethics of assessment. Second, the treatment of adult survivors of childhood abuse using recovered memories has resulted in high awards in malpractice cases. The best advice is simply to avoid this approach, and if you do use it to be very clear about boundaries.

TABLE 1. **Major Causes of Successful Malpractice Suits against Psychologists**

Cause	% of costs	% of claims
1. **Sexual impropriety**	53.2	20.4
2. **Incorrect treatment** (i.e., using treatments the therapist was not qualified to perform by lack of training or experience)	8.4	13.2
3. Loss (to the patient) from evaluation (performed by the psychologist)	2.6	8.5
4. **Breach of confidentiality or privacy**	1.3	6.4
5. **Countersuit for fee collection** (improper fee setting, billing, or fee collection methods)	1.3	6.2
6. Suicide of patient	11.2	5.8
7. **Diagnosis: Failure to or incorrect**	3.7	5.4
8. Defamation: Libel/slander	0.7	4.4
9. **Improper death of patient or others**	2.0	3.2
10. Miscellaneous (the meaning of this category was unclear to Pope)	0.8	3.1
11. Premise liability (e.g., a client was hurt in the office by falling)	0.1	2.4
12. Violation of legal regulations	0.5	2.6
13. Bodily injury	1.6	2.2
14. Loss of child custody or visitation	0.2	2.2
15. Violation of civil rights	1.1	2.1
16. Licensing or peer review	0.2	2.1
17. Poor results	0.1	1.7
18. Undetermined (i.e., the causes of action were undetermined)	7.9	1.5
19. Breach of contract	0.1	1.4
20. Assault and battery	1.5	1.2
21. Failure to supervise properly	0.3	0.9
22. **Undue influence** (these are basically dual relationships)	0.4	0.6
23. **Failure to warn**	0.6	0.4
24. Abandonment	0.1	0.3
25. False imprisonment/arrest	11 cases, average cost $935	
26. Failure to refer	1 case, cost $2,141	
27. Failure to treat	2 cases, average cost $38	

Note. The data are from Pope (1989a).

This may seem like a long list. Do you have to worry about everything you do as a therapist? The answer is no. Nearly all malpractice complaints stem from just a few issues, and most are in areas over which you have excellent control. Over 60% of the claims in Table 1 and the majority of complaints noted by the APA Committee on Ethics, originiated in sexual improprieties, dual relationships, substandard diagnosis or treatment, lapses in the duty to protect, and poor office administration. You can reduce or eliminate the vast majority of risks in these areas if you are clinically competent and self-aware, if you consult fully with others, and if you create an adequate written record to document your actions and the reasons for them. The good news in all this: **Almost all malpractice cases arise not from unforeseeable problems, but from ones that could have been avoided if only they were recognized and anticipated** (Bennett et al., 1990).

In some cases, the issues are so clear that lists of dos and don'ts can be created for them. I have included these in this book where appropriate. More importantly, some principles are so clearly formulated that they can be incorporated into your practice simply by using the forms, sample documents, guidelines, and checklists in this book. In fact, that is a major concept underlying this book: If you build the ethics into your paperwork, you greatly reduce your risk of malpractice.

Four Steps toward Ethical Self-Protection

1. **Be realistic.** Ethical dilemmas can and may happen to you.

   One barrier to improved ethical practice is arrogance. "Pride goeth before a fall," but arrogance is hard to avoid when capable people are asking your advice every day, listening carefully, paying you and being grateful. Do not let false pride, denial, panic, ignorance, or rumors cause you to avoid acting to protect yourself and your clients.

2. **Learn the rules.** The fact that you have the client's best interests at heart, are well intentioned, or like the client doesn't ensure that you are acting ethically. Don't assume that ethical niceties and picky little rules can be ignored because you are a "good guy/girl." These rules have usually been carefully worked out after painful experiences.

   First, get, read, and keep copies of your state's licensing law and all the ethical codes or principles you operate under. You need to be mindful of the legal context in which you operate. There are many codes of ethical standards available (Gorlin, 1990). Which ethical standards apply to you? It will be the code of the group you align with by education or by the title or description you offer of your services. You will also, perhaps surprisingly, be held to the standards of any group an ordinary citizen would see you as belonging to. Even if you are not certified by the American Association for Marriage and Family Therapy, a court is likely to hold your practice to this group's standards if you identify yourself as a "marriage counselor" or "family therapist."

   For a dozen perspectives on the APA code of ethics, see a special section of the journal *Professional Psychology: Research and Practice* (Vol. 25, No. 4, November 1994). For interpretations of each section of the new APA ethics code, see Canter et. al. (1994). Read the current literature, and attend continuing education programs in the areas of ethical practice. For short overviews of the issues, see Hulteng and Goldman (1986) and Ewing (1983). A readable and brief (140-page) survey of all the ethical issues from the perspective of the practicing clinician can be found in Haas and Malouf (1989).

   In addition, join your profession's associations. Their newsletters will keep you ahead of changes in laws, regulations, and court decisions. Their boards, ethics committees, and professional staffs are available to offer useful guidance.

3. **Develop an ethical consciousness.** Ethics education should result in a "learned dis-ease." This is an awareness of vulnerability, complexity, and multiple perspectives. It is almost an operational definition of an ethical consciousness. It will give you a "gut feeling" to guide and warn you. This anxiety should motivate thoughtfulness, consultation, conservatism, foresight, contingency planning, and empathy. The development of an ethical sensitivity will help alert you to the ethical aspects and implications of all your professional activities. For practice, a book by Stromberg et al. (1988, pp. 235–271) contains a table of more than 100 situations in which the practice of psychology raises legal or ethical questions.

   To develop and maintain an ethical awareness, repeatedly evaluate the ethical implications of your decisions. Ask yourself "What if . . . ?" questions from a "worst-case scenario" perspective and from the perspective of a hostile complainant (patient, peer, or lawyer). Be especially careful about novel or uncommon practices. If what you are doing with a client, or are considering doing, is unusual among your peer professionals, get at least one consultation on its ethical correctness *before* proceeding. My own rule is this: If you don't personally know anyone else who is doing what you are doing, be extraordinarily cautious.

4. **Tighten up your procedures.** By using checklists and similar procedural devices, you can anticipate problems and head them off. Such procedures can remind you of legal obligations, shape the questions you ask, and offer easily incorporated risk management strategies (Bennett et al., 1990, p. 45). Read each section of this book that applies to your practice, evaluate the forms and sample documents, modify them as necessary, make photocopies, and *use them* with every one of your patients.

3.2 Legal Aspects of Malpractice

When Do Patients Sue?

Lawsuits represent the last stage of breakdown in human relationships. They tend to occur in therapeutic contexts under the following conditions:

- When patients are disappointed with the outcome of treatment.

- When patients think they have had a bad outcome and attribute it to the therapist's incompetence or negligence.

- When patients believe they have been exploited or "used" financially, emotionally, or sexually.

- When patients are presented with a bill larger or later than they expected.

What Is Malpractice?

Negley (1985) offers this definition: "Malpractice is a deviation (by omission or commission) from the standards of professional care which then results in an injury" (p. 243). From the viewpoint of a plaintiff's attorney, a potentially successful case must have these three elements: a serious injury (worth at least $75,000), regardless of the extent of the violation of the standards; a "deep pocket" belonging to an insurance company or an institution; and someone's behavior that caused the injury.

Soisson et al. (1987) summarize what a plaintiff must demonstrate to support a malpractice claim as follows:

"a. The practitioner owed a duty to the plaintiff that was based on an established therapeutic relationship" (p. 498). This is the simplest part to demonstrate and is not of much concern here.

"b. The quality of care provided by the practitioner fell below the standard of care expected of the average practitioner" (p. 498). This standard used to be determined on a local basis, but is now interpreted by the courts on a regional or national basis. The comparison may be based on the specialty advertised or offered to the patient, or the care offered by other practitioners of a particular school of thought (Knapp & VandeCreek, 1990, p. 85).

"c. The patient suffered or was caused harm or injury" (Soisson et al., 1987, p. 498).

"d. The practitioner's dereliction of duty was the direct cause of the harm or injury" (p. 498).

Many kinds of behaviors can result in liability: negligence, breach of contract, intentional misconduct, defamation, invasion of privacy, failure to prevent an injury, and so on (King, 1977). Wilkinson (1982) adds liability for self-inflicted injuries and suicide, harm by the client to third parties, errors in judgment concerning patient management, harmful treatment methods, and sexual misconduct. Perhaps it should be emphasized that "mistakes are not proof of malpractice" (Knapp & VandeCreek, 1990, p. 86).

The Good News (for Us): The Real Risks Are Small

Medical malpractice suits are rarely successful; the risk of a loss at trial is surprisingly small. Although 100% of those consulting malpractice attorneys are angry at their doctors, only 20% have sufficient facts to file complaints (and some of these are mistaken). Only 10% of lawsuits against physicians go to trial, and in them defendants are exonerated 70–90% of the time; 75% of suits filed are won by the physicians and 60% are resolved without payment to the patients (Barge & Fenalason, 1989). Charles (cited in Barge & Fenalason, 1989) has reported that four of five cases are settled without payment to the plaintiffs, and that in three-fourths of those that go to trial, the physicians are vindicated. Furthermore, "For those who do win . . . the median award is $36,500" (Charles, in Barge & Fenalason, 1989).

The Bad News (for Us): Malpractice Accusations Hurt

As the saying goes, "You can't win a malpractice lawsuit, but you sure can lose one." And you can do so very badly. The actual costs, losses, and hassles pale before the self-doubt, public humiliation, and anxiety. You can be sued for more money than you have or will ever have. Your insurer will at best pay only part of the judgment (but generally most of your defense), and will try to settle the case early (if this is successful, you may be seen as guilty by your peers even if you are innocent). You will spend countless hours sitting in court (where you *are* on trial), giving depositions, having conferences with lawyers, getting support from friends, and engaging in endless self-reproaches and tears. If you are convicted of a felony, you will lose your license and have to find a new line of work. There is now a national data bank of practitioners, maintained by the Health Resources and Services Administration of the U.S. Department of Health and Human Services, in which you are listed if a single dollar is spent on your case—not if you lose your case (i.e., are found guilty). This will make it harder to get onto boards later. If this applies to you, you can review and comment on what is placed in your file. There are very sensitive portraits of the effects of just being accused in Charles (1985), and Charles et al. (1988), Rosenthal (1976), Wilbert et al. (1987), and Eidetics (1988).

Charles et al. (1985, 1988) have described the "malpractice stress syndrome"—a pattern of behaviors, feelings, and thoughts that is much more likely to appear in those involved in a malpractice case than in those not so involved. The sued are more likely to feel depressed, ashamed, misunderstood, defeated, tense, angry, and frustrated. They experience headaches, insomnia, and similar symptoms; drink alcohol excessively; and have suicidal ideation. They stop seeing certain kinds of patients, consider retiring earlier, and discourage their children from entering their profession.

What to Do If You Are Complained Against: A Checklist

The following checklist concerns lawsuits but also generally applies to having a complaint alleged against you with an ethics or licensing board. It is based on recommendations from Wright (1981a, 1981b), Woody (1983), the American Professional Agency (1992), and others.

❏ **If you are served a summons or a subpoena, accept it, but don't overreact to it.** Control your anxiety; don't panic. Keep these points in mind:

> If a large number of allegations are made, this "shotgun" approach is standard practice, and most of the time they are all settled at once.

> Exaggeration and "legalese" are to be expected.

> Lawsuits are not unusual in our society. The vast majority of complaints and lawsuits are frivolous and go nowhere.

> Resolution will take years (from 1 to 3 years usually).

❏ **Call your professional liability insurance agency immediately and supply the information its staff members request.** They will open a file, assign a claims manager at their office, and call a local lawyer. Meet with this attorney as soon as possible. Remember that these contacts with a lawyer *are* privileged communications. If you need more effort or a different approach, hire your own personal defense attorney. Do not make any notes until you have established this relationship, as these documents are not privileged.

❏ **Assemble all relevant documents and records.** Do not alter, add to, or destroy any documents. Show them to no one except your lawyer. Do not release any documents unless your attorney instructs you to do so. Make and keep copies and originals of everything. Do not offer more than is relevant.

❏ **Read the relevant literature.**

❏ **Educate your lawyer about the strengths and weaknesses of your case.** If this is a complaint to the licensing board, consult with your lawyer and prepare a carefully considered reply to the board. The client is likely to read this reply, so be circumspect. Do not divulge confidential information unless you have the client's consent or a subpoena from the board.

❑ **Assume a defensive stance.** Admit nothing and make no self-incriminating statements to *anyone* not covered by confidentiality. If it is a current client, end the therapy immediately with a letter (created with the help of your attorney) advising the client to transfer and offering a few referral names. See Section 6.3 on termination.

❑ **Do not communicate with the client or the client's lawyer by mail or in person.** Do not play therapist any more. Do not attempt to "therapeutically resolve" the issues or to "negotiate" a resolution. These communications are not privileged and can be used against you. Have everything from or to the client or the client's attorney go to and through your attorney.

❑ **Do not play lawyer and attempt to settle the matter.** Don't meet or talk with the client or the opposing lawyer unless your attorney is present. If you do meet with the client's attorney, be sure the client has consented to that conversation. Follow this rule even if you are told that another therapist is the target of potential litigation. Inform the patient's attorney and "Bill the [patient's] attorney for your time, just as you would bill the patient. To not bill might imply that you owe the patient something because of improper care" (Barge & Fenalason, 1989).

❑ **Do not discuss your claim with *anyone* (except your legal spouse) without the agreement of your personal attorney.** Consultation with a trusted colleague or close friend may seem valuable but such conversations are not privileged and can later be used against you. If you do talk to experts in ethics, any lawyers other than your own, or any institutional colleagues, do so only in hypothetical terms. Limit discussions with colleagues to the process of being sued or ways to cope with the stress, and do not discuss details of the case, the care you provided, or any other confidential information. Personal therapy for the stress and other personal issues related to a claim, however, may be valuable, and such conversations *are* considered privileged communications because you are then a client.

❑ Continue to work at your profession to the same high standards.

Do not feel ashamed because you are sued. Remember (as you have no doubt told clients), the fact that someone didn't like what you did does not prove you did anything wrong.

Don't let yourself get depressed or overly concerned. Control your anger as well. Learn to compartmentalize your life.

Remember that being complained against doesn't mean you are a jerk, stupid, or incompetent.

❑ At some point, attorneys will start to talk about a settlement. Discuss any proposals fully with your personal attorney, and weigh the many factors and implications carefully. Do not rush, and make sure you have the resources before you "do the right thing."

❑ When it is all over, create a summary of the case and its outcome. You will need this in later years, when you apply for panel membership and other opportunities. "When the ordeal is over and the dust settles, celebrate your survival and get on with your life. Acknowledge the lessons you've learned, make amends where you need to, and move on" (Boedecker, 1995, p. 3).

❏ If you are accused, read Wright (1981a, 1981b); if you are sued for malpractice, read Cohen (1979, pp. 274–283). It would even be wise to read both in advance.

3.3   Ways to Reduce Your Risk of Malpractice

Note. For a discussion of reducing you risk of malpractice in billing, see Section 2.7.

Twenty-Three Steps for Risk Reduction

As long as you are practicing, you can never totally eliminate your risk for malpractice, but here are 23 concrete steps that can very significantly reduce your risk.

1. **Assure the continuity of each patient's care.** You do not have to accept everyone as a patient, but once you have accepted a patient, don't abandon him or her. See Section 6.3 on termination.

2. **Practice competently.** The central protective rule of ethics is to stay within what you know. We all know how hard it is to know exactly what we don't know, or to know beforehand what we don't know well enough. Clinical knowledge comes from direct training by experienced teachers (e.g., internships); from work at regionally and professionally accredited educational institutions; from training workshops by leaders in the field; from relevant and prolonged supervision; from your own well-considered experience over substantial time; and from thoughtful reading, writing, and teaching. In general, always keep the following guidelines in mind:

   ▪ Never do what you are not legally entitled to do. Do not practice medicine, law, or pharmacy if you are uncredentialled.

   ▪ Do not try to do everything you *are* legally allowed to do. You are *not* competent to handle everything that walks in the door.

   ▪ Moreover, you are probably not really competent to do some things you were exposed to if you did not receive the necessary high quality of training.

   ▪ Make clear the real areas of your competence in your communications to patients, both orally and in writing. Inaccurate expectations can be the basis for a complaint.

   ▪ If you do assessments, use "a well-defined and systematic method of interpreting test findings and be able to support your findings in court" (Cohen, 1990, p. 660). See also Section 3.5 on malpractice in testing.

   ▪ Don't use shortcuts (sending tests home with clients, or depending excessively on computerized test interpretations) (Redlich & Pope, 1980).

- Don't do custody evaluations without evaluating all parties (Redlich & Pope, 1980).

- If you operate in the area of "health psychology" or "behavioral medicine," be especially careful not to "practice medicine without a license." Maintain full, continual, and two-way communication with physicians, and define your roles and knowledge base carefully (Knapp & VandeCreek, 1981b).

3. **Get fully informed consent.** Require competent, informed, and voluntary consent for everything you do. Inform clients fully about the limits of confidentiality. See Chapter 4 on obtaining consent.

4. **Maintain confidentiality.** Know the limits of the confidentiality you can offer, and do not promise more than you can deliver. Inform the client of these limits *before* he or she reveals something you cannot keep confidential. See Chapter 7.

5. **Communicate fully.**

   - Communicate completely. Keep your patients' expectations reality-based.

   - Communicate openly. Become curious about difficulties and failures of communication. Be willing to hear complaints nondefensively.

   - Communicate honestly. Don't pretend to clarity you don't have; the best direction is not always clear, and each case is a little different. Issues and decisions can remain clouded. We can only use our best judgment based on our knowledge, skill, and experience, but we can use all of it and share our concern.

   - Communicate clearly, especially in regard to money, fees, and insurance.

   - Communicate regularly. Your patient handout forms, initial evaluation remarks, and regular feedback on progress are crucial here.

   - Don't be distant. Be kind and warm where appropriate. Show that you care about the client's welfare and are "doing everything in [your] power to help" (Pressman & Siegler, 1983, p. 109).

6. **Supervise fully.** When you supervise, be thorough and be available. Monitor your students, teammates, and employees closely. Supervision is always a difficult balance between paternalism and the encouragement of autonomy, between risk assumption and self-protective fears. Bear in mind that your employees can commit malpractice. Prevention should include training in confidentiality, collections, filing, scheduling, and any other areas that occur to you. Have your supervisees obtain their own professional liability insurance, if possible. If not, you must provide it under your policy; in either case, remember that you will be held responsible for their malpractice.

7. **Keep abreast of new developments on both the clinical and legal fronts.** You must know what is considered high-quality in the field, so you have to keep up on current developments. Put aside time and energy for professional development (more than the minimum required for continuing education credits). Continuing education on

both your methods *and alternative ones* is essential; go to the presentations of those you disagree with. Keep aware of the development of the legal aspects of professional work as well. Remember that the half-life of the knowledge base gained in a PhD program is (at the very most) 10 years.

8. **Consult frequently and formally.** Get consultation when things aren't going well with a patient, whenever you have some unease about something, and definitely when you are considering breaking any rule. Do not delay! If you have doubts or are uncomfortable about your conceptualization or treatment, consult with a colleague and/or your attorney. "Consult" with clients' former therapists by getting records and asking questions. Nonmedical therapists (and many medical therapists) should consult clients' physicians about any medical questions.

9. **Take seriously and evaluate thoroughly any evidence of suicidal ideation or intent.** See Sections 3.9 and 3.10.

10. **Have a contingency plan.** It is much more difficult to plan after a client becomes dangerous to self or others. Your plan should include resources for family or support system contacts, special consultations for both you and the client, medications, referrals, hospitalization, police contacts, contacts with your lawyer, and so on. Tell your client about your options and your duty to warn (see Section 4.2). It may be too late to do this when the client is dangerous, so write this into your datebook this minute.

11. **Refer carefully.**

    ▪ Refer clients when the problem they present is one with which you have little experience or training.

    ▪ Refer only to others who have the necessary areas of competence. Get feedback from those clients you refer and respect, so that you know who is competent and who is not among your possible referral resources.

    ▪ Ethically, a client who does not improve under your care should be referred elsewhere, even when a colleague with the necessary competence seems hard to find or the client is reluctant to start again. At the minimum, the client must be informed and allowed to choose. Document the options, the choices made, and their rationales.

12. **Be conservative in your treatments.** You are required by the ethics of your profession to act prudently and reasonably. If you do not, you are exposing yourself to risk, because you are exposing your patient to substandard treatment.

Having a theoretical rationale for a treatment does not make it ethical; nonetheless, base all your psychotherapeutic interventions on a well-established theory (Woody, 1988a, p. 211). This does not mean that you must *always* follow a recognized "school" with at least a minority of adherents, but courts are likely to move in that direction. Your treatment does not have to have an empirical justification, but it must be seen as acceptable by a significant number of your peers. In general, it will be hard for a court to find fault with the prudently reasoned use of a new and professionally or scientifically supported method by a therapist with strong credentials and no personal gain in sight.

If your treatment lacks this prudence, call it "experimental," tell the patient of other treatment options, get special informed consent, and discontinue it at the first sign of harm to the patient. It is a continuing and difficult professional struggle to balance the use of a scientifically tested method, which (in theory) protects the patient, against the need to tailor any method to the unique client and the need to innovate (for future clients' benefit). This balancing is an inescapable ethical dimension of high-quality practice.

13. **Don't promise a cure.** Be careful when discussing the effectiveness of your treatment approach, and do not allow a client to develop expectations that will not be fulfilled. Promote realistic expectations of treatment outcomes, not overly optimistic expectations of success, by utilizing standardized conceptualizations and classifications and by making probabilistic statements (Cross & Deardorff, 1987, p. 75).

14. **Document.** Get a relevant case history, especially of substance use, violence, homicide, suicide, all previous episodes and treatments, lawsuits, and the like (see the intake materials in Chapter 5). Keep clear, concise, and complete records. Use behavioral descriptions, not just diagnoses, labels, or shortcut jargon. Record the essentials. Pressman and Siegler (1983) suggest: "One way to think about what the medical record should contain might be to think about what you would want to see if you were called in as a new consultant on the case in order to understand the history and to start a course of treatment" (p. 109).

Document your thinking, reasoning, and judgments as well. Record diagnoses, prognoses, progress, and evaluations of outcome. Record your instructions to clients, handouts given to clients, and after-hours calls. Document no-shows (and your responses), consultations, and your arrangements for another professional's covering for you, and for which patients. See Chapters 5 and 6 for a full discussion of clinical record keeping.

15. **Diagnose.** If a case should come to a courtroom, a therapist cannot "hide behind the notion that since his or her theory of therapy does not rely on psychodiagnostics, [no diagnostic evaluation was performed]" (Woody, 1988a, p. 211). A good history may be all that is necessary and *reasonable* (the key word). The extent and nature of this evaluation process depend on your professional discipline as well. Malpractice claims for "misdiagnosis [negligent or improper diagnosis] generally require the use of egregiously inappropriate" methods (Stromberg et al., 1988, p. 453).

A care provider has an obligation (a) to diagnose accurately and thus treat properly; (b) to ensure that a patient who presents with an emotional problem does not suffer from an undiagnosed and untreated coexisting or contributing medical illness; and (c) to provide adequate biological treatment. This burden is especially heavy on care providers who are biased against, lacking proficiency in, or reluctant to obtain consultation for such treatment. In a representative and most instructive case with a negative outcome, the court stated that "the question is not whether the physician made a mistake in diagnosis, but rather whether he failed to conform to the accepted standard of care" in his procedures and judgments (Stromberg & Dellinger, 1993, p. 7). In order to document your own clinical judgments, administer psychological tests as necessary.

16. **Avoid fee disputes and the accumulation of a large debt.** Never turn a debt over for collection without a personal conversation by you (not your secretary or office manager) with the client (not a spouse or other).

17. **Be alert to a patient's dissatisfaction with you.** This may be why the patient is not paying your bill, attending sessions regularly, or complying with treatments. Other early warning signs of dissatisfaction may include a patient's being overconcerned with your fees; being overly critical of a previous therapist or treatment (and therefore likely to be dissatisfied with yours); and having unrealistically high expectations of therapy's outcome (which are bound to be dashed). Of course, all of these should be dealt with as issues in therapy. In addition, factors such as lack of "psychological-mindedness" and entering therapy under external pressure may direct a patient to seek a way out of therapy, to gain revenge, and to make a profit all at the same time—by filing a complaint or suit.

   Pay careful and immediate attention to any patient's disappointment or to failure of any expectations. If you are distant, arrogant, not readily available, or hard to talk to, then a patient may begin to question your competence. Remember that patients are usually not qualified to judge your clinical competence; they can only judge you as they see you, based on your actions as a human being. This is why testimonials from patients were forbidden until the 1992 revision of the APA code of ethics (APA, 1992a), and even now testimonials from current patients are not allowed.

   Of course, any patient's dissatisfaction should be responded to immediately, but this may also be the first warning of a complaint or suit.

18. **Respect the complexities of families and couples.** Be aware that family and marital therapies raise sticky complexities regarding the therapist's responsibility to each person, particularly regarding confidentiality and informed consent. The therapist's own values (about preserving a marriage, extramarital affairs, sex roles, etc.) add to the complexities. Margolin (1982) addresses these issues sensitively and clearly, and advises being open and straightforward with the clients. Her article is required reading for anyone who is designing consent procedures for couples or families.

19. **Don't work if you are burned out.** A significant risk factor for unethical practice is therapist burnout. If you identify with several of the items on this short list, read some of the books on therapist burnout and seek consultation.

   ■ Do you feel pessimistic or even cynical toward clients?

   ■ Have you experienced persistent and interfering daydreams during sessions?

   ■ Have you had hostile thoughts toward any client?

   ■ Are you bored with your clients? Are they beginning to sound the same?

   ■ Do you find yourself overly quick to diagnose?

- Are you overusing medication as treatment for the client or yourself?

- Are you blaming the client?

20. **Respect client differences.** Respect each client's ethnic, religious, cultural, and gender differences. You have an ethical obligation to develop a sensitivity to these differences. There is guidance available from the APA's Office of Minority Affairs (1993). In addition, Section A.2 of the Appendix to this book is a list from Mark Leach, PhD, of Hattiesburg, MS, of a number of applied books to increase sensitivity in the area of cultural and ethnic differences. Respect should extend to religious values as well: Incorporating your spiritual and religious values into your psychotherapy can create conflicts with your training and with scientific findings, not to mention with clients' values. Note that "Having religious convictions is not sufficient qualification to practice pastoral counseling" (i.e., offering religious guidance based on beliefs and values about say, abortion, divorce, or homosexuality) (Younggren, 1993, p. 7).

21. **Terminate properly.** See Section 6.3 for guidance in avoiding abandonment and other problems.

22. **Consider screening clients for litigiousness.** You might think about excluding from your practice clients whom you believe are likely to file lawsuits at some point.

23. **Consider limiting the scope of your practice.** You might limit or plan in the future to limit your practice to a single or a few specialized clinical domains.

Other sources of guidance on malpractice prevention include lists from Cohen (1979) and Knapp (1980).

Other Risk Areas for Malpractice

The 23 steps above pertain to psychotherapy with *adults*. The assessment and treatment of children raise other issues, but there are no separate national guidelines to the ethics of work with children (Morris, 1993), so be careful.

In your writing and publishing, you should be alert to the ethical and legal consequences of scientific fraud, misinformation, plagiarism (uncredited taking of words), duplicate publication (publishing the same or essentially the same findings more than once in order to get more publication credits on your resume), piecemeal/serial publication (unnecessarily separating your findings so you can publish them in several articles to get more publications), and failure to credit authorship properly. An excellent guide to the last of these problems is provided by Fine and Kurdek (1993).

Risks in Repressed-Memory Therapy

Exercise extreme caution if you are considering doing repressed-memory work. In 1992, there were hardly any claims on this issue; by 1994, fully 16% of all professional liability claims against mental health professionals were connected with repressed memory (Marine, cited in "Repressed Memory Claims Expected to Soar," 1995). If you want to persist, Nagy (1994) and Marine and Caudill (1996) recommend that you do the following:

- Rule out, or at least investigate fully, any medical or physical causes for the client's symptoms.

- Consider all alternative methods that are appropriate to the goals. Document your weighing of these and your reasons for rejecting the alternatives and pursuing this method.

- Devise a complete and balanced statement of the risks and benefits of recovering memories, and have the client read, discuss, and sign it.

- Videotape or audiotape all sessions, if possible. Make sure your notes fully "reflect how the memories surfaced and [show] that you did not lead the patient to the conclusion that they were [sic] the victim of abuse" (Marine & Caudill, 1996, p. 12).

- Have clients complete, very early in therapy and in their own handwriting, a detailed personal and family history that will serve to document their "victimization" as to behaviors, affects, memories, family stories, and understandings. This is to prevent the later accusation that you "implanted" memories.

- Remain your patient's therapist, be objective, and do not become their advocate.

- If you plan a confrontation session with a nonpatient, make it clear to the guest that this session is not therapy for him or her and that it may be distressing or negative. Have the guest sign a statement to this effect. Also, make it clear that the guest may leave with no discussion, and that if the guest participates, he or she must agree "not to litigate over what happens during the session" (Marine & Caudill, 1996, p. 12). In addition, do not let the guest pay for the session; meet in a neutral site, not your office; invite a cotherapist or at least a neutral professional observer to be present; and have the neutral observer conduct the session, if possible and with the patient's permission.

- Do not suggest that Amytal or Brevital is a "truth serum."

- Do not use statistics extrapolated from small samples or other weak data correlating childhood abuse with symptoms or disorders as a basis for concluding that abuse occurred.

- Know your local laws (especially on the reporting of abuse) and local ethical codes about areas of competence, documentation, and so on.

- This area is rapidly evolving, so know and keep up to date with the flood of litigation in this area (so you will know how to respond if your clinical case becomes a forensic case), your professional liability coverage and obligations, the mental health professions' statements on these issues, and current research and practice.

3.4 Evaluating the Ethicality of Proposed Treatments

There are hundreds of types or schools of psychotherapy and thousands of interventions. How can you evaluate the ethicality of a technique with a particular client? Each psychotherapist should be able to answer the following questions about every treatment provided to every client. You may not usually consider these questions so formally, but if you are considering any treatment that is unusual, controversial, or experimental, it will be in your long-term best interest to consider answering these by "thinking out loud for the record" to show that you have arrived at your treatment plan thoughtfully. Table 2, a questionnaire prepared by the Association for Advancement of Behavior Therapy (1977), highlights these ethical issues.

3.5 Avoiding Malpractice in Psychological Testing

Pope (1988d) offers 17 specific ways for avoiding malpractice in the areas of assessment, diagnosis, and testing. This section is loosely adapted from his recommendations.

Require the Client to Give Consent

Note. For a full discussion of the meanings of consent, see Section 4.1.

Consent must be all of the following:

- **Competent.** The client must be both old enough and sufficiently intellectually competent to understand the consequences of giving consent, to understand the choices, to make a consistent decision, and to act in his or her best interests. Obviously, for children, the mentally retarded, and others, the substitute consent of a competent and appropriate adult needs to be obtained. This issue is of greater ethical concern when the purpose of testing is to determine competence (e.g., to make a will or life-planning decisions).

- **Voluntary.** Clients must know that they have the option to refuse or discontinue testing without punishment. They must also know the situational consequences if they do not participate (such as loss of disability benefits, promotions, etc.; Sweet, 1990). You and an unbiased peer should be able to agree that a client is not feeling threatened or just being agreeable in consenting.

- **Informed.** Clients must know the purposes, nature, and consequences of the assessment. Specifically, clients must be told all the significant consequences of the testing that can be anticipated, and they must understand the issues, such as conflicts of interest or the ramifications of the results. These are especially important in forensic evaluations. The issues must be explained in terms familiar to the clients. Also, you must be sure to document that these explanations have been given. Clients must be informed that they have the "right to know the results, interpretations made, and the bases for [the psychologists'] conclusions and recommendations" (APA, 1981, p. 637). Any local

C:\mydoc\PP\Therapst Forms\Ethicality Checklist

TABLE 2. Checklist for the Ethicality of Proposed Treatments

A. Have the goals of treatment been adequately considered?
1. To insure that the goals are explicit, are they written?
2. Has the client's understanding of the goals been assured by having the client restate them orally or in writing?
3. Have the therapist and client agreed on the goals of therapy?
4. Will serving the client's interests be contrary to the interests of other persons?
5. Will serving the client's immediate interests be contrary to the client's long-term interest?

B. Has the choice of treatment methods been adequately considered?
1. Does the published literature show the procedure to be the best one available for that problem?
2. If no literature exists regarding the treatment method, is the method consistent with generally accepted practice?
3. Has the client been told of alternative procedures that might be preferred by the client on the basis of significant differences in discomfort, treatment time, cost, or degree of demonstrated effectiveness?
4. If a treatment procedure is publicly, legally, or professionally controversial, has formal professional consultation been obtained, has the reaction of the affected segment of the public been adequately considered, and have the alternative treatment methods been more closely reexamined and reconsidered?

C. Is the client's participation voluntary?
1. Have possible sources of coercion on the client's participation been considered?
2. If treatment is legally mandated, has the available range of treatments and therapists been offered?
3. Can the client withdraw from treatment without a penalty or financial loss that exceeds actual clinical costs?

D. When another person or an agency is empowered to arrange for therapy, have the interests of the subordinated client been sufficiently considered?
1. Has the subordinated client been informed of the treatment objectives and participated in the choice of treatment procedures?
2. Where the subordinated client's competence to decide is limited, have the client as well as the guardian participated in the treatment discussions to the extent that the client's abilities permit?
3. If the interests of the subordinated person and the superordinate persons or agency conflict, have attempts been made to reduce the conflict by dealing with both interests?

E. Has the adequacy of treatment been evaluated?
1. Have quantitative measures of the problem and its progress been obtained?
2. Have the measures of the problem and its progress been made available to the client during treatment?

F. Has the confidentiality of the treatment relationship been protected?
1. Has the client been told who has access to the records?
2. Are records available only to authorized persons?

G. Does the therapist refer the clients to other therapists when necessary?
1. If treatment is unsuccessful, is the client referred to other therapists?
2. Has the client been told that if [he or she is] dissatisfied with the treatment, referral will be made?

H. Is the therapist qualified to provide treatment?
1. Has the therapist had training or experience in treating problems like the client's?
2. If deficits exist in the therapist's qualifications, has the client been informed?
3. If the therapist is not adequately qualified, is the client referred to other therapists, or has supervision by a qualified therapist been provided? Is the client informed of the supervisory relation?
4. If the treatment is administered by mediators, have the mediators been adequately supervised by a qualified therapist?

Note. Reprinted from the Association for Advancement of Behavior Therapy (AABT, 1977). Copyright 1977 by the AABT. Reprinted by permission.

variations on this theme must be included. Clients must be informed about the nature and therapeutic techniques you will use (while keeping in mind the constraints of test security, expectancies, and practice effects). Make certain that you know, and fully inform the clients about, *all* those who will have access to the test report and the raw data. And, lastly, all of this should occur before the testing begins, so you will be in compliance with all laws and your conscience will be clear.

Know the Rules

First, you must know the appropriate standards and guidelines of your discipline. Professional organizations have published many guidelines (see the Appendix, Section A.1d) with which you should be familiar. Generally, you will be held to the national standards, so learn them and provide services at a high level of quality and integrity.

In addition, you must know the current state and local laws. Conflicts between what you promise a client (such as confidentiality of some information divulged to you), and what the governing laws require can be avoided if you know all the applicable laws (such as those concerning clients with both substance abuse and developmental disabilities; Sweet, 1990). For example, which takes precedence—workers' compensation law or mental health law? Stromberg et al. (1988) is an excellent source for guidance.

Stay within Your Areas of Competence

Weiner (1989) has argued that it is possible to be competent at psychological testing without being ethical, but that it is not possible to be ethical without being competent. Don't do everything you are licensed, trained, or even degreed to do. Make certain you are fully trained and practiced in administering, scoring, and interpreting each test you use. If you were last trained in test administration years ago, a consultation with a colleague who observes you may be very enlightening and may improve the validity of your testing. Don't use a test if your administration will be invalid or if your knowledge is insufficient to interpret *all* potential findings validly and fully.

In a remarkably simple and elegant analysis, Moreland et al. (1995) identified seven factors and 86 areas of test user competence, and then, taking critical incidents of test misuse as guides, developed empirically based test purchaser qualification forms. They have listed 12 minimal areas of competence and the seven factors. Ethical guidelines can be drawn from this list such as "Don't coach anyone" and "Refrain from labeling people with derogatory terms like 'dishonest' on the basis of a test score that lacks perfect validity."

Administer Tests the Way They Were Designed

- You must understand the technical aspects of measurement, validation, and evaluation design; the tests, procedures, and materials used; and their limitations and appropriateness for the subject.

- Follow the standardized procedures *exactly* when you are administering and scoring a test, to ensure validity.

- Use only tests whose manuals have the necessary and currently appropriate reliability and validity data. The manuals should also have detailed procedural descriptions of the methods of administering, scoring, and interpreting the tests' results.

- Use the most current, reliable, and valid version of a test. Although, as Sam Knapp (personal communication, October 2, 1996) reminds me, "It can be justified to use an earlier version of a test under some circumstances, for example, in doing a test–retest with a particular patient."

- For test security reasons, do not quote the questions asked (especially from copyrighted tests) in your reports. Instead, describe the stimuli in general terms. Similarly, keep the tests, materials, and manuals unavailable to potential clients and to unsophisticated users. Do not let clients take a test home (this ensures that no one will assist the clients in answering).

Interpret and Report Your Findings Carefully

- It is probably a good idea to write your report as if persons besides the referrer will someday read it. If you are not fully comfortable justifying (perhaps in court and to a hostile opposition) any statement, either leave it out or modify it.

- Don't go beyond your findings: Do not, in your report or through defensiveness stirred up in the courtroom, go beyond your data. The APA ethics code reminds us that psychologists must recognize the "limits to the certainty" of diagnoses, judgments, and predictions (APA, 1992a, Section 2.05).

- Treat test results as hypotheses, not factual pronouncements. After all, they are only behavior samples from the universe of possible behaviors. Even when you use an automated scoring and interpretation service you must understand the decision rules that transform the raw data into interpretative statements, as well as the psychometric properties of the program (especially its reliability and validity). Again, the probabilistic statements generated by the service should be treated as hypotheses and not as facts.

Be Alert for Biasing Factors

- Know and keep in mind the assumptions behind your orientation, and struggle to understand how these can blind you to evidence, shape your expectations, and bias your results.

- Seek out and attend to personal, social, and cultural factors that can bias your results. These may include ageism; "beautyism" (the influence of weight, height, coloring, and prettiness); ethnic preferences and beliefs; racism; sex-role stereotypes; your social class; "personal allergies" to some people; your financial gain from some findings or diagnoses; sympathy with the "victim"; hostility to the "aggressor"; blaming the victim; supporting the downtrodden; your personal liberalism or conservatism; feelings about smokers, drinkers, abstainers, those "in recovery," the pious, or the agnostic; and other less well-defined feelings that can interfere with careful analysis.

- Understand and always weigh in the "low base rate" phenomenon, which can severely limit the accuracy of any variable's identification. Similarly, appreciate the effects of a high base rate, and know the local base rates of the phenomena of interest.

- In your report, state clearly all possible limitations of and reservations about reliability and validity:

  Environmental factors: room lighting, a client's poor hearing or need for glasses, interruptions, noise.

  Communicational factors: the client's hearing, speech, and facility in English (written, read, heard, and spoken). For example, the Minneapolis Multiphasic Personality Inventory (MMPI) requires an eighth-grade reading level.

  The client's personal aspects: age, sex, education, and ethnic/cultural background.

  Any differences between the client and the norming population, which might invalidate the use of a test for this client. When such differences exist, weight them.

Be Aware of Forensic Issues

Never take a contingency fee for forensic evaluations (because doing so appears to compromise your professional independence), and do not base custody evaluations on less than full evaluations of all parties. Anderten et al. (1980) add several other considerations for forensic evaluations:

- Be especially careful to be objective and impartial, resisting pressure to support the position of the side that hires you.

- Work with your attorney to assure that *all* of your relevant findings will be heard in court.

- Make your first priority the client's well-being, not your loyalty to the attorney or agency.

Be Thorough

- Consider possible physical causes of any and all findings and pursue their investigation.

- Always obtain and review previous testing and treatment records.

Finally, as always, you should stay current on the literature, the issues, and the evolving state of the assessment arts.

3.6 Boundary Issues

Several of the ethical problems described earlier can be understood as "boundary issues": failure to clarify or maintain differences between client and therapist; crossing the boundary between friend and therapist; not keeping your private life out of your work; forming sexually intimate relationships in therapy; and so on. Excellent reviews of these issues can be found in Smith and Fitzpatrick (1995) and Gutheil and Gabbard (1993). A very good self-educational questionnaire exploring the consequences of boundary confusion is the Exploitation Index (Epstein & Simon, 1990). Boundary issues stemming from "dual relationships" in general, and from client–therapist sexual intimacy in particular, are discussed in detail in the next two sections.

Take the time to answer the questionnaire presented in Figure 4. To gain most from it, consider all your clients when answering it, not just the one it asks about. The questions are likely to raise your consciousness of how these issues can distort your work. I am indebted to Estelle Disch, PhD, of Boston, MA, for her permission to reprint it, and to Sam Knapp, EdD, of Harrisburg, PA, for suggesting the addition of the last four items.

3.7   Dual Relationships

What Are Dual Relationships?

"Dual relationships" exist whenever a therapist interacts with a client in more than this one role or capacity as therapist, such as also being a business partner, teacher, consultant, or sexual partner. In psychiatry, most of these are called "double agentry."

Why Avoid Dual Relationships?

Performing any role besides that of therapist creates goals, needs, and desires that are yours and not the client's. Dual relationships seem inevitably to lead to conflicts between your interests and the client's, and so you may not put the client's interest first. **Thus, dual relationships impair your unselfish judgment which is the essence of being a professional.** In addition, such relationships can have these negative effects:

- They limit the effective handling of the transference and other relationship variables.

- They usually close the door to future therapy if it is needed.

- The power differential inherent in the therapy relationship may be exploited through seducing or intimidating the client into the other relationship.

- In addition, when clients are exploited in dual relationships, complaining about it is much more difficult for them than complaining about most other issues, like fees. The clients must overcome the power differential and transference in order to assert their own needs. The risks to a client are usually much greater than the risks to a therapist. For example, in a complaint, confidentiality may be broken and the therapist can say, allege, or deny almost anything about the client's life, thus putting the client on trial.

Dual relationships usually stem from "subtle, gradual, and innocuous beginnings" (Pope, 1988a, p. 17). They may arise from inattention to the dynamics of the therapeutic relationship, or from a desire to be of even more help to a patient. They can also arise from the patient's own manipulation (because of pathology, transference, or other sources); in these cases, "dual" relationships often become "duel" relationships.

Are You in Trouble with a Client?

The purpose of this checklist is to alert you to boundary issues that might be interfering with your ability to work effectively with a particular client. Be particularly attentive if the situation persists even after you have attempted to change it. Answer either true or false to each question and add any explanations or details.

Client's initials or pseudonym: _____ Date: _____

1. This client feels more like a friend than a client. ❏ True ❏ False

2. I often tell my personal problems to this client. ❏ True ❏ False

3. I feel sexually aroused in response to this client. ❏ True ❏ False

4. I want to be friends with this client when therapy ends. ❏ True ❏ False

5. I'm waiting for therapy to end in order to be lovers with this client. ❏ True ❏ False

6. To be honest, I think the good-bye hugs last too long with this client. ❏ True ❏ False

7. My sessions often run overtime with this client. ❏ True ❏ False

8. I tend to accept gifts or favors from this client without examining why the gift was given and why at that particular time. ❏ True ❏ False

9. I have a barter arrangement with this client. ❏ True ❏ False

10. I have had sexual contact with this client. ❏ True ❏ False

11. I sometimes choose my clothing with this particular client in mind. ❏ True ❏ False

12. I have attended small professional or social events at which I knew this client would be present, without discussing it ahead of time. ❏ True ❏ False

13. This client often invites me to social events and I don't feel comfortable saying either yes or no. ❏ True ❏ False

14. This client sometimes sits on my lap. ❏ True ❏ False

15. Sometimes when I'm holding or hugging this client during our regular therapy work, I feel like the contact is sexualized for one or the other or both of us. ❏ True ❏ False

16. There's something I like about being alone in the office with this client when no one else is around. ❏ True ❏ False

17. I lock the door when working with this client. ❏ True ❏ False

18. This client is very seductive and I often don't know how to handle it. ❏ True ❏ False

19. This client owes me/the agency a lot of money and I don't know what to do about it. ❏ True ❏ False

20. I have invited this client to public or social events. ❏ True ❏ False

21. I am often late for sessions with this particular client. ❏ True ❏ False

22. I find myself cajoling, teasing, or joking a lot with this client. ❏ True ❏ False

23. I am in a heavy emotional crisis myself and I identify so much with this client's pain that I can hardly attend to the client. ❏ True ❏ False

(cont.)

FIGURE 4. Are you in trouble with a client? Questionnaire for assessing boundary issues, devised by Estelle Disch, PhD, of Boston, MA, and reprinted here by permission of Dr. Disch. (Items 48–51 were suggested by Sam Knapp, EdD, of Harrisburg, PA.)

Figure 4 (*cont.*)

24. I allow this client to comfort me. ❑ True ❑ False

25. I feel like this client and I are very much alike. ❑ True ❑ False

26. This client scares me. ❑ True ❑ False

27. This client's pain is so deep I can hardly stand it. ❑ True ❑ False

28. I enjoy feeling more powerful than this client. ❑ True ❑ False

29. Sometimes I feel like I'm in over my head with this client. ❑ True ❑ False

30. I often feel hooked or lost with this client and supervision on the case hasn't helped. ❑ True ❑ False

31. I often feel invaded or pushed by this client and have a difficult time standing my ground. ❑ True ❑ False

32. Sometimes I hate this client. ❑ True ❑ False

33. I sometimes feel like punishing or controlling this client. ❑ True ❑ False

34. I feel overly protective toward this client. ❑ True ❑ False

35. I sometimes drink or take drugs with this client. ❑ True ❑ False

36. I don't regularly check out what the physical contact I have with this client means for the client. ❑ True ❑ False

37. I accommodate to this client's schedule and then feel angry/manipulated. ❑ True ❑ False

38. This client's fee feels too high or too low. ❑ True ❑ False

39. This client has invested money in an enterprise of mine or vice versa. ❑ True ❑ False

40. I have hired this client to work for me. ❑ True ❑ False

41. This client has hired me to work for her/him. ❑ True ❑ False

42. I find it very difficult not to talk about this client with people close to me. ❑ True ❑ False

43. I find myself saying a lot about myself with this client—telling stories, engaging in peer-like conversation. ❑ True ❑ False

44. If I were to list people in my caseload with whom I could envision myself in a sexual relationship, this client would be on the list. ❑ True ❑ False

45. I call this client a lot and go out of my way to meet with her/him in locations convenient to her/him. ❑ True ❑ False

46. This client has spent time at my home (apart from the office). ❑ True ❑ False

47. I'm doing so much on this client's behalf I feel exhausted. ❑ True ❑ False

48. I have given this client a ride home. ❑ True ❑ False

49. We have had lunch/dinner during sessions. ❑ True ❑ False

50. This client has performed minor favors for me, such as returning library books or picking up dry cleaning. ❑ True ❑ False

51. I have accepted valuable gifts from this client. ❑ True ❑ False

Types of Dual Relationships

There are many types of dual relationships, and therapists must be alert to all the possibilities. Pope (1988a) lists 18 real-life scenarios (and I have added some others), which can be simplified into the following general kinds of relationships.

Double Roles

Double roles include being a therapist as well as a supervisor, teacher (see below), dissertation committee member, evaluator, or research supervisor to the same person. Another example of double roles is providing therapy to current social acquaintances or business contacts, or to former ones when the old relationship was intense. Any such double roles are likely to distort the therapy relationship.

Being both a therapist and a friend is a third example of double roles. A "friend" is defined as someone with whom one socializes outside the therapy office (or the friend or close relative of such a person). There are many distinctions between friendship and therapy, and the patient handout provided a little later (Handout 1) describes some of them. A policy is also included in the sample client information brochure (Section 4.2), and you may wish to make additions to this list from your own experience. You may even wish to expand upon the list in Section 4.2 for a separate handout; if you do so, please share the results with me.

Other examples of double roles include the following:

- Having any kind of sexual relationship with a former or current client (see Section 3.8).

- Having any kind of business relationship with a former or current client (that of employer, coauthor, consultant, advisor, mentor, partner, lender, debtor, etc.).

- Providing any kind of psychological services to the children of your employees; to children of colleagues, friends, or frequent social, political, or business contacts; or to children you coach in an athletic activity.

- In regard to students (see above), always refer your current students seeking therapy, and be careful about relationships with those who might become your students. It may even be better to remain somewhat distant, have only casual contacts, or meet only at social events associated with the university until a student graduates and one of your roles terminates, before entering a closer friendship with this person (Keith-Spiegel & Koocher, 1985, p. 273).

Double Professions

The term "double professions" means serving in a second professional capacity with your patients, such as practicing law/medicine/financial advising (or any other profession) without a license (Pope, 1988a).

Double Financial Relationships

Double financial relationships are a third type of dual relationships. Trading or bartering therapy for legal or professional services (e.g., tutoring), goods, or discounts, either on a dollar-for-dollar value or on a task-for-task basis, puts you into an additional commercial role. In this role your goals are, or appear to be, in conflict with those of your clients. That is, you seem to be giving services at the lowest cost to you for the highest cost to them.

When Dual Relationships Are Not Avoidable: Weighing Their Effect

Dual relationships are unavoidable in rural areas, in the military, and in most small communities. The central issue is the avoidance of *conflicting* roles. The APA ethics code recognizes that "in many communities and situations it may not be feasible or reasonable" (APA, 1992a, Section 1.17A) to avoid nonprofessional encounters with clients, their parents, and so on. Thus the code does not forbid dual or multiple relationships, but puts the burden of keeping them harmless on the psychologist. Eleven guidelines for doing so are offered by Barnett and Yutrzenka (1994).

In an intelligent and thoughtful article, Gottlieb (1993) proposes that since dual relationships are often unavoidable and are not prohibited outright, their variable effects ought to be weighed on three dimensions: "power," "duration," and the clarity of the time limits of the relationship, which he calls "termination." Essentially, relationships with low power differentials, briefer contacts, and clear time boundaries are less risky for exploitation, require less consultation, require less extensive and detailed informed consent, and so on. For example, vocational testing consultation is lower on all three dimensions than intensive psychotherapy. For carefully reasoned arguments and suggestions about defining which multiple relationships are harmful and which are not, see Sonne (1994) and Gonsiorek and Brown (1989).

If you recognize that you are deep in conflicting and risky dual relationships with a patient, Kaplan (1990) recommends that you do the following[1]:

- Don't wait until the patient makes it clear that a problem has developed. Act.

- Get consultation about (1) the dynamics of the dual relationships, (2) how best to end the dual relationships, and (3) how to create the least harm to the patient.

- Review your insurance policy and inform your carrier.

- Talk to an attorney to learn how to limit your liability.

- With the patient's agreement, try to get a mediator to devise a "mutually agreeable, constructive solution which works toward restoration of a healthy therapeutic relationship or, in the alternative, develop a means to terminate both . . . relationship[s] without harming the patient through abandonment" (Kaplan, 1990, p. 30).

[1]This list is adapted from Kaplan (1990). Copyright 1990 by the Illinois Psychological Association. Adapted by permission.

- "Arrange for an independent evaluation of the patient to determine whether the patient has been harmed and to develop future treatment recommendations" (Kaplan, 1990, p. 30).

- Document all interactions with the patient and your memories of how the dual relationship arose.

- Document any agreements with the patient, and have them reviewed by both your own counsel and the patient's.

Preventing Trouble

HANDOUT 1 A handout on dual relationships is presented as Handout 1. It is intended to be used for patient education, and thus to lessen troubles in this area. It can be left in your waiting room or handed to a patient when questions or a potentially risky situation occurs.

Limits of the Therapy Relationship: What Clients Should Know

Psychotherapy is a professional service I can provide to you. Because of the nature of therapy, our relationship has to be different from most relationships. It may differ in how long it lasts, in the topics we discuss, or in the goals of our relationship. It must also be limited to the relationship of therapist and client *only.* If we were to interact in any other ways, we would then have a "dual relationship" which would not be right, and may not be legal. The different therapy professions have rules against such relationships to protect us both.

I want to explain why having a dual relationship is not a good idea. Dual relationships can set up conflicts between my own (the therapist's) interests and your (the client's) best interests, and then the client's interests might not be put first. In order to offer all my clients the best care, my judgment needs to be unselfish and professional.

Because I am your therapist, dual relationships like these are improper:

- I cannot be your supervisor, teacher, or evaluator.
- I cannot be a therapist to my own relatives, friends (or the relatives of friends), people I know socially, or business contacts.
- I cannot provide therapy to people I used to know socially, or to former business contacts.
- I cannot have any other kind of business relationship with you besides the therapy itself. For example, I cannot employ you, lend to or borrow from you, or trade or barter your services (things like tutoring, repairing, legal advice, dentistry, etc.) or goods for therapy.
- I cannot give legal, medical, financial, or any other type of professional advice.
- I cannot have any kind of romantic or sexual relationship with a former or current client, or any other people close to a client.

There are important differences between therapy and friendship. As your therapist, I cannot be your friend. Friends may see your position only from their personal viewpoints and experiences. Friends may want to find quick and easy solutions to your problems so that they can feel helpful. These short-term solutions may not be in your long-term best interest. Friends do not usually follow up on their advice to see whether it was useful. They may *need* to have you do what they advise. A therapist offers you choices and helps you choose what is best for you. A therapist helps you learn how to solve problems better and make better decisions. A therapist's responses to your situation are based on tested theories and methods of change. You should also know that therapists are required to keep the identity of their clients secret. Therefore, I may ignore you when we meet in a public place, and I must decline to attend your family's gatherings if you invite me. Lastly, when our therapy is completed, I will not be able to be a friend to you like your other friends.

In sum, my duty as therapist is to care for you and my other clients, but *only* in the professional role of therapist. Please note any questions or concerns on the back of this page so we can discuss them.

3.8 Sexual Intimacies in Therapy

Sexual relationships with patients are a particularly toxic type of dual relationship and they constitute a plague in the health professions. We must greatly extend our efforts to prevent them through consciousness raising, training, supervision, investigation, and punishment. The American Psychological Association's code of ethics (APA, 1992a, Section 4.05) says flatly: "Psychologists do not engage in sexual intimacies with current or former patients."

What Is Meant by "Sexual Intimacies"?

Although there is no precise agreement on the definition of "sexual intimacy," the following statements are made in the professional liability insurance policies of several professional organizations.

The American Professional Agency's (1995) policy (from the Executive Risk Indemnity, Inc.) defines "sexual misconduct" this way:

> any type of actual, alleged, attempted, or proposed physical touching or caressing or suggestions thereof by *You* or by any person for whom *You* may be legally responsible, with or to any of *Your* past or present patients or clients, or with or to any relative or member of the same household of any such patient or client, or with or to any person with whom such patient or client or relative has an affectionate personal relationship, which could be considered sexual in nature and/or inappropriate to any psychological services being provided. (American Professional Agency, 1995, p. 6; emphasis in original)

The policy sponsored by the American Psychiatric Association (Psychiatrists' Risk Retention Group, 1996) for its "Members" excludes coverage for "undue familiarity with the Claimant" and for "mishandling of the transference or counter-transference phenomenon":

> Undue familiarity means, with respect to a patient, a former patient, or a member of the patient's immediate family or household (hereinafter the "Claimant"), any actual or alleged sexual or social relationship between a Member and the Claimant or any actual or alleged physical contact by a Member of such Claimant, or any other demonstrated intention or act for the purpose of sexual gratification or stimulation, including but not limited to, with respect to such Claimant, any actual or alleged mishandling of the transference or counter-transference phenomena, harrassment, or abandonment. (Psychiatrists' Risk Retention Group, 1996, p. 12)

The policy available for psychologists (from the APA's Insurance Trust, Chicago Insurance Company) states that it

> does not apply to any *Claims* made or Suits brought against any *Insured* alleging, in whole or in part, sexual assault, abuse, molestation, or licentious, immoral, amoral, or any other behavior which threatened, led to or culminated in any sexual act whethere committed intentionally, negligently, inadvertently or with the belief, erroneous or otherwise, that the other party is consenting and has the legal and mental capacity to consent thereto, that was committed, or alleged to have been committed by the *Insured* or by any person for whom the *Insured* is legally responsible. . . . This exclusion applies regardless of the legal theory or basis upon which the *Insured* is alleged to be legally liable or responsible, in whole or in part, for any *Damages* arising out of such actual or alleged behavior, including but not limited to, assertions of improper or negligent hiring, employment or supervision, failure to protect the other party, failure to prevent the sexual misconduct, failure to prevent assault and battery or failure to discharge the employee. (Interstate Insurance Group, 1994, p. 4, emphasis in original)

As you can see, current policies are very broadly written. In addition, state laws differ in defining sexual behaviors; some indicate only intercourse, while others include kissing and sexual touching but may be silent on other kinds of sexual expression.

With Whom Are Sexual Intimacies Prohibited?

Sexual intimacies are not allowed with "clients" of any kind, including supervisees, trainees, students of yours, or any persons in a professional relationship with you (e.g., business partners or employees). In parallel, the APA ethics code (APA, 1992a) says that you should not do therapy with former sexual partners.

It also appears best to say no to sexualized relationships with relatives of clients and ex-clients, members of a client's household, or even anyone (such as an ex-spouse or a boyfriend or girlfriend) with whom any of these persons has or had a close emotional relationship. Although this is the most stringent exclusionary approach, it may be better to be safe that sorry, in light of the direction the field is going.

Stromberg and Dellinger (1993) raise the question of how state regulations define "patient." This may be of considerable importance to psychologists, who often have a wider spectrum of possible professional relationships than do psychiatrists or social workers. For example, psychologists see assessment subjects, organizational clients, research participants, employment counseling clients, and the like. Obviously, psychologists have to know the answer to this question and be circumspect; regulators tend to think in polarities, whereas psychologists may evaluate patienthood in terms of the intensity, duration, and intimacy of the relationship.

Who Is Prohibited from Engaging in Intimacies?

You as the therapist are prohibited from engaging in sexual intimacies, of course, but those you employ or supervise are also thus prohibited.

The Damage to the Client and to Therapy

Therapist–client sexual intimacies are universally prohibited because they betray trust, and so the harm to the client can be extensive (Pope, 1988b). There have been problems with the collection of empirical data in this area; as a result, we have only the upper and lower limits of occurrence rates, and descriptions of some of the damage from these relationships (Williams, 1992).

Frequently reported consequences to the client (Bouhoutsos et al., 1983) include ambivalence, distrust of men or women, and distrust of therapy. The victims become "therapeutic orphans." They may have flashbacks, nightmares, and other recollections, and/or depression, hospitalizations, and suicides. They may exhibit relationship problems, with confusion about identity, boundaries, and roles. They may experience feelings of anger, abandonment, exploitation, devastation, guilt, emptiness, and isolation; they may also show suppressed rage, emotional dyscontrol, and mood swings.

Pope (1988b) has described the "therapist–patient sex syndrome" as similar both to Posttraumatic Stress Disorder and to the sequelae of child or spouse abuse, rape, and incest. According to Pope, this syndrome involves "(a) ambivalence, (b) a sense of guilt, (c) feelings of emptiness and isolation, (d) sexual confusion, (e) impaired ability to trust, (f) identity, boundary, and role confusion, (g) emotional lability . . . , (h) suppressed rage, (i) increased suicidal risk, and (j) cognitive dysfunction . . . " (1988, p. 222). Folman (1990) has suggested that 11 psychotherapy processes are all affected negatively by sexual contacts: transference, countertransference, trust, confidentiality, resistance, privacy, intimacy, boundaries, self-disclosure, use of touch, and termination. Theory suggests that the effects may differ for men and women, may be worse if the therapist initiates the intimacies and is married, and may also be worse if the client has been victimized before. In summary, if any of the negative consequences described here is likely to occur, they are so serious that taking the chance that a patient *won't* be harmed is unethical. As clinicians, we do have a minimal ethical duty: "At least do no harm."

Negative Consequences to the Clinician

The helping professions no longer ignore sexual relations with clients. It appears that, in fact, the trend is toward greater enforcement, condemnation, and punishment. If you need reinforcements for abstaining from sexual intimacies, here are some from Keith-Spiegel (1977) and others:

- Subsequent therapists will support and encourage your ex-client to complain.

- Your client/lover will expect commitment, or at least a continuation of the relationship, from you; you will then have to deal with a spurned lover, not a helped client.

- The mass media love these cases. You will be publicly pilloried.

- Some states make ethical violations illegal, so you can lose your license.

- As of 1996, 15 states have criminalized sexual contact between therapists and clients. It is a felony and the maximum sentence is 20 years in prison and a fine of $150,000.

- Intimacy with a client is likely to result in multiple legal problems. Gary Schoener, an expert in this area, says, "I call it a triple whammy. First, a criminal case can result in a prison term or probation and a large fine. Second, a criminal conviction makes it more likely that a therapist will lose a civil case and have to cough up monetary damages. Third, criminal conviction usually makes it an easy and fast job for a state board to revoke professional licenses" (Schoener, quoted in Foster, 1996, p. 25).

- R. Folman (personal communication, August 29, 1996) reports that several therapists have made suicide attempts when confronted with accusations of sexual improprieties.

- You cannot really win if you are sued; you will experience excruciating stress, lost money, and marital conflict (if you are married). Your professional liability insurance probably won't cover the damages awarded: Insurers generally cover only up to $25,000 for sexual cases, and many will not cover these at all. Current practice is for the insurance company to offer the $25,000 only for the defense of the claim, and nothing to settle the claim or pay any damages awarded. Therefore, you alone will be fully responsible for any damage awards. Insurance companies argue that their policies don't cover intentional or knowing misconduct, and that your ethics code and the literature have put you "on notice" that these are wrong (Stromberg & Dellinger, 1993). Moreover, you can even be sued by the patient (and his or her spouse, if any) for such things as intentional infliction of harm (Stromberg & Dellinger, 1993, p. 9)

Not Me! I Would Never!

Misconceptions and distortions abound about sexually intimate and abusing therapists. Pope (1989b) has identified categories and scenarios for therapists who became sexually intimate with patients. On the basis of his work and that of others, we can debunk the following misconceptions:

- It is not true that only poorly trained therapists get sexually involved with patients.

- It is not true that only jerks get sexually involved; respected, influential, successful, or prominent therapists also do the same.

- It is not true that the sexually active therapist is seen as a hero. Such a therapist's sexual behaviors will be seen as exploitative and motivated by feelings of inadequacy (Keith-Spiegel, 1977).

- It is not true that sexual intimacies can be simply an extension of sex education or sex therapy.

- It is not true that sexual intimacies can be a component of trailblazing or innovative therapy.

- It is not true that sexual intimacies may be justified if the consequence of refusal would be the client's suicide or something else as serious. (If this idea even flickers though your mind, consult a peer to examine this rationalization and find ethical alternatives.)

- It is not true that abusing therapists will only abuse one sex, so confining their practice to the other sex will safeguard their clients.

- It is not true that the termination of therapy legitimizes the intimacy. You cannot simply discharge or refer a patient and then pursue a relationship.

- It is not true that waiting a year after discharge means "it can't be transference" and thus it is all right.

- It is not true that "anyone can get carried away with passion." You will be held responsible for your behavior.

- It is not true that sincerely believing that sexual attraction is totally inappropriate and harmful protects a therapist from being sexually attracted (Bennett et al., 1990).

- The Group for the Advancement of Psychiatry (GAP, 1990) offers some common rationalizations that have led therapists into trouble:

  "If we had met socially I'm sure we would have had a great relationship right from the start. Why should we be penalized by our bad luck in merting this way?"

  "We are both mature people, and basically healthy, so we can handle the relationship despite any transference distortions."

- It is possible that real, true love—not just transference—can happen in therapy, but it is not at all certain that a client and a therapist can accurately distinguish it. Therapists and clients have married after the therapeutic issues are resolved, but the burden of demonstrating that such a relationship is not exploitative rests completely on the therapist. See below.

Is Sexual Intimacy with a Client *Ever* Acceptable?

Sexual intimacy with a client is *never* acceptable, even if the therapy is over. **It is always your responsibility to say "No." "Never—without time limits"** is the safest course. As of December 1988, the American Psychiatric Association felt that "Sexual involvement with one's former patients generally exploits emotions deriving from treatment and therefore almost always is unethical" (quoted in GAP, 1990, p. 59).

For psychologists, the code of ethics (APA, 1992a, Section 4.07) sets a 2-year posttherapy time limit, but after that the psychologist is responsible for demonstrating that the relationship is not exploitative (Section 4.07(b)). This is slippery; a therapist in love/lust/loneliness is likely to be a poor judge of these issues. Adler (1988) offers guidance for consultation seekers in this area. It is also educational to read the APA code's list of criteria for evaluating potential exploitativeness: the amount of time that has passed since termination; the nature and duration of the therapy; the circumstances of termination; the client's personal history; the likelihood of adverse impact on the client *or others*; and any statements or actions made by the therapist during the course of therapy *suggesting or inviting* the possibility of a posttermination sexual *or romantic* relationship with the patient (APA, 1992a; modified and emphasis added).

Individual states, however, are enacting laws concerning the time limits. Florida (Fla. Stat. Chapter 21U-15004) considers the therapy relationship "to continue in perpetuity," whereas California believes in a 2-year limit (Cal. Civil Code Section 43.93), as do Ohio and Minnesota. There is also much uncertainty about the statute of limitations for suing. Generally it has run from the time of the incident, but courts are now accepting the idea that the statute may not start until the harm is discovered or recognized, and this may be years later. "Thus, in essence, most courts are bending over backwards to permit patients to proceed with suits against abusive therapists—even if their mental state caused considerable delay in doing so" (Stromberg & Dellinger, 1993, p. 10).

Because of the many options and factors involved, therapists who are sexually involved with clients or ex-clients can never be sure that they will not be sued for sexual intimacies, no matter how long it has been since the termination of therapy. For all these reasons, "never" is safest for both you and your clients.

Other "What If . . . ?" Situations

- Sex with a client is not allowed even if you believe it is in the client's best interest (as sex therapy, as a means of raising his or her self-esteem or sexual confidence, as a restitutive emotional experience, etc.) If you are afraid that discontinuing a sexual relationship will have negative consequences, these consequences may happen anyway. Consult.

- Sex is not allowed even if the client is a consenting adult who wants to have sex, initiates it, authorizes it, says it's OK, promises it will be no problem for you, pleads, or the like. In the laws making therapist–client sex a felony, consent (by the client) is specifically ruled out as a defense to be used by the therapist. So if you and a client have sexual intimacies, you are guilty *de jure.*

- Even if what you feel for a client is "true love," sex is not allowed. Sorry, but your feelings do not count here. It is probably unethical even when you fully intend to marry a client or ex-client. Plans change; promises don't.

- Sex, of course, is not allowed with force, seduction, drugs, threats, or intimidation.

- If you think, "Sex outside the office is OK because it is not therapy," think again. Sex is not allowed even if you never discuss therapy in bed.

- Sorry, but even *flirting* is out. This is not a legitimate or reliable way to raise the self-esteem of a patient.

- *No* kind of sex is allowed. Remind yourself that sexual activities are not just limited to intercourse, not just genital, not just heterosexual.

- Regarding touching: The safest rule, "never touch," seems too conservative and crippling to both parties. Some guidelines from Meiselman (1990, p. 138) were originally devised for treating adult women who were sexually abused as children, but seem sensible and well reasoned:

  "Wait for the client to spontaneously initiate touch or indicate a willingness to be touched." This allows the client to retain control and security.

  "Specifically ask for the client's permission before touching her in any way." This allows cognitive reinforcement of affects and supports the client's control of her (or his) body.

  "Avoid falling into a routinized pattern of touching," because "establishing a custom of touching can cause the client to feel coerced into allowing touching . . . when she would prefer to avoid it."

  "Decline any form of touch that seems likely to be sexually stimulating to either party." Be aware that *any* touch can be sexualized, and the contact may be erotic only to the patient. This rule reinforces boundaries and the rule that both parties have the right to say "No."

A Checklist of Preventive Measures

❏ Inform clients early in therapy about ethical limits. (See, e.g., Handout 1 and see Section 4.2)

❏ Reduce your vulnerability by doing nothing but therapy in the office, keeping the office businesslike, and perhaps never being alone in the office suite with some clients.

❏ Be sensitive to how each client may interpret your nonsexual or affectionate behaviors, conversation about sexual topics, jokes, efforts to be helpful, and so forth. Even simple touches and expressions of concern can be misinterpreted. Think how the patient will interpret your touching him or her. Explain what you are doing and why before you do it, so that it will not be seen as a sexual overture (Bennett et al., 1990).

❏ Monitor your feelings throughout the therapy. If your attraction or fantasies become strong or distracting, consult immediately.

❏ Ask yourself: What effects will a sexual relationship with this client have on my other important relationships?

❏ Remind yourself: You really need this career. You have worked hard and long for it, and you are, or will be, very good at it. Don't throw it away for a little "fun." There is an old saying (and not only for men): "Don't let the little head do the thinking for the big head."

What to Do If a Client Asks You for Sex

If a client asks you for sex, plan your reaction carefully, because this is a high-risk situation for you and a high-vulnerability time for the client. Maintain the client's self-esteem (say you are flattered), and clarify the request. In particular, explore the issues therapeutically:

■ Is the client attracted to your role or power, or to you as a person?

■ Are there transference, avoidance, authority, or parental issues?

■ Is the client subverting the therapy to avoid confrontation and change?

■ Is the client setting up another defeat of a therapist, failure of treatment, or failure of his or her own efforts? (Any of these could be a reflection of infantile, narcissistic, or helplessness needs.)

Rutter (quoted in Foster, 1996, p. 27) offers this observation:

> A client trying to seduce a therapist may be repeating past injuries, but is also most likely searching for a response that will discourage this repetition. The client is doing exactly what patients are supposed to do when they see their doctors: bringing her [sic] illness to her therapist, her self-destructive pattern, in the only way she knows how, by repeating it with her therapist, right there in the room. Along with her hunger for warmth and affection, she is showing her therapist that she has always been out of control of her own sexual boundaries. The therapist can either victimize her as others have, or he can offer her a way to begin recovering from her past injuries.

When you say "No" to the client (as you must), make the "No" solid. Do not be ambiguous. Don't say "Only if . . . ," or "When . . . ," or "However . . . ," or even "No, but . . . ". Say, "It is unethical and would be harmful to you. Not after therapy is over. Never, under any conditions." Set and keep rigid boundaries.

Consciousness Raising

In an appendix to their book, Pope and Bouhoutsos (1986), offer a list of situations in which the risk of sexual intimacy with a client is high. Their list is rephrased below, with some additions, for consciousness-raising purposes.[2]

You are at increased risk when you are:

- Preoccupied with your personal problems when in therapy.

- Playing the authority on everything and becoming angry when challenged.

- Dressing, talking, or acting in a flirtatious or seductive manner with a patient.

- Prescribing that a client dress, talk, or act in a flirtatious or seductive manner. You are at some increased risk of the patient's misunderstanding when you prescribe seductive behavior (as in dating skills training or sexual therapy), or especially when you have him or her rehearse with you. Therefore, be extra careful to get fully informed consent. Also, you might want to involve a consultant or even a witness to your therapy plan and methods.

- Prescribing sexual behaviors for your vicarious pleasure, curiosity, voyeurism, or sense of power.

- Prescribing abstinence or proscribing some relationship because you are jealous.

- Discussing sexual material because of your own interests rather than the patient's clinical needs.

- "Dating" your patient—taking him or her out for lunch, a drink, a film, or an art gallery. Treating agoraphobia *in vivo* might lead to these situations.

- Scheduling a patient so that you have lots of time with him or her (last patient of the day), or can be alone together, or can have extra sessions with him or her.

- Wallowing in a "mutual admiration society": giving or receiving excessive compliments, basking in the glow of the client's appreciation while ignoring or minimizing the distortion, rationalizing away either party's limitations.

---

[2]Most of this list is adapted from Pope and Bouhoutsos (1986). Copyright 1986 by the Greenwood Publishing Group, Inc. Adapted by permission.

- Not examining your attraction or arousal in light of the therapy's dynamics and your own psychological state and needs, and not offering an appropriate and therapeutic response.

- Isolating the patient from other sources of assistance so that you become his or her "lifeline," and he or she is less likely to tell another professional of your sexual relations.

- Isolating yourself from consultation, peers, supervision, and education.

- Believing that in the case of this patient, there are special mitigating factors that make sex OK (GAP, 1990, p. 58).

By far the most common scenario in which sexual improprieties arise is one in which a male therapist (or, rarely—5–10% of the time—a female therapist) has personal problems that temporarily distort his (or her) judgment. Therefore, if you are compromised by such problems, do not work. Rest and recuperate; get consultation and education. Everything is more difficult to get out of than into. If you discover or even suspect that you are at risk, **get help immediately!** Seek consultation, personal therapy, time off, or whatever you need.

What to Do If You Are Attracted to a Client

"Attraction" means finding a client strikingly physically attractive, amazingly witty or sensitive, alluringly comfortable for you, or the like. Here are some guidelines for what to do if you find yourself feeling this way:

- Step back mentally and ask yourself whether this presentation has previously been a strategy of the client's for getting his or her needs met. Ask how such a strategy plays into your own needs and situation. Consider your own issues, such as rescue fantasies and needs to be admired, found attractive, be in control, or be depended upon. In addition, how are your intimate relationships going now?

- How have you previously resolved such attractions? Remember, therapists should meet clients' needs, not vice versa.

- My own rule about fantasies is this: If you are highly attracted to or fantasizing about your client, and you can't or don't make it go away in three sessions, consult a peer or your supervisor.

- Irvin P. R. Guyett, PhD, of Pittsburgh, PA, adds: If you find yourself fantasizing about the client outside the session or your fantasies are amplified in the next session, consult a peer.

- If you are attracted, do *not* discuss this attraction with the client until you have consulted a peer first. You must fully understand your side before putting anything more on the client.

- It is still your responsibility to deal with both your own and the client's urges, fantasies, and attractions in a therapeutically productive way, or you may be at risk of malpractice even without the sexual contact. That is, you may be ignoring or not meeting the client's needs but meeting your own, and so you are providing inadequate or even incompetent services.

■ Some advise immediately referring a client to whom you develop romantic feelings; however, besides resembling abandonment and punishing the client, this is avoidance of your or the client's feelings. It is likely to be better in the long run to process these feelings with your supervisor or consultant and to resolve them.

■ Ask yourself: Can I control my impulses? Can I be open about this problem and my feelings with a colleague? If you cannot resolve the feelings, terminate the therapy and refer the client, before you get into deeper trouble.

■ Pope (1987) outlines a successful case treatment of a therapist who was highly attracted to a client. This may be useful reading.

Reporting Another Therapist

What if you recognize the damage done to a patient by a previous sexual relationship with a therapist, but the patient does not? Of course you will work with the patient on this issue, but do you have to report it? Generally, the answer is yes (APA, 1992a, Section 8.05), because you have a duty to care for the patient. Unfortunately, fewer than 3% of such cases are reported to licensing boards (Parsons & Wincze, 1995).

What if a client *falsely* accuses a previous therapist of sexual misconduct? Good starting sources for some information about false accusations of sexual improprieties are Gutheil (1992) and Sederer and Libby (1995).

Client–Therapist Intimacy: Appropriate and Inappropriate Conduct

HANDOUT 2   The purposes and functions of Handout 2, the patient education handout presented below, are as follows: (1) to reduce the rate of inappropriate sexual behaviors on the part of clients; (2) to increase the rate of clients' reporting of sexual exploitation by all kinds of professionals; and (3) to protect you if you are misunderstood or even accused of sexual improprieties, because this form states your rules of practice. The handout is valuable because it is written for consumers, in a narrative and casual style. Its message and tone are empowering; it addresses questions of ethics, harm, love, and discomfort with sexual behavior in therapy; and it offers options for reacting, taking action, and handling the emotions stirred up by sexual behaviors in therapy.

This handout is not suitable for routine distribution to every client, because the reading may be burdensome for those who have not had ideas or experiences along these lines. Also, it may stimulate inappropriate thoughts in clients who are borderline, psychotic, or dependent.

You should be the one to ask or bring up the subject of this handout, because the client may be feeling too ashamed, confused, or guilty to do so. It can be given to a patient when it is topically appropriate, or it can be made available in a three-ring binder, along with other patient education materials and some of your forms, in your waiting room. You might suggest that a client "look through the book when you have a chance because I want you to have this information." Perhaps 3–5% of new female clients will have had a sexual relationship with a previous therapist or other trusted professional. Although you should ask about this possibility in the first interview's history taking (this is why questions about it are included in the intake interview questions and guide—see Form 34), the client may not be ready to reveal this. You generally cannot ask this question repeatedly, but by leaving Handout 2 on your waiting room table, you have "normalized" the question, done some patient education, and told the client you are ready to hear about this relationship whenever she is ready to reveal it. The same applies to domestic violence and battering.

Thorn et al. (1993) found that the use of a brochure or handout such as Handout 2 raised clients' consciousness about specific kinds of sexual abuse, and was very likely to prevent such abuse by therapists. Some patients who read this or similar materials may come to recognize that a previous therapist was sexually exploitative. You should be prepared to deal with this contingency legally, emotionally, and professionally through education or through referral.

This form is based on one authored by the Alabama Psychological Association's (555 South Perry St., Suite. 113, Montgomery, AL 36104; phone 205-262-8245) Committee to Prevent Sexual Misconduct, which was in turn adapted from a longer brochure published by the APA's Committee on Women in Psychology (1989), entitled "If Sex Enters the Psychotherapy Relationship." Copies of that brochure may be ordered from the American Psychological Association, Order Department, P.O. Box 2710, Hyattsville, MD 20784.

Insert the names, addresses, and phone numbers of your state's associations on page 3 of the handout, above the associations listed there, before you photocopy the handout for distribution.

Client–Therapist Contact: Proper and Improper Conduct

This brochure has been written to help you understand what is proper and improper conduct for a therapist, and what responses are available to you as a consumer. It may raise issues that you have not considered before. However, if you are well informed, you will be better able to make sure your needs get met in therapy.

Although most therapists are ethical people (that is, good and law-abiding people) who care about their clients and follow professional rules and standards in their practice, there are a very few who do not consider what is best for their clients and who behave unethically. These issues apply to any mental health worker: psychologists, psychiatrists, social workers, counselors, clergy, nurses, or marriage and family therapists.

Therapist Behaviors That May Not Be OK

There will be times in your therapy when it might be important, even if it is very uncomfortable for you and your therapist, to discuss your feelings and concerns about sex. In fact, such discussions may be needed if you are to benefit from your therapy. **However, sexual contact is never a proper part of any sex education or sex therapy.**

Many caring therapists sometimes show their feelings through touch. These forms of physical contact in therapy, such as a handshake, a pat on the back, or a comforting hug, may not concern you. But you are the best judge of the effects that any touching may have on you. If your therapist engages in any type of physical contact that you do not want, tell him or her to stop, and explain how you feel about that contact. A responsible therapist will want to know about your feelings and will respect your feelings without challenging you.

If your therapist makes sexual comments or touches you in a way that seems sexual to you, you are likely to feel discomfort. Trust your feelings. Do not assume that your therapist must be right if it feels wrong to you.

There are warning signs that a therapist may be moving toward sexual contact with you. The therapist may start talking a lot about his or her own personal problems, giving you gifts, writing letters to you that are not about your therapy, or dwelling on the personal nature of your relationship. Or the therapist may create the idea that he or she is your only source of help by criticizing you for standing up for yourself, or by telling you how to behave with a sexual partner. A red flag should definitely go up if your therapist discusses his or her own sexual activities or sexual attraction to you. Other signs include making remarks intended to arouse sexual feelings, or forms of physical seduction, such as sexual touching.

(cont.)

Attraction to Your Therapist

It is normal for people in therapy to develop positive feelings, such as love or affection, toward a therapist who gives them support and caring. These feelings can be strong and may sometimes take the form of sexual attraction. It can be helpful to discuss these feelings with your therapist in order to understand them. A caring, ethical therapist would never take advantage of your feelings by suggesting sexual contact in therapy or by ending therapy to have a romantic relationship with you.

Though sexual feelings sometimes occur, and discussion about them is often useful, sexual contact with your therapist cannot be helpful. Sexual contact in therapy has been found to be harmful to the client in many ways, including damaging the client's ability to trust. The harmful effects may be immediate, or they may not be felt until later. For this reason, sexual contact with clients is clearly against the rules of all professional groups of mental health workers (psychologists, psychiatrists, social workers, and so on).

Actions You Can Take If You Believe That Your Therapist's Actions Are Not OK

Any time you feel uncomfortable about a part of your therapy, including therapist behavior that you think is improper, consider discussing this with your therapist. Your therapist should not try to make you feel guilty or stupid for asking questions, and your therapist should not try to frighten, pressure, or threaten you. If your therapist will not discuss your concerns openly or continues to behave in ways that are not OK with you, you probably have reason to be concerned.

When a discussion with your therapist about these behaviors does not help, you have the right to take some further action. You may wish to find another therapist and/or file any of several types of complaints. It is important for *you* to make the final decision about what course of action is best for your concerns and needs.

It may be very hard for you to think about making any kind of complaint against your therapist. You may worry that he or she will eventually find out about your complaint and be angry or hurt about it. You may also be concerned about possible harm to your therapist. There are several points to consider when you are trying to decide what is the best thing to do:

- Sexual contact between a therapist and a client is never a proper form of treatment for any problem. A therapist who suggests or engages in sexual contact in therapy is showing a lack of concern for you.
- Sexual contact in therapy is never your fault. Regardless of the particular things that have happened, you have placed your trust in the therapist, and it is his or her duty not to take advantage of that trust. If the therapist does this, you have been betrayed.
- A therapist who engages in sexual contact with a client is likely to do so more than once and with more than one client. If no one reports this behavior, **other people may be harmed by the same therapist.**

Specific Courses of Action

Remember that you have the right to stop therapy whenever you choose. At the same time, you may also wish to **make some type of complaint against the therapist** who has acted improperly.

If you choose to make a complaint against your therapist, the process may become long and difficult. Other clients taking such action have felt overwhelmed, angry, and discouraged. **It is very important**

(cont.)

that you have support from people you can depend upon. Good sources of support might be family members, friends, support groups, a new therapist, or some type of advocate. Identifying and using good sources of support will help you feel more secure about the plan of action you have chosen.

You may wish to see another therapist to help you continue with your therapy, including dealing with problems resulting from the experience with the unethical therapist. It would not be unusual for you to have confusing thoughts and feelings about your experience and your previous therapist. It would also be understandable if you felt frightened about seeking, or had difficulty trusting, a new therapist.

You may also want an advocate to actively help you in making and pursuing plans. Try to locate a mental health worker who has had experience with other clients who have been victims of therapist sexual misconduct. He or she will be able to understand your situation, provide you with important information, and support you in your choice of action.

Many therapists work in agencies or other offices with supervisors. Consider talking to your therapist's supervisor or agency director to see what can be done.

You may want to **contact the state and/or national professional group** to which your therapist belongs. For example, many practicing psychologists are members of this state's Psychological Association and the American Psychological Association. These organizations have specific rules against sexual contact with clients, and each has an ethics committee that hears complaints. State and national professional associations do not license their members to practice psychotherapy; however, they can punish an unethical therapist, sometimes by expelling that person from membership in the organization. Such an action may make it more difficult for the therapist to get or keep a license to practice.

If your therapist is a licensed professional, you may want to **contact this state's licensing board** of the profession to which your therapist belongs. It has the power to take away or suspend the license of a psychologist found guilty of sexual misconduct.

Another option is to **file a civil suit for malpractice**, which would be done through a lawyer. To get a referral to an advocate or therapist experienced in working with victims of sexual misconduct, or to obtain information on filing a complaint, call or write to this state's professional organization.

Here are the addresses of some of the organizations mentioned above:

American Counseling Association
5999 Stevenson Avenue
Alexandria, VA 22304
703-823-9800

American Psychiatric Association
1400 K Street, N.W.
Washington, DC 20005
202-682-6000

American Psychological Association
750 First Street, N.E.
Washington, DC 20002-4242
202-336-5500

National Association of Social Workers
750 First Street, N.E., Suite 700
Washington, DC 20002-4241
202 408-8600

There are groups in many communities to help victims of sexual abuse, and you can usually find them through the telephone book's "Human Services" section.

Please write your questions on the back of this handout so we can discuss them. Thank you.

3.9   The Duty to Protect (and Warn)

In addition to the ethical duties discussed previously, therapists also have ethical and legal obligations to prevent their clients from physically harming themselves or other persons. If you believe a client is dangerous, you have to use all reasonable care to protect the potential victim of your client's violence. You must use your professional judgment and position to *protect*, not just the more narrow duty simply to *warn*. Actually, your duty is to take appropriate action, which is not confined to warning. You probably also have an ethical duty to prevent violence. You have a less clear but more general obligation as a citizen to protect your fellow citizens.

The Legal Basis

The court's two decisions in the famous *Tarasoff* case (*Tarasoff v. Regents of the University of California*, 1976) established therapists' duty to protect. Since then, court cases have sent mixed messages about the limits of therapists' liability and required behaviors. But they have rarely held a therapist liable, and never when a professionally proper response was made. (This is good news for therapists.) **You will not be held responsible for a negative outcome if you have done what a good clinician should have—proper evaluation, planning, and implementation.** A recent review (Appelbaum, 1996) of suits against clinicians for warning others indicates that therapists should warn potential victims in order to avoid liability for subsequent violence, even though doing so opens the therapist to allegations of breach of confidentiality.

When adopting *Tarasoff*, the courts have usually followed three basic principles in assessing liability. These principles are "(a) 'foreseeability' of harm (a verbal threat to an identifiable victim), (b) identifiability of a victim, and (c) feasibility of therapist intervention" (Knapp & VandeCreek, 1990, p. 42). On the other hand, about 15 states have adopted "anti-*Tarasoff*" legislation or immunity statutes, which hold a therapist not liable if he or she fails to warn a victim. Furthermore, if therapists do break privilege in order to protect life, they generally will not be held liable for this breach under a doctrine of "qualified privilege" (i.e., if they can prove that there was a necessity to breach confidentiality). Some states have passed laws to limit a mental health practitioner's liability to situations where the therapist has actual knowledge of a danger to a specific person; even then, the liability is avoided if the therapist warns the target person and notifies the police. The states of California, Minnesota, Colorado, Kentucky, Louisiana, New Hampshire, Illinois, Indiana, and Maine require only warning the victim. (This listing is not a substitute for knowing your local laws in detail, however.)

When Do You Have a "Duty to Warn"?

You have a duty to warn, and should reveal the threat of violence, when you have reasonable cause to believe that the patient is dangerous to a specific person or property. But what are the characteristics of "reasonable cause"?

First, the threat must be toward *a specific and identifiable target*. This must be a particular person, identifiable persons, or even property, rather than a general group or category. The threat may arise through the patient's contemplation of a criminal act, so be attentive to all the consequences of such statements. The threat may also be toward the client's self, as in self-mutilation, suicide, or even self-neglect (such as failing to eat or drinking alcohol to the point of unconsciousness). Second, the threat has to be *believable*. It should be explicit, not vague; motives count, as does history.

In determining whether reasonable cause exists, you must use good judgment, professional skill, and knowledge at levels usually provided by your peers. However, you are "not liable for simple errors made in good faith and with reasonable professional judgment" (Brodsky & Schumacher, 1990, p. 668). You do not need to be a perfect predictor of dangerousness—only to exercise a standard of care that a reasonable member of your discipline, in your local community and in these particular circumstances, would use. Such a professional should have current knowledge in the areas of evaluating dangerousness and violence (the texts by Roth, 1987, and more recently by Eichelman & Hartwig, 1995, provide guidance in these areas). You must "take whatever other steps are reasonably necessary under the circumstances" (*Tarasoff v. Regents*).

What to Do When You Decide to "Warn"

"Discharging your *Tarasoff* duties" (as the lawyers call it) depends on many factors. You must take "reasonable" and "necessary" steps to protect the potential victim or victims. These will, of course, vary with the circumstances and the local laws, but *may* include the following options. Good sense suggests that you should implement as many of these options as reasonable, based on local rules and consultation:

- Warning the intended victim.

- Notifying local law enforcement authorities.

- Contacting relatives or others who can apprise the potential victim of the danger.

- Initiating voluntary or involuntary commitment. (This will shift the burden of decision making to the courts.)

- Taking whatever other steps seem appropriate and necessary under the unique circumstances.

- Documenting all your thoughts and efforts.

State laws vary from offering specific steps (reasonable efforts to communicate the threat to victim and police—California, Kentucky, Louisiana), to simply warning the victim (Indiana, Massachusetts, Minnesota). In New Jersey, the therapist must do "any of the following: (1) arranging for the patient to be admitted to a psychiatric facility; (2) initiating procedures for involuntary commitment of the patient; (3) notifying local law enforcement authorities; (4) warning the intended victim; or (5) in the case of a minor who threatens to commit suicide or injury to herself, warning the patient's parents or guardian" (Stromberg, Schneider, & Joondeph, 1993).

We can expect to see more variations on this issue of protecting clients, and at least one deserves mention here: Does the therapist of a patient who is HIV-positive have a duty to warn the patient's partner of the medical risks of sexual activity if the patient refuses to tell the partner? See Lamb et al. (1989) and the APA's position as stated in Fox (1992). If you find yourself in this situation, do not face it alone; I urge you to obtain local, up-to-date legal and ethical consultation immediately. (See also the end of Section 7.1.) The HIV-positive patient raises many ethical, legal, and professional questions. Excellent resources are the four appendices of references in Werth and Carney (1994) concerning ethical, legal, and professional issues; assessment and diagnosis; research design; and counseling diverse populations.

Suicide

The duty to protect often extends to protecting patients from themselves, as well as protecting others from them. Although courts have rarely held therapists responsible for outpatient suicides, this situation is now changing, especially where the situational facts are clear. In general, the therapist is protected by performing the proper professional activities—thorough evaluation, careful consideration, and appropriate interventions. The treatment of a suicidal crisis is beyond the scope of this book. The major references are Bongar (1991) and Blumenthal and Kupfer (1990), and a good overview can be found in Bongar (1992). The major journal is *Suicide and Life-Threatening Behavior*.

There is no one foolproof treatment plan to follow in dealing with a suicidal patient, but make certain to act aggressively by implementing the plan you choose. I suggest that you determine *right now* what your referral and support resources are in your community; trying to find them with a crisis on your hands may be too late and is certainly more stressful. Make it a goal for this week to ask all your peers and anyone else who would know about who can help in a suicidal crisis (or any other crisis—violence, abuse, homicide, etc.), and get their exact names and phone numbers.

When you realize that a patient is suicidal, take precautionary measures such as the following:

- Hospitalization.

- Close observation.

- Referral for appropriate services.

- Preventing access to means of self-harm (e.g., only small doses of risky medications).

- Providing backup services when you are unavailable.

- Consultation.

- Reviewing and keeping complete records.

You might also consider getting a more specific waiver of responsibility anytime a patient refuses to cooperate with an important treatment recommendation. The patient can sign a statement that he or she has been fully informed that refusing this treatment recommendation may seriously compromise his or her health, and that the patient is choosing to refuse the recommendation despite this warning (Liberman, 1990). You might add, for a suicidal patient, a "no-suicide contract" such as the following: "I accept that I am responsible for my own actions, and that if I come to feel my life situation has become too difficult, I will contact you, my therapist. If I cannot reach you, I will contact _____." This statement should be expanded and tailored to each individual client.

Family Violence and Abuse

Cervantes (1992) indicates specific steps therapists can take to respond to their ethical and legal responsibilities to protect spouses and children from abuse:

- Developing a safety plan with clients.

- Knowing the legal protections.

- Assessing for and reporting child abuse.

- Assessing for and reporting cruelty to animals.

The ethics of family therapy in cases of violence are considered by Willbach (1989). The APA's Committee on Professional Practice and Standards (1996) has recently offered guidance for those who treat abused children.

If you even suspect that a client is either the victim of abuse or an abuser, you may have a legal duty to report the situation and an ethical duty to protect victims (see Section 7.1). Precautionary measures should include the following:

- Examine all situations coming to your attention that might involve abuse.

- Just as hypochondriacs can get sick, even paranoids and liars can be victims. Be thorough.

- Keep your assumptions about abusers open (people of all classes, races, ages, etc., assault other people). In particular, be alert to your negative reactions to the abuser. If these continue to interfere with your objectivity, refer the case. Similarly, attend to your rescue fantasies.

- Know in detail, and obey, local laws' requirements about reporting abuse, and prepare your response thoughtfully.

- Get consultation if you are not familiar with the family members' or the abuser's personality patterns and choose not to refer.

- Document fully and sensitively the claims, your evaluation, and your actions. Because the abuser or family members may pressure victims to recant or modify their statements, be certain to record verbatim the information offered to you (about occurrences, circumstances, sequences, etc.).

3.10   Assessing a Client's Dangerousness to Self and Others

The preceding section has described, in general, your ethical duty to protect your client and potential victims of his or her violence. This section covers exactly how and when to carry out that obligation. If you have *any* reason to suspect any risk, a comprehensive evaluation of the risks of violence is necessary. Be sensitive to your feelings, which may lead you toward or away from full and accurate assessment. Truscott et al. (1995) offer a summary of the literature and a model for clinical decision making in the outpatient treatment of violent clients; their model is simple and yet comprehensive. The most recent comprehensive reference in violence prediction is Monahan and Stedman's (1994) book. Polythress (1992) addresses testimony.

Here are the steps you should ideally take in dealing with the risk of violence.

Prepare Ahead of Time

Monahan (1993) urges therapists to become educated in risk assessment, stay current with developments in the field, and be conversant with the laws of their jurisdictions. For example, you should obtain continuing education and otherwise keep up to date on working with spousal abuse.

In addition, indicate the limits of confidentiality in your educational procedures at the beginning of therapy (see Sections 4.2 and 7.1).

Gather Information to Assess Risk

"Obtain reasonably available records of recent prior treatment and carefully review current treatment records" (Monahan, 1993, p. 243). Note the use of "reasonably"; this is meant to exclude "all possible" records. If a record is very old, if it concerns problems irrelevant to the risks at hand, or if it is likely to be unobtainable, you do not need to obtain it to be seen as acting like a responsible professional. However, it is advisable to obtain any record known to be relevant to violence, and to obtain usual records and read them for violence-related information. In addition, it may be advisable to ask the client for a release to question others who may know of the client's behavior, history, or motives (you can amend Form 42). If the client refuses, document this refusal.

In your deliberations, attend to the client's motivation. Beck (1990, pp. 702–703) suggests asking, "Are you angry at anyone? Are you thinking of hurting anyone?" If the answer is yes, it is important to follow this up with questions about specific thoughts the patient is having; about whom these thoughs are occurring; when, where, and how long these thoughts are occurring; whether the patient is worried about the control of these impulses; and whether the patient has acted on them or come close to acting on them. Bennett et al. (1990) suggest also assessing for beliefs in justified revenge or in the appropriateness or efficacy of violence.

Evaluate the Risk Factors Present

The Issue of Suicide

If people are responsible for their own behavior, why are mental health workers held responsible when their patients commit suicide? "Courts often conclude that suicide occurs within the context of 'diminished capacity' or diminished functioning; therefore customary views that patients are responsible for their own behavior do not always apply" (Knapp & VandeCreek, 1983, p. 18). However, courts usually recognize that suicide cannot be well predicted, but "professionals have been held liable when they ignored or failed to assess indicators of suicide" (Knapp & VandeCreek, 1983, p. 18). "Courts usually consider two fundamental issues: (a) did the professional adequately assess the likelihood that a patient was suicidal? and, (b) If an identifiable risk of harm was determined, did the professional take sufficient precautions to prevent suicide?" (Knapp & VandeCreek, 1983, p. 18).

As noted above, Bongar (1991) is the standard reference on management of suicidality; see also Maltsberger (1986) on assessment. Jobes and Berman (1993) provide a thorough treatment of this area and offer incisive suggestions for managing risk. Their book also provides formats for recording the important issues for both therapists and clients, and some of their ideas have been incorporated into the materials offered here.

To perform ethically, you must collect all the relevant information, weigh this information to the best of your ability, and document your conclusions and decisions. You are not expected to predict the future perfectly, only to do your job well. Your assessment can be based most securely on different sources of information and different ways of acquiring it. For example, you can assess known risk factors, which produce a general probability or likelihood of suicide but can't predict the specific likelihood for an individual. The checklist of suicide risk factors (Form 7; see below) facilitates the recording of the most widely recognized risk factors. A second source of information, and obviously most crucial, is your interviewing of the client. Finally, you can integrate all the information you have obtained on the suicide risk assessment summary and recommendations (Form 34). It is designed not only to summarize the risk factors and interview information, but to document your professional judgments about suicide. You may not need to use both of the forms, especially when early indications are that the suicide risk is not great, but they are desirable when the risk appears to be high.

The Assessment of Suicide Potential: Risk Factor Analysis versus Predictions of Suicide. Summarizing much research, Hillard (1995) stated that "none of these studies has identified factors that successfully predict suicide by an individual." Why not? The main obstacle is well recognized: Suicide is quite uncommon. Only about 12 in 100,000 persons per year commit suicide in the United States (National Center for Health Statistics, 1988). It is so rare that even a highly accurate test for suicide potential results in unacceptably high levels of false positives (which mean that time and money are wasted in investigating these cases) or false negatives (which mean, tragically, that interventions are not offered when they might help).

Although we can't predict suicide, we can assess risk. Risk factors are those variables that are significantly correlated with suicide, according to grouped data, though they cannot predict individual cases. Using them, we can design levels of intervention appropriate to the level of risk, such as monitoring for active suicidality and implementing psychotherapeutic interventions aimed at lowering the risk (Jobes & Berman, 1993). For example, risk factors of race and sex are significant: 72% of suicides are white males; there are about 20 per 100,000 age-adjusted deaths for males, as opposed to 4.84 for females; nonwhite males make up 7% of all suicides, and nonwhite females 2% (Allen et al., 1994).

Risk Factors for Suicide among Psychiatric Patients. Among psychiatric patients, however, the suicide rates are much higher—about 6% on average, and as high as 20% among those with panic disorder (Rudd et al., 1993). These figures indicate that having a psychiatric disorder is a significant risk factor. Bongar (1992) and Hirshfeld and Davidson (1988), summarizing several studies, found the following points relevant:

- A psychiatric history (diagnosis, treatment, hospitalization) increases the risk of completed suicide. Having a psychiatric disorder/diagnosis raises the rate for males 8–10 times; having depression raises the male rate 80–100 times (and severe depression raises it 500 times). Risk is also increased with a diagnosis of schizophrenia or substance abuse. Caldwell and Gottesman (1990) report a lifetime suicide rate of approximately 15% for those with mood disorders (which is over 30 times the rate of the general population), and a rate of 10–13% for those with schizophrenia.

- Being an inpatient increases risk from 5 to 40 times the risk in the general population.

- In the general population, males have a greater risk for attempts than females by a ratio of about 2.5:1; however, this ratio falls to about 1.5:1 for psychiatric inpatients because of the increase in female suicide completers.

- Older white males are the greatest risk group outside institutions, but the riskiest inpatient age groups are 25–40 for males and 30–50 for females.

- Alcohol use is implicated in increased risk in several ways:

  One in five victims of completed suicide is intoxicated, and many more attempters have used alcohol immediately prior to their attempts.

  Alcoholics are more likely than individuals with other diagnoses to communicate suicidal intent.

  The rate of completed suicide is increased for alcoholics if there is a concurrent depressive disorder.

- A history of previous suicide attempts greatly increases the risk for completion, except among psychotics, who may offer little or no warning.

- Refusal or inability to cooperate with treatment increases risk.

FORM 7 | There are a number of other clusters of risk factors for suicide (see Zuckerman, 1995), and many of these have been incorporated into Form 7. Bear in mind that the factors have to be weighted; they change over time; and, of course, they have different meanings for different individuals. Also, remember (1) that low risk never means *no* risk; and (2) that risk factors are not simple predictors, have no established weights in a predictor equation, and must be integrated with other data. Form 7 is only a guide.

The purposes of this form are (1) to evaluate the risk of suicide, (2) to insure and document the thoroughness of this evaluation for ethical and protective purposes, (3) to reduce the risk of suicide based on this evaluation, and (4) to initiate appropriate treatment of the suicidal client.

[FORM 7—Use the top of this page for your letterhead.]

Checklist of Suicide Risk Factors

Client: _____ Date: _____

The following ratings are based on my:

❑ Review of records (specify): _____

❑ Interview with staff, friends, relatives (circle and name): _____

❑ Observations of this individual over the last ❑ interview ❑ day ❑ week ❑ month

❑ Other (specify): _____

Demographic risk factors

❑ Caucasian or Native American

❑ Male

❑ Lowest socioeconomic class

❑ Age: Young adult (15–24) or very elderly (75–85 or older)

❑ Medical, dental, or mental health professional, lawyer, etc.

❑ Protestant

❑ Suicidal partner

❑ Divorced status (especially repeated divorce or divorce in last 6 months)

❑ Never-married or widowed status

Historical risk factors

❑ A relative or close friend who died by suicide

❑ Criminal behaviors

❑ Self-mutilating behaviors

❑ Substance abuse or dependence

❑ Checking off "suicide" on intake form or other assessments

❑ Suicidal behaviors: ❑ Multiple threats/attempts of ❑ high lethality ❑ high violence ❑ high pain
                       ❑ Clearly intended death ❑ Secretive attempts ❑ Anniversary attempts

❑ Other risk factors: ❑ Chronic psychiatric problems ❑ Frequent accidents

❑ _____

Recent specific risk factors

In the last ❑ 24 hours ❑ few days ❑ week ❑ month ❑ few months ❑ year, the client has:

❑ Had passive death wishes   ❑ Experienced fleeting ideation

❑ Experienced persistent ideation   ❑ Made threats

❑ Made gestures   ❑ Engaged in actions, rehearsals   *(cont.)*

FORM 7. Checklist of suicide risk factors (p. 1 of 2). From *The Paper Office*, pp. 106–107. Copyright 1997 by Edward L. Zuckerman. Permission to photocopy this form is granted to purchasers of *The Paper Office* for personal use only (see copyright page for details).

❑ Made an attempt of ❑ high ❑ medium ❑ low lethality with ❑ high ❑ medium ❑ low potential for rescue

❑ Seen recent/relevant media reports

❑ Talked with therapist or other staff about suicide intentions/plans

❑ Made a clear statement of intent to others

❑ Written a suicide note

❑ Described a practical/available method or plan

❑ Given away an important personal possession

❑ Made a will

❑ Made funeral arrangements

❑ Made suicide plans that involve a highly lethal method and a time without interruption

❑ Established access to means/methods

❑ Had a minimal social support system (no nearby friends, close relationships, therapeutic alliance; lives alone)

❑ Experienced significant stressors (major losses, irrevocable losses, failure in life roles, humiliation)

❑ Other (specify): _____

Current psychiatric symptoms (circle a number)

❑ Psychological pain	Little	1	2	3	4	5	Intolerable
❑ Vegetative symptoms (sleep disturbances, restlessness)	Low	1	2	3	4	5	High
❑ Perceived external stressors	Low	1	2	3	4	5	High
❑ Agitation, irritability, rages, violence	Low	1	2	3	4	5	High
❑ Hopelessness	Absolutely hopeful	1	2	3	4	5	Absolutely hopeless
❑ Self-regard	Extremely positive	1	2	3	4	5	Extremely negative
❑ Impulsivity (low self-control, distractibility)	Low	1	2	3	4	5	High
❑ Depression (blunted emotions, anhedonia, isolation)	Low	1	2	3	4	5	High
❑ Cognitive disorganization (organic brain syndrome, psychosis)	Low	1	2	3	4	5	High
❑ Other factors (homicidal intent, few/weak deterrents, motivated by revenge): _____	Low	1	2	3	4	5	High
❑ _____	Low	1	2	3	4	5	High
❑ _____	Low	1	2	3	4	5	High

Additional information on the items checked can be found in/at: _____

Additional factors for a child or adolescent

❑ Gender: ❑ Female (more likely to attempt) ❑ Male (more likely to succeed)

❑ Age above 15

❑ Rural resident

❑ Strained family relationships

❑ Other stressors (legal difficulties, unwanted pregnancy, change of school, birth of a sibling, etc.)

Therapist: _____ Supervisor: _____

This is a strictly confidential patient medical record. Redisclosure or transfer is expressly prohibited by law.

More formal assessment measures include scales of suicidal ideation (Beck et al., 1979; Reynolds, 1991), suicidal intent (Beck et al., 1974), and hopelessness (Beck, 1986). There are many other suicide evaluation scales, most with good empirical support. For example, Western Psychological Services sells the Suicide Probability Scale (Cull & Gill, 1988), which has 36 questions that map onto four scales—Hopelessness, Suicide Ideation, Negative Self-Evaluation, and Hostility. There are norms for normals, psychiatric patients, and attempters, and it can be hand- or computer-scored. The Reynolds (1991) Adult Suicidal Ideation Questionnaire, and an adolescent version, are available from Sigma (see the Appendix, Section A.4). The questions offered on the next two forms are not a substitute for a reliable and validated scale but are simply useful questions to acquire information on a client's suicidal thoughts, emotions, and behaviors. Use them to guide an interview and ask those questions that seem relevant and productive.

To learn more about interviewing clients who may be at risk for suicide, you might want to read Wollersheim (1974), which offers specific phrasings and guidance for conducting a risk interview. Sommers-Flanagan and Sommers-Flanagan (1995) provide a structured way of asking and recording the relevant information on risk.

The Risk Factors for Interpersonal Violence

The following variables, according to Monahan (1981) and Beck (1990, p. 702), are associated with interpersonal violence:

- Being male

- Being 16–25 years of age

- Moving frequently

- Being unemployed

- Living or growing up in a violent subculture or family

- Abusing substances

- Having lower intelligence

- Having a history of violence (this is the best indicator)—fighting, hurting others, and violence against animals

- Having appeared in court for violence, or having had inpatient psychiatric treatment for violence

- Reporting own acts of violence

- Committing more severe, recent, and frequent violent acts

- Having weapons (or other means) available

- Having victims available (or accessible)

- Having multiple stressors (which may lessen frustration tolerance)

Obviously, there are no normative weights available for these factors, and they are based on grouped data rather than data on individuals, so use them with circumspection.

Analyze the Information Gathered

Consider what additional information is needed and obtain the assessments. Examples may include assessments of paranoia or sociopathy, or of membership in a social grouping that condones or promotes violence. Richard E. Jensen, PhD, of St. Charles, IL, helpfully suggests considering all potential problematic behaviors: aggression, arson, elopement, suicide, robbery, property destruction, terroristic threats, and any other situation-specific behaviors. Jensen also suggests attempting, from records or other data, to assess these intervention-relevant factors: the "triggers" of the negative behaviors; the client's compliance with previous treatment and likely compliance with future treatment; and the client's attitude toward therapists, programs, staff, members, and so on.

In addition, assess the client for lessened internal controls. For example, psychosis, paranoid suspiciousness, organic brain syndrome, and substance use can all cause lessened control (Beck, 1990, pp. 702–703). Bennett et al. (1990, p. 66) note that the following may also lower internal controls: a history of impulsiveness or volatile temper; affective illness; beliefs in justified revenge or the appropriateness or efficacy of violence; and medication interactions.

Be alert to threats. If the client makes any threats, Bennett et al. (1990) advise evaluating their purpose. Is a threat real or manipulative? Is it self-justifying or self-protecting, or is it made in order to avoid some other consequence? Be especially alert to threats with specific details. Beck (1990) cautions that mention of time, method, contingency, location, victim, and use of the active voice are all indicators of greater likelihood in a threat.

Get consultation as well. The demonstration of a consensus, especially among professionals of several disciplines, proves that your care did not fall below a reasonable standard. You may need someone's assistance if pharmacotherapy or hospitalization is necessary.

Finally, it may be valuable, but is not generally necessary, to consider other foreseeable victims (such as coworkers) beside those identified by the patient.

Document the Situation and Your Actions

"Record the source, content, and date of significant information on risk and the content, rationale, and date of all actions to prevent violence" (Monahan, 1993, p. 246). Your notes should show that you "understood the nature of the situation and that reasonable steps were taken in light of the facts" (Fulero, 1988, p. 186). Take full and thoughtful notes about any threat. Quote the patient's statements and answers to your questions; note your conclusions, your course of action, your rationale for choosing this course, and your reasons why you believe it is better than any other available choice. Your records should show how you thought out the issues in an ongoing way what happened, your evaluation, the options you considered, risk–benefit analyses, your judgments, the patient's involvement, the treatment plan to reduce risk factors, and so on. In cases involving the potential for suicide, Forms 7 and 34 are designed to assist with the documentation of the known risk factors and your formulation of the case.

Manage the Risk by Altering the Therapy

Make any environmental manipulations (e.g., removing guns) that may reduce the danger of impulsive actions.

Before you break confidentiality, weigh the costs against the benefits, such as protecting a possible victim. The costs can include losing the trust of the client or even the opportunity to continue to work with the client and help him or her. Discuss the issues with the client before disclosure. This is rarely unproductive when it is handled as a part of therapy, and harm seems more likely when it is not discussed. Beck (1982) suggests involving the client in warning the potential victim. It may even be possible to involve the potential victim in the therapy (Knapp & VandeCreek, 1990, p. 43). But be cautious and modest in considering your resources.

This may sound strange, but you should attempt to get a release (see Form 42) to break confidentiality if a serious threat is made. Most violent people are desperate and ambivalent about their aggression, and are still competent to consent. Violent behavior does not, in and of itself, justify breaking confidentiality. In addition, do not break confidentiality when you have only suspicions but no client words or deeds. If you are uncertain, use judgment, consultation, and thorough, honest documentation. Do not act to warn just out of fear of a *Tarasoff* suit.

As an alternative to breaking confidentiality, **consider intensifying the therapy** and documenting the alteration and its rationale. The following are good ideas:

- Increase the frequency of sessions.

- Focus on anger, aggression, controls, consequences, alternatives to violence, and topics that stimulate violent thoughts.

- Pay more attention to minor threats.

- Work with the client to attend to the "triggers" and to change the violent behaviors and risks, but be aware that the client may lie to you about his or her changes.

- Follow up on any lack of compliance with treatment (Monahan, 1993).

- Do anything that will increase the "therapeutic alliance" (Whiston & Sexton, 1993).

In addition, it is wise to **develop various protective interventions**:

- Develop a safety plan for both the potential victim and the perpetrator.

- If the spouse is a target, consider couple therapy, but only if safety issues can be addressed and documented.

- Know your community's resources for victims (shelters, support groups, etc.) (Cervantes, 1992).

- Work with family members who can more closely observe the client.

- Consider hospitalization or police actions that would serve to incapacitate the client (Monahan, 1993).

- Monahan (1993) also suggests "target hardening," or making the target less vulnerable (by decreasing salience or accessibility, hiring bodyguards, etc.). This is not a therapy area, so get consultation.

- "Communicate information and concerns about violence to the person responsible for making decisions about the patient, and make important items salient" (Monahan, 1993, p. 245).

Do Damage Control

If violence has occurred, do not make public statements of responsibility, and do not tamper with the record (Monahan, 1993). See Section 3.2.

Limit Your Personal Vulnerability to Violence

Therapists are as vulnerable to violence as others are. Guy et al. (1992) found that about half of all the psychotherapists they studied had been threatened, harassed, or physically attacked by patients during their careers. These unwanted behaviors and fears included unwanted calls to their offices or homes; threats of malpractice suits; verbal threats against therapists; destruction of the contents of their offices; physical attacks on therapists or on their loved ones; threats against their loved ones; destruction of their homes; and even murder of therapists or their loved ones (Guy et al., 1992).

As a result of such experiences, many therapists have taken protective measures. These include refusing to treat certain clients or to disclose personal data to patients; prohibiting clients from appearing at one's home; relocating one's office in a "safe" building; specifying intolerable patient behaviors; discussing safety issues with loved ones; having no home address listing in the telephone directory; developing contingency plans for summoning help at the office; avoiding working alone in the office; hiring a secretary; terminating a threatening client; obtaining training in management of assaultive behaviors and self-defense for oneself and one's loved ones; installing a home security alarm system; developing a contingency plan for family members if a client appears at the home; avoiding solo practice; installing an office alarm system; keeping a weapon at home and/or at the office; hiring a security guard; and other measures (Guy et al., 1992). It may be in your best interest to consider each of these for yourself and implement some of them before trouble strikes.

3.11 Ethical and Legal Issues in Working with Managed Care Organizations

Special ethical and legal issues are involved in working for managed care organizations (MCOs) and with their clients. Because these concerns must be described to potential clients before treatment is begun, Handout 3 is provided as a patient handout for this purpose at the end of this section. Please review and, if necessary, revise it. This section looks at the possible ethical dilemmas from the therapist's point of view. The issues of most concern are as follows:

- Patients must be told in detail about the limitations imposed by MCOs *before* treatment begins, in order for their consent to treatment to be fully informed.

- MCOs often restrict the range of clinicians a client may see to those on a preapproved "panel." This may or may not increase the quality of care available.

- MCOs tend to approve only very brief treatment, which may not be clinically appropriate for all patients.

- MCOs often require therapists to supply extensive and often sensitive information for treatment authorization and reauthorizations, and for other reviews. The fate of this information and its consequences are often unclear.

- MCOs often "micromanage" the therapy by requiring frequent, detailed consultations in order to authorize a small number of continuing treatment sessions.

- MCOs may sometimes "change their mind" and refuse to pay even for services they have authorized by phone or in writing. This changes the agreed-upon financial burdens.

- Under managed care, therapists have the additional obligation to appeal when services they recommend have been denied.

- Therapists sometimes have the ethical obligation—and may, under managed care, have a contractual obligation—to continue to treat patients whose benefits become unavailable or exhausted.

- MCOs can require "risk-sharing" financial arrangements and risk assumption when treatment is discontinued or when "hold harmless" contract clauses are signed. (This appears to be disappearing from contracts.)

- MCOs may require clinicians not to discuss treatments for which the MCOs will not pay; they may also forbid clinicians to discuss the incentives MCOs offer to clinicians to limit care, or the MCOs' other practices. These are called "gag rules," and they too may be disappearing because of public pressures and new laws.

These issues are discussed below in more detail. Bear in mind that although these issues are typical of the field at this writing, the field is changing rapidly.

Consent Issues

Besides the usual concerns involved in obtaining informed consent to treatment (covered in Chapter 4), there are additional concerns for MCO patients. Clients should be informed of the limits of the benefits available to them under their managed care coverage. This should include both the written limits and the therapist's own experience of the services frequently allowed (which are almost always even less than the written limits specify). Clients should be informed about the whole preauthorization and reauthorization process, the invasion of their privacy that this process may entail, and their rights (and often the necessity) to appeal MCO decisions. They should also be fully informed about the limitations on which clinicians they can receive treatment from without having to pay more out of pocket.

Confidentiality Issues

When an MCO refers a patient, it expects only one, or at most two, sessions for evaluation. The therapist must then provide the MCO with a diagnosis, a treatment plan, and a great deal of information on the patient's life functioning. The MCO's reviewers then assess the "medical necessity" of treatment. Because this process requires the gathering of much detailed information in many areas of life, it can be intrusive. Appelbaum (1993) notes that as a therapist, you must disclose to the patient the "nature and extent of information that may have to be released to managed care reviewers" (p. 254), as well as the lack of ethical and legal limitations on their disclosure.

Release of this confidential client information to the MCO is open to problems. This information is often transferred to the MCO by fax or electronic methods, which do not necessarily have the same legal and technical privacy protections as paper reports. When the information has left the therapist's office, there are few legal constraints and no effective ethical constraints on what happens to it. In addition, the training and skills of the MCO personnel receiving and evaluating this information are often uncertain. These people are not usually controlled by laws and ethics, as licensed psychotherapists are. Reviewers are not (at least at the lower levels) mental health professionals; even at higher levels, if they are mental health professionals, they may not be clinicians or therapists. Only a few MCOs require even a professional of your discipline to review your treatment. Given these factors, I advise the following:

- You should have a more detailed release-of-information form signed before talking to an MCO reviewer. (You can use Form 42.)

- You should discuss with the client the consequences of releasing this information to the MCO, where it will become part of a permanent medical record. It is possible that this record will be accessible to many other organizations over time, although in the past, indemnity insurance companies have been quite careful with such records.

- Releasing detailed information may be countertherapeutic with some borderline or paranoid patients. You should decide what to do, and may have to forgo MCO payments with these patients.

Treatment Issues

Problems may arise when an MCO refuses to authorize treatment that is not "medically necessary," but that you and the client believe will be valuable. Coping with this situation is called "transitioning the patient from necessary to optional care" and should be carefully based on your shared assessment of the client's functional levels and presenting symptoms. The patient must accept the MCO's intention to pay only for treatment to return him or her to baseline levels of functioning. When this has happened, you and the client must renegotiate your contract, including goals, methods, and payment for services.

Submitting authorization requests for treatment is important, because MCOs will deny payment for services they have not authorized. MCO reviewers can refuse to pay for any treatment at all or for treatment by a particular therapist. They may refuse to pay even though the client's benefits have not been used to the limits of the policy. They may only pay a small amount of money. They can prevent a client from paying for treatment himself or herself. Finally, they can require outside evaluations, which may be burdensome and intrusive.

The present and apparently universal treatment philosophy of MCOs seems to be that "briefer is better." In the experience of many clinicians, this seems to prevail no matter what a client's diagnosis, history, or need may be, but I have seen no good data on this point. An MCO's definition of "brief" is often too short (6–10 sessions) to be effective for many diagnoses, based on the literature (which frequently suggests 20–30 sessions for effectiveness). Yet MCO personnel themselves have little or no research support for requiring brief therapy. Because they are usually not clinicians, or your legal supervisors, they are unable to offer direction for treatment. To make a bad situation worse, they often will stop referring patients to therapists who take longer to treat patients than the MCOs think desirable. Even when authorizations for more sessions are considered, MCOs will require new documentation; MCOs have been able to shift this significant administrative burden onto clinicians, and they do not reimburse this time. Finally, Appelbaum (1993) notes the "possibility that payment for therapy might be terminated before either the patient or the clinician believes that the goals of treatment have been achieved." If your client could benefit from more treatment but is not severely incapacitated, authorization may be denied. You may not ethically falsify the client's level of functioning.

Yet, when an MCO refuses to pay, the clinician's obligation to care for the client does not stop. If the client continues in the clinician's opinion to need care, the clinician must appeal the MCO's decision. Note, however, that this process is entirely under the auspices of the MCO. which makes all the rules. Appelbaum (1993) says, "At a minimum, a clinician whose patient has been denied payment for care that he or she believes is indicated, may have an ethical obligation to contest, on the patient's behalf, the decision of the managed care entity" (p. 253). Stromberg and Dellinger (1993) make this point even more strongly: "If managed care refuses payment, you are legally required at least [to] (1) provide clinically necessary emergency services regardless of payment, and (2) energetically seek approval for additional services the patient genuinely needs" (p. 13). The clinician should make some effort at the initial appeal level. A decision on whether to continue to secondary levels of appeal needs to be made after "consultation with the patient, taking into consideration the likelihood of success, whether the patient still desires to proceed with treatment, and the availability of alternative means of paying for care" (Appelbaum, 1993, p. 253).

The following questions should be weighed when alternative treatment resources are considered:

❑ Can the client afford to obtain care from an out-of-network provider at higher cost?

❑ Can the client pay out of pocket for the therapy?

❑ Is the client willing to proceed with the therapy during the appeals process, risking being held responsible for the charges accrued in the interim?

❑ Are there free or less expensive alternative sources of care to which the client can be referred, if you find them competent to treat, and the client finds referral acceptable?

❑ Are you willing to continue care at a reduced rate or without payment?

❑ Are you willing to terminate the client?

However, read your contract with the MCO carefully. It may, in fact, require you to discharge the patient. Or it may require you to continue to treat the patient after benefits are exhausted, if he or she still needs treatment, and may even prevent you from charging the patient for this treatment.

The serious problems described above are being (poorly, slowly, and often counter-therapeutically) addressed in the courts, the state legislatures, and the boardrooms of MCOs. Most professional organizations have not been proactive or even in the forefront, but are now trying to respond (see, e.g., the series of five "practice guidelines" from the American Psychiatric Association, 1996).

Managed care appears to be the most serious threat to the current practices of psychotherapy yet to appear. At this writing, however, the pendulum is beginning to slow and may swing back somewhat in the other direction. Certainly there will be losses and perhaps gains. It is hard to know because of "Cannella's law": "Optimism about one's [professional] future is inversely proportional to the number of years out of training" (Cannella, 1995). Ideally, MCOs will use outcome and progress data to improve their services and to eliminate some of the dilemmas for therapists that have been described above.

Informing Clients about Managed Care

HANDOUT 3   Handout 3 is designed to inform clients of the managed care situation and its legal and ethical implications. Before using the handout, please review it to see whether it is accurate for your current experience. A few sentences are from Higuchi (1994), which is a good review of the legal issues. The next-to-last paragraph offers clients the possibility of paying directly and thus not creating any records outside your office; this may not be allowed under the contract you have signed with an MCO.

What You Should Know about Managed Care

Your health insurance may cover part of the costs of your therapy, but these benefits cannot be paid until a "managed care organization" (MCO) says they can be. The MCO has been selected by your employer, not by you or me. The MCO sets some limits on both of us, and you need to know what these are.

If you use your health insurance to help pay for your treatment, you must allow me to inform the MCO of your problem, of the treatment I am suggesting, and of how you are doing in many areas of your life. I will also have to supply the MCO with information on your progress during treatment. All of this information will become part of the MCO's records. All insurance companies claim to keep such information private, and there are federal laws about its release. But the laws and other rules that apply to me are stricter than the rules that apply at present to MCOs. If you are concerned, we should discuss these issues more fully before we start treatment and before I send the MCO any information. Also, if you wish, I will give you copies of any written reports that I send to the MCO.

The MCO will review the information I send in, and then will decide how much treatment I can provide to you. The MCO can refuse to allow me to treat you. It can refuse to pay for *any* of your treatment, or may pay only a very small part of its cost. Finally, it can limit the kinds of treatments I can provide to you.

Even if it does give the "go-ahead" to treatment, the MCO may put limits on the number of times we can meet. Your insurance policy probably has a maximum number of appointments allowed for therapy, but the MCO does not have to let you use all of those appointments. Also, it may not agree to more sessions even if I believe we need more to fully relieve your problems, or even if I think that undertreating your problems may prolong your pain or lead to backsliding. If the MCO denies payment before either of us is satisfied about our progress, we may also need to consider other treatment choices, which may not be the ones we would prefer.

We can appeal the MCO's decisions on payment and number of sessions, but we can only do so within the MCO itself. We cannot appeal to other professionals, to your employer, or through the courts without great effort. This state does not have laws regulating MCOs—that is, laws about the skills of their staff members, their legal status, their appeals process, and so on.

You should know that my contract or your employer's contract with a particular MCO may prevent us from taking actions against it if things go badly because of its decisions. My contract may prevent me from discussing with you treatment choices for which the MCO will not pay. I will discuss with you any efforts the MCO makes to get me to limit your care in any way.

The particular MCO in charge of your mental health benefits can be changed during the course of your treatment. If this happens, we may have to go through this whole process again.

If after reading this and discussing it with me, you are concerned with these issues, you have the choice of paying me directly and not using your health insurance. This will create no record outside of my files.

I have read and understood the issues described above, and willingly enter treatment accepting these limits. I give my therapist permission to submit information in order to secure payment for the mental health services to be provided to me.

_____   _____
                    Signature of client   Date

HANDOUT 3. Patient handout for informed consent to managed care. From *The Paper Office*, p. 116. Copyright 1997 by Edward L. Zuckerman. Permission to photocopy this form is granted to purchasers of *The Paper Office* for personal use only (see copyright page for details).

CHAPTER 4

Getting Informed Consent

4.1   The What and Why of Getting Informed Consent

> *Informed consent is actually a statement about the moral atmosphere of the relationship between clinician and patient. In more practical terms, informed consent is a dyadic process, or dialogue that begins at the moment of eye contact and continues throughout the relationship.''*
> —GUTHEIL (1993, p. 1005)

The relationship of therapist and client is complex and multidimensional. It evolves therapeutically, economically, and interpersonally. If this relationship is not spelled out, the client, therapist, ethics committees, insurance companies, and courts are all quite likely to interpret it differently. The relationship should thus be clarified as soon as clinically feasible; this process of clarification and of obtaining informed consent is not optional, but essential. But how can you be sure you have obtained such consent? What specific methods can you use to obtain it? This chapter answers these questions and offers five fully developed paths, or methods, you can use with clients to arrive at their informed consent. Any of these methods, however, requires that four basic conditions be met.

What Informed Consent Requires

Informed consent requires a **mentally competent** person who has a good **knowledge** of what will occur in treatment, freely **chooses** to be treated, and is **documented** in the record as such. If any of these is lacking, its absence must be documented, explained, and responded to. Let's look more carefully at each of these elements.

Mental Competence

Mental competence is presumed for all adults unless a court has decided that an adult is incompetent, or the adult has manifested clear signs of incompetence to you. Receiving a severe diagnosis or even being involuntarily hospitalized does not automatically presume incompetence. Some indicators of possible incompetence are psychosis, dementia, severe depression, suicidal behavior, and the like. In such cases, consult and/or refer if you lack the professional skills to evaluate the impact of these symptoms on the client's competence. Also note that the rationality of a decision is unrelated to the competence to make it (Group for the Advancement of Psychiatry [GAP], 1990, pp. 87 ff.) An irrational decision is defined as one that results in the person's suffering foreseeable harms without adequate reason (GAP, 1990, p. 87).

Competence is not "all or nothing." The extent of someone's competence depends on the issues of concern at the moment. A client may be competent to consent to some treatments and not to others; the latter may require resources he or she does not possess, now or at any time, such as the ability to foresee consequences in detail.

Competence is generally denied to minors, but local laws differ. A minor is usually anyone under 18 years of age. By law and presumption, minors cannot give consent or waive privilege because they are considered incompetent due to age. Consent must therefore be obtained from their parents or guardians. Residing with a child does not make an adult that child's legal guardian, and being a parent does not assure the parent's having legal custody to consent. If you need consent for a minor, find out who can give it.

In order to reduce barriers to treatment of minors, there are some legal exceptions concerning their competence to consent to treatment. For example, minors can generally seek treatment for sexually transmitted diseases or pregnancy without parental consent. Some states have extended this to drug and alcohol treatment and other diagnoses, or have allowed treatment in some settings. Consent to treatment by adolescents is complicated by their not-quite-adult legal and psychological status. The tendency is to give more weight to the thinking abilities of later adolescents and less to those of early adolescents. **You must know your local laws.** To illustrate, in Pennsylvania, the following questions need to be considered in deciding whether you need parental consent to treat an adolescent (Elwork, 1993): Is the treatment to be inpatient or outpatient? Is this a form of treatment an adolescent can consent to (e.g., drug/alcohol treatment), or not (e.g., treatment for mental illness)? Do you need parental consent to obtain records? Do you need parental consent for treatment, or do you only need to notify the parents of this treatment? Is parental notification a duty of yours or a right of theirs?

Knowledge

Consent is "informed if all the risks and possible consequences of the procedure . . . along with alternatives have been explained . . . and . . . [the client] understands" (Cohen, 1979, p. 248). Note that this has two aspects: (1) giving adequate information and (2) ensuring that the client understands it. We need to examine each aspect in turn. First, how much information needs to be disclosed? Must every *possible* side effect be described?

"If a doctor knows (or should know) of possible complication[s] of the treatment, he [*sic*] is under a legal duty to disclose that information to his patient" (Cohen, 1979, p. 248). Not every possibility must be covered, but "only those risks which a reasonable man would consider material to his decision whether or not to undergo treatment" (Cohen, 1979, pp. 248–249). Haas and Malouf (1989) recommend that if in doubt, it is probably better to give information and thus support the autonomy of the patient, than to withhold it and be accused later of paternalism. This is clearly subtle and complex in real-life practice, but some effort must be made in this direction with every patient.

Full knowledge involves giving the information that a rational person would want to have before making a decision. This usually requires you as the therapist to explain the following:

- Your approach and your qualifications.

- All procedures to be used, and any changes during treatment.

- The purposes of treatment—both the long-term and the short-term or immediate goals.

- Discomforts to be expected (e.g., side effects of medication).

- Foreseeable negative consequences, or "harms." "The harms which concern rational persons are death; pain (physical and mental); various disabilities; and loss of freedom, opportunity, or pleasure" (GAP, 1990, p. 80). They may also include some side effects of treatment.

- The anticipated benefits of this treatment.

- The option of no treatment and its consequences.

- Alternative treatments. A useful guideline for alternatives is to ask yourself whether some very differently trained but fully competent therapist might suggest some other treatment in this situation (GAP, 1990, p. 81).

Clients, even those without previous therapy experience, generally understand the ethical principles of therapy but are uncertain about more specific points (Claiborne et al., 1994). Furthermore, Jensen et al. (1991) found that clinicians and parents tended to agree on the content of informed consent discussions. Parents understood these purposes of therapy: to "talk things out"; to help problems get better; to get help for complex or very difficult problems; to improve parenting skills; and to improve relationships. They also understood the limits and risks of confidentiality (e.g., the mandatory reporting of child abuse, the possibility of having family secrets revealed). However, parents were more concerned than were clinicians with iatrogenic risks: the chance that problems might fail to improve or might get worse, as well as the effects of labeling (e.g., the children's being called mentally disturbed by others, the parents' being seen as inadequate) and other stigma-related issues (e.g., the possibility that having been in therapy might cause problems in employability, school admission, etc.). It is important to note that in this study, demographics did not affect these issues' rankings of importance. Therefore, a uniform approach, such as a handout plus a discussion that is relatively standard but can be tailored to the particular needs of clients, is empirically justified.

Clients' needs and therapists' approaches differ, and so different information needs to be provided accordingly. For example, the scheduling of therapy is more problematic for clients at lower socioeconomic levels, so it should be discussed more fully (Graziano & Fink, 1973). Similarly, a study found that when those with more pathology were given more information on the limits of confidentiality, they revealed less than those given less information; those with lower pathology revealed most (Taube & Elwork, 1990). Labeling and other stigma-related issues are more important for some patients or families with a history of being stigmatized or a high risk of being stigmatized (Lidz et al., 1984). Inpatients and outpatients need discussion of different issues (Lidz et al., 1984). Families have different concerns from those of single adults or minors (Gustafson & McNamara, 1987).

Discussions of different therapeutic approaches may also require different content. For example, Widiger and Rorer (1984) argue that disclosure of therapeutic methods may cripple free association. If specialized techniques (such as biofeedback or hypnotherapy) are later introduced, additional informed consent is appropriate, even though a more general informed consent to treatment was obtained early in treatment. Those who use paradoxical methods should proceed with caution; these methods raise some serious questions about consent and require a more extensive consent-getting process.

As mentioned above, the offering of adequate information is not sufficient to ensure that a patient has knowledge sufficient for consent. The second requirement now comes into play; that is, the client must understand how the information applies to him or her. Such competence has two aspects: the comprehension of the meaning of what has been told, and its appreciation—that is, the realization that what has been said applies to him or her at the present time (GAP, 1990, p. 13).

To assure the client's understanding, it is important to remember these guidelines:

- Use simple, declarative sentences.

- Give explanations in language that is free of jargon (clinical, legal, or bureaucratic) and adjusted for the client's education or reading skills. Handelsman et al. (1986) suggest sixth- to eighth-grade language skill for consent forms. The forms in the field have not improved, and the research done on forms to consent to participate in research (LoVerde et al., 1989) indicates that things are getting worse, not better: In the 7 years studied, the forms got 58% longer, and they still required too high a level of education to be understood (22% required graduate school!).

- Communicate that any questions that occur to the client will be answered at any time.

- Respect the client's levels of cognitive functioning (especially memory abilities). One pitfall is "that information overload can prevent the obtaining of informed consent, perhaps as much as underdisclosure" (Haas & Malouf, 1989, p. 10).

- Ask questions that probe the client's understanding, in addition to inviting and answering his or her questions.

- Make special efforts if English is the client's second language, or if there are hearing or cultural barriers.

■ Couch your risk–benefit statements to the patient in terms like these (GAP, 1990, p. 10):

" . . . while no completely satisfactory statistics are available, [I] believe that this combination of treatments offers the best chance of success."

"The success rate of this treatment is about __%. That is, about __% of all patients receiving this treatment experience complete or substantial relief of their symptoms."

Choosing Freely

Treating patients without their consent is one type of "paternalistic behavior" (see GAP, 1990, pp. 27–44). Freely choosing to be treated, or "voluntariness," requires that the consent must be free from coercion, that is, free from powerful negative incentives such as "threats of severe pain or significant deprivation of freedom" (GAP, 1990, p. 12), that a rational person would find hard or unreasonable to resist. There should be a clear absence of coercion on your part. Bear in mind that others, as well as simple reality, may exert coercion; this is not your responsibility unless you have control over the coercer (see GAP, 1990, p. 16, which is based on Mallory et al., 1986). Pressure is not the same as coercion; arguing forcefully for a course of action and voicing a degree of challenge are appropriate at times (GAP, 1990, p. 82), especially when you feel the client's best interests are not being attended to.

The other side of the coin is that the client must know that he or she can withdraw from treatment at any time without being punished or suffering any consequences other than the loss of any benefits derived from the treatment. If there are other consequences, they must be described fully.

Liberman (1990) wisely suggests obtaining a "written waiver" for situations where a patient's refusal to follow a treatment recommendation would threaten his or her health. The waiver states that the patient has been informed of the recommendation and its probable consequences (i.e., it may seriously compromise his or her health), and that the patient is choosing to refuse the recommendation despite this warning. Examples offered by Liberman include a patient with severe bipolar disorder who refuses lithium treatment, a severely anorexic patient who refuses hospitalization, and patients with signs of serious medical conditions who refuse medical consultation and treatment.

Documentation

All of this therapist–client communication and rapport are consummated in the signing of a form, but the form cannot substitute for the interpersonal process of gaining informed consent. The form is not itself the consent; it is only the written evidence of the discussion and agreement. If you do not get a signed form, you must carefully document in your notes what you have told the client about treatment, to demonstrate that you have indeed obtained informed consent.

If you cannot obtain consent before beginning treatment, document the reason why not (e.g., emergency, incompetence/proxy consent, court-ordered treatment, etc.) Then, if possible, get consent as soon as the crisis has passed. Everstine et al. (1980) recommend obtaining consent even in cases where treatment is compelled. The reason is that, though "legally empty, [consent] in many cases will very likely have clinical usefulness" (p. 832).

Remember also that a signed form, by itself, is not a guarantee that informed consent has been obtained. Vaccarino (1978) has reported that "legal actions for lack of informed consent have been brought despite the existence of a signed consent form" (p. 455). He emphasizes that consenting is an interpersonal, face-to-face, rapport-based, discussion process, and not a mechanical, paper-based one. Furthermore, studies of medical patients given written consent forms suggest that at best 60% of the information is retained, and so the discussion process is essential (Grunder, 1980; Ley, 1982).

The Three Steps to Obtaining Informed Consent

The discussion above emphasizes that informed consent is an ongoing process, not a single act. How can you be sure you have obtained it? The following three-step process offers the best procedures.

The first step is to have discussions covering the issues, because discussion is the essence of informedness. Use either your memory, or, better, one of the following as a basis for the topics to cover in your discussion:

- The topics covered in the client information brochure (see Section 4.2).

- The questions in "Information You Have a Right to Know" (see Section 4.3).

- The contents of clients' rights statements (see Section 4.4).

- The contents of treatment contracts (see Section 4.5).

- A checklist made up from the materials above and your own understanding and ideas about the nature of your treatment.

The second step is to document the client's agreement with one (or, in complex situations, both) of the following:

1. A signed consent form. Use one of these:

   - The client information brochure (see Section 4.2).

   - A treatment contract (see Section 4.5).

   - A consent-to-treatment form (see Section 4.6).

2. Your notes concerning each of the relevant issues. The notes must document the following about both the discussions and the client's consent:

   - That you and the patient discussed all the relevant issues (for informedness).

   - That you answered all the patient's questions (again for informedness).

- That the patient signed the form voluntarily.

- That the patient was competent to consent. Use a statement such as the following: "After interacting with the patient for __ minutes, observing his or her behavior and discussing many topics, I found no reason to suspect that the patient was not competent to consent to treatment."

The third step is to keep the discussions about your treatment and their documentation ongoing. This is especially important when there are difficulties or when you change the treatments you offer.

Do Written Consent Forms Have a Negative Effect on Clients or Treatment?

Many clinicians are reluctant to use specifically worded consent materials such as those offered in this book, for fear they might turn away clients. They fear that the materials will create an obstacle to treatment, or that their use will make a humane activity too formal and legalistic. Fortunately, empirical data are available to address these issues.

Handelsman (1990) has researched the effects of materials like these, in various combinations. He found that their use increased readers' positive judgments of the therapist's experience, likability, and trustworthiness; increased the readers' likelihood of recommending the therapist; and even increased self-referral by the readers. In an analogue but prospective study, Gustafson et al. (1994) found that providing information about risks and benefits did not affect parents' decision to seek psychological treatment for their children. Sullivan et al. (1993), in an analogue study, reported that subjects "gave higher ratings to a therapist who used an informed-consent procedure and reported more willingness to recommend him to a friend and go to him themselves" (p. 160).

In a more recent study with university students in counseling, Dauser et al. (1995) found that providing a great deal of information on ethical issues (such as the limits of confidentiality, right to terminate, etc.), on the therapist's professional experience, and on what to expect in therapy (anticipated results, risks, alternatives, etc.) had no negative effects. There were no differences in no-shows or client-initiated terminations between those receiving more and those receiving less information. Those receiving more information felt they had a better understanding of what counseling would be like than did those receiving less information.

The limits of confidentiality consitute the topic of most concern to patients (Beeman & Scott, 1991). These researchers found that therapists believed that pursuing informed consent enhances autonomy and control, enhances the therapeutic relationship, satisfies ethical requirements, increases motivation for therapy, ensures appropriate expectations, views older adolescents as adults, satisfies legal requirements, results in fewer divorced-parent complaints, and selects only those wanting therapy. It appears that a majority of therapists do seek informed consent, although almost exclusively through discussions, which are vulnerable to the pressures of current interests and the vagaries of memory.

To summarize, **the research does not support any negative effects of using consent forms, and suggests many benefits.** Yet, despite these findings, many therapists do not use a form for obtaining informed consent to treatment (Handelsman et al., 1986). It can be argued that a form has the advantages of being (1) a defense against malpractice; (2) a patient education tool; (3) an aid in socializing the patient into therapy; and (4) a means of therapist self-development. In my experience, about 60% of psychologists now use some paper form (usually a single page) for informed consent purposes. The main reason offered by the others for not doing so is the effort it takes to research its contents. This chapter offers the fruits of just such a research effort.

The Five Paths to Informed Consent

We have now examined the basic requirements for obtaining informed consent: that your client be mentally competent to consent to treatment; that you communicate information about your qualifications and the treatment; that you make certain the client understands these; that the client choose freely to be treated; and that you document the entire ongoing process.

The remainder of this chapter offers five methods for conducting this process. In essence, they are five differing *paths* to consent. These are (1) giving and discussing a client information brochure; (2) offering clients a list of questions to guide discussion (here called "Information You Have a Right to Know"); (3) offering a list of clients' rights as a basis for discussion; (4) using a psychotherapy treatment contract; and (5) using a consent-to-treatment form.

4.2   The First Path to Informed Consent: The Client Information Brochure

Kinds of Brochures

There are at least three kinds of brochures in wide use. Each is tailored to a specific purpose—namely, to advertise or market your service; to give patients specific information on specific conditions, procedures, and topics; or to initiate patients into, and assure informed consent for, therapy. Table 3 offers a more detailed description of each type.

In the table, I have named each of the brochure types according to its purposes. Other writers have called the advertising brochure, aimed at potential clients and possible referrers, a "practice" brochure; I find this ambiguous because it describes only some aspects of the practice. Similarly, note that though the topical and client information brochures both provide factual information (which sometimes even overlaps), their goals and approaches are quite different. Although the fourth kind of brochure is quite common, I cannot recommend it. Designing separate brochures for each purpose will avoid confusing the readers with extraneous details and assure that all issues have been addressed.

I concentrate here on the third type, the client information brochure. This needs to be as comprehensive and protective as possible in order to achieve the goals listed in Table 3. A comprehensive client information brochure is the *core document of the treatment relationship*. It establishes the boundaries of your way of practicing, and is a therapeutic contract between you and your client (Schwitzgebel & Schwitzgebel, 1980). It should be thoughtfully

TABLE 3. Types and Purposes of Brochures Used in Psychotherapy

Type	Purpose	Possible contents
Advertising/marketing brochure	Describing your services in a very positive light so as to attract new clients	Your resources, addresses, staff, credentials, ways to reach you, and so on. May also include testimonials (from ex-clients), invitations to visit, maps, photographs.
Topical brochure	Educating clients about specific topics. This is sometimes called "patient education."	Treatable conditions and the methods and benefits of therapy; health insurance, costs, and procedures; medications; child development and conditions; and many other possible topics.
Client information brochure	Assuring informed consent; conforming to ethical and legal concerns; creating a therapeutic alliance or contract; reducing malpractice risks; socializing clients into therapy; modeling openness; and so on.	Office procedures, such as intake, financial arrangements, appointments, clinical records, and the release of records. Also, the nature of therapy, goals, planning, and assessment of progress.
Combination	Simplifying your paperwork or reducing its costs.	Various combinations of the contents described above.

constructed because it initiates and structures your relationship, which is the heart of therapy. You will generally be seen as having obtained informed consent if your client has read your client information brochure and has acknowledged in writing that he or she has done so.

Besides being a legal/ethical contract, the client information brochure can also enhance the process of therapy. Based on open exchange, it models an ongoing negotiation process. Collaboration with an informed client not only satisfies legal requirements, but facilitates trust therapeutically. In addition, the process of informing clients through an advertising brochure alone can elicit their fears, fantasies, and erroneous beliefs; if these are not addressed, they could hinder therapy (Cross & Deardorff, 1987, p. 64). The client information brochure permits handling of these issues earlier. Finally, this document serves to "socialize" or introduce clients into the procedures and expectations of therapists, and can be tailored to this aim. If you develop particularly fine efforts at socialization, please share them with me.

How to Use the Model Client Information Brochure

At the end of this section, I offer an exhaustive model client information brochure. I have tried to include the full range of topics, not all of which may be relevant to your practice. It is designed to allow you to create a comprehensive and detailed brochure tailored for your own practice in just an hour or two. Spending the time to tailor a brochure to your needs will be a good investment, both ethically and professionally. Even weighing the parts you finally conclude are irrelevant can raise your awareness. To help with this task, I offer suggestions and commentary at appropriate points throughout the model brochure's text.

This brochure is very highly detailed, so as to be legally and ethically correct. It is written in standard U.S. grammar and word choice to make it widely applicable. Terms unfamiliar to the average client are explained in language the client can understand (APA, 1992a). Note also that I have chosen a personal "I" style over an institutional, passive voice or a formal "we" version. You may prefer one of the other two; choose what feels most comfortable for you, but be consistent across all your documents.

If you are using the computer disk of forms and figures from this book, you can import this text and make the changes to it. In either case, you can pick and choose sections from this long version to match your specific practice needs. You can also change the format or margins, and add suitable wording to tailor it to your working methods, your locality, your clients, and your understanding of your practice. I generally call the model brochure "Information for Clients," but alternative titles might include "Welcome to the Psychological Practice of [Name]," "Introduction to the [Name] Clinic," or "New Client Introductory Information." Meek et al. (1985) use "Office Policy Statement." The brochure could also be titled by goal, such as "Ensuring Fully Informed Consent for Counseling." Others might prefer "Starting Our Work Together" or "How I Do Therapy."

Having the brochure conveniently available on your word processor is advantageous, because you can then print copies when needed and update it as your practice evolves. As a rule, when you find yourself telling three clients the same information, you should probably add it to your version of the brochure.

Two other model brochures are widely available. Kachorek's (1990) is short and somewhat dated, but well worded, and Schlosser and Tower's (1991) is extraordinarily extensive for doing assessments.

I recommend the use of the client information brochure as the most comprehensive method for getting informed consent. However, the use of even a very complete brochure for informing clients of the nature of therapy and of your practice's procedures has some drawbacks:

- There is no way to be certain that a client has understood what he or she has read, or even that he or she has read the brochure.

- Risks and alternative treatments for an individual's particular difficulties are very difficult to convey in a generic, preprepared document.

- Most of these brochures require too high a level of sophistication and reading skill (although I have made every effort to simplify the one below).

- The client has effectively lost the right to refuse information.

Therefore, it is worth considering alternative methods.

The Model Client Information Brochure

The model brochure now begins with the indented sans serif text that follows. The headings are headings that you can use in your own brochure. As you will see, my comments and suggestions are interwoven throughout and are not indented.

INFORMATION FOR CLIENTS

Welcome to my practice. I appreciate your giving me the opportunity to be of help to you.

This brochure answers some questions clients often ask about my therapy practice. It is important to me that you know how we will work together. I believe our work will be most helpful to you when you have a clear idea of what we are trying to do.

This brochure talks about the following in a general way:

- What the risks and benefits of therapy are

- What the goals of therapy are, and what my methods of treatment are like

- How long therapy might take

- How much my services cost, and how I handle money matters

- Other areas of our relationship

After you read this brochure we can discuss, in person, how these issues apply to your own situation. This brochure is yours to keep and refer to later. Please read all of it and mark any parts that are not clear to you. Write down any questions you think of, and we will discuss them at our next meeting. When you have read and fully understood this brochure, I will ask you to sign it at the end. I will sign it as well and make a copy, so we each have one.

About Psychotherapy

Because you will be putting a good deal of time, money, and energy into therapy, you should choose a therapist carefully. I strongly believe you should feel comfortable with the therapist you choose, and hopeful about the therapy. When you feel this way, therapy is more likely to be very helpful to you. Let me describe how I see therapy.

My theoretical approach is based on . . .

The most central ideas in my work are . . .

The goals of my treatment are . . .

Here you should create a general statement about therapy as you see it. Woody (1988a, p. 207) calls this communicating your "standard of care." "The Therapy Process" by Meek et al. (1985) is an outstanding example of such a statement; it raises questions while asserting an approach. Eimer (1988) uses a three-stage model of therapy, the description of which is designed as a patient handout. Tailor your statement to your conception of the impact and value of your psychological services. It can include the general aims appropriate to therapy as you understand it. Include your model of working with patients (e.g., collaboration, education, problem solving, insight into dysfunctional patterns, redeciding, primal release, relearning through transference, working with outside groups, etc.). It is also appropriate to describe, under a separate heading, other services you offer (such as medication, court testimony, relationship counseling, or psychological assessment). If these service descriptions become quite detailed, you should make them into separate handouts. Services you do *not* offer can also be specified, such as custody evaluations for relationship therapy patients.

It may be useful to indicate, if applicable, that you are not a physician (say "medical doctor," not just the ambiguous "doctor"), and so you do not use physical interventions such as medications. When discussing the kinds of treatment you offer, you can indicate that when medications are appropriate, you will work closely with the client's physician.

Hawkins and Bullock (1995) suggest that it would be proper to **indicate here any moral values you hold** that might conflict with clients' religious beliefs, or that might be adopted by clients through a process of convergence in which clients adopt their therapists' ideas on many topics. Hare-Mustin et al. (1979) suggest specifying and elaborating on any technique that might be at odds with the clients' values. For example, if you do relationship counseling, be sure to indicate that your obligation is to the mental and emotional health of the individuals, not to the relationship. A relationship cannot be a client, according to Keith-Spiegel and Koocher (1985, p. 122), but Margolin (1982) differs on this point. If your treatment methods are experimental or even controversial, you should make this section even more detailed or prepare a special consent form. This applies, at present, to any therapy that aims to recover repressed memories of sexual abuse (see Section 3.3).

The following is the way my own brochure describes my approach, its central ideas, and its goals to clients:

> The type of therapy I do is called "rational–emotive therapy," or RET. It was developed by Albert Ellis, PhD, and is described in his dozens of books.
>
> We often believe that our behaviors and feelings are caused by what happens in the real world. However, this is not quite true. When we have any kind of experience, it does not affect us directly. Rather, we first give it a meaning through our beliefs about it. For example, if I hear a sound in the kitchen and believe it is made by my wife, I am not bothered at all. But if I believe I am alone in the house, the same sound can bother me a great deal. Here we see that feelings and behaviors (my actions about the sound) flow from the active process of thinking about or adding meaning to the actual event (the sound).
>
> Dr. Ellis separates beliefs into two kinds: "rational" beliefs, or ones based on reality, and "irrational" beliefs, or ones based on false or unrealistic ideas. When we have irrational beliefs, we suffer from strong negative emotions (like rage, depression, and anxiety). When we act on the basis of irrational beliefs, our actions are often not effective and can even be harmful. If we have rational beliefs, we will experience more of the positive emotions (like pleasure, hope, and joy). We can still feel the mildly negative emotions, like irritation, sadness, and concern, but our behaviors will be more effective.
>
> I think of my approach to helping people with their problems as an educational one. Anyone can learn to recognize irrational beliefs, dispute them, and replace them with more rational beliefs. We can, with practice, unlearn these beliefs and become happier persons who function better in the world. This is what I mean by an educational approach.
>
> I want you to be able to use RET without me. I encourage you to learn more about what methods are used in RET, how well it works, and what possible problems or side effects it may have. I can lend you books and articles that explain how it works. Please return them when you no longer need them so I can lend them to other clients. I may also give you copies of articles or handouts that are yours to keep. I usually take notes during our meetings. You

may find it useful to take your own notes, and also to take notes outside the office. You could also tape-record our meetings to review at your leisure at home.

By the end of our first or second session, I will tell you how I see your case at this point and how I think we should proceed. I view therapy as a partnership between us. You define the problem areas to be worked on; I use some special knowledge to help you make the changes you want to make. Psychotherapy is not like visiting a medical doctor. It requires your very active involvement. It requires your best efforts to change thoughts, feelings, and behaviors. For example, I want you to tell me about important experiences, what they mean to you, and what strong feelings are involved. This is one of the ways you are an active partner in therapy.

I expect us to plan our work together. In our treatment plan we will list the areas to work on, our goals, the methods we will use, the time and money commitments we will make, and some other things. I expect us to agree on a plan that we will both work hard to follow. From time to time, we will look together at our progress and goals. If we think we need to, we can then change our treatment plan, its goals, and its methods.

You might want to indicate that minor, major, and multiple problems take different amounts of therapy time (both frequency of sessions and duration of the therapy).

An important part of your therapy will be practicing new skills that you will learn in our sessions. I will ask you to practice outside our meetings, and we will work together to set up homework assignments for you. I might ask you to do exercises, to keep records, and perhaps to do other tasks to deepen your learning. You will probably have to work on relationships in your life and make long-term efforts to get the best results. These are important parts of personal change. Change will sometimes be easy and quick, but more often it will be slow and frustrating, and you will need to keep trying. There are no instant, painless cures and no "magic pills." However, you *can* learn new ways of looking at your problems that will be very helpful for changing your feelings and reactions.

In my brochure, **I do not address goals** except to suggest that they involve the reduction of symptomatic or distressing behaviors. I address the client's other specific goals during our interviews and in the treatment plan.

Most of my clients see me once a week for 3 to 4 months. After that, we meet less often for several more months. Therapy then usually comes to an end. The process of ending therapy, called "termination," can be a very valuable part of our work. Stopping therapy should not be done casually, although either of us may decide to end it if we believe it is in your best interest. If you wish to stop therapy at any time, I ask that you agree now to meet then for at least one session to review our work together. We will review our goals, the work we have done, any future work that needs to be done, and our choices. If you would like to take a "vacation" from therapy to try it on your own, we should discuss this. We can often make such a "vacation" be more helpful.

I will send you a brief set of questions about 6 months after our last session. These questions will ask you to look at our work together, and sending them to you is part of my duty as a therapist. I ask that you agree, as part of entering therapy with me, to return this follow-up form and to be very honest about what you tell me then.

The Benefits and Risks of Therapy

As with any powerful treatment, there are some risks as well as many benefits with therapy. You should think about both the benefits and risks when making any treatment decisions. For example, in therapy, there is a risk that clients will, for a time, have uncomfortable levels of sadness, guilt, anxiety, anger, frustration, loneliness, helplessness, or other negative feelings. Clients may recall unpleasant memories. These feelings or memories may bother a client at work or in school. Some people in your community may mistakenly view anyone in therapy as weak, or perhaps as seriously disturbed or even dangerous. Also, clients in therapy may have problems with people important to them. Family secrets may be told. Therapy may disrupt a marital relationship and sometimes may even lead to a divorce. Sometimes, too, a client's problems may temporarily worsen after the beginning of treatment. Most of these risks are to be expected when people are making important changes in their lives. Finally, even with our best efforts, there is a risk that therapy may not work out well for you.

The statement above presents a list of some risks in accordance with the requirements of informed consent. For example, Hurvitz (1976) found that progress in individual therapy may often disrupt a marital relationship. If you do this kind of work, you should include this point.

John Kachorek (1990, pp. 106–109) offers the most complete and well-reasoned handout of this type I have seen. It includes this statement:

In therapy, major life decisions are sometimes made, including decisions involving separation within families, development of other types of relationships, changing employment settings and changing life-styles. These decisions are a legitimate outcome of the therapy experience as a result of an individual's calling into question many of their [sic] beliefs and values. As your therapist, I will be available to discuss any of your assumptions, problems, or possible negative side effects in our work together. (p. 107)

Some other possibilities for risks, according to Soreff and McDuffee (1993), are that

symptom[s may be intensified;] the conflict may not be resolved; the emotional experience may be overwhelming or too intense to deal with at this time; the targeted behavior may not change; the patient may not be any more aware of himself [sic] than when therapy commenced; in spite of therapy, the patient still may not accept or forgive himself; the interpersonal experience may not be successful or corrective; the therapeutic experience may activate or reactivate conflicts, thoughts, or emotions that may in turn lead to disruptive behavior; new and different symptoms may develop during therapy; the patient may have difficulty in terminating therapy. (p. 491)

While you consider these risks, you should know also that the benefits of therapy have been shown by scientists in hundreds of well-designed research studies. People who are depressed may find their mood lifting. Others may no longer feel afraid, angry, or anxious. In therapy, people have a chance to talk things out fully until their feelings are relieved or the problems are solved. Clients' relationships and coping skills may improve greatly. They may get more satisfaction out of social and family relationships. Their personal goals and values may become clearer. They may grow in many directions—as persons, in their close relationships, in their work or schooling, and in the ability to enjoy their lives. I do not take on clients I do not think I can help. Therefore, I will enter our relationship with optimism about our progress.

In your description of the benefits of psychotherapy (either orally or in writing), be careful not to promise a cure, or benefits so substantial that they approach a complete cure. Again, you are not in control of all or even most of the factors determining the outcome, and you especially do not wish to cause disappointment. You might also want to cite the meta-analysis of Smith and Glass (1977). However, recommending, even energetically, is not insisting and is not coercion, so don't be shy about the therapy you offer. Everstine et al. (1980) also discuss the benefits of personal growth and maturity.

Consultations

This section of the brochure explains consultations. Depending on your practice, you might indicate here that you sometimes will suggest the need for psychological or educational testing, or for medication evaluation and prescription. If so, note the approximate cost of such referrals, and your usual arrangements for these referrals.

> If you could benefit from a treatment I cannot provide, I will help you to get it. You have a right to ask me about such other treatments, their risks, and their benefits. Based on what I learn about your problems, I may recommend a medical exam or use of medication. If I do this, I will fully discuss my reasons with you, so that you can decide what is best. If you are treated by another professional, I will coordinate my services with them and with your own medical doctor.

> If for some reason treatment is not going well, I might suggest you see another therapist or another professional in addition to me. As a responsible person and ethical therapist, I cannot continue to treat you if my treatment is not working for you. If you wish for another professional's opinion at any time, or wish to talk with another therapist, I will help you find a qualified person and will provide him or her with the information needed.

Try to present alternative treatments evenhandedly for two reasons: (1) to present yourself as truly having the client's best interests at heart and (2) to keep the client from thinking that, because you are discussing other helping programs so enthusiastically, you do not really want to work with the client (Hare-Mustin et al., 1979).

What to Expect from Our Relationship

Sam Knapp, EdD, of Harrisburg, PA, offers the following as an introduction to this topic:

> Psychological services are best provided in an atmosphere of trust. You expect me to be honest with you about your problems and progress. I expect you to be honest with me about your expectations for services, your compliance with medication, and any other barriers to treatment.

> As a professional, I will use my best knowledge and skills to help you. This includes following the rules and standards of the American Psychological Association, or APA. In your best interests, the APA puts limits on the relationship between a therapist and a client, and I will abide by these. Let me explain these limits, so you will not think they are personal responses to you.

First, I am licensed and trained to practice psychology—not law, medicine, or any other profession. I am not able to give you good advice from these other professional viewpoints.

Second, state laws and the rules of the APA require me to keep what you tell me confidential (that is, private). You can trust me not to tell anyone else what you tell me, except in certain limited situations. I explain what those are in the "About Confidentiality" section of this brochure. Here I want to explain that I try not to reveal who my clients are. This is part of my effort to maintain your privacy. If we meet on the street or socially, I may not say hello or talk to you very much. My behavior will not be a personal reaction to you, but a way to maintain the confidentiality of our relationship.

Third, in your best interest, and following the APA's standards, I can only be your therapist. I cannot have any other role in your life. I cannot, now or ever, be a close friend or socialize with any of my clients. I cannot be a therapist to someone who is already a friend. I can never have a sexual or romantic relationship with any client during, or after, the course of therapy. I cannot have a business relationship with any of my clients, other than the therapy relationship.

In the paragraph above, it would be appropriate to add any rules you have that the client might inadvertently break or misinterpret. For example, some therapists have a rule never to touch a patient, mainly to avoid miscommunication. See Kertay and Reviere (1993) for a full discussion of and guidelines about touch. Or you may have a rule that the client establishes (perhaps with some assistance) the goals of therapy, and that you serve as his or her consultant in providing the means for those ends. Such clarifications are especially useful with borderline patients and those with a history of manipulation.

You might also want to add more specific information on these points:

Even though you invite me, I will not attend your family gatherings, such as parties or weddings.

As your therapist, I will not give you gifts; I may not notice or recall your birthday; and I may not receive any of your gifts eagerly.

Haas and Malouf (1989) offer excellent guidelines on the subject of gift receiving: express positive and caring feelings; do not immediately clinically process the giving; suggest an alternative (such as a gift to charity); and relax about most of these situations.

About Confidentiality

The section of the brochure on confidentiality is one of crucial legal concern. The APA ethics code (APA, 1992a, Section 5.01) requires that the limits of confidentiality be communicated explicitly and in advance to all clients (clinical and organizational). It requires that you discuss the limits of confidentiality at the beginning of treatment and as any new circumstances warrant. As of 1990, Massachusetts law requires the therapist to furnish a handout to each client explaining the limits of confidentiality. Other states also require this kind of disclosure for informed consent, so this section of the brochure addresses this issue in detail. You might want to provide your clients (or selected clients) with a separate handout concerning only this issue; see Section 7.1 for such a handout and for more information.

I will treat with great care all the information you share with me. It is your legal right that our sessions and my records about you be kept private. That is why I ask you to sign a "release-of-records" form before I can talk about you or send my records about you to anyone else. In general, I will tell no one what you tell me. I will not even reveal that you are receiving treatment from me.

In all but a few rare situations, your confidentiality (that is, your privacy) is protected by state law and by the rules of my profession. Here are the most common cases in which confidentiality is *not* protected:

1. If you were sent to me by a court for evaluation or treatment, the court expects a report from me. If this is your situation, please talk with me before you tell me anything you do not want the court to know. You have a right to tell me only what you are comfortable with telling.

2. Are you suing someone or being sued? Are you being charged with a crime? If so, and you tell the court that you are seeing me, I may then be ordered to show the court my records. Please consult your lawyer about these issues.

3. If you make a serious threat to harm yourself or another person, the law requires me to try to protect you or that other person. This usually means telling others about the threat. I cannot promise never to tell others about threats you make.

4. If I believe a child has been or will be abused or neglected, I am legally required to report this to the authorities.

In the fourth exception above, I use the phrase, "If I believe a child . . . " I have used "believe," but this word may not be accurate in your state. State laws differ in their language. For example, if the legal criterion is "what a reasonable person would suspect," this means that the level of evidence for reporting is lower than if the law were to say "believe." You must know your local rules. You might post a copy of the law in your waiting room as suggested by David Clovard, MD, of Raleigh, NC.

An alternative phrasing for the third and fourth exceptions above is this: "As a therapist, my legal and moral duty is to protect your confidentiality, but I also have a duty under the law to the wider community and to myself, if there is harm, threat of harm, or neglect."

Obviously, you need to tailor the confidentiality section of your brochure to your specific situation, locality, and practice. For example, does your state have other exceptions to confidentiality besides those listed above, such as elder abuse? Be sure to modify this statement in light of your title, your profession's legal status, the state in which you practice, and the type of therapy you are doing. For example, if you see neuropsychology or rehabilitation clients and your state requires you to notify it of impaired drivers, you should indicate this rule. There is no substitute for exact knowledge and caution.

The statements above are not suitable for the treatment of minors. Set the ground rules with minors and their parents before therapy. See also Forms 9 and 10 for treatment contracts for minors, and Form 12 for a consent-to-treatment form for a child.

A different or fuller statement of the law in your locality, or for your profession, may be appropriate here. You may use the patient handout on the limits of confidentiality (Handout 8) as a basis for your version.

> There are two situations in which I might talk about part of your case with another therapist. I ask now for your understanding and agreement to let me do so in these two situations.
>
> First, when I am away from the office for a few days, I have a trusted fellow therapist "cover" for me. This therapist will be available to you in emergencies. Therefore, he or she needs to know about you. Generally, I will tell this therapist only what he or she would need to know for an emergency. Of course, this therapist is bound by the same laws and rules as I am to protect your confidentiality.
>
> Second, I sometimes consult other therapists or other professionals about my clients. This helps me in giving high-quality treatment. These persons are also required to keep your information private. Your name will never be given to them, and they will be told only as much as they need to know to understand your situation.

An alternative phrasing for consultation is offered by Constance Fisher, PhD, of Pittsburgh, PA: "We consult with colleagues and specialists about our ongoing work. This pursuit of quality assurance never involves your name or any specifics through which you might be identified."

> For the purpose of these consultations, I may want to make audio or video recordings of our sessions. I will review the tape with my consultant to assist with your treatment. I will ask your permission to make any recording. I promise to destroy this recording as soon as I no longer need it, or, at the latest, when I destroy your case records. You can refuse to allow this recording, or can insist that the recording be edited.

You should have the client sign a formal release (such as Form 15) if you are going to video-tape sessions for consultations.

> Except for the situations I have described above, my office staff and I will always maintain your privacy. I also ask you not to disclose the name or identity of any other client being seen in this office.
>
> My office staff makes every effort to keep the names and records of clients private. My staff and I will try never to use your name on the telephone; other clients may be in the office and overhear it. All staff members who see your records have been trained in how to keep records confidential.
>
> If your records need to be seen by another professional, or anyone else, I will discuss it with you. If you agree to share these records, you will need to sign a release form. This form states exactly what information is to be shared, with whom, and why, and it also sets time limits. You may read this form at any time. If you have questions, please ask me.

You might want to add the following, again suggested by Constance Fisher, PhD, of Pittsburgh, PA: "We do not divulge the fact that you are a client or anything about you or your sessions to anyone, unless you request us (in writing) to do so."

Because you cannot foretell the needs for your records, I suggest retaining them for many years, or forever (see Section 1.6 on retention of records), and your clients should be advised of your policy. Here is my own statement:

It is my office policy to retain clients' records for 20 years after the end of our therapy.

If you treat couples or families, the APA code (APA, 1992, Section 4.03) addresses some issues like confidentiality. Therefore, you might want to insert a notice like the following, before going on to address the topic of the information you give to insurance companies:

> If we do family or couple therapy (where there is more than one client), and you want to have my records of this therapy sent to anyone, all of the adults present will have to sign a release.

> Generally, your health insurance company will receive only my statement. This gives the dates of our appointments, my charges, and a diagnosis. It will become part of your permanent medical record. In my experience, this is not likely to reflect negatively on you. But if you are concerned, you should discuss this with me.

In 15 years of practice, I have been contacted about patients twice by the FBI when patients sought security clearances. However, this is not the only risk of receiving mental health treatment; other situations should be fully explored before a record is created and it is too late. For example, when all patient records are computerized, there is likely to be no way of segregating old records created under assumptions of confidentiality from new ones, or even from old medical records with different protections of confidentiality (as, for example, those created in different states).

> As part of cost control efforts, an insurance company will sometimes ask for more information on symptoms, diagnoses, and my treatment methods. I will let you know if this should occur and what the company has asked for. Please understand that I have no control over how these records are handled at the insurance company. My policy is to provide only as much information as the insurance company will need to pay your benefits.

> You can review your own records in my files at any time. You may add to them or correct them, and you can have copies of them. I ask you to understand and agree that you may not examine records created by anyone else and sent to me. I will keep your case records in a safe place.

Many states have laws concerning clients' review of their own records, but few of those apply to private practice. For example, federal law is silent on drug and alcohol clients' inspection of their records (Drug Abuse Office and Treatment Act of 1972, Public Law 92-255), even when such clients are seen in private practice. But it defers to stricter state laws. These laws usually concern the following points: A client has a right to inspect records; to request corrections of inaccurate, irrelevant, outdated, or incomplete information; and to submit rebuttal information or memoranda. The laws may allow a professional or an agency manager to remove part of the record temporarily, if he or she determines that it might be detrimental to the client. This person must document the removal and its rationale. The client may appeal any limitation of access. If you design your procedures to work within these guidelines, and indicate your rules in your brochure, you will reduce your risk exposure greatly.

> In some very rare situations, I may temporarily remove parts of your records before you see them. This would happen if I believe that the information will be harmful to you, but I will discuss this with you.

My Background

This section gives your clients information about your professional background and training. Mention only your clinically relevant background; do not list social or political accomplishments, as these are irrelevant to therapy. You can include your areas of special professional interest, your publications, your supervisor status, and/or positions you hold in your professional organizations. Few people are knowledgeable about therapists' credentials, so it may be helpful to offer explanations of such matters as licensure or levels of certification. You can also mention training, such as internships, qualifications, supervision, education, and positions held.

It is not unethical to include a statement of experience such as this: "I have over 20 years of experience in the delivery of psychotherapy, psychological assessment, and consultation to children, adults, and families." You can also list the full range of services you offer such as group, individual, relationship, and/or family therapy; evaluations of various kinds; consultations with schools, other clinicians, or lawyers; hospital and home visits; and so on. If you present yourself as having any specialty, you will have to perform at, and conform to, the standards of others with full certification in that specialty. See Section 1.2 on the ethics of credentials.

If you are being supervised, the APA code of ethics (APA, 1992a, Section 4.01) requires that you inform clients of this fact and the supervisor's name where the supervisor has legal responsibility. I would suggest also including the supervisor's address and phone number as well, with the intention of heading off problems.

> I am a psychologist with 20 years of experience. For the past 12 years, I have had my own office for the general practice of clinical psychology. I am trained and experienced in doing one-on-one and couple therapy with adults (18 years and over). Earlier in my career, I worked in clinics and similar settings. I hold these qualifications:
>
> - I have a doctoral degree in clinical psychology from the University of Pittsburgh, whose program is approved by the American Psychological Association (APA).
>
> - I completed an internship in clinical psychology, approved by the APA.
>
> - I am licensed as a psychologist in Pennsylvania.
>
> - I have been entered in the National Register of Health Care Providers in Psychology.
>
> - I am a member of the APA.
>
> - I am a fellow of the Pennsylvania Psychological Association.

I am a psychologist and I like the phrase "general practice of clinical psychology." But you might prefer to call yourself a "health psychologist," a "counselor," or another explanatory title. I have avoided the term "private practice," but an acceptable alternative phrase is "independent practice."

Although memberships do not certify competence, listing them informs the client of your adherence to that organization's codified ethical standards. Thus the client has recourse to the professional organization's ethics committee. You might consider stating in the brochure here that you accept and practice in conformity with the code of ethics of your license or certification in your state. This model brochure makes such a statement in a later section (see "Statement of Principles and Complaint Procedures").

About Our Appointments

The very first time I meet with you, we will need to give each other much basic information. For this reason, I usually schedule 1½ hours for this first meeting. Following this, we will usually meet for a 50-minute session once or twice a week, then less often. We can schedule meetings for both your and my convenience. I will tell you at least a month in advance of my vacations or any other times we cannot meet. Please ask about my schedule in making your own plans.

The paragraph above describes the general time frame for brief therapy. You might want to be more detailed about the first session. It could be called an "initial evaluation session," for example, and you could specify that it includes open discussion of problems and concerns, history gathering, testing or questionnaires, and completion of forms (e.g., Form 26, the financial information form).

The scheduling of weekly appointments is traditional but not empirical. Zhu and Pierce (1995) suggest that, to the degree that the learning in therapy resembles the learning–forgetting curves seen in laboratory studies, the schedule of meetings ought to be negatively accelerated. As an example, they suggest meetings at 1, 3, 7, 14, and 30 days for optimal prevention of relapse. I would very strongly encourage you to consider such a schedule, because I believe it will greatly facilitate success in therapy.

I suggest above that appointments can be scheduled for "both your and my convenience." An alternative wording might be "Changes in appointments should be made with as much advance notice as possible, as a sign of our mutual respect." Or, "While I am willing to be flexible, I have found that therapy is more effective when it occurs at a regular time each week. I hope we can work toward this regularity of schedules." Or, "Appointments can be scheduled during my office hours, Monday through Friday, 11:00 A.M. to 9:00 P.M." If you use this last format, you could indicate that appointments or calls outside these times will be charged at twice your usual rate.

Be careful not to use "session" and "hour" interchangeably (unless your session length truly is 60 minutes). Doing so may mislead some clients. Do not choose the length of your session on the basis of what your peers are doing; choose it on the basis of your particular style of doing therapy. Keep in mind your need for breaks, for time to write notes, and for moving around, as well as your office location. Therapists often schedule 1-hour sessions for individuals and 1½-hour sessions for couples. If you treat both individuals and couples, you can include both lengths at this point in your brochure.

An appointment is a commitment to our work. We agree to meet here and to be on time. If I am ever unable to start on time, I ask your understanding. I also assure you that you will receive the full time agreed to. If you are late, we will probably be unable to meet for the full time, because it is likely that I will have another appointment after yours.

A cancelled appointment delays our work. I will consider our meetings very important and ask you to do the same. Please try not to miss sessions if you can possibly help it. When you must cancel, please give me at least a week's notice. Your session time is reserved for you. I am rarely able to fill a cancelled session unless I know a week in advance. If you start to miss a lot of sessions, I will have to charge you for the lost time unless I am able to fill it. Your insurance will not cover this charge.

For the paragraph above, you can substitute the following:

I will reserve a regular appointment time for you into the foreseeable future. I also do this for my other patients. Therefore, I am rarely able to fill a cancelled session unless I have several weeks' notice. You will be charged the full fee for sessions cancelled with less than 72 hours' notice, for other than the most serious reasons.

Repetition of this point on your appointment cards, on your bills, and on a sign in the office is recommended.

Constance Fisher, PhD, of Pittsburgh, PA, suggests having a clear, specific policy, such as the following: "Except for unpredictable emergencies (or because of a situation that would be seen by both of us as an unpredictable emergency), I will charge you 50% of the regular fee for any missed sessions." She chooses to implement this only with the second missed session.

Another possible statement is "If the appointment is not kept or is cancelled with less than 24 hours' advance notice, you can expect me to charge you for it." Some therapists add, "A retainer against such sessions, or for the closing session, will be requested at the initial meeting." For some therapists, the minimum advance notice for cancellation is 24 hours; this might then make a provision for weekends necessary, such as "Cancellations for a Monday appointment should be made no later than Thursday morning."

Note that the cancellation policy above is addressed to an individual client. If you treat families or couples, you need to make clear what you will do when everyone does not attend. (See Section 4.5 for some points concerning family therapy contracting.)

If you see children or adolescents, you should modify the following statement to suit your practice:

I request that you do not bring children with you if they are young and need babysitting or supervision, which I cannot provide. I do not have toys, but I can provide reading materials suitable for older children.

You might also want to include a statement such as this: "You will be charged for any damage to, or theft of, property in this office by you or anyone for whom you are legally responsible." To this you might add, "I cannot be responsible for any personal property or valuables you bring into this office."

Depending on your methods, you might end this section with other information for clients, such as suggesting comfortable dress, requesting no smoking, asking that they avoid bringing food or drinks, or offering a note about your dog's or cat's presence.

Fees, Payments, and Billing

Payment for services is important in any professional relationship. This is even more true in therapy; one treatment goal is to make relationships and the duties they involve clear. You are responsible for seeing that my services are paid for. Meeting this responsibility shows your commitment and maturity.

My current regular fees are as follows. You will be given advance notice if my fees should change.

Regular therapy services: For a session of _____ minutes, the fee is $_____. Please pay for each session at its end. I have found that this arrangement helps us stay focused on our goals, and so it works best. It also allows me to keep my fees as low as possible, because it cuts down on my bookkeeping costs. I suggest you make out your check before each session begins, so that our time will be used best. Other payment or fee arrangements must be worked out before the end of our first meeting.

Telephone consultations: $_____ per hour, prorated for the time needed. (For example, if we talk on the phone for 30 minutes, you will be charged $_____.) I believe that telephone consultations may be suitable or even needed at times in our therapy. If so, I will charge you our regular fee, prorated over the time needed. If I need to have long telephone conferences with other professionals as part of your treatment, you will be billed for these at the same rate as for regular therapy services. If you are concerned about all this, please be sure to discuss it with me in advance so we can set a policy that is comfortable for both of us. Of course, there is no charge for calls about appointments or similar business.

Extended sessions: Sometimes it may be better to go on with a session, rather than stop or postpone work on a particular issue. When this extension is more than 10 minutes, I will tell you, because sessions that are extended beyond 10 minutes will be charged on a prorated basis.

Psychological testing services: $_____ per hour. Psychological testing fees include the time spent with you, the time needed for scoring and studying the test results, and the time needed to write a report on the findings. The amount of time involved depends on the tests used and the questions the testing is intended to answer.

Reports: I will not charge you for my time spent making simple reports to your insurance company. However, I will have to bill you for any extra-long or complex reports the company might require. The company usually will not cover this fee.

Other services: Charges for other services, such as hospital visits, consultations with other therapists, home visits, or any court-related services (such as consultations with lawyers, depositions, or attendance at courtroom proceedings) will be based on the time involved in providing the service at my regular fee schedule. Some services may require payment in advance.

I realize that my fees involve a substantial amount of money, although they are well in line with similar professionals' charges. For you to get the best value for your money, we must work hard and well.

You may want to specify different fees for activities with different time needs or costs. For example, fees for supervision may be lower. Fees for conducting in-service or other training sessions may be higher because of the preparation time involved. Court testimony may be priced by the half-day, since schedules may be uncertain. If you write reports for lawyers or others, you may want to state that these "must be fully paid for before they are provided in legally signed form or released to any third party." See also Form 46 for a release and contract with a lawyer.

You may wish to offer variations in your fee structure, but be careful to avoid seeming to have two fees—one for those who have health insurance and a lower one for those who do not—because the insurance company will see this as fraud. Instead, you can offer a discount on your regular fee, just as you do when you sign onto a panel of a MCO. You must however make this explicit on your bills by showing your regular fee, the discount, and the discounted fee. You could offer a discount to self-paying clients for payment in full at the time of billing or for payment in advance, but not for those who pay slowly. All of this must be explicitly stated in your information brochure for clients.

Other points that may need clarification can be included here:

- Will you accept a portion of the fee at the time of services, with the rest to be paid by the insurance company at a future date? If so, make this clear.

- Will you raise a client's fee during the course of therapy? The brochure has mentioned above that clients will be given advance notice of fee increases; this alerts them to the possibility. But if you anticipate a long treatment period and significant inflation, you should state your policy—for example, "I examine my fee schedule yearly, and so may change my fees each new year."

- Will you lower your fee if a client's insurance coverage is exhausted or if a client's financial circumstances change? (See Section 2.1 on financial policies.) You should decide and include a statement here.

- It's a good idea to repeat that payment is due at each session by hanging a sign about this in your waiting room. You can also have it printed on your appointment cards. Susan Hutchinson, DSW, LCSW, of Irvine, CA, advises clients in her office policy statement that she does not bill for the copayment; she thus reinforces payment for each session.

- If you offer payment by credit card, say so in this section. If you don't offer it, you may want to consider doing it (see Section 2.5).

- If your fee varies with the patient's managed care contract, you must indicate that this is so, or you may be misrepresenting your fee.

- If you make any other extra charges, such as a double rate outside your usual hours, it is helpful to put it here. This is the section clients will refer to when they check on charges.

I will assume that our agreed-upon fee-paying relationship will continue as long as I provide services to you. I will assume this until you tell me in person, by telephone, or by certified mail that you wish to end it. You have a responsibility to pay for any services you receive before you end the relationship.

At the end of each month, I will send you a statement. The statement can be used for health insurance claims, as described in the next section. It will show all of our meetings, the charges for each, how much has been paid, and how much (if any) is still owed. At the end of treatment, and when you have paid for all sessions, I will send you a final statement for your tax records.

The last paragraph obviously should fit your office procedures. If you provide a "walk-out" receipt (see Section 2.5) at the end of each session, this is what a client should submit to the insurance company, and you won't need to send a statement. As regards tax deductibility, you could add "Depending on your financial circumstances and total medical costs for any year, psychotherapy may be a deductible expense," and "Consult your tax advisor." Cost of transportation to and from appointments and fees paid may be deductible from the client's personal income taxes as medical expenses, but each client should check to be sure.

If you decide to bill some clients, you probably should put something like the two paragraphs below into your brochure:

Because I expect all payment at the time of our meetings, I usually do not send bills. However, if we have agreed that I will bill you, I ask that the bill be paid within 5 days of when you get it.

If you think you may have trouble paying your bills on time, please discuss this with me. I will also raise the matter with you so we can arrive at a solution. If your unpaid balance reaches $_____, I will notify you by mail. If it then remains unpaid, I must stop therapy with you. Fees that continue unpaid after this will be turned over to small-claims court or a collection service.

A simpler alternative to the last sentence above is offered by Sam Knapp, EdD, of Harrisburg, PA: "Patients who owe money and fail to make arrangements to pay may be referred to a collection agency." Another alternative is to set a session limit on the amount owed.

Charging of interest or offering of credit requires you to comply with federal and state laws and forms. Therefore, use late fees or charge no interest. You can use "A late fee of 1½% of the unpaid balance will be charged each month" or "A late payment fee of $_____ will be charged each month that a balance remains unpaid."

For informed consent about confidentiality, it is also a good idea to indicate the kinds of information you will provide to those you hire to collect your old bills. A collection agency may get only the client's name, address, phone number, the amount owed, and the name of the therapist. (Collection agencies usually want more information if they need to locate an ex-client.) Small-claims court will get only the client's name, address, proof of services, and the amount owed to you.

You may want to indicate that you do not give refunds to unsatisfied customers (or to explain when you do give refunds).

If there is any problem with my charges, my billing, your insurance, or any other money-related point, please bring it to my attention. I will do the same with you. Such problems can interfere greatly with our work. They must be worked out openly and quickly.

If You Have Traditional (or "Indemnity") Health Insurance Coverage

Because I am a licensed psychologist, many health insurance plans will help you pay for therapy and other services I offer. These plans include Blue Shield and most Major Medical plans. Because health insurance is written by many different companies, I cannot tell you what your plan covers. Please read your plan's booklet under coverage for "Outpatient Psychotherapy" or under "Treatment of Mental and Nervous Conditions." Or call your insurer's office to find out what you need to know.

If your health insurance will pay part of my fee, I will help you with your insurance claim forms. However, please keep two things in mind:

1. I had no role in deciding what your insurance covers. Your employer decided which, if any, of my services will be covered and how much you (and I) will be paid. You are responsible for checking your insurance coverage, deductibles, payment rates, copayments, and so forth. Your insurance contract is between you and your company; it is not between me and the insurance company.

2. You—not your insurance company or any other person or company—are responsible for paying the fees we agree upon. If you ask me to bill a separated spouse, a relative, or an insurance company, and I do not receive payment on time, I will then expect this payment from you.

To seek payment from your insurance company, you must first obtain a claim form from your employer's benefits office or call your insurance company. Complete the claim form. Then attach my statement to the claim form and mail it to your insurance company. My statement already provides the information asked for on the claim form.

You should insert here whatever procedures you will perform (such as doing all the verification of coverage, billing insurers, billing for copayments, etc.) and what procedures are expected of the patient.

If You Have a Managed Care Contract

If you belong to a health maintenance organization (HMO) or have another kind of health insurance with managed care, decisions about what kind of care you need and how much of it you can receive will be reviewed by the plan. The plan has rules, limits, and procedures that we should discuss. Please bring your health insurance plan's description of services to one of our early meetings, so that we can talk about it and decide what to do.

It may be helpful to list here the preferred provider organizations (PPOs), HMOs, managed care panels, and the like to which you belong, and then describe the procedures they require you to follow. Managed care issues are complicated, and to get informed consent you might want to use Handout 3.

I will provide information about you to your insurance company only with your informed and written consent. I may send this information by mail or by fax. My office will try its best to maintain the privacy of your records, but I ask you not to hold me responsible for accidents or for anything that happens as a result.

If you think that the loss of confidentiality, lessened professional control of treatment, and the impact of a psychiatric diagnosis are significant concerns for a client, consider giving them Handout 3. Ackley (1997) also has excellent educational handouts about fees and insurance and about payment plans.

If You Need to Contact Me

Because I do outpatient evaluation and therapy, I cannot promise that I will be available at all times. Although I am in the office _____ through _____, from _____ to _____, I usually do not take phone calls when I am with a client. You can always leave a message with my secretary or on my answering machine, and I will return your call as soon as I can. Generally, I will return messages daily except on Sundays and holidays.

If you have an emergency or crisis, tell this to my secretary, who will try to contact me. If you have a behavioral or emotional crisis and cannot reach me or my secretary immediately by telephone, you or your family members should call one of the following community emergency agencies: the county mental health office at _____, or the crisis center at _____, or the _____ Hospital emergency room.

You might indicate (only if it is true, of course) that you return all calls within 24 hours. The rule of immediate return is a good one to make, even if you have to work hard to keep it. You might also indicate hours for regular phone calls, such as 10 A.M. to 8 P.M., and say that calls outside these hours are treated as emergencies and charged accordingly. If it fits your style of practice, you could offer a regular hour each day during which you will be available to receive calls such as questions about homework. To reduce "telephone tag," you could specify a particular time each day during which you will return calls. Callers can then leave a number where they can be reached during that time.

For emergencies, you should add specific information for your situation. You might say, "In case of an emergency, call my answering service at _____. Tell the person who answers that you urgently need to speak with me, and ask him or her to locate me." Or, "In emergencies outside of my regular office hours, call me at home at _____. If you cannot reach me in a dire emergency, call your own medical doctor or go to the nearest emergency room." If you use a beeper or paging device, explain that here.

The following are some alternate phone policies: "I find that telephone therapy does not work as well as face-to-face therapy, and so I discourage it. I will generally suggest our meeting if you call with a problem that is not critical." Or, "I have found that brief telephone calls work quite well for some purposes, and I am willing to arrange this." Or, "If I feel that our work together calls for it, I will make special arrangements for telephone contact, and this service will be charged at my usual rate."

If I Need to Contact Someone about You

If there is an emergency during our work together, or I become concerned about your personal safety, I am required by law and by the rules of my profession to contact someone close to you—perhaps a relative, spouse, or close friend. I am also required to contact this person, or the authorities, if I become concerned about your harming someone else. Please write down the name and information of your chosen contact person in the blanks provided:

Name: _____

Address: _____

Phone: _____ Relationship to you: _____

Other Points

Although I share this office with other therapists, each of us works independently, and each alone is responsible for the quality of the care he or she provides.

The above is a protective and clarifying statement that is necessary if you are in a shared-office practice. If you are in a true group practice, you do share responsibility if another therapist commits an unethical or illegal act, so be explicit.

The APA code of ethics (APA, 1992a, Section 4.03(b)) suggests that you include the next point:

If you ever become involved in a divorce or custody dispute, I want you to understand and agree that I will not provide evaluations or expert testimony in court. You should hire a different mental health professional for any evaluations or testimony you require. This position is based on two reasons: (1) My statements will be seen as biased in your favor because we have a therapy relationship; and (2) the testimony might affect our therapy relationship, and I must put this relationship first.

As a professional therapist, I naturally want to know more about how therapy helps people. To understand therapy better, I must collect information about clients before, during, and after therapy. Therefore, I am asking you to help me by filling out some questionnaires about different parts of your life—relationships, changes, concerns, attitudes, and other areas. I ask your permission to take what you wrote on these questionnaires and what I have in my records and use it in research or teaching that I may do in the future. If I ever use the information from your questionnaire it will always be included with information from many others. Also, your identity will be made completely anonymous. Your name will never be mentioned, and all personal information will be disguised and changed. After the research, teaching, or publishing project is completed all the data used will be destroyed.

If, as part of our therapy, you create and provide to me records, notes, artworks, or any other documents or materials, I will return the originals to you at your written request but will retain copies.

This is protective of both you and the client (Berkowitz, 1995). A rare patient may ask you to remove or destroy some materials with the intention of removing your means of defense, and then complain against you or institute a lawsuit.

You can also indicate in this section any special rules you have—for example, about treating active substance abusers, criminal or court-referred patients, spouse/child abusers, suicidal patients, patients with paranoid disorders, and so on. If you work with adults who have a history of childhood abuse, it may be a good idea to consider informing them about the possibility of suing their abusers for monetary damages. States are now enacting laws extending the "statute of limitations" in such cases; thus it may be useful, in order to protect yourself from charges of negligence, to inform such clients of the legal situation in your area of practice.

Finally, you can leave a space here to write in any additional issues that bear on each individual case.

Statement of Principles and Complaint Procedures

I fully abide by all the rules of the American Psychological Association (APA) and by those of my state license.

The APA's rules include its Ethical Principles, its Standards for Providers of Psychological Services, its Guidelines for Delivery of Specialty Services by Clinical Psychologists, and others you care to mention.

Problems can arise in our relationship, just as in any other relationship. If you are not satisfied with any area of our work, please raise your concerns with me at once. Our work together will be slower and harder if your concerns with me are not worked out. I will make every effort to hear any complaints you have and to seek solutions to them. If you feel that I, or any other therapist, has treated you unfairly or has even broken a professional rule, please tell me. You can also contact the state or local psychological association and speak to the chairperson of the ethics committee. He or she can help clarify your concerns or tell you how to file a complaint. You may also contact the state board of psychologist examiners [note that this differs across states], the organization that licenses those of us in the independent practice of psychology.

It is helpful to list the professional ethical codes to which you conform, and to post these codes in the waiting room. You may want to add the telephone numbers of the groups listed above. Some would consider it unnecessary, pessimistic, or even masochistic to tell clients how to lodge a formal ethics complaint. But this information is essential for fully informing the consumer. Vinson (1987) found that the low level of reporting of sexual and other abuses by therapists was not attributable to lack of motivation, but to lack of information on how to file a complaint. Hare-Mustin et al. (1979) say that clients need to know what the legitimate grounds for complaints are, as well as what options are available for resolving them. Brown (personal communication in Branscombe, 1996) reported that in the state of Washington, where providing such information has been required since 1987, there has been no increase of complaints (frivolous or otherwise). This is, however, a complex clinical as well as ethical issue, with complicated options that are not well addressed in a small brochure. If a concern or complaint of any sort arises, document it. Do this even if you think it trivial or baseless.

In my practice as a therapist, I do not discriminate against clients because of any of these factors: age, sex, marital/family status, race, color, religious beliefs, ethnic origin, place of residence, veteran status, physical disability, health status, sexual orientation, or criminal record unrelated to present dangerousness. This is a personal commitment, as well as being required by federal, state, and local laws and regulations. I will always take steps to advance and support the values of equal opportunity, human dignity, and racial/ethnic/cultural diversity. If you believe you have been discriminated against, please bring this matter to my attention immediately.

In the list above of groups that can be discriminated against I have tried to be comprehensive—including, for example, "health status" as an indicator of HIV-positive individuals; "place of residence" in regard to low-socioeconomic-status areas or community mental health center catchment areas; and some other less usual factors. You should add to, or delete from, this list anything not applicable to your practice.

Our Agreement

I, the client (or his or her parent or guardian), understand I have the right not to sign this form. I understand I can choose to discuss my concerns with you, the therapist, before I start (or the client starts) formal therapy. I also understand that any of the points mentioned above can be discussed and may be open to change. If at any time during the treatment I have questions about any of the subjects discussed in this brochure, I can talk with you about them, and you will do your best to answer them.

I understand that after therapy begins, I have the right to withdraw my consent to therapy at any time, for any reason. However, I will make every effort to discuss my concerns about my progress with you before ending therapy with you.

To be sure you haven't promised a cure, you might want to insert language like this at the end of the brochure:

I understand that no specific promises have been made to me by this therapist about the results of treatment, the effectiveness of the procedures used by this therapist, or the number of sessions necessary for therapy to be effective.

I have read, or have had read to me, the issues and points in this brochure. I have discussed those points I did not understand, and have had my questions, if any, fully answered. I agree to act according to the points covered in this brochure. I hereby agree to enter into therapy with this therapist (or to have the client enter therapy), and to cooperate fully and to the best of my ability, as shown by my signature here.

_____   _____
Signature of client (or person acting for client)   Date

_____
Printed name

Relationship to client: ❏ Self ❏ Parent ❏ Health care custodial parent of a minor (less than 14 years of age) ❏ Guardian ❏ Other person authorized to act on behalf of the client.

Besides the signature, for your additional protection and assurance that the client has read every page, you could ask the client to initial each page at the bottom by including a statement like "Initial here to show that you have read this page."

I, the therapist, have met with this client (and/or his or her parent or guardian) for a suitable period of time, and have informed him or her of the issues and points raised in this brochure. I have responded to all of his or her questions. I believe this person fully understands the issues, and I find no reason to believe this person is not fully competent to give informed consent to treatment. I agree to enter into therapy with the client, as shown by my signature here.

_____   _____
Signature of therapist   Date

I truly appreciate the chance you have given me to be of professional service to you, and look forward to a successful relationship with you. If you are satisfied with my services as we proceed I (like any professional) would appreciate your referring other people to me who might also be able to make use of my services.

❏ Copy accepted by client   ❏ Copy kept by therapist

4.3   The Second Path to Informed Consent: The Question List as a Guide to Discussion

The second method for obtaining informed consent comes from Handelsman and Galvin's (1988) proposal to provide the client with a list of questions and then conduct a discussion of the points the client raises. They describe the advantages of their approach as follows:

> First, it informs clients what information they have a right to [ask about] but preserves their right to request it or not. Second, it may be less overwhelming for clients. . . . Third, because the answers are not spelled out, the form requires a conversation between therapist and client to take place. . . . Fourth, the form has a fourth-grade readability level. . . . (Handelsman & Galvin, 1988, p. 224)

In short, this approach is an admirably creative, flexible, and sensitive solution to a thorny problem.

The give-and-take of discussion incorporated into this approach is the essence of getting informed consent. In practice, you can give the questions to the client at the end of the first session to take home and read. The client can then be asked for questions during the second session, and the form can be signed. (If, as is fairly often the case, the client has forgotten it, a new copy can be offered, discussed, and signed.) This, then, is **a structured interview the client conducts with you.** After answering the client's questions, you can write a note such as this: "I believe I have obtained fully informed, voluntary, and competent consent to proceed with treatment because we have covered everything on my [question list]." This procedure simultaneously (1) meets your legal responsibility to get an informed consent form signed; (2) meets your ethical responsibility to have the dialogue (questions and answers) that must logically and technically underlie informed consent; and, most importantly, (3) is clinically elegant, as it starts therapy off with openness—putting everything on the table not only by answering the client's questions, but by even giving the client the questions to ask.

Because the questions are in simple English and the client signs the list to affirm that he or she has had a discussion of the points and understands them, I believe that this procedure makes a legal challenge to the effect that the patient simply signed a form, and that therefore the consent was not really informed, far less likely to succeed.

The questions offered below are adapted from the article by Handelsman and Galvin (1988). Several items have been added on the basis of Handelsman's later research (Bratten et al., 1993). Handout 4 (on p. 152) provides the question list in two-page format, which you can just photocopy and hand out.

HANDOUT 4

You may want to add questions or points suited to your practice. You could review the client information brochure (in Section 4.2) for ideas to include and for options in answering the questions about how you practice, such as your financial policies. It will be essential for you to review your procedures and rehearse your responses to each of these questions. The answers you offer can be based on straightforward facts about diagnoses and treatment, or they can be designed to serve clinical goals, such as restraining of change or predicting changes to gain control of a symptom.

Information You Have a Right to Know

When you come for therapy, you are buying a service to meet your individual needs. You need good information about therapy to make the best choice for yourself and your family. I have written down some questions you might want to ask me about how I do therapy. We may have talked about some of them already. You are free to ask me any of these questions, and I will try my best to answer them for you. If my answers are not clear, or if I have left something out, or if you have more questions, just ask me again. You have the right to full information about therapy.

A. About Therapy

    1. What will we do in therapy?

Obviously your answer to this should be tailored to your approach, but you might say something along these lines: "We will discuss fully what brought you to see me; explore your history and background; talk about all areas of your life, especially when, with whom, and in what settings you have problems; and discuss anything else that is important, so I can fully understand your situation." You could then discuss and describe treatments.

    2. What will I have to do in therapy?

Perhaps you could say: "I will expect you to be open and honest about your thoughts and feelings; to help design homework; to do the homework assignments; to try out new ways of dealing with your feelings, thoughts, or other people; to keep track of your feelings and behaviors . . . " (add anything else you think appropriate).

    3. Could anything bad happen because of therapy?

This question is designed to elicit a discussion of the possible risks involved in therapy, which might include the following: not improving, feeling worse temporarily, or a true worsening of the client's condition; conflicts with spouse, relatives, or peers; divorce or breakup of a relationship; or some depression, fears, and doubts. Almost every therapy client is concerned about these things, but most clients do get better.

    4. What will I notice when I am getting better?

Here you can focus the client's attention on specific areas chosen for their clinical utility. You might suggest that symptoms change in frequency, duration, intensity, or latency. You can predict reduced anxiety or increased optimism, self-confidence, energy, and courage.

    5. About how long will it take for me to see that I am getting better?

The response to this question will depend on the client's presenting problems and prognosis. I often tell my clients that they should feel increased optimism in a few sessions, with lessened anxiety or depression in 10–15 sessions. I also tell them that others may notice changes before they do.

    6. Will I have to take any tests? What for? What kind?

Obviously this depends on your approach and discipline, but symptom measures may be useful for assessing and documenting progress and outcome for both insurers and clients.

7. How many (that is, what fraction) of your clients with my kind of problem get better?

DSM-IV (American Psychiatric Association, 1994) has information on the life course of some diagnoses.

8. How many (that is, what fraction) of your clients get worse?

Most of us don't have this information, but we should. This may stimulate you to do some follow-up data collection calls.

9. How many (that is, what fraction) of people with the same kinds of problems I have get better without therapy? How many get worse?

This is a tough but critical question. Again, data collection may be needed.

10. About how long will therapy take?

Be realistic. Don't try to offer a low number of sessions because this is all the client's insurance will pay for, in cases where you know a low number will be insufficient. You can also discuss this in terms of short- and long-term goals.

11. What should I do if I feel therapy isn't working?

You might say this: "You should discuss this with me. We may be able to modify our treatment or your expectations might be inappropriate. We may need to add additional treatment methods. If we are not making progress I will seek consultation and may ask you to go to another therapist for a consultation. If we are really not making progress, I have an ethical obligation to discontinue treatment."

B. About Other Therapy and Help

1. What other types of therapy or help are there for my problems?

You can select from counseling, medications, group therapies, support groups, self-help groups, readings, and so forth, and from social agencies, clinics, schools, other practitioners, other orientations, and other disciplines.

2. How often do these other methods help people with problems like mine?

This is often a hard question for therapists to answer, because of interdisciplinary rivalry, ignorance of others' approaches, and fears of others' inadequacy in regard to training or skill. However, just as you would want complete and accurate information on alternatives before making a major decision, your clients deserve this discussion. Don't let your selfish interests in comfort outweigh a client's needs.

3. What are the risks or limits of these other methods?

You can indicate the costs, availability, location, and entry criteria of each alternative.

C. About Our Appointments

1. How will we set up our appointments?

2. How long will our sessions last? Do I have to pay more for longer ones?

3. How can I reach you in an emergency?

4. If I can't reach you, to whom can I talk?

5. What happens if the weather is bad or I'm sick and can't come to an appointment?

Options for all of these are offered in the client information brochure (see Section 4.2).

D.   About Confidentiality

1. What kinds of records do you keep about my therapy?

Describe your records to the client, or, better yet, show the client the record forms you use.

2. Who is allowed to read these records?

Some possibilities are the client, members of the client's family, other clinicians, the referrer, the courts, insurance companies and managed care organizations, government departments, supervisors, lawyers, and collection agencies. You can explain release forms and their
required contents (see Section 7.3).

3. Are there times you *have* to tell others about the personal things we might talk about?

Yes, and the usual situations are suicidal or homicidal threats, child or elder abuse/neglect,
and court referral of cases. See also Section 7.1 on confidentiality and its limits.

E. About Money

Here is the time to discuss your financial policies. Make sure to rehearse answers to these
questions, as this is hard for almost all therapists. See Section 2.1 on financial policies, as
well as Section 4.2.

1. What will you charge me for each appointment?

2. When do you want to be paid?

3. Do I need to pay for an appointment if I don't come to it or call you and cancel it?

4. Do I need to pay for telephone calls to you?

5. Will you ever raise the fee that you charge me? When?

6. If I lose some of my income, can my fee be lowered?

7. If I do not pay my bill, what will you do?

F. Other Matters

    1. How much training and experience do you have? Do you have a license? What are your other qualifications?

    2. What kind of morals and values do you have?

Some clients seek out religious therapists, believing that such therapists will share their values. All therapists have a moral philosophy, as do all therapies. Besides general values such as trustworthiness and flexibility, it may be useful to discuss value issues that are most relevant to the presenting problem (e.g., loyalty, openness despite fear of consequences, gender role preferences, respect for authority or age, etc.).

    3. To whom can I talk if I have a complaint about therapy that you and I can't work out?

You could say something like this: "If you have a complaint that we try to work out but can't, I may ask you to see another therapist for a consultation. The consultant can give both of us another perspective. If this doesn't help and you believe the issue is crucial, you can call the local psychological association and talk to the professional affairs officer to get direction and help."

The list above deals with the most commonly asked questions, but many people want to know more. Feel free to ask me any questions you have at any time. The more you know, the better our work will go. You can keep the "Information for Clients" brochure (if given) and this list. Please read them carefully at home, and if any questions come up, write them on this page so we can talk about them when we meet next time.

Information You Have a Right to Know

When you come for therapy, you are buying a service to meet your individual needs. You need good information about therapy to make the best choice for yourself and your family. I have written down some questions you might want to ask me about how I do therapy. We may have talked about some of them already. You are free to ask me any of these questions, and I will try my best to answer them for you. If my answers are not clear, or if I have left something out, or if you have more questions, just ask me again. You have the right to full information about therapy.

A. About Therapy
    1. What will we do in therapy?
    2. What will I have to do in therapy?
    3. Could anything bad happen because of therapy?
    4. What will I notice when I am getting better?
    5. About how long will it take for me to see that I am getting better?
    6. Will I have to take any tests? What for? What kind?
    7. How many (that is, what fraction) of your clients with my kind of problem get better?
    8. How many (that is, what fraction) of your clients get worse?
    9. How many (that is, what fraction) of people with the same kinds of problems I have get better without therapy? How many get worse?
    10. About how long will therapy take?
    11. What should I do if I feel therapy isn't working?

B. About Other Therapy and Help
    1. What other types of therapy or help are there for my problems?
    2. How often do these other methods help people with problems like mine?
    3. What are the risks or limits of these other methods?

C. About Our Appointments
    1. How will we set up our appointments?
    2. How long will our sessions last? Do I have to pay more for longer ones?
    3. How can I reach you in an emergency?
    4. If I can't reach you, to whom can I talk?
    5. What happens if the weather is bad or I'm sick and can't come to an appointment?

D. About Confidentiality
    1. What kinds of records do you keep about my therapy?
    2. Who is allowed to read these records?
    3. Are there times you *have* to tell others about the personal things we might talk about?

(cont.)

E. About Money

1. What will you charge me for each appointment?
2. When do you want to be paid?
3. Do I need to pay for an appointment if I don't come to it, or if I call you and cancel it?
4. Do I need to pay for telephone calls to you?
5. Will you ever raise the fee that you charge me? When?
6. If I lose some of my income, can my fee be lowered?
7. If I do not pay my bill, what will you do?

F. Other Matters

1. How much training and experience do you have? Do you have a license? What are your other qualifications?
2. What kind of morals and values do you have?
3. To whom can I talk if I have a complaint about therapy that you and I can't work out?

The list above deals with the most commonly asked questions, but many people want to know more. Feel free to ask me any questions you have at any time. The more you know, the better our work will go. You can keep the "Information for Clients" brochure (if given) and this list. Please read them carefully at home, and if any questions come up, write them on this page so we can talk about them when we meet next time.

I, the client (or his or her parent or guardian), have gone over this list with the therapist, and I understand these questions and the therapist's answers.

_____   _____
Signature of client (or parent/guardian)   Date

_____
Printed name

I, the therapist, have discussed these issues with the client (and/or his or her parent or guardian). I believe this person fully understands the issues, and I find no reason to believe that this person is not fully competent to give informed consent to treatment.

_____   _____
Signature of therapist   Date

❏ Copy accepted by client   ❏ Copy kept by therapist

<u>4.4</u> The Third Path to Informed Consent: Lists of Clients' Rights

The third path to informed consent is less formal and more fluid, and therefore better suited to some therapists and clients than the question list. It is the offering of a listing of clients' basic rights in psychotherapy.

If you are going to use this approach, you should review the three lists presented below, add your own ideas, and then devise a list tailored to the style and needs of your practice. You must also modify these rights statements to fit your local and current circumstances before you distribute the list, and you should keep it current by consulting with your local ethics committee.

About Handouts 5, 6, and 7

HANDOUT 5   The first list (Handout 5) is based on one first published by Everstine et al. (1980), which has been widely reprinted. In regard to point 6, see Form 15 for a consent-to-record form.

HANDOUT 6   The second list (Handout 6) is adapted and simplified from one provided by Bennett et al. (1990), who describe it as a list of "rights generally agreed upon" (p. 119).

HANDOUT 7   The third list (Handout 7) is modified from a publication of the California Department of Consumer Affairs entitled *Professional Therapy Never Includes Sex* (Quinn, n.d.). This free, 20-page booklet describes the California laws and details how to report abuse, take legal and administrative actions, and find help for the victim.

Please examine each rights statement and modify it to suit your locale and style of practice. For example, telling a client that he or she cannot refuse court-ordered testing or therapy may insert you into a conflict between the client and the court, which would be better handled by them (Sam Knapp, personal communication, October 2, 1996).

The Rights of Clients

1. You have the right to decide not to enter therapy with me. If you wish, I will provide you with the names of other good therapists.

2. You have the right to end therapy at any time. The only thing you will have to do is to pay for any treatments you have already had. You may, of course, have problems with other people or agencies if you end therapy—for example, if you have been sent for therapy by a court.

3. You have the right to ask any questions, at any time, about what we do during therapy, and to receive answers that satisfy you. If you wish, I will explain my usual methods to you.

4. You have the right not to allow the use of any therapy technique. If I plan to use any unusual technique, I will tell you and discuss its benefits and risks.

5. You have the right to keep what you tell me private. Generally, no one will learn of our work without your written permission. There are some situations in which I am required by law to reveal some of the things you tell me, even without your permission, and if I do reveal these things I am not required by the law to tell you that I have done so. Here are some of these situations:

   a. If you seriously threaten to harm another person, I must warn that person and the authorities.
   b. If a court orders me to testify about you, I must do so.
   c. If I am testing or treating you under a court order, I must report my findings to the court.

6. If I wish to record a session, I will get your informed consent in writing. You have the right to prevent any such recording.

7. You have the right to review your records in my files at any time, to add to or correct them, and to get copies for other professionals to use.

Clients' Rights in Therapy

Clients generally have the right to:

- Know all about the therapist's experience and training.

- Discuss their therapy with anyone they choose, including another therapist.

- Know all about the terms of therapy, such as its cost, appointment times, privacy issues, and so on.

- Have any therapy procedure or method explained to them before it is used.

- See all the information about them in the therapist's files, or have it shared with another professional or group at their request.

- Ask the therapist about anything about therapy—and, if not satisfied, complain to the therapist's superior, or even file a complaint with the government or the therapist's professional group.

- Read a copy of the therapist's guidelines or rules about practicing therapy, such as the therapist's code of ethics.

- Refuse any test, evaluation, or therapy of any kind.

- If a client is ordered to be evaluated or to come to therapy by a court, however, there may be legal problems when he or she stops treatment.

In this list your rights are described in very brief terms, and this state's laws or rules may give them somewhat differently. If you want more information, please ask me, and we can discuss your actual rights in this state under its current laws and rules.

Client Bill of Rights

You have the right to:

- Get respectful treatment that will be helpful to you.

- Have a safe treatment setting, free from sexual, physical, and emotional abuse.

- Report immoral and illegal behavior by a therapist.

- Ask for and get information about the therapist's qualifications, including his or her license, education, training, experience, membership in professional groups, special areas of practice, and limits on practice.

- Have written information, before entering therapy, about fees, method of payment, insurance coverage, number of sessions the therapist thinks will be needed, substitute therapists (in cases of vacation and emergencies), and cancellation policies.

- Refuse audio or video recording of sessions (but you may ask for it if you wish).

- Refuse to answer any question or give any information you choose not to answer or give.

- Know if your therapist will discuss your case with others (for instance, supervisors, consultants, or students).

- Ask that the therapist inform you of your progress.

HANDOUT 7. Third clients' rights form.   Adapted from Quinn (n.d.). This document is in the public domain.—From *The Paper Office*, p. 157.

4.5 The Fourth Path to Informed Consent: Psychotherapy Contracts

> *All treatment proceeds with a contract or a series of contractual agreements between therapist and patient that are either explicit or implicit in therapeutic discourse. The danger of an unarticulated contract is that it can be misunderstood, tacitly reconceptualized, or inconsistently applied, and thus misused. Such misunderstandings can increase exponentially in their impact, meaning and consequence over the course of treatment, resulting in an unexamined diffusion of and diversion from the therapeutic work.*
> —LIPMAN (1995, p. 996)

Contracts are not substitutes for the a client information brochure. But they can establish a different therapeutic relationship from that established by the brochure. Contracts focus on more specific aspects of therapy activities. Some of the contract forms offered here expand information on the techniques or methods of therapy, and some focus more on the goals of treatment, the "rules" for therapy, or the risks of treatment versus the probability of success.

The treatment contract can be one component of the process of getting informed consent. The form is evidence of consent, but it is not a substitute for it; as mentioned earlier, courts have held in some cases that consent was not obtained despite the signing of a form. The client must be fully informed through discussions if consent is to be effectively and legally given. Only then should a contract form be completed and signed. As treatment evolves, the contract should also be renegotiated and redrafted. If you prefer less legalistic-sounding terminology than "contract," you can call such a form an "understanding" or an "agreement."

The Nature of Contracts

Contracts have many advantages, as pointed out by Hare-Mustin et al. (1979):

- They reinforce equality, mutuality, and cooperation because they require negotiation.

- They clarify the relationship's goals, boundaries, and expectations.

- They "prevent misunderstandings about the responsibilities, methods, and practical arrangements of therapy" (p. 8).

- They clarify the roles of each person in the relationship: the therapist as possessing special skills, the client as offering personal knowledge.

- They increase both parties' accountability.

Contracts can also be made therapeutic for some clients by the planful placement of ideas under headings such as "Responsibilities" (e.g., completing all homework assignments) or "Possible Negative Effects of Treatment" (e.g., disappointment with therapy for not making the client's life better without the client's making any efforts). In phrasing a contract, as in phrasing a client brochure, do not underestimate the difficulties of therapy or promise change over which you have little control. Continually reevaluate progress and modify the goals as issues become better understood.

I want here to make a distinction between a "treatment contract" and a "consent to treatment form." An agreement can be negotiated that leaves out many of the goals, problem definitions, methods, and tactics; only the most critical items are stated. However, this form should be considered a consent-to-treatment form rather than a psychotherapy contract. These pared-down consent forms constitute the fifth path to consent and are covered in the next section. Here I offer the more detailed and specific contract approach.

Contracts should be tailored to your practice and to the client's individual situation. Sample contract forms are offered in the following pages: a contract for individual psychotherapy, two for treating children and adolescents, and one for group therapy. I also discuss important issues for contracts with families and couples.

A Checklist for a Psychotherapy Contract: Elements and Options

The contracts offered here do not cover all possible variations, and they may not quite suit your way of practicing. Below, I provide a list of the basic elements that a contract should include, together with a few additional options. This checklist is designed to help you create your own contracts. You can use one of the forms that follow as a general model, then pick and choose items from the list below. Any items included in the client information brochure (see Section 4.2) could also be incorporated into a contract; I have not, however, duplicated all these possible inclusions here. This checklist is partially based on ideas developed by the Health Research Group (Adams & Orgel, 1975), as modified in Kachorek (1990, p. 105). It also incorporates ideas from Stromberg et al. (1988, pp. 164–165), Hare-Mustin et al. (1979), Bennett et al. (1990, p. 54), and Stuart (1975). The checklist's items are worded as questions about the content of the contract form.

Agreement and Consent

❏ Does the form indicate clearly that this is an informal "agreement"? Its purpose is to indicate an understanding, or set of mutual expectations, between the client and therapist; its ultimate goals are clarification and communication. It is not an exhaustive, complete specification of all treatment variables and issues.

❏ Does the form fully inform the client of all relevant aspects and decisions, so that the client can consent to treatment as an autonomous adult?

❏ Does the form state that the client's consent to treatment is voluntary, and that he or she is free to withdraw from or discontinue treatment without penalty?

❏ Does the form tell the client that the contract will become part of the treatment record?

❏ Does the contract provide space for the signatures of both client and therapist and the dates signed?

Goals

❏ Are the goals of the psychotherapy with this client stated?

❑ Are they based on assessment of, and consultation with, the client?

❑ Have both long-term goals and short-term objectives been developed?

Description/Listing of Techniques

❑ Does the form describe treatment techniques, or confirm that the client has been informed of them through discussion with the therapist or reading materials?

❑ Has the client been informed of any techniques that might be at odds with his or her values?

Risks and Benefits

❑ Are the benefits to the client described fully, accurately, and without any promise of specific outcomes, results, cures, or guarantees?

❑ Are the risks to the client described, including contraindications, side effects, and undesirable or negative effects?

Client Responsibilities

❑ Does the form state that the client will "cooperate fully" and "to the best of my ability"?

❑ Are specific client responsibilities indicated? These could include being on time for appointments, paying on a timely basis, doing homework, reading patient education materials, cooperating with educational efforts, and the like. On a more therapeutic level, responsibilities could include acting "as if" when initiating new behaviors, not canceling appointments when afraid, examining resistances to doing homework, and working courageously to overcome shame or humiliation.

Therapist Responsibilities: Treatment

Does the form state that the therapist will:

❑ Use his or her best efforts, skills, resources, training, experience, and good faith?

❑ Make use of the specific techniques in which he or she has been trained in the best interests of the client?

❑ Continually monitor the progress of the therapy?

❑ Operate responsibly, such as being on time, responding promptly to calls, being prepared, and the like?

❑ Fulfill other therapeutic responsibilities, such as encouraging the client's independence or rights to self-determination, not siding with one partner, and so forth?

Therapist Responsibilities: Confidentiality

Does the form indicate that:

❏ Professional standards and ethics will be respected?

❏ There are exceptions to confidentiality (see Chapter 7)?

❏ Permission is granted to the therapist to take notes and to record the sessions (see Form 18)?

❏ Permission is granted to the therapist to collect and publish anonymous and grouped treatment data?

❏ Written permission will be needed to disclose information about any specific clients?

Meetings and Fees

❏ Are the location, frequency, and length of meetings indicated together with how they are arranged?

❏ Is the client's assumption of financial responsibility stated?

❏ Are fees and charges explicitly stated, including fees for missed sessions?

❏ Is the form clear about when payment is expected?

❏ Are future adjustments to the fee, if they will be made, specified?

Changing the Contract and Terminating Treatment

❏ Does the form state that any of the contract's contents may be renegotiated? Specifics may be mentioned, such as changing the nature, priority, or definition of the goals.

❏ Are the conditions of termination of therapy made clear? Specifically, the contract may be terminated by either party, but with some explicit advance notice.

Provisions When Treating Families or Couples

❏ Does the form state your policy on nonattendance by a family member or one member of a couple?

❏ Does the form state your policy on how you will handle family secrets?

Provisions When Treating Children or Adolescents

❏ Have you included a statement on parents' or guardians' legal rights to certain information?

❑ Does the form address a minor's right to a private life and your use of discretion in communicating with parents?

❑ Does the form state your policy on disclosing a minor's drug use, sexual behavior, or illegal actions, as well as confessions and similar privacies?

Provisions for Group Therapy

❑ Does each group member agree to keep other group members' identities and information confidential? (Note: Client information revealed in group therapy is generally not considered to be legally privileged. Do not assert that it is unless you know that it is in your state.)

Other Issues

❑ Are remedies for client dissatisfaction stated?

❑ Is a statement that the professional believes the client is fully competent to consent to treatment included?

A Contract for Individual Therapy with an Adult

FORM 8   Form 8 is a generalized agreement for adult clients. Modify it to suit your way of working.

Agreement for Individual Therapy

I,_____,the client, agree to meet with the therapist named below at the appointment times and places we agree on, starting on _____, _____, for about _____ sessions of _____ minutes each.

I have read the following materials on the therapy, which have been provided to me by this therapist:

1. _____ 3. _____

2. _____ 4. _____

I believe I understand the basic ideas, goals, and methods of this therapy. I have no important questions or concerns that the therapist has not discussed. In my own words, I understand the following:

1. According to this therapy, the causes of my problems lie in: _____

_____

2. The main methods to be used in this therapy are: _____

_____

3. During these sessions, we will focus on working toward these goals:

a. _____ b. _____

I understand that reaching these goals is not guaranteed.

4. I understand that I will have to do the following things/take the following actions:

a. _____ b. _____

With enough knowledge, and without being forced, I enter into treatment with this therapist. I will keep my therapist fully up to date about any changes in my feelings, thoughts, and behaviors. I expect us to work together on any difficulties that occur, and to work them out in my long-term best interest.

At the end of _____ meetings, we will evaluate progress and may change parts of this agreement as needed. Our goals may have changed in nature, order of importance, or definition. If I am not satisfied by our progress toward goals, I will attempt to make change in this agreement, and I may stop treatment after giving this therapist at least 7 days' notice of my intentions and meeting with the therapist for one last time.

This agreement shows my commitment to pay for this therapist's services. It also shows this therapist's willingness to use and share his or her knowledge and skills in good faith. I agree to pay $_____ per session, and to pay at the end of each session. I agree to pay for uncancelled appointments or those where I fail to give enough notice that I will not attend. The only exceptions are unforeseen or unavoidable situations arising suddenly. I understand and accept that I am fully responsible for this fee, but that my therapist will help me in getting payments from any insurance coverage I have. I understand that this agreement will become part of my record of treatment.

I also give my permission for the therapist to audiotape/videotape our sessions for personal review and use with a consultant, who is also bound by the legal framework of privacy and confidentiality. I understand that any information in this recording that could identify me in any way will not be published or given out without my written consent.

My signature below means that I understand and agree with all of the points above.

_____   _____
Signature of client   Date

I, the therapist, have discussed the issues above with the client. My observations of this client's behavior and responses give me no reason, in my professional judgment, to believe that this person is not fully competent to give informed and willing consent.

_____   _____
Signature of therapist   Date

❏ Copy accepted by client   ❏ Copy kept by therapist

This is a strictly confidential patient medical record. Redisclosure or transfer is expressly prohibited by law.

About Contracts for Couples and Families

When you go from individual to couple and family therapies, the number of ways of interacting increases; the number of ethical complexities also increases enormously. Although these complexities cannot be detailed here, there are two excellent reviews available: those by Patten et al. (1991) and by Hansen et al. (1989). The two most common ethical problems are the situations when only one partner comes for therapy and when there are secrets in the family. The provisions below can be incorporated into any of the paths to informed consent you select.

Nonattenders

What can you do when one partner comes in without the other(s)? Here are some options:

- Do an individual therapy session in which you explore family-of-origin issues.

- Refuse to meet.

- Make a tape recording for the missing individual(s).

- Do a session and review it when you all meet next. You must decide what is to be shared, so as to prevent revelation of secrets and the development of an unfair alliance with the person who was present.

Deciding which option is best depends on the specific circumstances. If the session is early in therapy, before a full commitment and therapeutic alliance have been established, it may be best not to meet. You can explain how it would not be fair, describe how it could be counterproductive for the relationship with all parties, and ask the person present to trust you that this is better in the long run.

Although the treatment of choice in family therapy is to have all the family members attend, this may not be realistic for many families. Teisman (1980) has several suggestions: offering a single individual session to the nonattender(s), in exchange for attending a single family session; having short family sessions whose only goal is developing plans for engaging the nonattender(s); taping parts of sessions for review by the nonattender(s); having only one to three sessions for the attender(s); using leverage from the referral source; and cancelling sessions at which all are not present.

In couple therapy where one partner refuses to attend, Wilcoxon and Fenell (1983) suggest the clever use of a letter to the nonattender summarizing the research literature on one-partner therapy (which has a negative prognosis for the relationship), proffering an invitation to attend, and requesting a statement signed by both parties that they accept the risks of one-partner therapy.

Secrets

A couple's secrets typically concern an affair, wanting a divorce, or sexual attraction to another. There are several schools of thought on secrets:

- Wendorf and Wendorf (1985) argue that the therapist's position should be siimilar to the following: "I will decide when and how any information I become aware of is to be shared amongst all of us. I will do so in the best interests of the family."

- Hines and Hare-Mustin (1978) advise the therapist not to keep secrets, and to refuse calls between sessions to reveal secrets. They do offer another policy: The therapist will keep the secret only with the intent of helping the individual divulge the secret.

- Margolin (1982), respecting the needs of the individuals present, argues for keeping secret only what one is asked to keep secret.

You will need to decide on a policy and communicate it to your patients *before* they reveal secrets.

Don-David Lusterman, PhD, of Baldwin, NY, includes this phrasing in his client information brochure:

> I will sometimes see you as a member of a family; if so my task may be to facilitate or improve your communication. At other times I may meet with one or another of you alone. If we do meet this way, the normal rules of confidentiality will apply. If issues come up in these sessions which you believe importantly concern your whole family, I generally will not communicate this information for you but will help you to speak to your family about any of these issues.

Contracts for Therapy with Minors

A Contract for Parental Consent to Therapy with a Minor

When a parent brings a child to your office, always ask about the other parent's involvement. You need to consider whether the other parent might have any objections; this can help you prevent later disagreements and perhaps legal/ethical complaints by feuding parents. Goldberg (1995) offers this advice:

> It is best to get both parents' agreement to treatment before you begin, especially if they are separated, divorced and sharing custody, if one parent is paying the bill, or they live in the same geographic area. Sometimes I meet with the parents jointly, if they are not too angry. Otherwise I meet with them separately in the hope of reassuring each of them about my care of their child. (p. 7)

FORM 9

Form 9 includes the minimum for written parental consent to assessment and/or treatment of a child, as suggested by Morris (1993). He indicates the need for a written consent unless the evaluation is court-ordered, the situation is a true emergency, or the child is committed to an institution employing you.

Agreement for Psychotherapy with a Minor

I,_____, the parent/legal guardian of the minor,_____,give my permission
for this minor to receive the following services/procedures/treatments/assessments:

1. _____
2. _____
3. _____

These are for the purpose(s) of:

1. _____
2. _____
3. _____

These services are to be provided by the therapist named above, or by another professional as the therapist sees fit.
The fees for these services will be $_____ per hour of service, or $_____ for the full services.

This therapist's office policies concerning missed appointments have been explained to me. I have been told about
the risks and benefits of receiving these services and the risks and benefits of *not* receiving these services, for both this
minor and his or her family.

I agree that this professional may also interview, assess, or treat these other persons:

1. _____
2. _____
3. _____

Because of the laws of this state and the guidelines of the therapist's profession, these rules concerning privacy will
be used:

1. _____
2. _____
3. _____

A report or reports concerning the therapist's findings will be available after this date: _____. Progress
in this minor's treatment will be reviewed on or about this date: _____ and on a regular basis after that.

My signature below means that I understand and agree with all of the points above.

_____   _____
Signature of parent/guardian   Date

I, the therapist, have discussed the issues above with the minor client's parent or guardian. My observations of this
person's behavior and responses give me no reason, in my professional judgment, to believe that this person is not fully
competent to give informed and willing consent to the minor client's treatment.

_____   _____
Signature of therapist   Date

❏ Copy accepted by parent/guardian   ❏ Copy kept by therapist

This is a strictly confidential patient medical record. Redisclosure or transfer is expressly prohibited by law.

FORM 9. Contract with parent/guardian for psychotherapy with a minor.   From *The Paper Office*, p. 166. Copyright
1997 by Edward L. Zuckerman. Permission to photocopy this form is granted to purchasers of *The Paper Office* for personal use only (see
copyright page for details).

A Contract for Therapy with an Older Minor

When you are dealing with a minor, especially an older child or adolescent, the minor as well as the parent/guardian needs to be properly informed and to consent. Form 9, above, is a contract for parents' signature; Form 10 is a contract for older minors themselves and their parents to sign.

FORM 10

A major concern in treating minors, especially older children and adolescents, is balancing the degree of legal confidentiality available (little or none) with a minor's needs for privacy and trust in the professional. No perfect solution exists, but clarity about your rules, stated at the initiation of therapy, is essential. Taylor and Adelman (1989) encourage reframing the problem as finding ways to establish a working relationship in which information can be best shared.

Young people may become "emancipated" and have adult rights when they marry, graduate from high school, or live on their own. It is important to clarify the legal status of young people in your community and your caseload. Likely exceptions to the need for parental consent are emergencies, treatment for drug/alcohol abuse, and some sensitive medical conditions.

Form 10 is designed to be understood and signed by an older child or adolescent. It was originally written by Glenn W. Humphrey, OFM, PhD, of New York, NY, and is adapted here with his kind permission. To make it fit the client, replace or select the gender pronouns, and perhaps replace "the therapist" with your name and title.

Agreement for Meetings with My Therapist

I, _____, agree to meet with the therapist named below, _____ time(s) a week starting on _____. Our meetings will last about _____ minutes. When we meet, we may talk, draw pictures, play games, or do other things to help this therapist get to know me better and understand my problems.

I understand that my parent (or parents) or my guardian has a right to know about how I am doing in therapy. I agree that this therapist may talk with my parent/guardian to discuss how I am doing. They may also talk about concerns and worries they may have about me. Or they may talk about things the therapist and I decide my parent/guardian needs to know about. Sometimes this therapist may meet with my parent/guardian without me. At other times we may all meet together.

The things I talk about in my meetings with the therapist are private. I understand this therapist will not tell others about the *specific* things I tell him or her. He or she will not repeat these things to my parent/guardian, my teachers, the police, probation officers, or agency employees. But there are two exceptions. First, because of the law, the therapist *will* tell others what I have said if I talk about seriously hurting myself or someone else. This therapist will have to tell someone who can help protect me or the person I have talked about hurting. Second, if I am being seriously hurt by anyone, this therapist has to tell someone for my protection.

I understand that sometimes I may not feel good about some things we may talk about in our meetings. I may feel uncomfortable talking to this therapist because I don't yet know him or her very well. I may feel embarrassed talking about myself. Some of the things we talk about may make me feel angry or sad. Sometimes coming to meetings may interfere with doing other things I enjoy more. But I also understand that coming to therapy should help me feel better in the long run. I may find that I will trust this therapist and can talk about things that I can't talk to anyone else about. I may learn some new, important, and helpful things about myself and others. I may learn some new and better ways of handling my feelings or problems. I may feel less worried or afraid and come to feel better about myself.

Any time I have questions or am worried about the things that are happening in therapy, I know I can ask this therapist. He or she will try to explain things to me in ways that I can understand. I also know that if my parent/guardian has any questions, the therapist will try to answer them.

I understand that my parent/guardian can stop my coming to therapy any time he or she wishes. If I decide therapy is not helping me and I want to stop, this therapist will discuss my feelings with me and with my parent/guardian. But, I understand that the final decision about stopping is up to my parent/guardian.

Our signatures below mean that we have read this agreement, or have had it read to us, and agree to act according to it.

_____   _____
Signature of child   Date

_____   _____
Signature of parent/guardian   Date

I, the therapist, have discussed the issues above with the minor client and his or her parent/guardian. My observations of their behavior and responses give me no reason, in my professional judgment, to believe that these persons are not fully competent to give informed and willing consent.

_____   _____
Signature of therapist   Date

❑ Copy accepted by client and parent/guardian   ❑ Copy kept by therapist

This is a strictly confidential patient medical record. Rediscisure or transfer is expressly prohibited by law.

FORM 10. Contract for psychotherapy with an older child or adolescent.   Adapted from a form devised by Glenn W. Humphrey, OFM, PhD, of New York, NY, and used by permission of Dr. Humphrey.—From *The Paper Office*, p. 168. Permission to photocopy this form is granted to purchasers of *The Paper Office* for personal use only (see copyright page for details).

A Contract for Group Therapy

Orienting a client to a group experience is complex, and only the legal and ethical issues are addressed here, not the clinical ones. You may want to construct one or more additional handouts (about the "ground rules," ways members "work" to promote growth, the roles of leaders, contacts with member's partners, use of drugs/alcohol, violence, permission to make recordings, etc.) to support your initial evaluation and orienting efforts.

FORM 11

There are some unique risks and benefits you might discuss with the group or add to the contract in Form 11. Some possible risks, according to Soreff and McDuffee (1993, p. 492), include "disclosure of one's name or other information by a group member; emergence of extreme reactions, including disruptive behavior, in response to the intensity of the group experience; acquisition of others' symptoms and behavior from exposure to their psychopathology." Some possible benefits, also according to Soreff and McDuffee (1993, p. 492), include "insight into one's relationships; opportunity to practice interpersonal communication skills; recognition of how [one affects] others (group feedback); diminished isolation; increase in sensitivity to the reactions and feelings of others."

Many of the issues are the same in group therapy as in other therapy formats, but there are some important differences. **The legal and ethical rules of confidentiality** do not apply to group therapy, because the members are not professionals (or even cotherapists in the professional/ethical sense). The legal model in most states (except where there are laws specifically addressing confidentiality in groups) is that information shared with anyone besides a therapist, or a therapist's employee, is no longer privileged. Therefore, the central issue of ethical concern in groups appears to be the maintenance of confidentiality. For a wide-ranging discussion of ethical issues in group therapy (such as screening risks, informed consent, termination, etc.), see Corey (1984).

To increase the likelihood of confidentiality's being maintained, you can stress the rationale and importance of maintaining it from the first meeting onward, and model it in the discussions of earlier group interactions. Repeat the rationale when any new member joins or the topic comes up in a session, even in an indirect way. Offering many examples of breaking confidentiality seems to help people control their natural desire to gossip. If you see a member of the group in individual therapy as well, be especially cautious when raising issues with this person in the group to make certain the information was not given to you in the confidence of the individual session. If it was, do not share it or act on it in group sessions. Keep separate records for each kind of therapy.

Form 11 is a contract designed for groups. For various reasons, it may need to be modified or amended to be appropriate for a particular group:

- This version is designed to be given to *individual* group members. When anonymity is unnecessary, a single contract signed by all group members might do instead of separate contracts.

- There is a provision prohibiting socialization outside the group meetings, but this may not be appropriate for some support groups. Or you might alter it to require full disclosure of all members' relationships to the group.

■ If the group concerns domestic violence, you might want to add a paragraph giving permission for full and continuing contact with the group member's partner.

■ If you charge a down payment to reserve a place in the group, you may want to include that in your discussion of costs. You may also want to indicate that some fees are not refundable.

■ You may want to require each individual to meet separately with the leaders on a regular basis.

■ The provision for a monetary payment for damages in rule 6 is to support a breach-of-contract suit in the future if a member should reveal the contents of group discussions, identity of group members, or other confidential matters. This paragraph is loosely based on one from Morrison et al. (1975) as quoted in Bindrim (1980).

Agreement for Group Therapy

As a group member, I have rights and benefits as well as duties, and I understand that some of them are described in this agreement.

This group will be called _____ and will meet from _____ to _____ on _____ at _____. The total cost of this group is $_____, or $_____ per session. I agree to pay this fee even for group meetings I do not attend, unless I make other arrangements in advance.

The purpose of this group is to provide me with the opportunity to achieve the following goals:

1. _____
2. _____
3. _____

I agree to work in this group. This means openly talking about my thoughts and feelings, honestly reporting my behaviors, keeping my promises, and exchanging helpful feedback with other members of the group.

I will attend all meetings of this group from start to finish, even if I do not always feel like it. If I cannot attend, I will tell the group a week in advance (at the beginning of that meeting), or, if it is an emergency, call one of the leaders as soon as I know I cannot attend. If I decide not to go on or am unable to go on with the group, I will discuss my reasons with the group and its leaders, and I will give 2 weeks' notice to the group.

I will not socialize outside the group with any of its members or leaders. This is needed so that everyone will be equals in the group. If I happen to meet a member outside, I will tell the group at our next meeting.

I understand that this group experience is not a replacement for individual therapy. If issues arise that are not suitable for the group's process, I may benefit from individual therapy sessions, for which I will have to pay separately from the cost of the group therapy.

I understand that the leaders are required by law to report any suspected child or elder abuse, or serious threats of harm to myself or another person, to the proper authorities.

With full understanding of the need for confidentiality (that is, privacy) for all group members, I accept these rules:

1. We will use only first names.

2. We will permit no children, spouses, journalists, or other visitors in our sessions.

3. We will not permit any kind of recordings of our sessions, even by our members or leaders.

4. I promise to tell no one the names of the group members, or in any other way allow someone not in the group to learn their names.

5. I promise not to tell anyone outside the group of any of the problems presented by any group member, even if I conceal the name of the member.

(cont.)

---

6. I understand and agree that if I break rules 1–5 often without meaning to, or if I ever break one of these rules on purpose, I will be asked to leave the group. I will also face a possible lawsuit in which I may have to pay damages. If I reveal private information, I give the offended person or persons the right to recover for damages to his, her, or their reputation for at least $_____. Also, this person or persons may recover for any other damages that can be proven.

7. I understand and agree that the leaders will keep a record on each individual member, and that this record will not contain information by which any other members can be identified. This record, kept in each member's name, can be shown to other professionals only with the member's written consent.

8. I understand that the leaders will keep another record about the group's meetings and the interactions of the members, and that this record will not be included in any member's records. This record may not be shown to anyone without the written agreement of all the members and the leaders.

9. Other points:

_____

_____

_____

_____

_____

I have read the points stated above, have discussed them when I was not clear about them, and have had my questions answered fully. I understand and agree to them, as shown by my signature below.

_____   _____
Signature of member (or parent/guardian)   Date

_____
Printed name

Please return a completed and signed copy of this agreement to one of the group's leaders, and you will receive a copy for you to keep.

I, a leader of this group, have discussed the issues above with the client (and/or his or her parent or guardian). My observations of this person's behavior and responses give me no reason to believe that this person is not fully competent to give informed and willing consent.

_____   _____
Signature of leader   Date

_____
Printed name

_____   _____
Signature of leader   Date

_____
Printed name

❑ Copy accepted by group member ❑ Copy kept by leader

This is a strictly confidential patient medical record. Redisclosure or transfer is expressly prohibited by law.

4.6 The Fifth Path to Informed Consent: Consent to Treatment and Other Services

I use "consent-to-treatment forms" when a contract is too detailed or comprehensive, but agreement to participate in treatment must be documented. These consent forms leave out many of the goals, problem definitions, methods, and tactics, and they state only a few of the most critical items.

This section offers several different consent forms, covering the following:

- Generic consent to the treatment of an adult

- Generic consent to the treatment of a minor child

- Consent to counseling for a child whose parents are divorcing

- Permission to make electronic recordings of sessions, and to make various uses of case material

- Consent to psychological testing and evaluations

No doubt other occasions would benefit from a written consent form. If you have developed such a form, please share it with me for the next edition (see the introduction to this book).

Generic Consent to an Adult's Treatment

FORM 12   Form 12 is a brief form for obtaining generic consent to the treatment of an adult. As with all of the photocopiable forms in this book, you can use it "as is" or modify it to suit your own setting and practice.

Generic Consent to a Minor Child's Treatment

FORM 13   Form 13 is a brief form for generic consent by a parent or legal guardian to the treatment of a child. Essentially, it certifies that you and the parent have had discussions on the issues relevant to the treatment.

Consent to Treatment

I acknowledge that I have received, have read (or have had read to me), and understand the "Information for Clients" brochure and/or other information about the therapy I am considering. I have had all my questions answered fully.

I do hereby seek and consent to take part in the treatment by the therapist named below. I understand that developing a treatment plan with this therapist and regularly reviewing our work toward meeting the treatment goals are in my best interest. I agree to play an active role in this process.

I understand that no promises have been made to me as to the results of treatment or of any procedures provided by this therapist.

I am aware that I may stop my treatment with this therapist at any time. The only thing I will still be responsible for is paying for the services I have already received. I understand that I may lose other services or may have to deal with other problems if I stop treatment. (For example, if my treatment has been court-ordered, I will have to answer to the court.)

I know that I must call to cancel an appointment at least 24 hours before the time of the appointment. If I do not cancel or do not show up, I will be charged for that appointment.

I am aware that an agent of my insurance company or other third-party payer may be given information about the type(s), cost(s), date(s), and providers of any services or treatments I receive. I understand that if payment for the services I receive here is not made, the therapist may stop my treatment.

My signature below shows that I understand and agree with all of these statements.

_____   _____
Signature of client (or person acting for client)   Date

_____   _____
Printed name   Relationship to client
                                                       (if necessary)

I, the therapist, have discussed the issues above with the client (and/or his or her parent, guardian, or other representative). My observations of this person's behavior and responses give me no reason to believe that this person is not fully competent to give informed and willing consent.

_____   _____
Signature of therapist   Date

❑ Copy accepted by client   ❑ Copy kept by therapist

This is a strictly confidential patient medical record. Redisclosure or transfer is expressly prohibited by law.

FORM 12. Form for generic consent to treatment of an adult.   From *The Paper Office*, p. 174. Copyright 1997 by Edward L. Zuckerman. Permission to photocopy this form is granted to purchasers of *The Paper Office* for personal use only (see copyright page for details).

[FORM 13—Use the top of this page for your letterhead.]

Consent to Treatment of a Child

Name of child client: _____

The therapist named below and I have discussed my child's case. I have been informed of the risks and benefits of several different treatment choices. The treatment chosen includes these actions and methods:

1. _____
2. _____
3. _____

These actions and methods are for the relief of:

1. _____
2. _____
3. _____

I have had the chance to discuss all of these issues, have had my questions answered, and believe I understand the treatment that is planned. Therefore, I agree to play an active role in this treatment as needed, and I give this therapist (or another professional, as he or she sees fit) permission to begin this treatment, as shown by my signature below.

_____   _____
Signature of parent/guardian   Date

I, the therapist, have discussed the issues above with the child's parent or guardian. My observations of this person's behavior and responses give me no reason, in my professional judgment, to believe that this person is not fully competent to give informed and willing consent to the child's treatment.

_____   _____
Signature of therapist   Date

❑ Copy accepted by parent/guardian   ❑ Copy kept by therapist

This is a strictly confidential patient medical record. Redisclosure or transfer is expressly prohibited by law.

FORM 13. Form for generic consent to treatment of a child. From *The Paper Office*, p. 175. Copyright 1997 by Edward L. Zuckerman. Permission to photocopy this form is granted to purchasers of *The Paper Office* for personal use only (see copyright page for details).

Consent to Counseling for a Child of Divorce

The children of divorcing parents often have an obvious need for treatment. Yet a therapist can easily stumble into a minefield of accusations. By definition, about half of the persons involved in a custody dispute will be dissatisfied with the outcome, and this area has been a very frequent source of ethics complaints and suits. Knapp and Tepper (1992) offer this preventative suggestion:

> If it appears that a child custody dispute may emerge, then the treating psychologist should inform the parent(s) that a court-appointed child custody evaluator, or an independent psychologist, may be a better person to provide psychological expert testimony. Treating psychologists may be accused of being biased since they have a therapeutic alliance with one of the parents. The psychologist also may fear that the courtroom testimony would jeopardize the quality of the needed psychotherapy. (p. 16)

If it is too late to warn, Saunders (1993), in a very worthwhile article, offers these "practical steps a psychologist can take if he or she has been a therapist to one or more of the parties" (p. 55) to avoid additional problems:

1. Directly inform all parties of pertinent facts. E.g., the therapist, has no opinion on the matter before the Court; formulation of such an opinion may jeopardize the treatment relationship; the parties have had no opportunity for informed consent.

2. Suggest an independent evaluation of all parties, and make a referral where necessary.

3. Invoke the privileged communication statute if applicable in that state.

4. Have the existing record redacted by a trial judge, to exclude potentially harmful clinical material.

5. File a motion to quash the subpoena.

6. If called as a witness, withhold any expert opinion. (Serve only as a fact witness.) (p. 55)

Saunders (1993) goes on to suggest ways to operate properly and reduce your risk when you are working as a custody evaluator to one party:

1. Provide informed consent to all parties.

2. Set out anticipated procedures in advance.

3. Verify as much of the available clinical material as possible.

4. When working with attorneys, consider using letters of engagement.

5. Take as elaborate or detailed a clinical history as possible. (p. 55)

Additional guidance comes from Garber (1994), in a sophisticated review of the issues. He points to some practical aspects that must be considered for maximal success and minimal professional liability: "1) educating referral sources, 2) inclusion of both parents, 3) establishing a contract for therapy, 4) anticipating triangulation, and 5) considerations affecting the duration and termination of treatment" (p. 254). Another outstanding reference is a book by Hodges (1991), especially its Chapter 12.

FORM 14 Garber (1994) offers the agreement given below (Form 14), as a means of educating the parents and informing them about the role you will assume. Although the language of Garber's form may be a bit difficult for some parents, it does an admirable job of covering the important points. If the parents endorse this agreement beforehand, this should greatly reduce your risk exposure, in addition to supporting meaningful therapeutic interventions. Modify numbered paragraph 4 to suit your resources.

Authorization to Record Sessions and Use Case Materials

FORM 15 If you think you will ever use any of your clinical notes or cases in any future professional work, you should probably get Form 15 signed during treatment (but not at the beginning, because the client will not be able to give informed consent without knowing what will come up in therapy). For the same reasons, it is inadequate to ask for the client's consent as you are starting the recording; this is not likely to provide the client with sufficient information about what will be discussed or revealed to give informed consent. Use this form afterward.

- Most situations are covered through simply making identification impossible by altering the facts of the case, but sometimes these cannot be changed, and sometimes information slips through. So the use of this signed form may be double protection for little additional effort.

- According to the rules of the Federal Communications Commission (Rule 64, subpart E), you may record telephone conversations without using a beep tone every 15 seconds if you simply inform the other party that you are recording the conversation. There may be state or other regulations as well as the federal ones, however, and so you should check locally.

- If you are going to use videotape or show the client in such a way that he or she can be recognized, you will probably need to explain, in detail and in writing, exactly what is to be done with the materials (by whom, for what purposes, etc.). Form 15 can assist with that process.

Form 15 is based on ideas from the "Release and Permission to Tape Form" by Elizabeth A. Schilson, PhD, and from "Client Informed Consent for Videotaping." Both forms are in Piercy et al. (1989). Piercy et al.'s book also includes model release forms in legal language for the commercial use of photographs.

Agreement for Parents

Psychotherapy can be a very important resource for children of separation and divorce. Establishing a therapeutic alliance outside of the home can:

- Facilitate open and appropriate expression of the strong feelings which routinely accompany family transitions, including guilt, grief, sadness and anger

- Provide an emotionally neutral setting in which children can explore these feelings

- Help children understand and accept the new family composition and the plans for contact with each member of the family

- Offer feedback and recommendations to a child's caregivers based on knowledge of the child's specific emotional needs and developmental capacities

However, the usefulness of such therapy is extremely limited when the therapy itself becomes simply another matter of dispute between parents. With this in mind, and in order to best help your child, I strongly recommend that each of the child's caregivers (e.g., parents, step-parents, day-care workers, *Guardian Ad Litem* [GAL]) mutually accept the following as requisites to participation in therapy.

1. As your child's psychotherapist, it is my primary responsibility to respond to your child's emotional needs. This includes, but is not limited to, contact with your child and each of his or her caregivers, and gathering information relevant to understanding your child's welfare and circumstances as perceived by important others (e.g., pediatrician, teachers). In some cases, this may include a recommendation that you consult with a physician should matters of your child's physical health be relevant to this therapy.

2. I ask that all caregivers remain in frequent communication regarding this child's welfare and emotional well-being. Open communication about his or her emotional state and behavior is critical. In this regard, I invite each of you to initiate frequent and open exchange with me as your child's therapist.

3. I ask that all parties recognize and, as necessary, reaffirm to the child, that I am the child's helper and not allied with any disputing party.

4. I strongly recommend that all caregivers involved choose to participate in Parenting Apart psycho-educational groups. These are six-week groups in which separating and divorced parents learn basic strategies for conducting a divorce in the best interests of the child.

5. Please be advised regarding the limits of confidentiality as it applies to psychotherapy with a child in these circumstances:

   - I keep records of all contacts relevant to your child's well-being. These records are subject to court subpoena and may, under some circumstances, be solicited by parties to your divorce, including your attorneys.

   - Any matter brought to my attention by either parent regarding the child may be revealed to the other parent. Matters which are brought to my attention that are irrelevant to the child's welfare may be kept in confidence.

(cont.)

However, these matters are best brought to the attention of others, such as attorneys, personal therapists or counselors.

- **I am legally obligated to bring any concern regarding health and safety to the attention of relevant authorities. When possible, should this necessity arise, I will advise all parties regarding my concerns.**

6. This psychotherapy will not yield recommendations about custody. In general, I recommend that parties who are disputing custody strongly consider participation in alternative forms of negotiation and conflict resolution, including mediation and custody evaluation, rather than try to settle a custody dispute in court.

7. Payment for my services is due, in full, at the time of service in a manner agreed to by all parties involved. Any outstanding balance accrued (for example, in conference with attorneys, the GAL, or teachers), must be paid promptly and in full. An initial retainer of $_____ will be required prior to commencing this therapy to be held against charges incurred and subject to reimbursement at the conclusion of this therapy, as appropriate.

Your understanding of these seven points and agreement in advance of starting this therapy may resolve difficulties that would otherwise arise and will help make this therapy successful. Your signature, below, signifies that you have read and accept these points.

_____   _____
Caregiver name   Date

_____
Printed name

_____   _____
Caregiver name   Date

_____
Printed name

_____   _____
Caregiver name   Date

_____
Printed name

_____   _____
Caregiver name   Date

_____
Printed name

_____   _____   _____
Child's name   Date of birth   Age

_____   _____
Mental health professional   Date

❑ Copy accepted by client   ❑ Copy kept by therapist

This is a strictly confidential patient medical record. Redisclosure or transfer is expressly prohibited by law.

Release and Permission to Record Sessions and to Use Case Materials

As a therapist, I naturally want to know more about how therapy helps people. To understand therapy better, I must collect information about clients before, during, and after therapy. Therefore, I am asking you to help by allowing me to record our sessions, and also by filling out some questionnaires about different parts of your life—relationships, changes, concerns, attitudes, and other areas. Video and audio recordings are sometimes used as aids in the therapy process, in the education of mental health professionals, and in research. I need to have your written permission to make and use these recordings for these purposes.

I would also be grateful for your consent to use your case material in my other professional activities. Your material may help in the development of the mental health field or in the training of future mental health workers. It is possible that I could use your material in teaching, supervision, consultation with other therapists, publishing, or scientific research. For these purposes, I might use any of the following:

- Notes I have taken during or after our sessions

- Psychological test responses and scores

- Audio or video recordings of our sessions

- Other materials

When I use materials from my testing or therapy work, I do not want anyone who hears, reads, or sees it to be able to identify the clients involved. Therefore, I would conceal your identity by one or both of these two methods:

1. Report the results as grouped data (that is, publish only numbers like averages, and not publish anyone's names).

2. Remove (or, if this is not possible, greatly change) all names, dates, places, descriptions, or any other information by which you or anyone else involved could be identified. In particular, I will not use, or allow anyone else to use, your real name in any presentation of any of these materials.

These materials will be shown only to other mental health professionals and to their students. All of these persons are bound by state laws and professional rules about clients' privacy. I will keep all these materials in a safe location, and destroy them as soon as they are no longer needed.

(cont.)

Therefore, I am asking you to read and sign the following:

I, the client (or his or her parent or guardian), consent to the recording of my therapy sessions for the purposes described above. This recording may be done by video and/or audio taping, by video cassette, by video disc, or by any other means. The purpose and value of recording have been fully explained to me, and I freely and willingly consent to this recording.

This consent is being given in regard to the professional services being provided by the therapist named below. I agree that there is to be no financial reward for the use of the recordings. I understand that I will not be punished in any way if I do not wish a particular session to be recorded. I understand that I may ask for the recording to be turned off or erased at any time during my sessions. I also understand that within 5 days following a session, I may choose to request a viewing of the recording with the therapist. I further understand that I may then ask for the recording to be destroyed. If I choose to ask this, I will deliver a written statement to this effect to the therapist within 5 days following the viewing.

I understand that I am fully responsible for my own participation in any and all exercises and activities suggested by the therapist. I agree not to hold the therapist legally responsible for the effect of these exercises on me, either during the therapy session or later.

I give the therapist named below my permission to use the recordings of me for research, teaching, and other professional purposes. I understand that they will be used as an aid in the process of improving mental health work or training mental health workers. I agree that the recording may be sold or otherwise made available to mental health professionals for educational, training, and/or research purposes. These professionals and their students are bound by state laws and by professional rules about clients' privacy.

I hereby give up my rights to any and all interests that I may have in the recordings. I agree to let the therapist be the sole owner of all the rights in these recordings for all purposes described above.

_____   _____
Signature of client (or parent/guardian)   Date

_____
Printed name

I, the therapist, have discussed the issues above with the client (and/or his or her parent or guardian). My observations of this person's behavior and responses give me no reason to believe that this person is not fully competent to give informed and willing consent.

_____   _____
Signature of therapist   Date

❑ Copy accepted by client   ❑ Copy kept by therapist

This is a strictly confidential patient medical record. Redisclosure or transfer is expressly prohibited by law.

Consent to Psychological Testing

Younggren (1995) reminds us:

> Patients have a right to know what a test is designed to measure, whether it is reliable and valid for the expected use, how the data will be used, how they will be stored and who will have access to the results. Psychologists who use scoring services and various electronic devices in conducting assessments should outline how these systems are constructed and what protections are provided. (p. 7)

On a related note, you should always ask clients you are testing whether they have been tested before, when, with what tests, by whom, and for what purposes. If a client is not very aware, I delay these questions until the Wechsler Block Design subtest and then ask, "Have you seen these designs before?" In forensic and disability testing, you should expect that a client is likely to have been coached (sometimes extensively) by his or her lawyer or relatives, and so you should ask, "What have you been told about these tests, who told you, and what did they tell you?" Of course, the client does not have to tell the truth, but at least you can document what he or she says.

FORM 16

Form 16 is both a consent form for testing and an agreement to pay for such evaluations; it covers the most common and simplest cases. This form is based on one created by John M. Smothers, PhD, ABPP, of Kensington, MD.

Consent to Being Evaluated for a Third Party

Problems may arise when either a child or an adult is referred for an evaluation whose results are to be used by the referrer (such as a court or lawyer or agency) for its own purposes, which may not overlap with the client's preferences or even best interests. If you take such a case, you may be placed in a position where your obligations (to the client, to the referring agency, to the payer, to principles of beneficence, etc.) conflict. A form is needed that combines the elements of consent to be evaluated and release of the results of the evaluation;

FORM 17

Form 17 does this. Some of the wording in this form has been provided by David A. Miller, PhD, of Kansas City, MO.

Consent and Agreement for Psychological Testing and Evaluation

I, _____, agree to allow the psychologist named below to perform the following services:

❑ Psychological testing, assessment, or evaluation
❑ Report writing
❑ Consultation with lawyers
❑ Deposition (that is, written testimony given to a court, but not made in open court)
❑ Testimony in court
❑ Other (describe): _____

This agreement concerns ❑ myself or ❑ _____

I understand that these services may include direct, face-to-face contact, interviewing, or testing. They may also include the psychologist's time required for the reading of records, consultations with other psychologists and professionals, scoring, interpreting the results, and any other activities to support these services.

I understand that the fee for this (these) service(s) will be about $_____, and that this is payable in two parts: a deposit of $_____ payable before the start of this (these) services, and a second payment of the balance due on the completion and delivery of any report (or, for depositions, testimony, or other services, at the time these services take place). Though my health insurance may repay me for some of these fees, I understand that I am fully responsible for payment for these services.

I understand that this evaluation is to be done for the purpose(s) of:

1. _____

2. _____

I also understand the psychologist agrees to the following:

1. The procedures for selecting, giving, and scoring the tests, interpreting and storing the results, and maintaining my privacy will be carried out in accord with the rules and guidelines of the American Psychological Association and other professional organizations.

2. Tests will be chosen that are suitable for the purposes described above. (In psychological terms, their reliability and validity for these purposes and population have been established.) These tests will be given and scored according to the instructions in the tests' manuals, so that valid scores will be obtained. These scores will be interpreted according to scientific findings and guidelines from the scientific and professional literature.

3. Tests and test results will be kept in a safe place.

I agree to help as much as I can, by supplying full answers, making an honest effort, and working as best I can to make sure that the findings are accurate.

_____   _____
Signature of client (or parent/guardian)   Date

I, the psychologist, have discussed the issues above with the client (and/or his or her parent or guardian). My observations of this person's behavior and responses give me no reason, in my professional judgment, to believe that this person is not fully competent to give informed and willing consent.

_____   _____
Signature of psychologist   Date

❑ Copy accepted by client   ❑ Copy kept by psychologist

This is a strictly confidential patient medical record. Redisclosure or transfer is expressly prohibited by law.

FORM 16. Consent form and contract for psychological testing and evaluation.   Adapted from a form devised by John M. Smothers, PhD, ABPP, of Kensington, MD, and used by permission of Dr. Smothers.—From *The Paper Office*, p. 183. Permission to photocopy this form is granted to purchasers of *The Paper Office* for personal use only (see copyright page for details).

Consent to Evaluation

I agree to undergo (or I give consent for this person, _____, to undergo) a complete psychological/psychiatric/mental health/family evaluation at the direction of this third party: _____
_____. I understand and agree that the results of this evaluation are to be the sole property of this third party. I agree that I will not hold this third party legally responsible for any events resulting from this evaluation or the records created by it.

I understand that the purpose(s) of this evaluation are:

1. _____

2. _____

3. _____

I understand and agree that no doctor–patient or therapist–client relationship exists between myself (or the person being evaluated) and the evaluator.

I understand that I may withdraw my consent to this evaluation and to the transfer of information at any time by means of a written letter. However, I also understand that my withdrawal will not be retroactive (that is, it will not apply to testing and information transfer that have already taken place). If I do not withdraw my consent, it will automatically expire in 90 days from the date I signed this form.

I agree that a photocopy of this form is acceptable, but that it must be individually signed by me and a witness. I understand I have the right to receive a copy of this form upon my request.

_____   _____
Signature of client (or custodial parent/guardian of young child)   Date

_____
Printed name

_____   _____
Signature of adolescent client   Date

_____
Printed name

I, the psychologist, have discussed the issues above with the client (and/or his or her parent or guardian). My observations of this person's behavior and responses gives me no reason to believe that this person is not fully competent to give informed and willing consent.

_____   _____
Signature of psychologist   Date

❏ Copy accepted by client   ❏ Copy kept by psychologist

This is a strictly confidential patient medical record. Redisclosure or transfer is expressly prohibited by law.

FORM 17. Form for consent to being evaluated for a third party.   Adapted from a form devised by David A. Miller, PhD, of Kansas City, MO, and used by permission of Dr. Miller.—From *The Paper Office*, p. 184. Permission to photocopy this form is granted to purchasers of *The Paper Office* for personal use only (see copyright page for details).

CHAPTER 5

Intake and Assessment Forms and Procedures

5.1   Creating the Client's Chart

Most clinicians dislike paperwork, but the keeping of clinical records is not optional. How, then, should it best be done? How can you be sure your records are legally and ethically adequate to protect you? How can you best document your effectiveness for supervisors or third-party payers?

The Chronology of Record Keeping

This chapter and the next one offer standards for keeping clinical case records, and detailed suggestions for how to meet those standards. **They follow the natural chronology of recording a case.** I cover various types of records at the places in the chronology where you need to give them attention.

- I begin with a brief overview of what client records should contain.

- Then I start where you will start with a case—at the first telephone contact and the agreement to meet as therapist and client. I call this Phase 1.

- Next, in Phase 2, I collect the basic intake information, or make other types of preappointment contact. I offer forms that can constitute a preappointment package, to be mailed before the first meeting. If time is short, these can be completed by the client in the office before the first meeting (Phase 3).

- Phase 3 occurs during the client's first office visit, just before I interview the client. This is the time for filling out informational forms (histories, financial data, reasons for seeking services) that must precede the face-to-face interview.

- Then, for the actual interview (Phase 4), I offer forms for structuring the collection of more detailed data. This information is often sensitive, and its collection requires face-to-face interaction with the client. Examples include information on suicide risk, physical or sexual abuse, and mental status. The interview should also include broad screening questions, where the client's reactions may suggest to the clinician that clinically significant information may be obtained by probing further.

- In Phase 5, the last phase, the data collected are integrated and summarized. I offer forms for summarizing suicide risk, drug and alcohol use, and the formulation of the client's case. These form the basis for the next chapter, Chapter 6, which continues the chronology by looking at treatment planning, case progress notes, and termination.

The Contents of the Record

I believe there are 10 categories of information we need to keep on each client. Each of these categories is described below.

Intake and Assessment

1. *Intake forms.* The client's record should contain basic information on the client, the reasons for referral, and the client's chief concerns. This chapter offers three examples: the first-contact record and two client information forms.

2. *Histories.* The record can include personal and family histories, as well as histories of previous interventions or treatments. This chapter includes an interview guide and a form for parents to fill out on a child's developmental history.

3. *Evaluations and assessments.* The client record needs to include clinical assessments, previous evaluations, and any testing. This chapter offers two problem checklists (one for adults and one for children) and focused guides for the evaluation of chemical use, mental status, health information and medication, and suicide risk.

4. *Diagnoses and case formulations.* Each client record should include formal diagnoses and a case formulation. Offered here is an intake summary, which can help in case formulation and treatment planning.

Treatment Planning, Progress, and Termination

5. *Treatment plan.* Each client's record should document the treatment plan. The plan should include the target problems, methods of intervention, reviews, and outcomes. Chapter 6 offers several plan formats.

6. *Progress notes.* These might include regular summaries of treatment sessions. See Section 6.2 for more on progress notes.

7. *Termination summary.* This should consist of a summary of treatment provided, the progress made, any remaining problems, the client's prognosis, the reasons for termination, and any clinical recommendations. (See Section 6.3.)

Other Important Client Information

8. *Correspondence.* This might include correspondence and records from past treaters and notes of nontrivial phone calls with the client or with other professionals about the client.

9. *Financial records.* These might include a signed agreement to pay; the dates of services; the charges, payments, bills, and collection phone calls; and notes to the client, insurance companies, and managed care organizations (MCOs) about bills and payments.

10. *Legal documents.* These would include any releases signed by the client and documentation of informed consent through contracts or the client information brochure (see Chapter 4).

It is a challenge to keep all of this information logically separated and yet easily accessible. See Section 1.4 for more on structures for organizing your records, and Section 6.2 for more on structuring the contents of what you record in your notes.

5.2   Phase I: The Initial Telephone Contact

> *Nobody, as long as he moves about among the chaotic currents of life, is without trouble.*
> —CARL JUNG

The client's record should begin at the beginning—with your first contact with him or her as a prospective client. This is almost always by telephone. Your goals during this initial conversation should be the following:

- To assess whether you are an appropriate clinician to treat this person and problem.

- To discover if there are reasons for refusing this person as a client (see below).

- If you discover no such reasons, make efforts that will increase the likelihood that the person will show up for treatment. (Section 5.3 discusses this in greater detail.)

- To begin the chart or record of your treatment so that it is professional, usable, and effective.

Your first contact with future clients can be a source of both satisfaction and income; do it right. Ideally, you should sound competent, efficient, and knowledgeable, as well as eager to listen. As the saying goes, you have only one chance to make a good first impression. Practice until you are comfortable, smooth, and confident when offering information and answering common questions. Be prepared to give information about office hours, insurance accepted, fees, and your credentials. Practice until your statements are anxiety-free and almost routine, so that your mind can attend to the clinical aspects of the call.

Remember, confidentiality extends to this first contact, so make sure no one can overhear you. If you suspect that some highly sensitive information is about to be revealed, make sure to defer it until you can meet with your caller and discuss the implications of its disclosure more fully.

Reasons for Refusing a Caller as a Client

A caller may not be an appropriate client for you for a variety of reasons:

- You do not have the time available, and placing the caller on a waiting list is inappropriate or unacceptable.

- You and the caller are not able to establish a working relationship for some reason (e.g., your personalities or belief systems differ sharply).

- The caller is a relative, coworker, trainee, or the like. (See Section 3.7 on dual relationships.)

- The client cannot afford your fees (and your low-fee and *pro bono* hours are filled).

- The client may not be suitable for voluntary treatment because he or she has a significant or recent history of violence, is in an acute medical crisis, is an active and severe substance abuser, is unable to consent to treatment, has repeatedly discontinued treatment against professional advice, or has refused prescribed treatments.

- The client has problems outside your area of expertise. Remember, you are not a master of every effective treatment, and therefore you are not competent to treat every problem or every person seeking treatment (because of his or her special needs, language skills, etc.).

Getting the Essential Data

FORM 18

The simplest way to ensure the collection of basic data is to fill out the first-contact record (see Form 18, below) as you talk to the caller. You might keep blank copies in your briefcase or datebook, so as to have one available when you get a referral.

Form 18 will help you to cover these essential points:

1. Get the client's name, address, and phone number, spelled correctly (ask). Clarify the relationship to the identified patient if the caller is not the client, and get a practi-

cal telephone number. This is essential later if the client does not show or fails to keep the appointment, and you have to contact the client (or other person) to cancel, reschedule, or respond. (See Section 5.3.)

2. Identify the referrer by asking, "And how did you get my name?" This answer is needed for many insurance companies; more importantly, however, it tells you about your reputation and professional network, and perhaps the client's understanding of the problem. When appropriate later, you can ask for permission to send thanks to the referrer and confirmation that the referral was completed. Having the caller offer a name may also increase the likelihood of his or her coming in. If the referrer is someone the client will see again, such as a physician, he or she may be likely to ask about the referral. If the client got your name from an advertisement or presentation you made to a group, it may be helpful to ask, "What most appealed to you? What moved you to call?" The answer to this question is central to your marketing efforts. Both this question and the referrer question are natural bridges to discussing the presenting problem.

3. Focus on the chief complaint or chief concern. This information is needed so that you can decide whether the client has reached the wrong helper, and you can then make a better referral. It also gives you insight into the level of the client's understanding of his or her difficulties, which can guide your interventions. Elicit this information by asking the caller, "Please tell me briefly what problem has caused you to call me?" or "Please tell me about what is troubling you," or "Please try to tell me the problem in one sentence."

4. Determine the urgency of the problem. Get enough information about the situation so that you can decide how urgent the problem is, and can then set the first appointment, refer, or add other treatment resources.

5. Schedule the first appointment, and write its date and time in your appointment book. The longer the caller has to wait to see you, the less likely he or she is to come in (see the discussion of reducing dropout in Section 5.3). Less than 24 hours is ideal service; you would want that for yourself.

6. Tell the client you want to use the first meeting to get an understanding of the situation, history, and problem, and the ways the client has been coping with the situation. A useful phrasing is "This will be an opportunity for you to find out if I can understand your situation in a way that is useful to you."

7. Tell the caller that "This time is set aside exclusively for you," and, that if he or she cancels it will be "impossible to fill this time." Indicate what a loss it would be to the caller (delay in resolving problems, getting clarity or relief, taking action, etc.) if this appointment is not kept.

8. Briefly tell the caller how to cancel, so you won't be waiting in your office at 10 P.M. You can try to charge the caller if he or she cancels or fails to show, but it won't usually work and it creates bad feelings. If you see many people who are self-referred through the Yellow Pages, clinics, advertising, or unknown sources, you might try getting a credit card number to bill them or to "cover" the first appointment. Irvin P. R. Guyett, PhD, of Pittsburgh, PA, has successfully used this technique in a number of doubtful cases.

This procedure is also a test of the client's motivation, which may be appropriate for some clients and some issues.

9. Ask whether the caller needs directions to your office. Keep in mind the time of day (for light, landmarks, and safety) and the parking situation.

10. Ask, "Do you have any questions?" The most usual question is about fees. Prepare a short and simple explanation and rehearse it several times, *today*. Most of us are uncomfortable talking plainly about money.

11. Consider asking for the financial information indicated Form 18. This is optional, but it can serve two purposes: (a) If you suspect that something is not quite right in this call or that there is unstable or insincere motivation for treatment, gathering this information can be used to screen the client, along with the statement that you will charge the client the full fee if he or she does not show up for the appointment; and (b) raising these questions and making this statement will indeed enable you to charge for your (lost) time and effort if the client fails to keep the appointment.

12. The bottom of Form 18 reminds you of what needs to be done before the first meeting. Make notes here and follow up immediately by making calls, sending your pre-appointment package, or whatever is most appropriate to each case.

After the first interview, in which the client information forms (see Forms 22, 23, and 24) are completed, place the first-contact record at the back of the new chart. The form has a place for entering a case number. If you file records by name, you don't need to use a number; however, if you want to keep all the records for members of a family together, or if the client's name changes, then an anonymous case number may be useful. If you need more room for responses, you can use the back of the form.

To recap, the purposes of Form 18 are to enable you to gather data (both demographic and clinical) for the initial appointment, and to support clinical decision making (triage) as early as possible. In addition, when completed, it can be used for "performance monitoring" of your practices at a later time. You can discover how long it takes to set up an appointment after an inquiry—information that MCOs believe to be important. You can also evaluate the distributions of your clients by age, gender, location, presenting problem, referral source, and so forth, in order to enhance or focus your practice.

First-Contact Record

Date: _____ Time: _____ A.M./P.M. Case record #: _____

Identification
Name of client: _____

Name of spouse/other: _____ Client's phone (home/work/day/evening): _____

Address: _____

_____

Caller's name (if not the client): _____ Relationship to client: _____

Referral source ("How did you get my name?"): _____

_____

Chief complaint (in client's exact words): _____

_____

_____

Urgency estimate: ❑ Emergency; immediate interventions ❑ Serious disruption of functioning; act in next 24 hours ❑ Treatment needed; act soon/routine ❑ Wait for: _____

Triage
❑ Referral to: _____ for: _____

❑ First appointment scheduled for: _____ at _____ A.M./P.M. at (location): _____

Given: ❑ **Directions?** ❑ **Cancellation method?**

Any questions? _____

_____

_____

Financial information
Credit card: Name on card: _____ Card #: _____ Exp. date: _____

Social Security #: _____ Driver's license #: _____

Things to do before first appointment
Call: _____ at: _____ about: _____

❑ Send preappointment letter, client information brochure, and these forms: ❑ Client demographic and clinical information forms ❑ Adult/child concerns checklist ❑ Developmental history ❑ Financial information form ❑ Agreement to pay ❑ Other: _____

Performance monitoring
Our return call: Date: _____ Time: _____ A.M./P.M. Initials of call returner: _____

Call response latency: Days: _____ Hours: _____

Appointment response latency: Days: _____ Hours: _____

This is a strictly confidential patient medical record. Redisclosure or transfer is expressly prohibited by law.

5.3   Phase 2: The Preappointment Package and Other Types of Preappointment Contact

The purposes and functions of sending the client some paperwork (including forms to fill out) before the first appointment include the following:

- It provides material evidence of your response to the client's needs; it solidifies the relationship and demonstrates your caring.

- Because it provides this evidence, it is likely to reduce the rate of no-shows.

- It can present you in a very professional manner—as organized, attentive, responsive, and thorough.

- It confirms the existence of an appointment and the beginning of treatment.

- It can help you to collect the basic information you need about the client.

- The financial information form (Form 26) can get the client used to the idea of paying directly for your services, and can provide necessary information about insurance coverage. Other forms that are discussed in Section 5.4 could also be included in a preappointment package.

- Seeing how the client fills out the forms you send can give you information on motivation and competence for therapy.

- Sending your client information brochure (see Section 4.2) can help to socialize the client into the role of patient, answer unasked questions, and give him or her permission to express further concerns. It can also teach about informed consent, confidentiality, and your way of doing therapy.

However, not all therapists prefer to send new clients a preappointment package. Various ways of making preappointment contact are discussed next.

Ways to Respond before the Initial Appointment

The Appointment Card

The simplest response to a new client is to do nothing after the initial phone call. However, if there is time, confirming the appointment in some way has value. Even a simple card will maintain the connection. Appointment cards are available in many clever and functional formats from medical printers (see the Appendix, Section A.3b), including cards that clients can peel off and stick onto their own calendar, bulletin board, or appointment book. FORM 19 Form 19 is a sample card or slip. Note the possibility of appointments on Sunday, as well as the location blank for therapists with several offices.

_____ has an appointment

at _____ A.M./P.M. on the _____ (date) of _____ (month), which

is a Monday Tuesday Wednesday Thursday Friday Saturday Sunday

with _____

at _____ (location).

     If you are unable to keep your appointment, please cancel it at least 48 hours

in advance by calling _____ (name)

at _____ (number). If you have an emergency,

call _____ (name)

at _____ (number).

_____ has an appointment

at _____ A.M./P.M. on the _____ (date) of _____ (month), which

is a Monday Tuesday Wednesday Thursday Friday Saturday Sunday

with _____

at _____ (location).

     If you are unable to keep your appointment, please cancel it at least 48 hours

in advance by calling _____ (name)

at _____ (number). If you have an emergency,

call _____ (name)

at _____ (number).

FORM 19. Appointment card or slip.   From *The Paper Office*, p. 193. Copyright 1997 by Edward L. Zuckerman. Permission to photocopy this form is granted to purchasers of *The Paper Office* for personal use only (see copyright page for details).

The Appointment Confirmation Letter

Confirming the appointment by means of a form letter allows you to add more information than is possible in a card. It can indicate how to cancel, how long to expect the appointment to take, and other possibilities. A letter also gives you the opportunity to give detailed instructions or to express your feelings. Form 20 is an appointment confirmation letter that you can use or modify for your practice. It includes language designed to prevent a no-show because of ambivalence and anxiety. It incorporates some ideas from Browning and Browning (as applied in a book of forms by Berk et al., 1994).

FORM 20

Dear _____ ,

First, let me thank you for choosing me for help with your personal problems. I intend and expect to provide you with high-quality professional services.

Your first appointment is scheduled as follows:

Day: _____ Date: _____ Time: _____ A.M./P.M. With: _____ .

Please note the location of your appointment: _____ .

Your first appointment may take 2 hours or more, because my office staff and I will ask you to fill out some forms. So plan your schedule with this in mind.

If you are unable to keep this appointment, please reschedule it at least 48 hours in advance by calling _____ .

It is common for those new to therapy to feel both eager to get going and uncomfortable about starting the process of therapy. Do not let some awkwardness keep you from beginning what you know will be in your long-term best interest. If you have some questions and you feel you need answers before this appointment, please call and let us discuss these. I hope that, as in most situations in life, you will find that if you forge ahead, your worries will soon lessen rapidly.

It may be very helpful to jot down some notes about what you want to get from your therapy, so that we can discuss these as well.

In order for us to serve you best, please bring *all* of your health insurance cards, so my staff and I can help determine your coverage, find out whom to bill, and give you some idea of what your costs will be.

The fee for this first visit will be $_____ . My office policy is that payment must be made or insurance coverage must be arranged at the time of each visit. Even when you or the person legally responsible for the bill gives information about insurance coverage or other methods of payment, paying the charges for therapy is your responsibility.

I look forward to a productive and successful relationship.

Yours truly,

A Personal Letter

You may want to use a more personal response to new clients than this form letter. Marc Andrews, ACSW, of Pittsburgh, PA, does not schedule initial appointments during the first phone contact. He tells callers, "I feel it is in your best interest if you first have some information about who I am and how I conduct my private practice." He then sends them a long letter, modeled on the client information brochure. It outlines questions that might come up in the first several meetings. He feels that clients can make better decisions without the pressure to decide on the phone. He believes that this method has reduced his level of no-shows and increased the commitment of those who do follow through.

The Preappointment Package

Sending a confirmation letter can also allow the enclosure of other information to create a package. Mention of any specific enclosures can be added to the letter. As noted earlier, the client information brochure (see Section 4.2) may be useful to enclose, and several of the preliminary assessment forms provided in Section 5.4 can also be included with instructions for the client.

For example, the letter might say, "In order to get a head start on our work, I would like some information. Please complete the enclosed forms and bring them to our first meeting," or "Please read through the 'Information for Clients' brochure and note your questions on it." Specific enclosures might include the adult concerns checklist, the child characteristics checklist, the financial information form, or the client demographic information form. If these forms are not sent in advance, they should be given at the first session. Again, see Section 5.4 for these forms and more detailed discussions of them.

Including a self-addressed stamped envelope with the package, or instructions to bring the forms to the first meeting (if time is short), will increase the likelihood that the client will complete the forms.

Ways of Dealing with No-Shows and Early Dropouts

When patients drop out of treatment even before the first appointment, it wastes time and energy, depresses new therapists, limits the interpretation of therapy research, and (of course) fails to benefit the patients. Patients who do not show, or who drop out early, can be encouraged to continue into therapy with appropriate interventions like those described below. Also, at a minimum, you need to protect yourself legally from complaints of abandonment. (*Note:* For issues of termination and procedures for managing it, see Section 6.3.)

Following Up No-Shows for the First Appointment

If a client does not show for a first appointment, there is not yet a treatment contract or a *strong* legal obligation upon the therapist. Making a phone call is better than sending a note. If you reschedule the initial appointment and the patient again fails to show, a simple note is all that is necessary; more than this may be seen by some patients as harassment.

FORM 21   Form 21 is such a note.

Dear _____,

You did not keep your appointment on _____ or the rescheduled appointment you agreed to on _____. I believe you can still benefit from treatment. Because of my concern for your health and well-being, I will be available to you in the future. Or, if you like, I can refer you to another professional, therapist, or agency.

If you no longer desire my services, and do not wish me to make a referral, I suggest you seek out another therapist immediately.

Yours truly,

FORM 21. Letter to a second-time no-show for an initial appointment.   From *The Paper Office,* p. 196. Copyright 1997 by Edward L. Zuckerman. Permission to photocopy this form is granted to purchasers of *The Paper Office* for personal use only (see copyright page for details).

Following Up No-Shows beyond the First Appointment

Although the following discussion goes somewhat beyond the preappointment context, I feel it is helpful and even essential to include it here. Of relevance at this point is Beckham's (1992) finding that missed and cancelled early sessions were highly predictive of treatment dropout. This suggests that therapists should make great efforts to build high rapport and to respond intensively to missed sessions.

Many therapists will not call a client who did not show for a regular appointment (or failed to keep or cancel an appointment), out of fear that they will hear complaints about their competence, helpfulness, or treatment. Therapists should be more tough-skinned and realistic, and should follow up on every missed appointment. There are many reasons including the ethical responsibility for continuity of care, and the need to avoid the possible abandonment of a patient. You can say, "I understood [or thought or believed] that we had an appointment at [date/time]. What happened?" Even though you are frustrated, if you express not hostility but acceptance of the client's anxiety, you will always be remembered fondly. But remember that you should not then try to solve large (or even medium-sized) problems on the phone. Lastly, calling is a way to practice your assertiveness (just what a therapist usually preaches) in the face of (fears of) rejection and overconcern with others' opinions, anger, or disappointment.

If the problem was not a simple mixup, ask why the client did not come in. If you sense some resistance, try using one of these responses:

- "Almost everyone would like to solve his or her problems without depending on someone else. This is the universal human need for independence. But there are times when. . . . "

- "We therapists sometimes say that 'everyone wants to be happy but no one wants to change.' Change is always painful, no matter how desirable or necessary it may be. Perhaps this may be a reason why you missed our recent appointment."

- "Sometimes we think we're ready to start to change, but find we have underestimated the forces holding us back. What is true, however, is that if you face a fear, the fear subsides. If you understand that it is the right thing to do but still feel afraid, pushing yourself to come to therapy can really work."

In my experience, about 50% of no-show cases can be attributed to a mixup in appointment times or some other easily resolvable or nonrecurring cause. A call is best for a missed appointment, and it should be made as soon as you realize a client hasn't shown—perhaps 20 minutes. Never wait more than 24 hours to make this important contact. If you call a no-show, he or she will usually come in, and the result will be a good course of treatment. The client may have had an attack of resistance or reactance, forgotten, "felt better," had an emergency, or simply been ashamed of not showing up and too embarrassed to call.

Research seems to indicate that the only predictor variables for treatment dropout are lower socioeconomic class, initial negative impression of the therapist, and therapist–client differences in understanding of the disorder and its therapy (Beckham, 1992). The following have *not* been found to be consistent predictors of dropout: age, sex, psychiatric diagnosis, level of education, patient–therapist racial similarity (Satler, 1977), Minnesota Multiphasic Personality Inventory variables (Walters et al., 1982), and therapist rating of patient motivation (Affleck & Garfield, 1961). For an earlier review of this literature, see Garfield (1986).

Other Strategies for Preventing No-Shows and Dropouts

Getting clients to show-up, to attend longer, or not to drop out can also be aided by the following methods (Pekarik, 1985):

- Shortening the waiting time until an appointment or between appointments.

- Offering services at alternative hours or days (e.g., seeing clients on Sundays or at 7 A.M. or 10 P.M.).

- Using letter and telephone prompts for future appointments.

- Rapidly promoting a therapeutic alliance.

- Setting a focus of treatment.

- Writing contracts and treatment plans.

- Contracting for a specific time limit to therapy (say, 12 sessions).

- Demonstrating greater therapist activity. Passivity, awaiting the best time to intervene, or using anxiety-arousing techniques may be counterproductive.

- Providing usable feedback. (Videotapes can demonstrate progress.)

- Providing pretherapy socialization or preparation through readings.

However, bear in mind that therapists and clients may view "dropping out" differently. Patients seem to expect significant improvement in only a few sessions. Some 40% of community mental health center patients attend only 1–2 visits, and less than a quarter attend even brief therapy's minimum of 10 visits (Ciarlo, 1979). In private practice, over half of the patients do not attend for 10 visits (Koss, 1979). Although those who attend for only 1–2 sessions have poor overall therapy outcomes (Gottschalk et al., 1967), a substantial percentage report being satisfied with the improvements gained in 4–6 sessions. Clients apparently expect therapy to last for fewer than 10 sessions, and anticipate improvement within 5 visits (Garfield & Wolpin, 1963).

5.4 Phase 3: The New Client's Arrival for a First Meeting

Ways of Collecting Further Client Information

The initial telephone call with the new client should give you guidance for the additional information you need to gather. You can note the specific forms you want to have completed at the bottom of the first-contact form. If the client has not been mailed these forms in advance, they can be filled out in the waiting room before your first meeting. Using your notes, you or your receptionist can have the forms ready and waiting for the client on his or her arrival for the first appointment. The client can be asked to arrive 20 to 30 minutes before the interview "to complete some necessary paperwork while you wait for the therapist." Be clear with whether or not you will charge the client for this time.

Having this information before you first meet the client face to face is very desirable. For example, without the financial information, you might start a relationship with a client whom you really cannot afford to see. Also, the client clinical information form (Form 23) will tell you whether you need to ask the client to fill out more detailed information on his or her drug/alcohol use or legal problems.

An alternative, but less reliable, procedure is to give these forms to the client after the first session and ask him or her to return them by mail the next day. Include a self-addressed stamped envelope, to increase the likelihood of return.

Information materials and forms suitable for completion by the client in the waiting room (or in the preappointment package) include the following:

- The client demographic information form (Form 22) collects basic factual identifying information. It expands on and will replace the first-contact form.

- The client clinical information form (Form 23) is for more personal information, and so it may be better in some situations to offer it when the client is alone in the waiting room, or even to wait until the interview to give it.

- The brief health information form (Form 24) collects information on health problems, medications, and treatment sources. The chemical use survey (Form 25) collects more specific data on alcohol and drug use.

- The financial information form (Form 26) collects essential information about insurance and other resources.

- For those clients who do not use insurance, or for whom insurance will not cover the entire fee charged, the agreement to pay for professional services (Form 27) assures payment.

- Problem checklists efficiently survey the client's functioning and understanding of problem areas; they also encourage the identification of difficulties, which the client may be reluctant to state during the initial call. I offer two forms, an adult checklist of concerns (Form 28) and a child checklist of characteristics (Form 29). For children, there is also a child developmental history record (Form 30). You could add to this package symptom checklists (e.g., the Symptom Checklist 90), specialized questionnaires (say, attention-deficit/hyperactivity disorder), or pre–post measures (e.g., the Beck Depression Inventory). However, do not give clients these standardized clinical questionnaires or other tests to take home, because of test security and ethical considerations.

Let us now look at each of these in more detail.

Obtaining Client Demographic Information

FORM 22 When completed, the client demographic information form (Form 22) replaces the first-contact form, because it is more complete and can be placed first in the client's file, thus becoming the "face sheet." Again, it can be included in the preappointment package to be completed at home or given to the client in the waiting room at the first meeting. As its name implies, it is straightforward, is primarily demographic, and can easily be filled out by the client alone. By contrast, the client clinical information form (see Form 23, below) seeks more private and detailed information that may need your interpretation, and it may be better to complete this form with the client during your first interview. Both of these forms are designed for those over 18 years of age.

The following are possible additions to Form 22. However, they may be seen as intrusive or irrelevant at this stage of the relationship, so decide whether you wish to include them.

K. Emergency information

If some kind of emergency arises and we cannot reach you directly, or we need to reach someone close to you, whom should we call?

Name: _____ Phone: _____

Address: _____

Significant other/nearest friend or relative not residing with you: _____

_____

Note: If you include the following questions, it may be useful also to include here the "no discrimination" clause from the client information brochure (Section 4.2).

L. Religious and racial/ethnic identification

Religious denomination/affiliation: ❑ Protestant ❑ Catholic ❑ Jewish ❑ Islamic ❑ Buddhist ❑ Other (specify): _____

Activity: ❑ Practicing ❑ Nonpracticing

Which (if any) church, synagogue, temple, or meeting do you belong to? _____

Ethnicity/national origin: _____ Race: _____

Or other similar way you identity yourself and consider important: _____

[FORM 22—Use the top of this page for your letterhead.]

Client Information Form 1

Today's date: _____

Note: If you have been a patient here before, please fill in only the information that has changed.

A. Identification

Your name: _____ Date of birth: _____ Age: _____

Your nicknames or aliases: _____ Social Security #: _____

Home street address: _____ Apt.: _____

City: _____ State: _____ Zip: _____

Home/evening phone: _____ Calls will be discreet, but please indicate any restrictions: _____

_____

B. Referral: Who gave you my name to call?

Name: _____ Phone: _____

Address: _____

_____

May I have your permission to thank this person for the referral?   ❑ Yes   ❑ No

How did this person explain how I might be of help to you? _____

_____

_____

C. Your medical care: From whom or where do you get your medical care?

Clinic/doctor's name: _____ Phone: _____

Address: _____

If you enter treatment with me for psychological problems, may I tell your medical doctor so that he or she can be fully informed and we can coordinate your treatment?   ❑ Yes   ❑ No

D. Your current employer

Employer: _____ Address: _____

_____

Work phone: _____ Calls will be discreet, but please indicate any restrictions: _____

_____

(cont.)

FORM 22. Client demographic information form (p. 1 of 3).   From *The Paper Office*, pp. 201–203. Copyright 1997 by Edward L. Zuckerman. Permission to photocopy this form is granted to purchasers of *The Paper Office* for personal use only (see copyright page for details).

E. Your education and training

Dates		Schools	Special classes?	Adjustment to school	Did you graduate?
From	To				

F. Employment and military experiences

Dates		Name of military or employers	Job title or duties	Reason for leaving
From	To			

G. Family-of-origin history

Relative	Name	Current age (or age at death)	Illnesses (or cause of death, if deceased)	Education	Occupation
Father					
Mother					
Stepparents					
Grandparents					
Uncles/aunts					
Brothers					
Sisters					

(cont.)

H. Marital/relationship history

	Spouse's name	Spouse's age at marriage	Your age at marriage	Your age when divorced/widowed	Is spouse remarried?
First					
Second					
Third					

I. Significant nonmarital relationships

	Name of person	Person's age when started	Your age when started	Your age when ended	Reasons for ending
First					
Second					
Third					
Current					

J. Children (Indicate which are from a previous marriage or relationship with the letter P in the last column)

Name	Current age	Sex	School	Grade	Adjustment problems?	P?

Obtaining Client Clinical Information

FORM 23 As noted earlier, the client clinical information form (Form 23) asks for more personal and detailed information, and so perhaps it should not be mailed to the client or completed when others are present. It should normally be completed during the first interview, but because it is useful to have this information *before* the first interview, it can be completed in the waiting room if you decide the client would not be uncomfortable doing so. I have seen forms like this one entitled "Application for Psychological Services."

In section G, questions 1–4 ask about the "CAGE" criteria for alcoholism, described by Ewing (1984). Depending on the client's answers, your observations, and any referral information, you may want to complete the chemical use survey (Form 25). These questions are widely used but may not be the most sensitive measures of change or of dependence. Two 10-item tests are found in Zung (1979) and Skinner (1982) and, for more current and validated measures, Allen and Columbus (1995) is recommended.

Some possible additional questions (the first two of which are from Eugene Snellings, CSW-ACP, of Baton Rouge, LA) are:

- List five things you like about yourself.

- List five things about yourself that you would like to change.

- What are your major strengths?

- Have any anniversaries of important or stressful events in your life occurred recently or are any due to occur soon?

- List any major problems or stressful events that other family members or close friends are currently dealing with.

- What solutions or efforts have you tried to solve the problems that bring you here?

You might also add client information questions relevant to your setting or practice, such as language spoken in the home, sources of income, living situation, and so on.

Client Information Form 2

Note: If you were a patient here before, please fill in only the information that has changed.

A. Identification

Name: _____ Date: _____

B. Chief concern

Please describe the main difficulty that has brought you to see me: _____

_____

_____

_____

C. Treatment

1. Have you ever received psychological or psychiatric or counseling services before? ❑ No ❑ Yes If yes, please indicate:

When?	From whom?	For what?	With what results?

2. Have you ever taken medications for psychiatric or emotional problems? ❑ No ❑ Yes If yes, please indicate:

When?	From whom?	Which medications?	For what?	With what results?

(cont.)

D. Relationships in your family of origin. Please describe the following:

1. Your parents' relationship with each other: _____
_____
_____
_____

2. Your relationship with each parent and with other adults present: _____
_____
_____
_____

3. Your parents' physical health problems, chemical use, and mental or emotional difficulties: _____
_____
_____
_____

4. Your relationship with your brothers and sisters, in the past and present: _____
_____
_____
_____

E. Abuse history: ❑ I was not abused in any way.   ❑ I was abused.   If you were abused, please indicate the following. For kind of abuse, use these letters: P = Physical, such as beatings. S = Sexual, such as touching/molesting, fondling, or intercourse. N = Neglect, such as failure to feed, shelter, or protect you. E = Emotional, such as humiliation, etc.

Your age	Kind of abuse	By whom?	Effects on you?	Whom did you tell?	Consequences of telling?

F. Present relationships

1. How do you get along with your present spouse or partner? _____
_____
_____
_____

2. How do you get along with your children? _____
_____
_____
_____

(cont.)

3. Your important friends, past and present:

Names	Good parts of relationship	Bad parts of relationship

G. Chemical use

1. Have you ever felt the need to cut down on your drinking? ❑ No ❑ Yes

2. Have you ever felt annoyed by criticism of your drinking? ❑ No ❑ Yes

3. Have you ever felt guilty about your drinking? ❑ No ❑ Yes

4. Have you ever taken a morning "eye-opener"? ❑ No ❑ Yes

5. How much beer, wine, or hard liquor do you consume each week, on the average? _____
   _____

6. How much tobacco do you smoke or chew each week? _____

7. Which drugs (not medications prescribed for you) have you used in the last 10 years? _____
   _____
   _____

   Please provide details about your use of these drugs or other chemicals, such as amounts, how often you used them, their effects, and so forth: _____
   _____
   _____

H. Legal history

1. Are you presently suing anyone or thinking of suing anyone? ❑ No ❑ Yes If yes, please explain:
   _____
   _____
   _____

2. Is your reason for coming to see me related to an accident or injury? ❑ No ❑ Yes If yes, please explain:
   _____
   _____
   _____

3. Are you required by a court, the police, or a probation/parole officer to have this appointment? ❑ No ❑ Yes
   If yes, please explain: _____
   _____
   _____
   _____

(cont.)

4. List all the contacts with the police, courts, and jails/prisons you have had. Include all open charges and pending ones. Under "Jurisdiction," write in a letter: (F = federal, S = state, Co = county, Ci = city). Under "Sentence," write in the time and the type of sentence you served or have to serve (AR = accelerated or alternate resolution, CS = community service, F = fine, I = incarceration, Pr = probation, Po = parole, O = other, R = restitution).

Date	Charge	Jurisdiction (F, S, C, Ci)	Sentence (AR, I, Pr, Pa)	Probation/parole officer's name	Your attorney's name

5. Your current attorney's name: _____ Phone: _____

6. Are there any other legal involvements I should know about? _____
_____
_____
_____

I. Other

Is there anything else that is important for me as your therapist to know about, and that you have not written about on any of these forms? If yes, please tell me about it here or on another sheet of paper:

_____
_____
_____
_____

Please do not write below this line.

- -

J. Follow-up by clinician

Based on the responses above and on ❑ interview data ❑ records I reviewed ❑ other information I have requested the client to complete and/or I have completed the following forms:

❑ Chemical use survey

❑ Suicide risk assessment summary and recommendations

❑ Mental status evaluation report

❑ Other: _____

This is a strictly confidential patient medical record. Redisclosure or transfer is expressly prohibited by law.

Obtaining Client Medical Information

FORM 24   The purposes and functions of Form 24, the brief health information form, are as follows: (1) to gather basic information on the client's health status; (2) to document that this information was gathered; (3) to support consultation with the client's medical caregivers; and (4) to assess psychobiological conditions for intervention.

Gathering health-related and medical information about a client in psychotherapy has several goals:

- A key goal is making sure the client does not have an undiagnosed or untreated medical condition that is causing the psychological symptoms you observe; this presentation is called "psychiatric masquerade." (For a summary of medical conditions that may result in such "masquerade," see Zuckerman, 1995.) By being sensitive and informed about the psychological presentation of medical conditions, the competent therapist (medical as well as nonmedical) can make appropriate medical referrals for evaluation and treatment.

- Second, mental health clinicians can contribute to the psychological management of clients' medical conditions. For example, diabetes has painful and complex management needs that are often resisted, despite the well-known health and life threats its poor management presents. Psychological interventions can greatly facilitate patient compliance, and so can enhance both physical functioning and the quality of life.

- Through gathering health information, clinicians may also be able to discover and thus to treat psychophysiological disorders with specific interventions. For example, temperature biofeedback can be used for migraine and Reynaud's phenomenon. More general techniques, such as stress management or family therapy, can be helpful for hypertension and irritable bowel syndrome.

- Psychological techniques can lessen suffering from physiological conditions such as chronic pain, which often can be effectively managed with hypnosis or behavioral treatments.

- Depression and anxiety may be hidden in the presentation of medical complaints or frequent help-seeking patterns. When they are discovered their treatment becomes possible, and the reduced overutilization of medical resources (called "medical cost offset") becomes a very significant financial benefit.

There are other benefits of behavioral medicine for specific conditions; these are too numerous to describe here, but they are well worth the efforts of the professional therapist.

Many detailed checklists and forms for gathering health-related information about clients are available from the medical arts publishers (see the Appendix, Section A.3b). These ask clients to indicate their symptoms, histories, surgeries, and similar medical data. However, those who cannot interpret this data probably should not acquire it. The brief form offered here does not ask for details, but only for general problem areas (to be further investigated by both medical and psychological means), diagnoses that have been already established, and the name of the client's physician.

If you want a more formal assessment of symptoms or health, there are numerous instruments with empirical validation and norms based on large or varied populations. A commonly used questionnaire is the Cornell Medical Index Health Questionnaire which has 223 questions in 22 areas. A very complete form with 236 simple questions in eight areas is the Health Problems Checklist (Schinka, 1989), available from Psychological Assessment Resources (see the Appendix, Section A.4). As noted above, there are many psychobiological conditions which require careful analysis by those expert in both the mind and the body. Whether you are a physician or not, consultation with the client's primary care physician is appropriate both before and during your treatment. Of course, make certain not to make such a contact before getting the patient's agreement and a signed release.

A word about **medication** in particular is in order here. Is it proper for psychologists and other nonphysicians to discuss medications with clients? Littrell and Ashford (1995) argue that both ethically (there is a requirement for coordination of treatment) and legally (co-treating nurses and pharmacists already do it), nonphysician therapists can and should discuss medications with clients. Many prescription medications are taken by people who become therapy patients, and these may cause psychiatric symptoms, which may mislead the unwary professionals assessing or treating these persons. Meyer and Fink (1989) offer some helpful ideas for nonphysicians in obtaining a full and accurate medication history:

❏ Ask the patient to bring all current and recent medications to the introductory or intake session.

❏ Review with the patient all medications: prescribed, borrowed, over-the-counter, recently discontinued, recreational. For each drug obtain the dose, schedule (both prescribed and actual), source, side effects noted, efficacy, and other comments. Ask the patient to tell you of any future changes in medications.

❏ Review the possible psychiatric side effects of each medication. This is difficult, but Meyer and Fink (1989) offer a short list. However, no list is complete; effects are variable; and drugs interact. There is no substitute for a consulting relationship with a well-informed, sensitive psychiatric physician.

❏ Continually evaluate for the presence of these psychiatric conditions or symptoms.

❏ If a psychiatric condition is present, consider whether its onset appears to correlate strongly with the onset of or change in the medication.

❏ If such a correlation exists, obtain a release of information and contact the patient's physician or help the patient to do so.

❏ Seek out the consultation and provide the physician with a thorough evaluation of all the relevant factors (psychological, social, stress-related, developmental, etc.) that you are able to evaluate.

Again, Form 24 is designed to meet the documentation needs of the nonmedical psychotherapist, so it only asks about health status and records the medical resources available to the client. This form is not a substitute for a medical evaluation or any appropriate consultations with physicians.

Brief Health Information Form

A. Identification

Client's name: _____ Case #: _____ Date: _____

B. History

1. Starting with your childhood and proceeding up to the present, list *all* diseases, illnesses, important accidents and injuries, surgeries, hospitalizations, periods of loss of consciousness, convulsions/seizures, and any other medical conditions you have had. (Describe pregnancies in section E.)

Age	Illness/diagnosis	Treatment received	Treated by	Result

2. Describe any allergies you have.

To what?	Reaction you have	Allergy medications you take

3. List *all* medications or drugs you take or have taken in the last year—prescribed, over-the-counter, and others.

Medication/drug	Dose (how much?)	Taken for	Prescribed and supervised by

(cont.)

4. Have you done any kinds of work where you were exposed to toxic chemicals?

Date	Kinds of chemicals	Kind of work	Effects

C. Medical caregivers

1. Your current family or personal physician or medical agency:

Name	Specialty	Address	Phone #	Date of last visit

2. Other physicians treating you at present or in last 5 years:

Name	Specialty	Address	Phone #	Date of last visit

D. Health habits

1. What kinds of physical exercise do you get? _____
   _____
   _____

2. How much coffee, cola, tea, or other sources of caffeine do you consume each day? _____
   _____
   _____

3. Do you try to restrict your eating in any way? How? Why? _____
   _____
   _____

(cont.)

4. Do you have any problems getting enough sleep? _____

_____

_____

E. For women only

1. At what age did you start to menstruate (get your period): _____

2. Menstrual period experiences:
   a. How regular are they? _____
   b. How long do they last? _____
   c. How much pain do you have? _____
   d. How heavy are your periods? _____
   e. Other experiences during period? _____

3. Please list all of your pregnancies:

Your age	What happened with this pregnancy?			Problems?
	Miscarriage	Abortion	Child born	
1.				
2.				
3.				
4.				
5.				
6.				

4. Menopause:
   a. If your menopause has started, at what age did it start? _____
   b. What signs or symptoms have you had? _____

_____

F. Other

Are there any other medical or physical problems you are concerned about? _____

_____

_____

_____

_____

Note: Significant aspects of family medical history should be recorded on "Client Information Form 2."

This is a strictly confidential patient medical record. Redisclosure or transfer is expressly prohibited by law.

Assessing Chemical Use

FORM 25   The purposes and functions of Form 25, the chemical use survey, are as follows: (1) to screen all new clients for chemical use problems, such as dependence, abuse, or withdrawal; (2) to document that information on these issues was sought and obtained, and options were weighed; and (3) to assist with the formulation of the case in its full biopsychosocial context.

Chemical use is a complex biopsychosocial phenomenon, and so there is no checklist (no matter how large) that will substitute for a comprehensive evaluation by an experienced clinician. If you want interview questions, there is a very complete set of questions to evaluate most aspects of chemical use in Zuckerman (1995). Form 25 can be given to clients to complete when there is any indication—from the referrer, from your observations, or in responses to your screening interview questions—that chemical use may be a problem.

Because of the denial and shame centering around chemical use problems, it is especially important to get objective or confirmatory data beyond what the client tells you. Try to interview a friend or family member of a suspected drug or alcohol user. Later in this chapter, Form 33, the chemical user's case formulation, is provided to aid you in summarizing all of your findings, formulating the case in a biopsychosocial context, and planning treatment for a client with a substance use problem.

Because chemical use problems can be understood from many perspectives, Form 25 offers several ways to document the findings; you can add or delete elements according to your preferences. (For example, you could add other chemicals to the list in section A.) Furthermore, the individual's patterns of use/overuse/misuse/abuse may change with availability, resources, setting, decision, treatment, and aging, and may involve cross-addictions, temporary substitutions or preferences, and many other factors, so a detailed and individualized history is desirable. Obviously, the central dynamic of denial will significantly affect your information gathering. Therefore, follow your clinical intuition and the client's lead (or avoidances) in history taking to get all the relevant facts.

Chemical Use Survey

Name: _____ Date: _____

In order to treat you effectively, I need information about the ways you and your family have used alcohol, drugs, and other chemicals that can affect you psychologically. So please answer these questions fully.

A. What have you used?

1. Think about any and all chemicals you have used, and indicate how much you used (amount) and how often (frequency). Then indicate all the effects it had on you (mental, physical, family, legal, etc.).

Chemical	First use		Last use		Over the last 30 days		See question 3, below
	Age	Amount	Date	Amount	Amount and how often	Effects/consequences	
Caffeine							
Tobacco							
Smoked							
Chewed							
Alcohol							
Marijuana							
Cocaine/Crack							
Injected							
Smoked							
Inhalants							
Others: Specify							

2. Write "P" above next to your primary drug of choice.

3. For each chemical you currently use, what causes you to stop? Enter one or more of these letters in the last column above: A = The money runs out. B = I use up my supply. C = Personal choice. D = Unconsciousness. E = Achieved my purpose. F = Other reasons: _____

4. What are or were your sources of money for buying the chemicals you have used? _____

_____

_____

B. Which of these have you had? ❏ Blackouts ❏ Bad reactions ❏ Withdrawal symptoms ❏ Overdoses
❏ Detoxification in a hospital ❏ Other problems: _____

(cont.)

C. Family patterns of chemical use

Please describe the chemical(s) used by family members.

	Name	Chemical	First use Age	First use Amount	Last use Date	Last use Amount	Over the last 30 days Amount	Over the last 30 days How often	Over the last 30 days Effects
Father									
Mother									
Brothers/ sisters									
Spouse									
Other relatives									

Please add any other information you think is important: _____

_____

_____

D. Treatment for chemical use

Dates From	Dates To	Agency/provider	Type of program*	Voluntary? (Yes or no)	Length of treatment	Methods used	Participation in aftercare programs (No/Which?)	Effects of treatment[†]

*In the fourth column, use these codes: AA/NA = Alcoholics Anonymous/Narcotics Anonymous; O = Outpatient counseling; ID = Inpatient detoxification; IT = Inpatient treatment (e.g., 28-day); O = Other.

[†]In the last column, use these codes: W = made situation Worse; N = No change; U = better Understanding of addiction; R = Reduction of use; BA = Brief abstinence; LA = Long-term abstinence; O = Other: _____

F. Self-description of use

1. Would you say you ❑ are a social drinker ❑ are a heavy drinker ❑ are an alcoholic or ❑ have a drinking problem? Or how would you describe your use? _____

_____

2. Would you say you ❑ are a recreational drug user ❑ are an addict or ❑ have a drug problem? Or how would you describe your use? _____

_____

G. Other

Has your drinking/drug use caused you any spiritual problems? _____

_____

_____

This is a strictly confidential patient medical record. Redisclosure or transfer is expressly prohibited by law.

Obtaining Financial Information

FORM 26   The purposes and functions of Form 26, the financial information form, are as follows:

1. It collects all the essential data you need for evaluating the client's insurance "benefits," and thus the true costs to you and to the client of your services.

2. It allows you to decide whether a client can afford your charges. If you do not use it before seeing the client, you should discuss fees and resources early in the interview, to avoid engaging anyone in a process and relationship that must then be canceled. That is why it is best to mail this form to new clients or to give it to them while they wait for their first visit.

Do not trust clients to understand their coverages or the technicalities of today's insurance marketplace. When they come in, ask for and make photocopies of any insurance wallet cards they have. With those numbers and a Social Security number, you can call the insurer(s) to verify their coverage. Do not start therapy without such verification.

You may need to make some changes to this form. For example, if your state has a special name for its health insurance program, or you see a lot of patients covered by CHAMPUS (Civilian Health and Medical Program of the Uniformed Services) or another specific carrier, you may need to change some of the wording of this form.

Finally, the question asking for the secondary insurance company (question 2 in part D) is for "coordination of benefits," in which insurers set priorities about who will cover services first. Ideally, the secondary insurer will cover any remaining amount due you.

Financial Information Form

I truly appreciate your choosing to come to me for psychological help. As part of providing high-quality services, we need to be clear about our financial arrangements.

- If you have health insurance, it may pay for a part of the cost of your treatment here. To find out if this is so, my staff and I need the information requested below. We will explain any part of this form that you do not understand.

- If you have no health insurance coverage, or do not intend to use it, please check here ❏ , complete sections A and E below, and return this form to me or my secretary.

A. Patient's name: _____ Birthdate: _____ Soc. Sec. #: _____

Address: _____ Home phone: _____

(If the patient is a dependent) Insured's/policy holder's name: _____ Occupation: _____

Employer: _____ Work phone: _____

Address of employer: _____

B. (If applicable) Spouse's name: _____ Birthdate: _____ Soc. Sec. #: _____

Occupation: _____ Employer: _____ Work phone: _____

Address of employer: _____

C. If you (or your spouse) have any of these kinds of insurance, please fill in the numbers and names for each one.

  1. Blue Cross/Blue Shield

    Name of subscriber (if different from patient): _____

    Identification/agreement/policy #: _____ Group or enrollment #: _____

    Plan #/code or BS #: _____ Effective date: _____

    Location of plan: _____ Reciprocity #: _____

    Phone: _____ Provider's phone: _____

  2. Commercial health insurance carrier/company

    Name of company: _____ Policy holder (if different from patient): _____

    Policy #: _____ Certificate #: _____

    Phone: _____ Provider's phone: _____

    Address to send claims: _____

  3. Health maintenance organization (HMO)

    Name of HMO: _____ Policy holder (if different from patient): _____

    Authorization #: _____ Agreement #: _____

(cont.)

Phone: _____ Provider's phone: _____

Address to send claims: _____

4. Medical Assistance

List all numbers: _____

(*Note:* Copayments by you are required.)

5. Medicare

Agreement # with any letters: _____

Railroad Medicare/Mine Workers Medicare: _____

6. Workers' compensation insurance

Name of company: _____

Policy #: _____ Certificate #: _____

Address to send claims: _____

Phone: _____ Treatment authorized by: _____ Date of accident: _____

7. Do you or your spouse have any other insurance coverage that applies here (CHAMPUS, motor vehicle insurance for an injury, etc.)? If yes, check here ❑ and fill in an empty section above.

D. For each kind of insurance you intend to use, you and I will have to make two decisions. First, we have to decide who will find the information to answer the questions below. Will you do this, or do you want this office to do it? The information will come either from your company's benefits office or from the insurance company. Then, when we have this information, we have to examine the treatment choices allowed by the coverage you have.

1. Company: _____ Effective date of coverage: _____

Deductible: $_____ ❑ per person or ❑ per family? ❑ per fiscal year or ❑ per calendar year or ❑ per policy year? ❑ per diagnosis?

How much of this deductible has been used so far? $_____

Benefit: _____% of ❑ charges ❑ Usual, customary, and reasonable (UCR) ❑ Maximum charge of $_____ ❑ Other benefits: _____

Percent reduction, if any, for mental health? _____%

Limitations: Number of visits: _____ Monetary limits: $_____ per _____

Lifetime limits: $_____

Is outpatient group psychotherapy covered? ❑ Yes ❑ No

Must a physician refer the client? ❑ Yes ❑ No

Is psychological testing covered? ❑ Yes ❑ No

Does any rule about preexisting conditions apply here? ❑ No ❑ Yes: _____

Are there any other limitations (such as conditions not covered, service settings, maximum per-session charges, need for DSM or ICD diagnostic codes or CPT service codes)? _____

_____

_____

_____

(*cont.*)

2. Company: _____ Effective date of coverage: _____

    Deductible: $_____ ❑ per person or ❑ per family? ❑ per fiscal year or ❑ per calendar year or
❑ per policy year? ❑ per diagnosis?

    How much of this deductible has been used so far? $_____

    Benefit: _____% of ❑ charges ❑ Usual, customary, and reasonable (UCR) ❑ Maximum charge of $_____
❑ Other benefits: _____

    Percent reduction, if any, for mental health? _____%

    Limitations: Number of visits: _____ Monetary limits: $_____ per _____

    Lifetime limits $_____

    Is outpatient group psychotherapy covered? ❑ Yes ❑ No

    Must a physician refer the client? ❑ Yes ❑ No

    Is psychological testing covered? ❑ Yes ❑ No

    Does any rule about preexisting conditions apply here? ❑ No ❑ Yes:_____

    Are there any other limitations (such as conditions not covered, service settings, maximum per-session charges, need for diagnostic codes or service codes)? _____
_____

E. If you do not have insurance, how will you pay for services from this office? _____
_____
_____
_____

F. I give this office permission to release any information obtained during examinations or treatment of this patient that is necessary to support any insurance claims on this account and secure timely payments due to the assignee or myself.

G. I understand that I am responsible for all charges, regardless of insurance coverage.

H. Assignment of benefits

I hereby assign medical benefits, including those from government-sponsored programs and other health plans, to be paid to the therapist above. Medicare regulations may apply. A photocopy of this assignment is to be considered as good as the original.

_____   _____
Client's (or parent/guardian's) signature,   Date
indicating agreement to all of the statements above

_____
Printed name

Assuring Financial Responsibility

FORM 27   The purpose of Form 27, the agreement to pay for professional services, is to formalize a client's (or someone else's) assumption of financial responsibility for therapy and other services. You may wonder "Isn't the client's stated promise to pay sufficient?" Simon (1992) indicates that an oral contract is valid and enforceable in simple circumstances where a client makes a simple promise such as "I will pay for his treatment," but where there is a condition such as "I will pay if he fails to pay," a written contract is needed. The client may harbor hidden assumptions—for example, that he or she will pay only if the problem is cured, or that he or she will need only a few sessions, or that psychotherapy services will be fully paid for by insurance or the government. Presenting this form (or the first paragraph as part of another form) brings these assumptions to the surface for resolution and clarification. Keller and Ritt (1982, p. 223) have a more formal version with legal language covering other relationship and financial possibilities. See also Meek (1990).

If any of the following situations apply, make certain to get a responsible person's signature before you become too involved in treatment:

- A noncustodial parent brings a child in for services.

- A divorcing spouse whose assets are likely to be in dispute or inadequate to pay for services comes for treatment.

- An adolescent without assets seeks your services.

- Treatment is going to be long or expensive, and you want someone besides the client to share the cost.

- You suspect that the client isn't sincere in offering to pay for your services.

- You feel that the client doesn't fully appreciate the responsibility involved.

Note that a statement indicating acceptance of financial responsibility is included at the end of the financial information form (Form 26, section G): "I understand that I am responsible for all charges, regardless of insurance coverage." It is always a good idea to repeat this point, and if you have any doubts about the client's full appreciation of this point, Form 27 can then be used.

Form 27 indicates that the client has read and agreed to the client information brochure (see Section 4.2), because the client cannot be expected to assume financial responsibility without knowing basic information about therapy (its duration, probable costs, etc.). It is best to include this form with the preappointment package; if it is offered in the waiting room before the first visit, it should be accompanied by the brochure.

Agreement to Pay for Professional Services

I, the client (or person acting for the client), request that the therapist named below provide professional services to me or to _____, who is my _____, and I agree to pay this therapist's fee of $_____ per session for these services.

I agree that this financial relationship with this therapist will continue as long as the therapist provides services or until I inform him or her, in person or by certified mail, that I wish to end it. I agree to meet with this therapist at least once before stopping therapy. I agree to pay for services provided to me (or this client) up until the time I end the relationship.

I agree that I am responsible for the charges for services provided by this therapist to me (or this client), although other persons or insurance companies may make payments on my (or this client's) account.

I have also read this therapist's "Information for Clients" brochure and agree to act according to everything stated there, as shown by my signature below and on the brochure.

_____   _____
Signature of client (or person acting for client)   Date

_____
Printed name

    I, the therapist, have discussed the issues above with the client (and/or the person acting for the client). My observations of the person's behavior and responses give me no reason to believe that this person is not fully competent to give informed and willing consent.

_____   _____
Signature of therapist   Date

❑ Copy accepted by client   ❑ Copy kept by therapist

Problem Checklists

It isn't that they can't see the solution. It's that they can't see the problem.
—G. K. Chesterton

People come for "help" for many reasons (physician referral, threat of divorce, intolerable pain, desires for the cure of symptoms, need for answers or advice, support for their views, desperation, etc.) and with many different understandings of the cause and possible cure of their difficulties. It has been shown repeatedly that the more closely client and therapist agree on the nature, cause, and methods of relieving the presenting problem, the better the outcome of therapy. Yet the professional's role often involves relabeling or reformulating the "referral reason" into something he or she understands and has the skills to relieve.

The intent of problem checklists is to offer new clients the widest range of possible choices and ask them to select from among these. This allows the exploration of all concerns early in therapy. If you simply ask, "What brings you here today?", you will get an abridged list of items, probably emphasizing the most recent and most memorable events (critical incidents). Or you might get the "referral reason," which is simply the "problem" defined by another professional, or a request for a specific treatment methods (such as hypnosis). Although clients may come seeking a particular kind of therapy, this should be a professional's decision.

The checklists offered here are labeled to avoid excessive pathologizing of the client's experience. The adult's version is called a checklist of "concerns" rather than "problems." The child's version, called a checklist of "characteristics," offers both problematic and helpful behaviors so that you will have at least some positives to build upon. Form 28 is the adult checklist, and Form 29, the checklist for children and adolescents, is to be completed by parents or caregivers. As an alternative, a very simple yet quite large form with 208 questions in 12 areas is the Personal Problems Checklist (Schinka, 1994), available from Psychological Assessment Resources.

FORM 28
FORM 29

You can of course tailor these two lists to your own practice by adding some items, and if you do so I would also suggest removing some, so that the lists do not become burdensome for clients. (For example, if you do more behavioral health work you can add "Headaches," "High blood pressure," "Pain management," etc., and delete less relevant items.) You can modify the format as well, by asking for a rating of severity or duration for each problem checked. Or, you can ask patients to "Circle any of the following if they were a concern in the past, and underline those that are presently of concern to you."

If you have clients complete the checklist before the first meeting, you can follow up those items checked to clarify exactly what is understood by each term and what difficulties are being presented.

Finally, I should note that under "Abuse" I have included cruelty to animals, which is both illegal in all states and highly related to violence against humans. For more information or resources, contact the American Humane Association (800-227-4645) or the Animal Legal Defense Fund (707-769-7771).

Adult Checklist of Concerns

Name: _____ Date: _____

Please mark all of the items below that apply, and feel free to add any others at the bottom under "Any other concerns or issues." You may add a note or details in the space next to the concerns checked. (For a child, mark any of these and then complete the "Child Checklist of Characteristics.")

❑ I have no problem or concern bringing me here
❑ Abuse—physical, sexual, emotional, neglect (of children or elderly), cruelty to animals
❑ Aggression, violence
❑ Alcohol use
❑ Anger, hostility, arguing, irritability
❑ Anxiety, nervousness
❑ Attention, concentration, distractibility
❑ Career concerns, goals, and choices
❑ Childhood issues (your own childhood)
❑ Children, child management, child care, parenting
❑ Codependence
❑ Confusion
❑ Compulsions
❑ Custody of children
❑ Decision making, indecision, mixed feelings, putting off decisions
❑ Delusions (false ideas)
❑ Dependence
❑ Depression, low mood, sadness, crying
❑ Divorce, separation
❑ Drug use—prescription medications, over-the-counter medications, street drugs
❑ Eating problems—overeating, undereating, appetite, vomiting (see also "Weight and diet issues")
❑ Emptiness
❑ Failure
❑ Fatigue, tiredness, low energy
❑ Fears, phobias
❑ Financial or money troubles, debt, impulsive spending, low income
❑ Friendships
❑ Gambling
❑ Grieving, mourning, deaths, losses, divorce
❑ Guilt
❑ Headaches, other kinds of pains
❑ Health, illness, medical concerns, physical problems

(cont.)

❑ Inferiority feelings
❑ Interpersonal conflicts
❑ Impulsiveness, loss of control, outbursts
❑ Irresponsibility
❑ Judgment problems, risk taking
❑ Legal matters, charges, suits
❑ Loneliness
❑ Marital conflict, distance/coldness, infidelity/affairs, remarriage
❑ Memory problems
❑ Menstrual problems, PMS, menopause
❑ Mood swings
❑ Motivation, laziness
❑ Nervousness, tension
❑ Obsessions, compulsions (thoughts or actions that repeat themselves)
❑ Oversensitivity to rejection
❑ Panic or anxiety attacks
❑ Perfectionism
❑ Pessimism
❑ Procrastination, work inhibitions, laziness
❑ Relationship problems
❑ School problems (see also "Career concerns . . . ")
❑ Self-centeredness
❑ Self-esteem
❑ Self-neglect, poor self-care
❑ Sexual issues, dysfunctions, conflicts, desire differences, other (see also "Abuse")
❑ Shyness, oversensitivity to criticism
❑ Sleep problems—too much, too little, insomnia, nightmares
❑ Smoking and tobacco use
❑ Stress, relaxation, stress management, stress disorders, tension
❑ Suspiciousness
❑ Suicidal thoughts
❑ Temper problems, self-control, low frustration tolerance
❑ Thought disorganization and confusion
❑ Threats, violence
❑ Weight and diet issues
❑ Withdrawal, isolating
❑ Work problems, employment, workaholism/overworking, can't keep a job

Any other concerns or issues:

❑ _____

❑ _____

Please look back over the concerns you have checked off and choose the one that you most want help with. It is:

_____

This is a strictly confidential patient medical record. Redisclosure or transfer is expressly prohibited by law.

Child Checklist of Characteristics

Name: _____   Date: _____

Age: _____   Person completing this form: _____

Many concerns can apply to both children and adults. If you have brought a child for evaluation or treatment, first, please mark all of the items that apply to your child on the "Adult Checklist of Concerns." Then review this checklist, which contains concerns (as well as positive traits) that apply mostly to children, and mark any items that describe your child. Feel free to add any others at the end under "Any other characteristics."

- ❏ Affectionate
- ❏ Argues, "talks back," smart-alecky, defiant
- ❏ Bullies/intimidates, teases, inflicts pain on others, is bossy to others, picks on, provokes
- ❏ Cheats
- ❏ Cruel to animals
- ❏ Concern for others
- ❏ Conflicts with parents over persistent rule breaking, money, chores, homework, grades, choices in music/clothes/hair/friends
- ❏ Complains
- ❏ Cries easily, feelings are easily hurt
- ❏ Dawdles, procrastinates, wastes time
- ❏ Difficulties with parent's paramour/new marriage/new family
- ❏ Dependent, immature
- ❏ Developmental delays
- ❏ Disrupts family activities
- ❏ Disobedient, uncooperative, refuses, noncompliant, doesn't follow rules
- ❏ Distractible, inattentive, poor concentration, daydreams, slow to respond
- ❏ Dropping out of school
- ❏ Drug or alcohol use
- ❏ Eating—poor manners, refuses, appetite increase or decrease, odd combinations, overeats
- ❏ Exercise problems
- ❏ Extracurricular activities interfere with academics
- ❏ Failure in school
- ❏ Fearful
- ❏ Fighting, hitting, violent, aggressive, hostile, threatens, destructive
- ❏ Fire setting
- ❏ Friendly, outgoing, social
- ❏ Hypochondriac, always complains of feeling sick
- ❏ Immature, "clowns around," has only younger playmates
- ❏ Imaginary playmates, fantasy
- ❏ Independent
- ❏ Interrupts, talks out, yells
- ❏ Lacks organization, unprepared

(cont.)

- ❑ Lacks respect for authority, insults, dares, provokes, manipulates
- ❑ Learning disability
- ❑ Legal difficulties—truancy, loitering, panhandling, drinking, vandalism, stealing, fighting, drug sales
- ❑ Likes to be alone, withdraws, isolates
- ❑ Lying
- ❑ Low frustration tolerance, irritability
- ❑ Mental retardation
- ❑ Moody
- ❑ Mute, refuses to speak
- ❑ Nail biting
- ❑ Nervous
- ❑ Nightmares
- ❑ Need for high degree of supervision at home over play/chores/schedule
- ❑ Obedient
- ❑ Obesity
- ❑ Overactive, restless, hyperactive, overactive, out-of-seat behaviors, restlessness, fidgety, noisiness
- ❑ Oppositional, resists, refuses, does not comply, negativism
- ❑ Prejudiced, bigoted, insulting, name calling, intolerant
- ❑ Pouts
- ❑ Recent move, new school, loss of friends
- ❑ Relationships with brothers/sisters or friends/peers are poor—competition, fights, teasing/provoking, assaults
- ❑ Responsible
- ❑ Rocking or other repetitive movements
- ❑ Runs away
- ❑ Sad, unhappy
- ❑ Self-harming behaviors—biting or hitting self, head banging, scratching self
- ❑ Speech difficulties
- ❑ Sexual—sexual preoccupation, public masturbation, inappropriate sexual behaviors
- ❑ Shy, timid
- ❑ Stubborn
- ❑ Suicide talk or attempt
- ❑ Swearing, blasphemes, bathroom language, foul language
- ❑ Temper tantrums, rages
- ❑ Thumb sucking, finger sucking, hair chewing
- ❑ Tics—involuntary rapid movements, noises, or word productions
- ❑ Teased, picked on, victimized, bullied
- ❑ Truant, school avoiding
- ❑ Underactive, slow-moving or slow-responding, lethargic
- ❑ Uncoordinated, accident-prone
- ❑ Wetting or soiling the bed or clothes
- ❑ Work problems, employment, workaholism/overworking, can't keep a job

Any other characteristics:

- ❑ _____

Please look back over the concerns you have checked off and choose the one that you most want your child to be helped with. Which is it? _____

This is a strictly confidential patient medical record. Redisclosure or transfer is expressly prohibited by law.

Obtaining Developmental Information

FORM 30

When the client is a child, collecting developmental history is essential. Much basic history information can be obtained on a form such as the one offered next (Form 30, the child developmental history record). However, more information will be required when there is a significant clinical problem with a child, and this information is better acquired during an interview. When all the information has been collected, Form 35, the Intake summary and case formulation, will help you integrate it. The purposes and functions of Form 30 are therefore (1) to gather and record information about major historical issues in development, and (2) to support the later summarization of information to support treatment planning and initiation. Some items are adapted from a very complete set of forms by Robert E. McCarthy, PhD, of Myrtle Beach, SC.

Child Developmental History Record

A. Identifications

1. Child's name: _____ Birthdate: _____ Age: _____

   Person(s) completing this form: _____ Today's date: _____

2. Mother's name: _____ Birthdate: _____ Home phone: _____

   Address: _____

   Currently employed: ❑ No   ❑ Yes, as: _____ Work phone: _____

3. Father's name: _____ Birthdate: _____ Home phone: _____

   Address: _____

   Currently employed: ❑ No   ❑ Yes, as: _____ Work phone: _____

4. Parents are currently   ❑ Married   ❑ Divorced   ❑ Remarried   ❑ Never married   ❑ Other: _____

   Child's custodian/guardian is: _____

5. Stepparent's name: _____ Birthdate: _____ Home phone: _____

   Address: _____

   Currently employed: ❑ No   ❑ Yes, as: _____ Work phone: _____

B. Development

Please fill in any information you have on the areas listed below.

1. Pregnancy and delivery

   Prenatal medical illnesses and health care: _____

   _____

   _____

   Was the child premature? _____   Weight and height at birth: _____ _____

   Any birth complications or problems? _____

   _____

   _____

2. The first few months of life

   Breast-fed? _____   If so, for how long? _____

   Any allergies? _____

(cont.)

FORM 30. Child developmental history record (p. 1 of 3).   From *The Paper Office,* pp. 229–331. Copyright 1997 by Edward L. Zuckerman. Permission to photocopy this form is granted to purchasers of *The Paper Office* for personal use only (see copyright page for details).

Sleep patterns or problems: _____

_____

_____

Personality: _____

_____

_____

3. Milestones: At what age did this child do each of these?

Sat without support: _____ Crawled: _____

Walked without holding on: _____ Helped when being dressed: _____

Ate with a fork: _____ Stayed dry all day: _____

Didn't soil his/her pants: _____ Stayed dry all night: _____

Dressed self completely: _____

4. Speech/language development

Age when child said first word understandable to strangers: _____

Age when child said first sentence understandable to a stranger: _____

Any speech, hearing, or language difficulties? _____

_____

_____

C. Health

List all childhood illnesses, hospitalizations, medications, allergies, head trauma, important accidents and injuries, surgeries, periods of loss of consciousness, convulsions/seizures, and other medical conditions.

Condition	Age	Treated by whom?	Consequences?

(cont.)

D. Residences

1. Homes

Dates		Location	With whom	Reason for moving	Any problems?
From	To				

2. Residential placements, institutional placements, or foster care

Dates		Program name or location	Reason for placement	Problems?
From	To			

E. Schools

School (Name, district, address, phone)	Grade	Age	Teacher

May I call and discuss your child with the current teacher? ❑ Yes ❑ No

F. Special skills or talents of child

List hobbies, sports; recreational, TV, and toy preferences; etc.: _____

_____

G. Other

Is there anything else I should know that doesn't appear on this or other forms, but that is or might be important?

_____

_____

_____

This is a strictly confidential patient medical record. Redisclosure or transfer is expressly prohibited by law.

5.5 Phase 4: First Meeting with a New Client

What is the best way to go about identifying a new client's problems? There is a continual struggle in the helping professions between using either broad or highly focused methods of collecting data. Sadly, you can't have both precision and comprehensiveness in data collection without expending enormous amounts of time. Should you use a questionnaire or checklist to ensure that you have missed nothing in the range of possible presenting symptoms, or should you rely on your interviewing skills ("clinical flags") and the conscientious patient to discover all of the important aspects of the case? Each approach has advantages and disadvantages, and so I have chosen to offer materials to support a combination approach, which is a multistep process.

Step 1. Use standard questionnaires to capture all the presenting problems, such as the two client information forms (Forms 22 and 23), the two checklists (Forms 28 and 29), and the child developmental history record (Form 30). At least some of these forms can be filled out by the client before the first meeting.

Step 2. Do an interview to follow up on the presenting problems in more detail, so that you and the client can come to a shared understanding of their nature and priority, and can establish a positive alliance.

Step 3. Because there may be other clinical issues that the client has not identified or was unwilling to indicate initially, do a survey interview with questions directed at some areas of known importance to all patients. The intake interview questions and guide (Form 31) provides structure when structure is desired, without imposing it.

Step 4. Follow up any new concerns with detailed interviewing methods. A very complete list of questions, organized according to clinical symptoms or syndromes, can be found in the *Clinician's Thesaurus* (Zuckerman, 1995).

Step 5. Use very specialized and focused questionnaires, behavioral schedules, and checklists only when the presentation is very complex or detailed documentation is essential. These syndrome-specific materials are beyond the scope of this book.

Step 6. Summarize and organize your data, using the forms provided in Section 5.6 for suicide risk, chemical use, and overall case formulation.

Another way to collect many of these data is to have the client write his or her own history, from a comprehensive outline given by you. Joan Anderson, PhD, of Houston, TX (a member the ethics committee of the Texas Psychological Association), suggests that this is especially useful in any case you expect may go to court because you will have the data in the client's own words (and usually his or her handwriting as well).

The purposes and functions of the forms presented in this section and in Section 5.6 are as follows: (1) to enable you to identify and assess the client's problems in clinical terms and decide how to intervene; (2) to document your assessment so that it is concise, accessible, productive, and professional; and (3) to help you begin building a productive therapeutic alliance. Some specific comments on the use of Form 31 follows.

Using the Intake Interview Questions and Guide

FORM 31

Rather than use a printed form (which always seems to have either too much or too little space) for recording the responses to interview questions, you can ask the questions from the intake interview questions and guide (Form 31) and record the client's responses, numbered to correspond to the question asked, on plain lined filler paper (see Section 1.4). As each question is answered, you can cross out its number on the form. Irvin P. R. Guyett, PhD, of Pittsburgh, PA, has used his laptop computer while interviewing patients and found it is not as distracting as one might expect. It allows the answers to be placed under the questions, and wastes no space when the answers are printed out for the chart. Here are a few more suggestions about the use of Form 31:

- Just before "Introductory Questions" the form lists the item "Entered into birthday book." This pertains to the sending of birthday cards, which may be appropriate for some child clinicians.

- The introductory questions repeat those of the client information forms (Forms 22 and 23), and so it may not be necessary to ask these again. However, if it has been a while since the first contact, they can be asked as a way of reestablishing rapport and making sure you and the patient agree on the problems to be dealt with. You may also discover changes that have occurred since the earlier contact. Finally, if you have doubts or concerns about what the client indicated earlier, ask these questions again to gain more detailed information or check for inconsistencies.

- As always, you should add or delete questions to this form to suit your clientele or practice.

- If you prefer to use a written questionnaire, you can rephrase, reformat, and delete some of the questions in Form 31 for your clients to complete in writing.

Special Considerations for Interviewing a Child

During your interview of a child patient or his or her caregiver(s), you might want to consider collecting data and your impressions about these points:

Social Context

1. Relationship between this child and each parent or significant adult.

2. Ways affection is shown and emotions are expressed and controlled.

3. Parenting skills. (Empathy, appropriateness of expectations, methods of control/discipline, by whom.)

4. Chores expected and performance.

5. Autonomy. (Age-appropriateness; allowances; selection of clothes, friends, music; etc.)

6. Relationships with siblings, relatives.

7. Social skills. (Friendships, peers, older vs. younger playmates, skill level.)

8. Social context. (Cultural, ethnic, religious, economic, immigrant, etc.)

9. Other.

Parental Understanding of Problem(s)

1. Parent's view of child's main problem.

2. Parental efforts to handle, change, or cure the child's problems.

3. Parental ideas of what the school or consultant can do for the child.

The Evaluation of Mental Status

FORM 32

The purposes of Form 32, the mental status evaluation report, are as follows: (1) to record observations about the customarily noted aspects of cognitive functioning in a systematic way; (2) to document the client's current mental status for baseline and treatment planning; and (3) to help a treating therapist, who may not be a clinician experienced in full-scale and precise mental status evaluations, document later observations.

There is no paper substitute for a comprehensive evaluation by an experienced clinician, because mental status is a complex biopsychosocial phenomenon. There are more formal mental status tests, such as the Folstein et al. (1975) Mini-Mental State, and clinical neuropsychological evaluation instruments, such as the Halstead–Reitan.

This form does not offer the interview questions that would produce the data it summarizes, because there are so many possibilities. It is adapted from Zuckerman (1995), which contains detailed resources for evaluating and describing mental status: a large collection of mental status questions under all headings, and 20 pages of words and phrases describing all aspects of cognitive functioning commonly evaluated in a mental status evaluation.

Intake Interview Questions and Guide

Client's name: _____ Date: _____ Interviewer's initials: _____

❑ OK to thank referrer? ❑ Yes ❑ No   ❑ Entered into phone book   ❑ Entered into birthday book

Introductory questions

1. Who suggested that you come to see me? _____ Referral code: _____

2. What is the problem, in your own words? How do you see the situation? (Chief complaint/concern, presenting problem; symptoms—frequency, duration, intensity, latency, recurrence, course; distress caused, change efforts; why help is being sought *now*—precipitants, stressors, consequences; contexts, relevant history; needs, goals, strengths.)

Essential information

3. Previous psychological episodes, treaters, and treatments.

   a. For what?

   b. Where/by whom?

   c. Treatment?

   d. When (from–to)?

   e. Outcome?

   f. Satisfaction/difficulties? (Especially follow up any hints of problems/abuse by therapists—e.g., dual relationships, sexual intimacies, litigation.)

   g. Release for records signed?

4. History of abuse. (Interview partners separately: Disagreements and decisions; verbal, physical, sexual abuse; marital, elder, childhood, family-of-origin abuse; kinds of violence; coping and protections; actions taken against abuser; fears, danger.)

5. Follow-up on responses to client information forms.

   a. Health problems. (Injuries, illnesses, allergies, eating patterns, exercise, sleep, sex; all current medications; last exam by an MD?)

   b. Legal history. (Involvement with the law/police, arrests; charges lodged—civil and criminal, not paying bills, fraud, violence; consequences, sentences; litigation anticipated, pending or in past, especially against therapists; lawyer's name and phone number.)

(cont.)

    c. Family of origin. (Make genogram. Parents: ages, health, education, etc.; Sibs: number, ages, relationships, etc.; Important friendships; For all relatives: issues of abuse, affection, control, discipline, expectations, aspirations, personalities, mental health, religion, schooling, occupations, marriages, legal issues.)

    d. Substance use history. (For client, family of origin, current family: Alcohol, drugs—street and prescription, chemicals, caffeine, tobacco; current and past use.)

    e. Current relationship/family situation. (How client met current partner; attraction, love; family's role; duration, transitions, stressors, and affectual tone of relationship; number and ages of children; problems with or concerns about children.)

Optional questions

6. What changes do you hope therapy will lead to? (Realism, readiness to change, changes of self vs. others, consistency with therapist.)

7. What do you want to change about yourself? (Locus of responsibility, control.)

8. How will therapy help you make these changes? (Understanding, sophistication, dependence.)

9. What do you think a therapist should be like?

10. How long do you think these changes will take? (Realism of time frame.)

11. What are your major strengths? (Abilities, resources, education, employment, personality, feelings, habits, relationships.)

12. What have been your major crises of the last 1–5 years, and how have you handled them? (Precipitants, coping mechanisms/skills, defenses.)

13. What are your goals? (Ambitions, family situation and satisfaction, school/work situation and satisfaction.)

14. What persons, ideas, or forces have been most useful or influential to you in the past?

15. When are you happy? What are the positive factors in your life right now? (Hobbies? Sports? Family? Security?)

16. What spiritual or religious issues are important to you? How does your culture influence you?

17. Is there anything we haven't talked about that is relevant or important, or that you feel I should know about?

18. [Add other questions that seem called for or appropriate.]

19. Examiner's confidence in accuracy of information obtained (high, adequate, marginal, poor)

20. Quality and intensity of alliance (positive, meshing; positive, building; neutral, cautious; negative, distant/guarded; negative, hostile/suspicious)

Mental Status Evaluation and Report

Directions: Rate current observed performance, not reported, historical, or projected. Circle the most appropriate descriptive terms in part C, and feel free to write in others. If an aspect of mental status was not assessed, cross out the heading. Write additional observations, clarifications, and quotations in part D.

Client: _____   Date: _____   Evaluator: _____

A. Informed consent was obtained about:

❑ The recipient(s) of this report   ❑ Confidentiality   ❑ Competency   ❑ Other: _____

B. Evaluation methods

1. The information and assessments below are based on my observation of this client during:

   ❑ Intake interview   ❑ Psychotherapy   ❑ Formal mental status testing   ❑ Group therapy
   ❑ Other: _____

2. We interacted for a total of _____ minutes.

3. Setting of the contact: ❑ Professional office   ❑ Hospital room   ❑ Clinic   ❑ School   ❑ Home   ❑ Work
   ❑ Jail/prison   ❑ Other: _____

C. Mental status descriptors (Circle all appropriate items)

1. **Appearance and self-care**

Stature	Average	Small	Tall	(For age, if a child)		
Weight	Average weight	Overweight	Obese	Underweight	Thin	Cachectic
Clothing	Neat/clean	Careless/inappropriate	Meticulous	Disheveled	Dirty	
	Appropriate for age, occasion, weather	Seductive	Inappropriate	Bizarre		
Grooming	Normal	Well-groomed	Neglected	Bizarre		
Cosmetic use	Age appropriate	Inappropriate for age	Excessive	None		
Posture/gait	Normal	Tense	Rigid	Stooped	Slumped	Bizarre	Other:_____
Motor activity	Not remarkable	Slowed	Repetitive	Restless	Agitated	Tremor

   Other notable aspects: _____

2. **Sensorium**

Attention	Normal	Unaware	Inattentive	Distractible	Confused	Persistent	Vigilant
Concentration	Normal	Scattered	Variable	Preoccupied	Anxiety interferes		
	Focuses on irrelevancies						
Orientation	×5	Time	Person	Place	Situation	Object	
Recall/memory	Normal	Defective in: Immediate/short-term	Recent	Remote			

(cont.)

3. Relating

Eye contact	Normal	Fleeting	Avoided	None	Staring
Facial expression	Responsive	Constricted	Tense	Anxious	Sad Depressed Angry

Attitude toward examiner   Cooperative   Dependent   Dramatic   Passive   Uninterested   Silly
Resistant   Critical   Hostile   Sarcastic   Irritable   Threatening
Suspicious   Guarded   Defensive   Manipulative   Argumentative

4. Affect and mood

Affect   Appropriate   Labile   Restricted   Blunted   Flat   Other: _____

Mood   Euthymic   Pessimistic   Depressed   Hypomanic   Euphoric
Other: _____

5. Thought and language

Speech flow   Normal   Mute   Loud   Blocked   Paucity   Pressured   Flight of ideas

Thought content   Appropriate to mood and circumstances   Personalizations   Persecutions
Suspicions   Delusions   Ideas of reference   Ideas of influence   Illusions

Preoccupations   Phobias   Somatic   Suicide   Homicidal   Guilt   Religion   Other: _____

Hallucinations   Auditory   Visual   Other: _____

Organization   Logical   Goal-directed   Circumstantial   Loose   Perseverations

6. Executive functions

Fund of knowledge   Average   Impoverished by: _____

Intelligence   Average   Below average   Above average   Needs investigation

Abstraction   Normal   Concrete   Functional   Popular   Abstract   Overly abstract

Judgment   Normal   Common-sensical   Fair   Poor   Dangerous

Reality testing   Realistic   Adequate   Distorted   Variable   Unaware

Insight   Uses connections   Gaps   Flashes of   Unaware   Nil   Denial

Decision making   Normal   Only simple   Impulsive   Vacillates   Confused   Paralyzed

7. Stress

Stressors   Money   Housing   Family conflict   Work   Grief/losses   Illness   Transitions

Coping ability   Normal   Resilient   Exhausted   Overwhelmed   Deficient supports
Deficient skills   Growing

Skill deficits   None   Intellect/educ.   Communication   Interpersonal   Decision making
Self-control   Responsibility   Self-care   Activities of daily living

Supports   Usual   Family   Friends   Church   Service system
Needed: _____

8. Social functioning

Social maturity   Responsible   Irresponsible   Self-centered   Impulsive   Isolates

Social judgment   Normal   "Street-smart"   Naive   Heedless   Victimized   Impropriety

D. Other aspects of mental status

_____
_____
_____

This is a strictly confidential patient medical record. Redisclosure or transfer is expressly prohibited by law.

This report reflects the patient's condition at the time of consultation or evaluation. It does not necessarily reflect the patient's diagnosis or condition at any subsequent time.

5.6 Phase 5: Summarizing the Intake Information

During the previous phases of the intake process, you have collected data about the client from the client, your observations, forms and perhaps other sources. Now it is time to review, sift, and integrate those data. This section offers three forms to assist with this process.

Summarizing Chemical Use and Suicide Risk Data

FORM 33
FORM 34

The processes of assessing clients' chemical use and suicide risk have already been discussed in Sections 5.4 and 3.10, respectively. Form 33, the chemical user's case formulation, and Form 34, the suicide risk assessment summary and recommendations, are designed to assist you in summarizing and integrating all the relevant information in cases where one or the other of these factors plays a significant role.

Formulating the Whole Case

When the information presented by a new client has been collected, the data must be organized for the making of clinical decisions. If treatment is appropriate, what should be the goals, and what methods should be used? A treatment plan is needed. Also, what should be the disposition of the case: Should the client be referred elsewhere, be sent for further assessments or consultations, receive treatment from you, or be sent to a specialized treatment program?

FORM 35

The purposes and functions of Form 35, the intake summary and case formulation, are to gather and formulate the findings so as to (1) focus your and the client's attention on the most important and immediate problems; (2) facilitate all appropriate referrals for evaluation or treatment; (3) support consultations and coordination with other professionals; (4) document the need for services to funding sources (e.g., health insurers and MCOs); (5) concentrate the data needed to develop a treatment plan; and (6) provide for continuity and comprehensiveness of care. Completion of this form should precede treatment of any patient. If your patient requires MCO approval, complete this first and then see Form 36, the individualized treatment plan for MCOs, at the end of Section 6.1.

Among other changes you might make to this form, DSM-IV (American Psychiatric Association, 1994) has proposed three axes for future study; it may be useful to start using these now, so that outcome changes on these can be scored in the future. They should go at the end of section D, part 3 ("Diagnoses").

Social and Occupational Functioning Assessment Scale (SOFAS: 0–100): Currently: _____ Past year: _____

Global Assessment of Relational Functioning (GARF) Scale (0–100): Currently: _____ Past year: _____

Defensive Functioning Scale (DFS): List up to seven defenses, most prominent first:

_____

_____

Predominant current defense level: ❏ High adaptive ❏ Mental inhibitions ❏ Minor image-distorting ❏ Disavowal ❏ Major image-distorting ❏ Action ❏ Defensive dysregulation

Chemical User's Case Formulation

Based on the data collected during this evaluation process, here are my conclusions. (The best descriptors are checked.)

A. Identification

Name: _____ Date: _____ Case #: _____

B. Observations

Client was intoxicated at interview	❑ Not at all	❑ Possibly	❑ Mildly	❑ Clearly ❑ Hung over
Consumption history was	❑ Acknowledged	❑ Minimized	❑ Denied,	❑ but confirmed
Legal consequences were	❑ Acknowledged	❑ Minimized	❑ Denied,	❑ but confirmed
Financial consequences were	❑ Acknowledged	❑ Minimized	❑ Denied,	❑ but confirmed
Health consequences were	❑ Acknowledged	❑ Minimized	❑ Denied,	❑ but confirmed
Spiritual consequences were	❑ Acknowledged	❑ Minimized	❑ Denied,	❑ but confirmed
Vocational consequences were	❑ Acknowledged	❑ Minimized	❑ Denied,	❑ but confirmed
Familial consequences were	❑ Acknowledged	❑ Minimized	❑ Denied,	❑ but confirmed

What brought the patient in now? _____

_____

The patient's goals (realism, comprehensiveness, resources needed): _____

_____

_____

C. Degree of identification/denial as an alcoholic/addict

- ❑ Denies any intemperate use, denies need for treatment
- ❑ Minimizes consequences of drinking
- ❑ Is "treatment-wise" or "just going through the motions"
- ❑ Identifies self as "an alcoholic/addict," "in recovery," has made sobriety his/her first priority
- ❑ Is willing to and did do whatever is necessary to maintain sobriety, has a positive and optimistic attitude toward the future

D. Stage in the progression of the disease (for alcoholics only)

- ❑ None ❑ Prealcoholic ❑ Prodromal ❑ Crucial ❑ Chronic ❑ Periodic excessive drinking
- ❑ Blackouts ❑ Sneaking drinks ❑ Loss of control over drinking ❑ Remorse and rationalization
- ❑ Changing the pattern of drinking ❑ Morning drinking ❑ Benders/binges ❑ Defeat

(cont.)

E. Important personal variables

Gender/sex role training   ❑ Not relevant   ❑ Minimal   ❑ Important   ❑ Crucial

Social class   ❑ Not relevant   ❑ Minimal   ❑ Important   ❑ Crucial

Ethnicity   ❑ Not relevant   ❑ Minimal   ❑ Important   ❑ Crucial

Self-esteem/sense of efficacy   ❑ Normal   ❑ Helpless/passive/defeated   ❑ Control in other life areas   ❑ Blames others/denial   ❑ Self-destroying

Impact of abuse   ❑ None   ❑ Mild   ❑ Significant   ❑ Severe/prolonged

Attitude toward treatment   ❑ Eager for   ❑ Neutral   ❑ Pessimistic   ❑ Hopeful

Other: _____

F. Important social variables

Residence   ❑ Comfortable, stable   ❑ Unstable   ❑ High-risk

Employment   ❑ Regular, consistent   ❑ Irregular or inconsistent   ❑ High-risk

Friends   ❑ No abusers   ❑ Some abusers   ❑ Only abusers   ❑ No friends

Addiction of spouse   ❑ None   ❑ Minimal   ❑ Important   ❑ Crucial

Addiction of close relatives   ❑ Not relevant   ❑ Minimal   ❑ Important   ❑ Crucial

Spouse/significant other   ❑ Supportive   ❑ Uncooperative   ❑ Not involved   ❑ In denial   ❑ Enabler   ❑ Codependent   ❑ Addicted

Family involvement   ❑ Cooperative   ❑ Exhausted   ❑ Punitive   ❑ In denial   ❑ None

Support system for sobriety   ❑ Excellent, stable, broad   ❑ Some   ❑ Minimal   ❑ Counterproductive

Other factors: _____

G. Diagnosis (DSM-IV or ICD diagnosis is on intake summary)

❑ Abstainer   ❑ In recovery   ❑ Social drinker/controlled drinker   ❑ Heavy drinker   ❑ Problem drinker

❑ Alcoholic   ❑ Uncontrolled drinker/Alcohol addict/Compulsive drinker   ❑ Terminal alcoholic

❑ "Dry drunk"   ❑ At risk   ❑ Addict   ❑ Cross-addicted   ❑ Controlled user   Other: _____

H. Additional assessments needed

❑ Mental status exam   ❑ Diagnostic evaluations for presence of concurrent psychiatric disorders

❑ Assessment of relationship/marital/sexual difficulties   ❑ Assessment of risk for suicide, homicide, abuse, violence

I. Prognosis

The prognosis, with treatment as specified in the individual treatment plan, is considered to be as follows:

1. For participation in and benefit from treatments: ❑ Optimistic ❑ Good ❑ Guarded ❑ Poor ❑ Negative.

2. For improvement of symptoms: ❑ Optimistic ❑ Good ❑ Guarded ❑ Poor ❑ Negative.

3. For recovery to previous level of functioning: ❑ Optimistic ❑ Good ❑ Guarded ❑ Poor ❑ Negative.

4. For growth and wellness: ❑ Optimistic ❑ Good ❑ Guarded ❑ Poor ❑ Negative.

Suicide Risk Assessment Summary and Recommendations

Client's name: _____ Date: _____

This assessment is based on information collected from the following:

❏ My interview(s) with these persons: On these dates: _____

  ❏ The client

  ❏ Family members: _____

  ❏ Friends: _____

  ❏ Other people: _____

❏ Reading of records (specify): _____

❏ Knowledge of the risk factors this client and situation present

❏ Other sources: _____

It is my professional judgment that this person currently presents the following risk of suicide:

❏ Almost nonexistent	No direct or indirect evidence for suicidal ideation, rumination, or behaviors from client or others (It is against strongly held beliefs; the client has many or valued reasons for living.)
❏ Low	Only passive/death wishes (tired of living/pain; fleeting ideation).
❏ Moderate	Ideation without plan, means, motivation (ambivalence, wondering, considering).
❏ Significant/likely	Persistent ideation, making plans, acquiring means. (The client has made statements, rehearsals, threats, low-lethality/symbolic/ineffective attempts. The client has discussed suicide).
❏ Very high	Serious/high-lethality attempt is likely in near future. (The client has arranged some affairs, has acquired some means, and has some plan of action and privacy).
❏ Acute and immediate	Persistent and preoccupying thoughts, continual efforts. (The client has acquired high-lethality means and is deliberate and focused. The client has an effective plan of action and the necessary privacy).

Therefore, I recommend the following interventions:

❏ No intervention is needed at present.

❏ Reevaluate by this date: _____

(cont.)

❑ Consultation with these people or organizations:

   ❑ Relatives: _____

   ❑ Other professionals: _____

   ❑ Mental health authorities: _____

   ❑ Law enforcement authorities: _____

   ❑ Other: _____

❑ Changes to therapy or new therapeutic interventions:

   ❑ Confrontation and concerned discussion by client's therapist to explore issues and motives

   ❑ No-suicide contracting

   ❑ Intensive psychotherapy

   ❑ Medications

   ❑ Intensive family interventions and support

   ❑ Partial hospitalization with intensive treatment

   ❑ Psychiatric inpatient hospitalization

   ❑ Other recommendations: _____

   _____

   _____

_____   _____
Signature   Date

_____
Printed name

A copy of this form should now be sent to: _____

This is a strictly confidential patient medical record. Redisclosure or transfer is expressly prohibited by law.

This report reflects the patient's condition at the time of consultation or evaluation. It does not necessarily reflect the patient's diagnosis or condition at any subsequent time.

Intake Summary and Case Formulation

Where space is insufficient, use an asterisk and write the information under section I on the last page.

A. Basic information

Client: _____ Date: _____ ID #: _____

Purpose of this intake: ❑ New client evaluation ❑ Readmission; previous intake on _____

❑ Consultation; copy to be sent to _____ ❑ Reevaluation or review

❑ Other purpose: _____

Documents reviewed

Name	Date created	Source/organization	Signed by	Date reviewed

B. Dynamics of difficulties

1. Risk factors/vulnerabilities/diatheses: a. _____

   b. _____ c. _____

2. Stressors and precipitants:

   Acute: a. _____ b. _____

   Enduring: a. _____ b. _____

3. Contributors to relapse (e.g., cognitions, moods, interactions, situations): a. _____

   b. _____ c. _____

4. Resources/support systems/coping skills available (describe and then write "Yes" or "No" in right-hand column to indicate whether it is currently being used):

   a. In the client (motivations, resilience, own efforts for change): _____ _____

   _____ _____

   b. Other persons: _____ _____

   _____ _____

   c. Organizations: _____ _____

   _____ _____

(cont.)

C. Present level of functioning/limitations/impairment (describe specific impairments at left, and rate degree of functional impairment at right with GAF number [100 = none, 70 = little, 30 = significant, 10 = incapacitated] or use descriptors):

Area of functioning	Rating
1. School/work: _____	_____
_____	_____
_____	_____
2. Intimate relationship/marriage: _____	_____
_____	_____
_____	_____
3. Family/children: _____	_____
_____	_____
_____	_____
4. Social relationships: _____	_____
_____	_____
_____	_____
5. Psychological/personal functioning: _____	_____
_____	_____
_____	_____
6. Other areas: _____	_____
_____	_____
_____	_____

D. Assessment conclusions

1. Assessment of currently known **risk factors**:

   a. *Suicide*: ❑ Not assessed   Behaviors   ❑ None known   ❑ Ideation only   ❑ Plan
                                                  ❑ Intent without means   ❑ Intent with means

   b. *Homicide*: ❑ Not assessed   Behaviors   ❑ None known   ❑ Ideation only   ❑ Plan
                                                  ❑ Intent without means   ❑ Intent with means

   c. *Impulse control*: ❑ Not assessed   ❑ Sufficient control   ❑ Moderate   ❑ Minimal   ❑ Inconsistent

   d. *Compliance with treatments*: ❑ Not assessed   ❑ Full compliance   ❑ Minimal noncompliance
                                  ❑ Moderate noncompliance   ❑ Variable   ❑ Little or no compliance

   e. *Substance abuse*: ❑ Not assessed   ❑ None/normal use   ❑ Overuse   ❑ Dependence
                          ❑ Unstable remission of abuse   ❑ Abuse

   f. *Current physical or sexual abuse*: ❑ Not assessed   ❑ No   ❑ Yes   Legally reportable? ❑ Yes ❑ No

   g. *Current child/elder neglect*: ❑ Not assessed   ❑ No   ❑ Yes   Legally reportable? ❑ Yes ❑ No
       If yes, client is   ❑ Victim   ❑ Perpetrator   ❑ Both   ❑ Neither, but abuse exists in family

   h. *If risk exists*: Client ❑ can ❑ cannot meaningfully agree to a contract not to harm ❑ self ❑ others ❑ both

   i. *History* that may affect current level of risk or impairment of functioning:
   _____
   _____

   j. *Other concerns*: _____

(cont.)

2. **Urgency** estimate ❑ Emergency; immediate interventions ❑ Serious disruption of functioning; act in next 24 hours ❑ Treatment needed; act soon/routine ❑ Wait for: _____

3. **Diagnoses**—Current best formulation

Name (indicate which is primary diagnosis with "P")	Code # ❑ DSM-IV or ❑ ICD?
Axis I _____	_____
_____	_____
_____	_____
Axis II _____	_____
_____	_____
_____	_____

"Rule-outs" (other possible diagnoses to be evaluated over time): _____
_____
_____

Axis III—Significant and relevant medical conditions, including allergies and drug sensitivities:

Condition	Treatment/medication (regimen)	Provider	Status

Axis IV—Psychosocial and environmental problems in last year; overall severity rating:

❑ Problems with primary support group   ❑ Problems related to the social environment

❑ Educational problems   ❑ Occupational problems

❑ Housing problems   ❑ Economic problems

❑ Problems with access to health care services

❑ Problems related to interaction with the legal system/crime

Other psychosocial and environmental problems (specify): _____
_____
_____

Axis V—Global Assessment of Functioning (GAF) Scale (100 down to 0): Currently: _____ Past year: _____

V Codes—Other problems that may be a focus of clinical attention: _____
_____
_____

(cont.)

E. Treatment plan (if additional problems are to be addressed, use copies of this page):

Significant improvement is to be expected, with treatment as specified, for:

Problem 1: _____

- Behaviors to be changed: _____
  _____
  _____

- Interventions (who does what, how often, with what resources; modality, frequency, duration): _____
  _____
  _____

- Observable indicators of improvement (behaviors, reports): _____   ■ Expected number of visits to achieve each indicator: _____
  _____
  _____

- Discharge level of problem behaviors: _____   ■ Review date: _____
  _____

Problem 2: _____

- Behaviors to be changed: _____
  _____
  _____

- Interventions (who does what, how often, with what resources; modality, frequency, duration): _____
  _____
  _____

- Observable indicators of improvement (behaviors, reports): _____   ■ Expected number of visits to achieve each indicator: _____
  _____
  _____

- Discharge level of problem behaviors: _____   ■ Review date: _____
  _____

Problem 3: _____

- Behaviors to be changed: _____
  _____
  _____

- Interventions (who does what, how often, with what resources; modality, frequency, duration): _____
  _____
  _____

- Observable indicators of improvement (behaviors, reports): _____   ■ Expected number of visits to achieve each indicator: _____
  _____
  _____

- Discharge level of problem behaviors: _____   ■ Review date: _____
  _____

(cont.)

F. Recommended program of coordinated liaisons, consultations, evaluations and services

1. Psychotherapy: ❑ Individual ❑ Family ❑ Marital/relational ❑ Hypnosis ❑ Biofeedback ❑ Other:

   Session length: ❑ 30 min. ❑ 50 min. ❑ 90 min.

   Frequency: ❑ twice weekly ❑ weekly ❑ twice monthly ❑ monthly

   ❑ Focal group therapy—type: _____

2. Support groups: Twelve-Step program: ❑ AA ❑ NA ❑ Overeaters ❑ Gamblers ❑ Other

   ❑ Other community support groups: _____

   Psychoeducational groups: ❑ Parenting skills/child management ❑ Communication skills

   ❑ Stress management ❑ Assertiveness ❑ Women's issues ❑ Other: _____

   Ancillary services: ❑ Pain clinic ❑ Back school ❑ Physical therapy ❑ Other: _____

3. Legal services: ❑ Offender program ❑ Sex ❑ Substance abuse ❑ Other: _____

   ❑ Victim support ❑ Referral to advocates: _____

4. **Referrals for continuing services**

Referred to	For (kind of service)	Date of referral
	Psychotropic medications Physical medical care Psychiatric evaluation Patient education Nursing care Educational/vocational services Occupational/physical therapy Other: _____	

5. **Further assessments,** based on current clinical evaluation, are needed to answer these concerns or rule out these possible coexisting conditions:

   ❑ Psychological presentation/symptoms of medical condition

      Likely possible sources: ❑ Thyroid ❑ Diabetes ❑ Alcohol/drug abuse ❑ Circulatory problem

      ❑ Neurological problem ❑ Poor nutrition ❑ Medication interactions ❑ Toxin exposure

      ❑ Other: _____

   ❑ Sexual dysfunctions   ❑ Factitious disorders   ❑ Substance abuse

   ❑ Psychophysiological disorders   ❑ Learning disabilities   ❑ Physiatrist

   ❑ Genetic disorders/counseling   ❑ Other: _____

6. **Documents to be obtained** (have requests for records completed and signed, photocopied, and placed in client's file so that receipt can be assured):

Type of record	Source	Date of first request
❑ Medical/physician/hospital		
❑ School		
❑ Agency		
❑ Other: _____		

7. **Other needed resources and services:** _____

   _____

CHAPTER 6

Planning and Then Documenting Treatment

After intake and assessment have been completed and recorded, planning treament, documenting its progress, and finally case termination are the next clinical and record-keeping tasks. This chapter of *The Paper Office* covers these aspects in detail.

6.1 Treatment Planning

The whole subject of treatment planning is in flux. There is neither a widely accepted set of essentials for a plan, nor any universally accepted format in use. The following general guidelines, as well as the forms and formats offered in this chapter, are intended to provide ideas and a framework rather than to be prescriptive or final.

Issues

Many therapists working today resist the planning of treatment, because they believe it interferes with the immediacy and spontaneity they value in therapy. It also seems to require the prediction of what they see as unpredictable—the evolving branching dance of client and therapist, problem and intervention.

249

The research has not resolved the question of whether a planful or a spontaneous approach is better, and it may never. Funding sources, manualized treatment methods, and clinical experience all suggest that at least some degree of organization is beneficial. However, as Hare-Mustin et al. (1979) point out, goal setting is extraordinarily difficult for some situations: when a client is unable to be specific; when children do not conform to their parents' goals (e.g., obedience); when spouses/partners have conflicting goals; when the client's goals stem from an ineffective conceptualization of the problem; when the client's symptomatic behaviors seem understandable or even socially acceptable to the therapist; and so forth. Obviously, we must constantly readjust the balance between rigid adherence to plan and spontaneous therapeutic innovation.

Developing a treatment plan jointly with each client requires the kind of thoughtful, comprehensive, insightful effort that ensures successful therapy. It can be a productive focusing of therapeutic time. This process can be used cooperatively to involve the client in planning, homework/self-monitoring, revision of methods, and overall evaluation. Such a model of joint decision-making strengthens the connections among consultation, planning, treatment, and evaluation. It also implements beliefs in mutuality and equality.

In addition, a treatment plan serves to limit distractions from the central goals. Without a plan, sequence, or map, both you and your client can easily be distracted from what is most important. You can both easily lose your "vision" in the welter of data, intercurrent events, levels of analysis, and so on, and fail to integrate the immediate into the important. As the saying goes, when we are up to our ears in alligators, it is hard to remember that we came here to drain the swamp.

Guidelines for Treatment Planning

Typically, a client comes in with complaints or problems, some ideas of their causes, and some desired outcomes. His or her presentation is reformulated by the therapist within a framework that allows for intervention and change. The therapist's favorite (or even just familiar) methods are offered to the client, and change is assessed irregularly. A more systematic and yet realistic sequence for treatment planning would proceed as follows:

- **Identify and assess** all the current problematic or symptomatic behaviors, affects, or cognitions. First, list, with the client, the major problems and related effects of these problems on his or her life. Review all areas of functioning. Prioritize these concerns. Chapter 5's forms support this process, and problem list formats are offered in Section 6.2.

- **Define the outcomes desired**—both long-term "goals" and short-term "objectives." Some view the relationship between goals and objectives as analogous to strategic and tactical efforts in military terms. One way to seek objectives is to ask, "If we are to achieve this long-term goal by this specific date [such as next year], what smaller steps would have to be accomplished and by when [such as next month]?" These smaller steps, or objectives, are usually more behavioral, measurable, and concrete than goals. For a simple and yet reliable and valid way of assessing the accomplishment of goals, see the discussion of goal attainment scaling later in this section.

- **Consider the interventions and resources needed** to achieve the goals. The selecting and sequencing of interventions is the responsibility of the therapist.

- **Provide reliable ways to evaluate** the client's current status, progress, and outcomes.

These steps are considered in more detail below.

Systems and Formats of Treatment Planning

If you are seeking a comprehensive system of planning treatment, consider the following. Some are more comprehensive or more detailed than others, and some will suit your setting or needs better. They are presented here roughly in the order of their complexity.

The One-Sentence Format

A brief but elegant guide for treatment planning is presented in the following sentence: "Who is going to do what, how often and for how long, to whom, for what problems, with what desired outcome by what date, and when are we going to check on how it is going?"

The PIC Treatment Plan

A simple, practical, and unique format is described by Levenstein (1994a). It has the advantages of coordinating treatment plans and progress notes, and of addressing obstacles to the progress of treatment. After a comprehensive evaluation, the clinician does the following:

1. Identifies the primary issues, and formulates a tentative explanation of how the problems occurred.

2. Gives a formal diagnosis (DSM-IV).

3. Creates the goal plan (in essence, the treatment plan).

4. Assigns a target date for each goal.

The format for the goal plan uses the acronym "PIC":

- P is for the problem (current behavior) or goal (desired end state).

- I is for the intervention(s).

- C is for the indicators of change (specific, overt behaviors to be tracked, how they will be assessed, and by whom).

With the addition of R for resistance or obstacles (Levenstein, 1994b), this format can be easily adapted for progress notes. See Section 6.2 for various types of progress notes.

The BASIC ID Model

Arnold A. Lazarus (1976) developed a model of assessment and treatment in which treatments of choice (those whose effectiveness for a specific problem has been supported by empirical research) are matched to each problem as analyzed at each of seven levels. The acronym for the levels is, irrelevantly, "BASIC ID." There are no limitations on the methods of treatment that can be used, and so it can fit any paradigm, but proper diagnosis or problem specification is crucial to this model.

- B is for behavior.

- A is for affect.

- S is for sensation.

- I is for imagery (fantasies, expectations).

- C is for cognition (beliefs).

- I is for interpersonal relations.

- D is for drugs (included here are all medical conditions and physiological functioning).

You would then create the goals, objectives, and target dates for each intervention.

The Problem-Oriented Record

The problem-oriented record (POR) is a comprehensive and logical method that is widely used in medicine. It is discussed in detail in Section 6.2.

The Expanded Problem-Oriented Record

The expanded POR is simple, flexible, and comprehensive, and is readily accepted in medical settings. It can be written in paragraphs devoted to these topics:

1. The problem.

2. The outcome or goal sought; foci of treatment (immediate and long-term issues); measurable performances or operationalizations of levels of progress.

3. The client's strengths or assets.

4. The client's liabilities, or the barriers to change in the client or elsewhere.

5. The treatment(s)/methods used: What, when, by whom? (Include interventions/methods/means/modalities, resources required, staff members and others involved, frequency of contacts, expected dates of achievement, dates of review.)

6. The means and dates of evaluation.

Individualized Treatment Plan for Managed Care Organizations

Managed care organizations (MCOs) require that an individualized treatment plan be developed in the first or second session. Form 36 (see below) will assist you in developing such a plan.

Levels of Functioning

Kennedy (1992), using DSM-III-R (American Psychiatric Association, 1987b) Axis V, has built master treatment plans around levels of functioning in the areas of psychological impairment, social skills, dangerousness, activities of daily living, occupational skills, substance use patterns, and so on.

Impairment Profile

Goodman et al. (1992) cleverly suggest using a patient impairment profile to document and communicate treatment needs, to develop a rationale for treatment and a treatment plan, and to predict outcome of care. The list of impairments (in their Appendix A) becomes a common language for helpers from different disciplines. When combined with a severity rating, it suggests an appropriate level of service or care. They add outcome objectives, selections from a list of interventions (their Appendix B), and progress measures to assess the effectiveness of treatment (basically, changes in the ratings of severity). Their system is neat and complete, but requires a new model—that of impairments.

The Seven P's

Sperry et al. (1992) offer a well-thought-out but elaborate approach. It focuses on "seven dimensions for articulating and explaining the nature and origins of the patient's presentation" and then their "subsequent treatment" (p. 132). The seven dimensions are as follows:

1. *Presentation:* Symptoms, history, course of illness, and diagnosis.

2. *Predispositions:* Physical, psychological, and social predisposers. (These are all diatheses.)

3. *Precipitants:* Stressors of all biopsychosocial kinds.

4. *Pattern:* In all three spheres (biological, psychological, social/interpersonal), "the predictable and consistent style or manner in which a person thinks, feels, acts, copes, and defends the self both in stressful and non-stressful circumstances" (p. 134). The individual's capacity for treatment is also included here.

5. *Perpetuants:* Any factors that reinforce, nurture, or encourage the pathology, or otherwise induce it to persist.

6. *Plan:* Treatment plan and outcome goals (both short- and long-term), in biological, psychological, and social areas. The treatment plan includes its setting, format, duration, frequency, strategy, somatic treatments, rationale, and approach.

7. *Prognosis:* A statement of future outcome with and without specific treatments.

Other Points in Planning Treatment

Focusing Your Efforts

You undoubtedly already know that in most psychotherapy, the diagnosis does not determine the treatment and the presumed historical causes of the problems are not usually the focus of treatment. This is different from most medical interventions. Psychological treatment focuses on the presenting problems or current (although perhaps historically determined) behaviors, affects, and cognitions.

Taking Account of Resistance

> *Everybody wants to be happier. No one wants to change.*
> —ANONYMOUS

If a treatment plan is to be truly effective, it must anticipate and respond to the obstacles to change. A great deal of the elegance and effectiveness of psychotherapy is found in its sophistication about handling "resistance." Here are some questions I like to ask a client in the course of planning treatment. The client's responses to these questions can be built into the plan, and this increase the chances of a successful outcome.

- "What would happen if you were to make the changes you say you want? How would these changes affect your partner, family, and friends? What would be the negative consequences?" (This question identifies demotivators, resistances, and blind spots.)

- "What are the blockages/obstacles to change?" (This lets you see how the client conceptualizes the problem)

- "What has not worked in the past?" (This will keep you from repeating unsuccessful approaches.)

- "What *has* been helpful in the past in dealing with these problems?" (You can build on these.)

- "When were there situations like this, but you were able to manage them successfully?" (This is a solution-focused approach.)

- "Who are your best allies in helping you deal with these problems?" (This question identifies the client's social and other supports.)

- "Who do you know who has successfully dealt with these same problems?" (This identifies potential role models.)

- "What do you think is necessary to make things better, and how long might each of these take?" (This question explores the client's conceptualization of treatment, so that you can blend into it or work to change it. Carl Whitaker called this "learning the family's dance; teaching them some new steps.")

Coordinating Treatment Efforts

Integrating comprehensive treatment to be provided by multiple agencies is always difficult. If the agencies are sequential providers, ideally they should all agree on a pairing of entry and discharge criteria for each organization. In other words, a level 2 agency should have entry criteria that are identical to a level 1 agency's discharge criteria, and discharge criteria that are identical to a level 3 agency's entry criteria.

Knowing Your Limits and Applying Your Skills

Do not suppose that the method or two you learned in graduate school will suit all problems brought to you. Turn away clients who do not fit your skills, or else run the risk of legal complications for your failing to attend to the ethical rule of staying in your areas of competence. Moreover, if you hold yourself out as an expert on treatment and accept the relevance and validity of scientific knowledge, you must know which methods the research has supported and which it has failed to support for the disorders you seek to treat. Learn those methods well and apply them energetically.

Evaluating Outcomes

How can you evaluate the changes a client makes? The methods of planning described earlier generally use symptom reduction as the criterion of change. However, alternative, more flexible models exist. The best-known one is *goal attainment scaling,* which is a very simple but powerful method of documenting progress toward goals (Kiresuk & Sherman, 1968; Kiresuk et al., 1994). It consists of the following components:

1. Specifying at least five goals. Goals can be described in *any* terms or areas; this is a major strength of this method.

2. Specifying a date in the future when progress toward the goals is to be evaluated.

3. Defining possible outcomes, in observable terms, at five levels for each goal. These five levels are as follows (slightly reworded):

   -2 = The worst outcome that is likely to occur.

   -1 = An outcome less successful than expected.

   0 = An outcome that achieves the expected level of success.

   $+1$ = An outcome more successful than expected.

   $+2$ = The most favorable outcome thought likely.

4. At the previously decided point or points in time, the level of attainment of each goal is scored.

5. Statistical tests can be applied to this score to determine whether it happened by chance. Scores can be compared over time, across clients, or across programs.

Some difficulties will arise if expectations are low and the true cause of the change cannot be determined. But the method is simple, easily learned (as by a client), and widely applicable. Its greatest advantage is that it can be applied to almost any kind of goal, and is thus independent of any theory or orientation.

Evaluating the Ethics of a Proposed Treatment

Table 2 in Section 3.4 is a checklist for evaluating the ethicality of a proposed treatment. This table should be reviewed whenever you are contemplating any treatment that is in any way nonstandard.

Formulating Treatment Plans for Managed Care Organizations

We should not let the current and substantial differences between the objectives of MCOs and those of clinicians obscure the commonalities. Thoughtful planning of treatment interventions is always desirable and in the patient's best interest. For dealing with MCO reviewers, here are some very revealing guidelines[1]:

Good managed care relations don't just happen. You have to understand the company's expectations and be willing to complete the seemingly endless paperwork. The treatment plan is one crucial device that keeps tabs on your managed care work and determines whether you get paid as you should.

Keeping an eye on treatment plans is managed care's preferred method for tracking "quality and appropriate care," says Scott Harris, PhD, co-director of the Center for Behavioral Health Care in Los Angeles. "It provides a structured mechanism for periodic review and authorization, monitoring providers for appropriateness, competence, and effectiveness."

Harris provides the following guidelines for writing a treatment plan (with special attention to the expectations of MCOs):

1. **Comprehensive overview.** Provide a full profile of the patient. Outline both the nature of the crisis and the focus of treatment.

2. **Goals and progress.** State treatment goals in measurable, behavioral terms. Indicate specific progress to be made within a given time period. Link clinical improvement to specific interventions and detail a pre-discharge level of progress.

3. **Action.** [The plan should] reflect the thinking, planning, and actions taken by the therapist with the patient. Interventions must promote change and movement through the therapy.

[1]The following passage, including the remarks and guidelines by Scott Harris, PhD, is reprinted from "Ten Steps to Create a Successful Treatment Plan" (1993). Copyright 1993 by Ridgewood Financial Institute. Reprinted by permission.

4. **Timeliness.** Treatment planning must correspond with the [MCO's] authorization as well as the clinician's billing. Without coordinated documentation, a delay in claims processing and reimbursement may result. That means frustrating phone calls and, perhaps, filing the claim a second or third time.

5. **Benefit awareness.** Know the limits and structure of the specific benefit being administered by the managed care firm. Some benefits may include only 3 to 5 sessions, while others allow as many as 50.

6. **Alternative services.** Show that you are aware of, and willing to refer to, other levels of care such as day treatment, hospitalization, etc., as well as other resources that complement and reinforce treatment goals. This may mean specifying patient involvement in 12-step programs, support groups, parenting classes, or medication consultations with a psychiatrist.

7. **Professional liaisons.** Specifically state the role of other professionals essential to the outcome of the case.

8. **Crisis** and other potential red flags. Understand, identify, and plan for potential crisis situations. Responses and steps for crisis intervention need to be clearly detailed for cases involving potential suicide or child abuse. Use case managers as resources.

9. **Chemical dependency.** Address and plan treatment for potential or existing chronic chemical dependency problems.

10. **Copies.** Always keep copies of treatment plans and authorizations. This prevents multiple frustrations when you learn that a plan has not been received, or received and then lost.

FORM 36   Form 36 is an individualized treatment form for MCOs that will enable you to follow these guidelines. Its purposes and functions are (1) to serve as a checklist to assure that all evaluations and treatments have been considered; (2) to document the recommendations for treatment; (3) to support consultation with MCO reviewers to assess needed level of care and "medical necessity"; and (4) to enable you to initiate the first phase of treatment. To simplify record making, this form is nearly identical to Form 35: it has a different first page and an additional last page. Thus, after summarizing your understanding of a case and developing a treatment plan on Form 35, you can easily reuse that material to create a treatment plan suitable for MCOs. Simply fill out the first and last pages of Form 36, photocopy pages 2–5 of Form 35, and insert those pages into Form 36. Your letterhead must contain any additional identifying information that the MCO requires (provider number, supervisor, credentials, license number, etc.).

Individualized Behavioral/Mental Health Treatment Plan

This is for ☐ Preauthorization for initial certification ☐ Concurrent review for reauthorization of care

Date present treatment began: _____ Date last plan created: _____

A. Identification

Client's name: _____ Soc. Sec. #: _____ ID #: _____

Membership #: _____ Date of birth: _____ Sex: _____

Group name/#: _____ Certificate #: _____

Name of subscriber/member, and address (if other than client): _____

Release-of-records form(s) signed: ☐ Yes ☐ Not yet

B. Case formulation/overview

1. Presenting problem(s)/reason(s) for seeking treatment:

Problem	Severity*	Duration
a.		
b.		
c.		

   *
   Code severity as follows (per GAF scale): 80–90 = mild, 60–70 = moderate, 40–50 = severe, 30 or less = very severe.

2. History of presenting problem(s) and current situation (precipitants, motivations, stressors, resources/coping skills, comorbid conditions, living conditions, relevant demographics): _____

   _____

   _____

   _____

   _____

3. Summary of mental status evaluation results: _____

   _____

   _____

(cont.)

C. Present level of functioning/limitations/impairment (describe specific impairments at left, and rate degree of functional impairment at right with GAF number [100 = none, 70 = little, 30 = significant, 10 = incapacitated] or use descriptors):

Area of functioning	Rating
1. School/work: _____	_____
2. Intimate relationship/marriage: _____	_____
3. Family/children: _____	_____
4. Social relationships: _____	_____
5. Psychological/personal functioning: _____	_____
6. Other areas: _____	_____

D. Assessment conclusions

1. Assessment of currently known **risk factors**:

   a. *Suicide*: ❑ Not assessed   Behaviors ❑ None known ❑ Ideation only ❑ Plan
   ❑ Intent without means   ❑ Intent with means

   b. *Homicide*: ❑ Not assessed   Behaviors ❑ None known ❑ Ideation only ❑ Plan
   ❑ Intent without means   ❑ Intent with means

   c. *Impulse control*: ❑ Not assessed ❑ Sufficient control ❑ Moderate ❑ Minimal ❑ Inconsistent

   d. *Compliance with treatments*: ❑ Not assessed ❑ Full compliance ❑ Minimal noncompliance
   ❑ Moderate noncompliance ❑ Variable ❑ Little or no compliance

   e. *Substance abuse*: ❑ Not assessed ❑ None/normal use ❑ Overuse ❑ Dependence
   ❑ Unstable remission of abuse ❑ Abuse

   f. *Current physical or sexual abuse*: ❑ Not assessed ❑ No ❑ Yes   Legally reportable? ❑ Yes ❑ No

   g. *Current child/elder neglect*: ❑ Not assessed ❑ No ❑ Yes   Legally reportable? ❑ Yes ❑ No
   If yes, client is ❑ Victim ❑ Perpetrator ❑ Both ❑ Neither, but abuse exists in family

   h. *If risk exists*: Client ❑ can ❑ cannot meaningfully agree to a contract not to harm ❑ self ❑ others ❑ both

   i. *History* that may affect current level of risk or impairment of functioning:
   _____

   j. *Other concerns*: _____

(cont.)

2. **Urgency** estimate ❏ Emergency; immediate interventions ❏ Serious disruption of functioning; act in next 24 hours ❏ Treatment needed; act soon/routine ❏ Wait for: _____

3. **Diagnoses**—Current best formulation

	Name (indicate which is primary diagnosis with "P")	Code # ❏ DSM-IV or ❏ ICD?
Axis I	_____	_____
	_____	_____
	_____	_____
Axis II	_____	_____
	_____	_____
	_____	_____

"Rule-outs" (other possible diagnoses to be evaluated over time): _____
_____
_____

Axis III—Significant and relevant medical conditions, including allergies and drug sensitivities:

Condition	Treatment/medication (regimen)	Provider	Status

Axis IV—Psychosocial and environmental problems in last year; overall severity rating:

❏ Problems with primary support group   ❏ Problems related to the social environment

❏ Educational problems   ❏ Occupational problems

❏ Housing problems   ❏ Economic problems

❏ Problems with access to health care services

❏ Problems related to interaction with the legal system/crime

Other psychosocial and environmental problems (specify): _____
_____
_____

Axis V—Global Assessment of Functioning (GAF) Scale (100 down to 0): Currently: _____ Past year: _____

V Codes—Other problems that may be a focus of clinical attention: _____
_____
_____

(cont.)

E. Treatment plan (if additional problems are to be addressed, use copies of this page):

Significant improvement is to be expected, with treatment as specified, for:

Problem 1: _____

- ■ Behaviors to be changed: _____
_____
_____

- ■ Interventions (who does what, how often, with what resources; modality, frequency, duration): _____
_____
_____

- ■ Observable indicators of improvement (behaviors, reports):   ■ Expected number of visits to achieve each indicator: _____
_____
_____
_____

- ■ Discharge level of problem behaviors: _____   ■ Review date: _____
_____

Problem 2: _____

- ■ Behaviors to be changed: _____
_____
_____

- ■ Interventions (who does what, how often, with what resources; modality, frequency, duration): _____
_____
_____

- ■ Observable indicators of improvement (behaviors, reports):   ■ Expected number of visits to achieve each indicator: _____
_____
_____
_____

- ■ Discharge level of problem behaviors: _____   ■ Review date: _____
_____

Problem 3: _____

- ■ Behaviors to be changed: _____
_____
_____

- ■ Interventions (who does what, how often, with what resources; modality, frequency, duration): _____
_____
_____

- ■ Observable indicators of improvement (behaviors, reports):   ■ Expected number of visits to achieve each indicator: _____
_____
_____
_____

- ■ Discharge level of problem behaviors: _____   ■ Review date: _____
_____

(cont.)

F. Recommended program of coordinated liaisons, consultations, evaluations and services

1. Psychotherapy: ❑ Individual ❑ Family ❑ Marital/relational ❑ Hypnosis ❑ Biofeedback ❑ Other:

   Session length: ❑ 30 min. ❑ 50 min. ❑ 90 min.

   Frequency: ❑ twice weekly ❑ weekly ❑ twice monthly ❑ monthly

   ❑ Focal group therapy—type: _____

2. Support groups: Twelve-Step program: ❑ AA ❑ NA ❑ Overeaters ❑ Gamblers ❑ Other

   ❑ Other community support groups: _____

   Psychoeducational groups: ❑ Parenting skills/child management ❑ Communication skills

   ❑ Stress management ❑ Assertiveness ❑ Women's issues ❑ Other: _____

   Ancillary services: ❑ Pain clinic ❑ Back school ❑ Physical therapy ❑ Other: _____

3. Legal services: ❑ Offender program ❑ Sex ❑ Substance abuse ❑ Other: _____

   ❑ Victim support ❑ Referral to advocates: _____

4. **Referrals for continuing services**

Referred to	For (kind of service)	Date of referral
	Psychotropic medications Physical medical care Psychiatric evaluation Patient education Nursing care Educational/vocational services Occupational/physical therapy Other: _____	

5. **Further assessments,** based on current clinical evaluation, are needed to answer these concerns or rule out these possible coexisting conditions:

   ❑ Psychological presentation/symptoms of medical condition

   Likely possible sources: ❑ Thyroid ❑ Diabetes ❑ Alcohol/drug abuse ❑ Circulatory problem
   ❑ Neurological problem ❑ Poor nutrition ❑ Medication interactions ❑ Toxin exposure
   ❑ Other: _____

   ❑ Sexual dysfunctions   ❑ Factitious disorders   ❑ Substance abuse

   ❑ Psychophysiological disorders ❑ Learning disabilities   ❑ Physiatrist

   ❑ Genetic disorders/counseling   ❑ Other: _____

6. **Documents to be obtained** (have requests for records completed and signed, photocopied, and placed in client's file so that receipt can be assured):

Type of record	Source	Date of first request
❑ Medical/physician/hospital		
❑ School		
❑ Agency		
❑ Other: _____		

7. **Other needed resources and services:** _____

_____

(cont.)

G. Administrative

1. Case manager's additional suggestions for treatments and resources:

Date	Name	Suggestions

2. Services:

Sessions requested*	Date of request	Start of sessions	Number of sessions authorized	Date of authorization	Date of next review

*Code sessions with a number (number of sessions) and letter: C = Collateral contacts, E = Evaluation, F = Family therapy, G = Group therapy, I = Individual therapy.

H. Additional comments and information _____

_____

_____

_____

_____

_____

I. Cooperative treatment planning

Our signatures below mean that we have participated in the formulation of this treatment plan, understand and approve of it, and accept the responsibility to carry out our parts of the plan fully.

_____   _____
Signature of client (or person acting for client)   Date

_____   _____   _____
Signature of service provider   Provider number   Date

This is a strictly confidential patient medical record. Redisclosure or transfer is expressly prohibited by law.

This report reflects the patient's condition at the time of consultation or evaluation. It does not necessarily reflect the patient's diagnosis or condition at any subsequent time.

You can make various changes to Form 36. For example, you can elaborate on crisis management with this under heading E:

Plans for possible crises:

Crisis	Risk level (1–10)	Intervention	Resources
❏ Suicide			
❏ Homicide			
❏ Violence			
❏ Substance abuse			
❏ Child or other abuse			
❏ Impulse dyscontrol			
❏ Noncompliance			
❏ Other: _____			

Under each problem in section E ("Behaviors to be changed," "Interventions," "Observable indicators of improvement," "Expected number of visits to achieve each indicator," and "Discharge level of problem behaviors"), you can substitute one of a number of alternative formats:

- "Goal," "Interventions," "Observable indicators of improvement," and "Time frame."

- "Target symptoms," "Target date," and "Expected outcome."

- "Diagnosis-related symptoms," "Symptom-related goals," "Interventions," and "Target date."

- "Short-term objectives," "Target date," "Long-term goals," and Target date."

For the present section F, you could substitute a statement or checklist with options of the services you have available, in order of intensity of service/need:

F. Recommended level of care
- ❏ Emergency/immediate psychiatric hospitalization
- ❏ Regular psychiatric hospitalization
- ❏ Residential treatment center
- ❏ Inpatient medical detoxification
- ❏ Inpatient substance abuse/dependence program
- ❏ Specialized inpatient program for: _____
- ❏ Group or supported housing
- ❏ Partial hospitalization/day treatment program
- ❏ Structured/intensive outpatient program for: _____

Or, depending on the likely needs of your clientele, you can add these to the present section F.

Residential care: ❏ Shelter   ❏ Partial hospitalization   ❏ Inpatient 24-hour hospitalization
    ❏ Group home   ❏ Family support   ❏ Other: _____
Educational/vocational services: ❏ Agency evaluation   ❏ GED classes   ❏ Work hardening
    ❏ Sheltered workshop   ❏ Special school services   ❏ Other: _____
Economic supports: ❏ Welfare/AFDC   ❏ Soc. Sec. Disability   ❏ Other: _____

6.2 Documenting Treatment's Progress

Change is certain. Progress is not.
—E. H. CARR

After treatment has been planned and initiated, records of its implementation need to be kept. The interactions between you and the client that result in progress (or its absence) must be noted. The treatment planning formats offered earlier in this chapter often include ways to monitor the progress of the case. This section discusses those and other options in more detail. Specifically, it discusses the following options for keeping treatment records:

- Note taking, including guidelines for when and how to take notes

- The problem-oriented record (POR), including a POR progress note form

- Structured progress notes for individual and for group therapy

- Client-generated records

Note Taking: Guidelines and Suggestions

Most clinicians write without a system, and so their notes only partially describe the facts of their therapy. Such notes will not protect these therapists or support understanding of their therapy. If this description applies to you, find or invent a system you can live with—one that makes sense for your way of working, helps you do your job, and protects you. The following ideas may help.

When to Write Notes

Writing notes during a treatment session saves time, but may lead to incompleteness and (because of lack of reflection or excess brevity) later incomprehensibility. It also reduces eye contact and rapport with the client. One position is to "Never take notes when an individual is talking about his feelings, or discussing matters which are sensitive, emotionally laden or difficult to express" (Wilson, 1980, p. 7). Other therapists find that taking notes uses little time, is seen as thoroughness, and gives them time to weigh what is happening and to consider their responses carefully. However, saying "Let me just make a note of that," or even the minimal cue of writing after a client says something, may reinforce that topic, mood, or pattern even when you don't want to increase symptomatic behavior. If a client becomes uneasy, discontinue your note taking and offer to share the notes with him or her.

Two additional suggestions for taking notes during a session are as follows:

- Take notes about the major issues in a "headline" or "telegraphic" format, leaving space. As soon as the session is over, write in the details and your well-considered formulations.

- Take real-time notes of things you suspect you will forget or any factual data that you may not remember accurately without a reminder (Wilson, 1980, p. 7).

Taking notes immediately after a session allows for perspective on the whole session, as well as for the identification of themes and the most important events. Make certain to schedule enough time and to charge the client for it.

The problem with taking notes at the end of the day is that writing so far removed from the experience leads to contamination of your memories of one client by those of other clients or events, as well as to other errors or distortions in your recollections. This is not fair to you or your clients.

By the way, *not* keeping notes is not an option; you are ethically required to have such records. (See Section 1.4 for information on record-keeping obligations.) And, whatever note-taking schedule you adopt, always keep you notes current. Periodically, or at case closing, you can revise your working notes into formal records and destroy the notes.

How to Write Notes: Formats

Progress versus Process Notes. Some authorities recommend keeping progress notes separate from process notes because they differ so much. Progress notes are the official "chart" and are available to the client and others. They include the following:

- Dates of appointments

- Problems addressed

- Treatment efforts

- Contents of interviews

- Referrals

- Homework assignments

- Objective data

Process or working notes contain the following:

- Sensitive information

- The therapist's reactions, fantasies, feelings, speculations, hypotheses, reflections, and so on.

- Notes to the therapist by the therapist

- Notes on process that would make no sense to anyone outside the session

Some therapists think it best not to include these working notes in the client's regular record; however, this is controversial and risky. (See "What to Write Down: Guidelines," below.)

Various formats for recording both process and progress notes follow.

Process Recording in Social Work. Social workers are often trained in the use of process recording, which includes the following:

- An almost verbatim record of what each person said, in a format like C (Client): . . . and W (Social Worker): . . .

- Notes on the client's nonverbal behaviors.

- The workers' feelings and reactions to the client.

- Observations and analytical thoughts about the client's internal processes and the events of the interview.

- A section headed "Diagnostic Summary" or "Worker's Impressions," which summarizes the worker's analytical thoughts and understandings.

- A section headed "Social Service Plan," "Casework Plan," "Comprehensive Service Plan," or "Treatment Plan."

This format is helpful with a confusing case or for documentation for training and supervision.

The Individual Psychotherapy Session Note. A process-focused format designed for individual dynamic therapy, modified from that of Presser and Pfost (1985), calls for the following:

A. A brief, narrative summary of the session.

B. The therapist's observations of:

1a. The client's behaviors

2a. The therapist's behaviors

3a. The client–therapist interaction

Items 1a, 2a, and 3a are paralleled by the therapist's interpretations, questions, and hypotheses about each of these (which can be called 1b, 2b, and 3b). A new heading, C, could be considered the therapist's interventions for change, their rationales, and their predicted effects. One could also include D, the trends of the session in light of previous sessions, and E, the trends in relation to the problem list.

Should you record process or record progress/content for family therapy? Brock and Barnard (1988) have this to say:

> Historically, clinical case notes have been more content oriented than process oriented. Process notes are more specific regarding systemic notions such as the family's rules, roles, evident communications styles, and patterns that appear to be operational. Attending to the organization and structure of a family in notes lends itself to the development of direction, goals, and possible interventions, for the therapist. Merely recording the content of who said what and where the session left off ignores such systemic information and may, in fact, get in the way of the therapist's appropriately conceptualizing the family in systemic fashion. We can all be entranced and diverted by stories. (pp. 139–140)

More is said later in this section about keeping notes in family or couple therapy.

Progress Recording in Social Work. According to Kagle (1991, p. 18), a progress-oriented record in social work must contain the following logical elements: (1) the client, the situation, and the available resources, which form the basis for (2) service decisions and actions, including (3) the purpose, goals, plan, and process of service, and (4) the effects service is expected to have upon the client, the situation, and the available resources. She offers this set of headings (p. 124):

- What happened during the session

- New problems/issues/needs that surfaced

- Interventions used

- New referrals, plans (e.g., for the next session), or recommendations made

To this can be added:

- Session goals

- Homework plan

The Problem-Oriented Record. The problem-oriented record (POR) format is largely a progress-oriented format, but it includes elements of process recording as well. It is discussed in detail later in this section.

How to Write Notes: A Checklist of Tips

Although notes should be concise, they must also be coherent, accurate, current, relevant, and handled in ways to assure and maintain confidentiality.

❑ All entries should be dated, sometimes timed, and signed. A signature may be unnecessary when the notes are in your handwriting, but initials should indicate where a particular note ends.

❏ The sources of all information recorded should be indicated.

❏ Make subheadings of the session's notes for clarity. <u>Underline important information if you will have to search for it later.</u> (See how well it works?) Number issues and subjects in your notes. You can also circle some numbers. If you use a problem list, you can cross-reference each entry to a problem (by its number P1, P2, etc.).

❏ Write paragraphs giving full explanations, which are better than phrases or cryptic notations.

❏ Use words that help the reader visualize; make your words a camera. Terms such as "No change" or "Improving" are too open to varying interpretations.

❏ Ignore set lengths as required on a printed form. Write as complete a note as necessary to achieve the record's purpose (Wilson, 1980, p. 113).

❏ Use direct quotations whenever possible to indicate the client's experiences and thought processes. Separate your judgments and conclusions from the facts and observations. A simple and practical notation scheme is as follows:

   All unmarked notations are the client's ideas and reports.

   Quotes from the client can be indicated by standard double quotation marks: " ".

   Statements from others reported to you by the client can be indicated by both double and single quotes " ' ' ".

   Words in parentheses are (your statements to the client).

   Words in square brackets are [your unspoken hypotheses or conclusions].

   Also, you can use HW for homework assignments and Rx for topics to cover in the future.

❏ Never alter any notations you have already made. If corrections are made to the record, it should be clear that they were made later than the entry being corrected, because not to make this clear is misleading and suspicious. For very small changes, it is best to draw one line through the error and to date and initial the correction. For larger changes make a notation at the earlier date, such as "See also entry of [today's date]"; then indicate in the later note that "My present recall differs, in that . . . " or "I was misinformed at that time, and now believe. . . . " If you later recall something you did not record earlier, you can write it with a notation that it is "Prior knowledge [or understanding or recollection] presently recorded."

❏ Do not add comments near a previously recorded entry in your notes. This may also appear to be tampering with the record. Instead, write notes at the end with today's date and cross-reference them to the original location in your notes (Gutheil, 1980). For example, "August 1: In rereading my notes of July 4, I note that I neglected to mention the fireworks, which. . . . "

What to Write Down: Guidelines

There are legal risks to be considered in excluding anything form your notes (Fulero & Wilbert, 1988). For example, omitting material on sex may leave you with little defense against an accusation of impropriety during a session. Releasing records with premature diagnoses or speculations could be the basis of a malpractice claim. This is why some therapists have kept dual records—one set not to be released, in order to protect both themselves and their clients, and a second or redacted set to be released upon request or court order. However, keep in mind that **there can no longer be secret records,** even as the obligation remains to try to keep information private. If you work in a setting covered by federal law, the Privacy Act of 1974 (Public Law 93-579) and the Freedom of Information Act of 1974 (Public Law 93-502) give clients rights of access to all your notes about them. Furthermore, state law or case law, or just filing a suit against you, will also give them access (Fulero & Wilbert, 1988). Therefore, create records with the expectation that they will be read by someone else and should be clear when read years later. Your clients may someday see your notes, so consider their psychological and legal implications. The best policy may be to write your records so that all will be well when a client or a client's parents read your notes.

Since you can't record everything, you need to choose what to note while bearing in mind the purpose of the record. I suggest the following priorities.

First, make a record of your clinical decision making for your own later review. Ask yourself, "Will I need to know this later? For the next session? Later in treatment or after treatment, for another purpose?" If having this information will not change some aspect of treatment, do not bother to record it. In particular, record any event or decision that precedes a change in the patient's condition (a new problem develops or is recognized, there is a response or a lack of response to adequate treatment, etc.).

Klein et al. (1984) (as summarized in Soisson et al., 1987) recommend the documentation of *all* significant decisions during therapy. Specifically, the record should include the following:

1. What the treatment choice is expected to accomplish (goals, objectives).

2. Why you believe it will be effective (a rationale).

3. Any risks involved and why they are justified.

4. Which alternative treatments were considered.

5. Why they were rejected or delayed.

6. Any steps taken to improve the effectiveness of the chosen treatments.

7. Evidence of informed consent provided by the client's statements or your own observations supporting the client's consent.

8. The rationales for any referrals made.

Second, make a record of your clinical decision making for self-defense. A useful rule of thumb may be "If it might make a mess, make a note." In a similar vein, Gutheil (1980,

p. 482) intelligently suggests that when taking any risky actions, you should "think out loud for the record" so that if the unfortunate happens, it can be traced only to an error in judgment and not to negligence. The following specific pointers may be helpful:

- Explicitly note where information isn't clear.

- Document all clinically significant events, such as nonroutine calls, missed sessions, and consultations with other professionals (Soisson et al., 1987).

- When forensically significant events or possible malpractice situations are anticipated, the record should be written from the perspective of future readers (Gutheil & Appelbaum, 1982), especially unfriendly readers. An example of such a situation might be a suicidal patient.

- Emergency treatment situations are responsible for a disproportionately large share of malpractice claims, and so should be documented with extra care (Gutheil & Appelbaum, 1982). Get full consultations, and document any resistance from significant others, so that responsibility can be placed accurately (Cohen, 1979).

- Your statements about the limitations of a treatment should be noted; its success should not be guaranteed, and excessive optimism should be shunned to avoid responsibility for a failure (Gutheil & Appelbaum, 1982).

What Not to Write Down: Guidelines

Do not record anything that is unnecessary for or irrelevant to treatment. I suggest that you generally exclude the following:

- Excessive detail.

- Gossip and hearsay.

- Emotional statements, editorializing, or hunches.

- Moral or personal value judgments about the client or others (e.g., "fat," "lazy," "weak," or "stupid").

- The client's political, religious, or other personal beliefs.

- Difficulties you had with other professionals or agencies in this client's case.

- Names of paramours (use initials?) or specific indicators of affairs.

- Reports of most illegal activity in the past.

- Incriminating information about illegal activity in the present (e.g., details of drug use).

- Medical diagnoses or other judgments that your training and experience do not qualify you to make.

- Most sexual practices.

- Sensitive, embarrassing, or harmful statements.

Special Considerations for Keeping Notes in Family or Couple Therapy

If you see several members of a family, or a couple, you will have particularly complex decisions to make about record keeping.

You can keep separate records (separate pages) on each person involved in a conjoint session, so that you do not have to release all the records when just one set is sought. Confidentiality can then be maintained. Margolin (1982) offers an extensive and thoughtful discussion of the privacy issues in marriage and family therapy. On the other hand, separate records create a fiction that there were not several interacting people in the room. Because the family members' issues involve each other, separate notes on each person cannot be considered truly independent and so cannot rationally be released separately.

The suggestion that all participating members must give permission for the release of the record seems logical. However, this must be implemented before the therapy is begun, by means of a paragraph in your client information brochure and paragraphs in your release-of-records forms. Two problems can arise: You are initially asking family members to agree to conditions for the release of records whose content they do not know, because the therapy and the records of it have not happened yet. This cannot be considered informed consent. Second, problems may arise when one member does not consent to the release that another member seeks.

Other Ideas about Documenting Treatment

For some purposes (clinical, research, protective, forensic, or administrative), recording sessions on audiotapes or videotapes may make sense. Tapes can be given to the client for review or kept privately. You will need permission to make such recordings, since they are not usual and have the potential to breach confidentiality. See Section 4.6 for a discussion and a permission-to-record form.

Client-created records (which are discussed at the end of this section) may be another way of getting around some of these issues. Although certainly the clients know what is in such records, they may not understand the implications of their release.

The Problem-Oriented Record

When you are documenting the progress of a case, the challenge is to record treatment-relevant information in an accessible form. However, clinicians, because of their differing training and interests, may record such diverse topics as the process of therapy, the symptoms of a disorder, the relationship with the client, the contents of interactions and outside events, the goals of recovery or growth, or many other possibilities.

In this diversity, the word "problem" has become a label acceptable to clinicians of many disciplines and backgrounds. Lawrence Weed (1971) invented a new record-keeping method because he found that the information necessary to treat a patient was being recorded in medical charts in too many places to be useful. Instead of being entered under arbitrary topical or discipline-based headings ("Intake," "Diagnoses," "Social History," "Psychological Evaluations," "Nursing Notes," "Consultant's Reports," etc.), all notes must be keyed to numbered problems. This method is called the "problem-oriented record" (POR), the "problem-oriented medical record," the "Weed system," or "SOAP notes." It is widely used in medicine and has been adapted to the psychotherapy setting.

As slightly modified for the psychotherapy context (see Sturm, 1987), the format consists of four main components: (1) the problem list, which remains on top of the chart and which serves as a table of contents to it; (2) the data base of history and findings; (3) the initial treatment plan; and (4) progress notes, or the continuing record of the clinician's observations and understanding of the patient. Each progress note entry is recorded in the "SOAP" format (see below) and is cross-referenced to a problem on the problem list by number. Therefore, all the information in the chart is organized around problems. All evaluations and their results are thus tied to their sources and their implications for treatment. To find all of the information in the chart about a concern, the reader has only to look for its problem number on all pages.

The Problem List

FORM 37

The problem list is simply a numbered listing of all problems identified by you or the client and used as a guide to the POR system. Forms 28, 29, and 30 offer several ways to identify problems. Once created, the list is placed on top of the chart to serve as a table of contents for the continuing record. Problems are defined at their current level of understanding, and are rewritten and renumbered as they become better or differently understood. Problems can be added and, when resolved, closed by making an entry and by not reusing that number. Added to this listing should be a psychiatric diagnosis with all axes considered; an evaluation of difficulties with activities of daily living; and a description of all functional impairments. Form 37 permits you to create a problem list for a POR.

Problem List for a Problem-Oriented Record (POR)

Client: _____   Page #: _____

Problem number	Date problem recognized	Problem title/formulation	Prob. # where problem is now included, *or* →	Date problem resolved
		Problems currently active	Problems now inactive	

This is a strictly confidential patient medical record. Redisclosure or transfer is expressly prohibited by law.

FORM 37. Problem list for a problem-oriented record (POR). From *The Paper Office*, p. 274. Copyright 1997 by Edward L. Zuckerman. Permission to photocopy this form is granted to purchasers of *The Paper Office* for personal use only (see copyright page for details).

The Data Base

The data base consists of the following usual and expected psychological topics, with each entry tied to the list of problems:

- Chief complaint.

- Mental status examination results.

- Social situation—personal, familial, environmental factors.

- Personal and social history.

- History of other medical and psychological conditions and their treatments.

- Records obtained from other treaters.

- Results of testing, or other relevant data.

The Paper Office does not provide separate forms for all of these, because they can be recorded in whatever format and size you may prefer. However, Chapter 5 includes forms and guides for recording some of this information.

The Initial Treatment Plan

Psychological interventions usually require the consideration of many dimensions simultaneously, and so a treatment plan is necessary. See Section 6.1 for suggested treatment plan formats and essentials. The POR treatment plan is simply a listing of therapeutic responses to each currently recognized and defined problem. It is the starting point for treatment, and is modified or added to through changes in the progress notes as the case progresses. The plan may include every kind of treatment by anyone (patient education, collection of more information, treatment of and by others, etc.), as well as the usual therapies.

Progress Notes Using the SOAP Format

"SOAP" is an acronym for four kinds of information that needs to be documented for each problem addressed during each client meeting. This is where the POR shines. Every note begins with the problem number for cross-reference and completeness, and continues as follows:

- S is for subjective data—the client's reports of complaints, symptoms, efforts made, problems, changes, and difficulties. S also includes notes of the statements of others.

- O is for objective data—your observations and the observations of others; measurable signs (especially changes); the results of psychological testing of the client; and his or her observable behaviors, appearance, and social situation.

- A is for assessment—your conclusions, diagnoses, interpretations, impressions, judgments, case formulations, and analyses of the meaning of the data.

- P is for the plan of treatment (both immediate and future), as created by you and by the others concerned. Diagnostic studies, patient education, and follow-up would also be placed here.

FORM 38   Form 38 is a photocopiable form for making POR progress notes according to the SOAP format, and Figure 5 is a completed example of this form. Of course, you can make various changes both to the SOAP format and to Form 38. First, progress notes can be made "SOAP-IER," which is well suited for the current direction of psychotherapies. Use the SOAP format as described above, and then add the following:

- I is for intervention or implementation of the plan—what you have done to, for, or with the patient relative to this problem. In this version you would put the longer-term goals into the plan (P), and use implementation (I) for the shorter-term objectives.

- E is for evaluation/effectiveness of the intervention—that is, the outcomes of intervention, positive or negative. These, of course, could be recorded under S and O, but in this framework they are separated for greater specificity.

- R is for revisions of the plan if it was ineffective. Again, these could be recorded under P as a new plan, but using this new heading makes the changes more salient.

An alternative to the SOAP format is to use a "DAR" format:

- D is for data.

- A is for the action you take based on this data.

- R is for the response of the patient or other.

POR Progress Note Form

Client: _____ Page #: _____

Problem number	Date of note	Problem status[*]	Progress notes[**]

[*]Problem status codes: C = continuing focused treatment; R = problem resolved; I = inactive problem; IT = inactive due to ongoing treatment; D = treatment deferred; N = newly identified problem; ReDf to # = problem redefined or combined with another problem whose number is indicated.

[**]Each entry must be related to a problem number; coded S for subjective, O for objective, A for assessment, or P for plan; and signed.

This is a strictly confidential patient medical record. Redisclosure or transfer is expressly prohibited by law.

POR Progress Note Form

Client: ___Last name, First name_____ Page #: ___1____

Problem number	Date of note	Problem status*	Progress notes**
1. Depression	9/9/99	C	S: No suicidal thoughts this week More energy—started painting project Fears of being fired Spouse confirms more optimism O: Increased facial expressions, more hand and arm gestures, faster movements BDI score = 9 A: Lessened depression P: Maintain or add treatments as follows: − Spousal reinforcement for activities as scheduled − Cognitive therapy 1/week − Continue meds − Consider adding new group activity—9/23/99 − Reevaluate medication—10/9/99 *Anna F. Therapist*

*Problem status codes: C = continuing focused treatment; R = problem resolved; I = inactive problem; IT = inactive due to ongoing treatment; D = treatment deferred; N = newly identified problem; ReDf to # = problem redefined or combined with another problem whose number is indicated.

**Each entry must be related to a problem number; coded S for subjective, O for objective, A for assessment, or P for plan; and signed.

FIGURE 5. Completed sample of a POR progress note form.

Advantages of the POR

- The POR is a complete record. It is logical and tidy. The information in it is accessible to other care providers, supervisors, or reviewers, and is easily defended in court.

- The POR is a means of keeping the focus of treatment on the client's larger concerns ("keeping your eye on the ball"). It is all too easy to go along with the client's desire to avoid change; to be distracted by interesting and *possibly* relevant side paths; or to avoid doing the hard work of being a therapist ("It's not fun any more"). The POR can help you keep such distractions to a minimum.

- The POR can keep both of you focused when the going gets confusing or slow, by keeping the horizon in view and allowing you to mesh the immediate and lively with the long-term and important.

- At another level, the problem list, treatment plan, and SOAP notes are the negotiated map of the territory of the client's life situation.

Disadvantages of the POR

- The POR format tends to oversimplify the complexity of psychotherapy's understandings and interventions.

- It can lessen the attention paid to the client's strengths and resources.

- Because it is person-focused, rather than focused on the person in his or her situation, context, or system, it may underemphasize the client's relationships. Environmental and case management interventions may be overlooked as a result.

- Its weakest point is defining what exactly is a problem. The good news, however, is that problems can be described at whatever level of understanding is currently available, and redescribed when they are understood differently. Simply close a problem entry with a cross-reference to the newer definition.

Two Structured Progress Note Forms

A Structured Form for Individual Clients

FORM 39   The form presented below, the structured progress note form (Form 39), is an efficient way of recording a client's progress when you do not use the POR system described above. The purposes of this form are (1) to document the progress of your treatment and the client's response to it; (2) to enable you to do this with as little time and effort as possible; and (3) to support evaluation of the treatment by you, the client, and other interested parties.

Form 39 is designed to be rather broadly useful for many kinds of treatment; it offers choices that may fit many practices, but you can enter specifics to fit your practice under the headings. This form is based on an excellent one from Ronnie M. Hirsch, PhD, of New York,

NY. If you need a more elaborate form, the "Professional Progress Notes" form from Psychological Assessment Resources (see the Appendix, Section A.4) is similar, but more elaborate in its coverage and evaluation of such risk areas as suicide potential, referrals needed, health problems, and allegations of sexual improprieties. In addition, its manual is a very thorough resource regarding record keeping and the use of good records as a malpractice risk reduction method. It is recommended.

To tailor Form 39 even more specifically to your practice, you might want to delete the "Next appointment . . . " or "Symptoms" items and add "Instructions, suggestions, directions" under Treatments (as suggested by Muriel L. Golub, PhD, of Tustin, CA). If you work in an agency setting, you might want to add such options as "Chart reviewed," "Case consultation," Treatment team meeting attended," or "Aftercare planning meeting." Specific target symptoms taken from Form 32 or elsewhere can be added to the listing, as well as a section on medications.

A Structured Form for Group Therapy

FORM 40

In keeping notes about the progress of individual clients in a therapy group, a simple checklist reduces the paperwork burden. You can use either Form 39, which contains several sections not in this one, or Form 40, which records more information about interventions, interactions, and participation in the group. Your can, of course, add items from Form 39 to Form 40—for example, the "Symptoms," "Stressors," "Level of functioning," and/or "Changes to diagnoses" items.

Progress Note

If a checkbox (❏) is inappropriate or insufficient, enter a letter and write additional comments on a separate page.

A. Client and meeting information

Client: _____ Date: _____

Meeting #: _____ of _____ authorized on this date _____ with provider # _____.

Meeting was: ❏ Scheduled ❏ Emergency Others present: _____.

Meeting lasted: ❏ 15 ❏ 30 ❏ 45–50 ❏ 60 ❏ 90 ❏ ____ minutes

Client: ❏ Was on time ❏ Was late by ____min. ❏ Did not show ❏ Cancelled and was rescheduled for ____

Meeting took place at: ❏ Office ❏ By phone ❏ Clinic ❏ Hospital ❏ Client's home ❏ Workplace

Mode of treatment: ❏ Individual therapy ❏ Family ❏ Group ❏ Couple ❏ Consultation

B. Topics/themes discussed   Notes

❏ Homework assignments _____

❏ Relationship(s) _____

❏ Stressors _____

❏ Identity/role _____

❏ Work problem _____

❏ Alcohol/drug problem _____

❏ Childhood/fam. of origin _____

❏ Sexual problem _____

❏ Parenting _____

❏ Dream(s) _____

❏ Other _____

C. Treatments/interventions/techniques

❏ Insights _____

❏ Behavioral _____

❏ Cognitive _____

❏ Homework given _____

❏ Family _____

❏ Relationship _____

❏ Problem solving _____

❏ Support _____

(cont.)

D. Assessments

1. Symptoms

Symptom/concern/complaint	Current severity rating*	Change since last evaluation (enter a check mark)					
		No change	Less severe	Much improved	Resolved/ absent	More severe	Much worse

*Rate from 0 to 10 as follows: 0 = not a problem/resolved; 5 = distressing/limiting; 10 = very severe distress, disruption, harm/risk.

2. Stressors

Stressor	Current severity rating*	Changes in severity?	Current level of coping/functioning†	Changes in coping level?	Coping skills employed

*Rate from 0 = not a problem to 10 = very severe, continuous, omnipresent, preoccupying.

†Rate from 0 to 10 as follows: 0 = much less able to cope; 5 = no change from last meeting/evaluation; or 10 = much improved level of coping.

3. **Mood:** ❑ Normal/euthymic ❑ Anxious ❑ Depressed ❑ Angry ❑ Euphoric
   Affect: ❑ Normal/appropriate ❑ Intense ❑ Blunted ❑ Inappropriate ❑ Labile

4. **Mental status:** ❑ Normal ❑ Lessened awareness ❑ Memory deficiencies ❑ Disoriented
   ❑ Disorganized ❑ Vigilant ❑ Delusional ❑ Hallucinating ❑ Other: _____

5. **Suicide/violence risk:** ❑ None ❑ Ideation only ❑ Threat ❑ Gesture ❑ Rehearsal ❑ Attempt

6. **Sleep quality:** ❑ Normal ❑ Restless/broken ❑ Insomnia ❑ Nightmares ❑ Oversleeps

7. **Participation level:** ❑ Active/eager ❑ Variable ❑ Only responsive ❑ Minimal ❑ None ❑ Resistant

8. **Treatment compliance:** ❑ Full ❑ Partial ❑ Low/noncompliant

9. **Response to treatment:** ❑ As expected ❑ Better than expected ❑ Much better ❑ Poorer ❑ Very poor

10. **GAF** (Global Assessment of Functioning) from 100 to 0 is currently: _____

11. Other observations/evaluations: _____

E. Changes to diagnoses: ❑ None or _____

F. Changes to treatment plan: ❑ None or _____

If treatment was changed, indicate rationale, alternatives considered/rejected/selected in notes.

G. Follow-ups

❑ Next appointment is scheduled for next ❑ week ❑ month ❑ 2 months ❑ 3 months ❑ as needed.

❑ Referral/consultation to: _____ For: _____

❑ Call/write to: _____ For: _____

I. Clinician's signature: _____ Date: _____

This is a strictly confidential patient medical record. Redisclosure or transfer is expressly prohibited by law.

Group Therapy Progress Note

Client and group information

Client: _____ Date: _____ Meeting attended is #: _____ for this client.

Group's name: _____ Time: _____ A.M./P.M.

Location: _____ # present: _____

Leader(s): _____ Signature(s): _____

_____ _____

Assessment of client

1. Participation level: ❑ Active/eager ❑ Variable ❑ Only responsive ❑ Minimal ❑ None ❑ Resistant

2. Participation quality: ❑ Expected ❑ Supportive ❑ Sharing ❑ Attentive ❑ Intrusive ❑ Monopolizing
   ❑ Resistant ❑ Other: _____

3. Mood: ❑ Normal/euthymic ❑ Anxious ❑ Depressed ❑ Angry ❑ Euphoric ❑ Other: _____
   Affect: ❑ Normal ❑ Intense ❑ Blunted ❑ Inappropriate ❑ Labile ❑ Other: _____

4. Mental status: ❑ Normal ❑ Lessened awareness ❑ Memory deficiencies ❑ Disoriented
   ❑ Disorganized ❑ Confused ❑ Vigilant ❑ Delusional ❑ Hallucinating ❑ Other: _____

5. Suicide/violence risk: ❑ None ❑ Ideation only ❑ Threat ❑ Gesture ❑ Rehearsal ❑ Attempt

6. Change in stressors: ❑ Same ❑ Less severe/fewer ❑ More/more severe ❑ Chronic stressors

7. Change in coping ability/skills: ❑ No change ❑ Improved ❑ Less able ❑ Much less able

8. Change in symptom severity: ❑ Same ❑ Less ❑ Much improved ❑ Resolved ❑ More severe ❑ Much worse

9. Other observations/evaluations: _____
   _____

Modes of interventions/treatments

❑ Support ❑ Clarification ❑ Education ❑ Exploration ❑ Problem solving ❑ Limit setting

❑ Socialization ❑ Orientation ❑ Reminiscence ❑ Reality testing ❑ Activity ❑ Confrontation

❑ Other: _____

Topics/themes/critical incidents

❑ Relationship(s) ❑ Work problems ❑ Alcohol/drug problems ❑ Parenting ❑ Abuse

❑ Childhood/fam. of origin ❑ Sexual ❑ Homework assignments ❑ Process ❑ Logistics/structure

❑ Other: _____

Further comments: _____

_____

This is a strictly confidential patient medical record. Redisclosure or transfer is expressly prohibited by law.

FORM 40. Structured progress note form for group therapy. From *The Paper Office*, p. 283. Copyright 1997 by Edward L. Zuckerman. Permission to photocopy this form is granted to purchasers of *The Paper Office* for personal use only (see copyright page for details).

Client-Generated Records

When clients take notes, or make drawings or flow charts of problems' causes and interactions, they bring additional cognitive resources to bear on their issues. These can be especially valuable activities; when accompanied by at-home review, they should be encouraged.

- Diaries of associations, dreams, and relationship interactions in dynamic therapies help the client to see connections. Similar records are called "client memoranda" in social work, and "diaries," "logs," and "frequency counts" in behavioral therapies.

- There are many kinds of affect and behavior checklists to help identify situations for clinical interventions. In rational–emotive therapy, the use of antecedent–behavior–consequence analyses will reinforce teaching in the session and build a pattern for approaching stressful situations.

- I have asked some patients to keep their notes in a three-ring binder, which they may call "The Book of My [or Our] Therapy" and use for many purposes. The binder can also house handouts; notes the patients have made from assigned readings; notes taken and questions raised during reviews of audiotapes of their therapy sessions; observations of their family members, friends, or television characters; self-study and journal writings; poetry and artwork; and many other items. When such materials are collected in one place, they are much more likely to be reviewed (and therefore to generate awareness and change) than if they are scattered in space and time.

- I have also encouraged patients to audiotape their sessions for themselves, telling them that many times things said in a session may be missed if they are only heard once (especially if there are difficult truths that require getting used to). Often, the patients are convinced when I tell them, "This way you get two sessions for the price of one." Some therapists are reluctant to offer this option because it creates some legal risks. A tape could, for example, show discrepancies between your actions and the treatment plan, which could be seen as incompetence on your part.

- There are guides for diary writing as therapy, usually called "journal keeping" (e.g., Baker, 1988).

6.3 Case Termination

If we can turn neurotic pain into normal misery we have done a lot.
—SIGMUND FREUD

A lack of clear goals may prevent both client and therapist from knowing whether therapy is finished. However, therapy should have a distinct ending even if its goals have not been accomplished. The absence of a message of closure is not only confusing to both parties, but can expose you legally. For example, if you agree to a client's decision for a premature termination or terminate a client for nonpayment of fees, it may be legally seen as negligent unless the client's welfare is protected. By far the most important point in terminations, regardless of reason, is the client's welfare. The American Psychological Association's code of ethics (APA, 1992a, Section 4.09) concerns the termination of professional relationships.

Reasons for Terminating or Transferring a Patient

First, **you simply cannot terminate a patient in crisis or at high risk.** On the other hand, you can terminate a patient for any of the following reasons:

- The patient has failed to pay fair and negotiated fees. Termination in such a case is often therapeutic as well.

- The patient is not cooperating with treatment. You must first try to work through the patient's resistance to treatment and document these efforts, but failure to follow an agreed-upon and appropriate treatment plan is very important.

- There are conflicts of interests, disruptive romantic thoughts, countertransference, or similar issues that you have not been able to resolve.

- The APA ethics code (APA, 1992a) says that you are ethically obligated to terminate when there has been little progress. (See "No-Improvement Terminations," below.)

- Although this is not explicit in the code, you should terminate and transfer when another, and incompatible, therapist or therapy appears to be in the patient's best interest. The patient may need services you cannot offer, such as medical interventions, inpatient care, or neuropsychological rehabilitation.

- Your own needs may require you to terminate the patient (e.g., you are leaving the area).

Termination issues are best dealt with early and continually in treatment. Remember that they are a major focus in the quite successful time-limited therapies. Be alert to your possible reluctance to terminate a successfully treated and functional patient who pays his or her bills reliably, is not difficult, and perhaps is pleasant to see. Being a responsible professional can be bittersweet.

How to Terminate Treatment in Different Situations

The options offered below are designed for five kinds of termination situations. The section on dealing with premature or early terminations is based upon ideas from the Philadelphia Society of Clinical Psychologists' Committee on Ethics (1988) and from Ewing (1990), whose discussion is brief and highly recommended. Kramer (1990) has written a thorough book on "bringing meaningful closure" to therapy.

Appropriate Terminations

When the therapy is finished and the termination is mutually agreed upon, document the following:

- The reasons for termination. (Ideally, the goals of therapy have been met and the client no longer needs your services.)

- The client's reactions.

- Any continuity-of-care needs.

- Any referrals.

- Any other unfinished details.

Although it's not necessary, you can send to each appropriately terminated patient, either 1 month after the end of treatment or 3, 6, or 12 months later, a follow-up note. If you do so, keep a copy. Some therapists may see such a note as purely self-promotional; you could, of course, deal with all these points in the final interview(s) instead of sending a note. It can be argued, however, that using the patient's paid time is more manipulative than using your (unpaid) time to construct the note. The note should include the following:

- Your hope that all is going well for the patient.

- A summary of treatment—progress, successes, high points, any unfinished work, or recommendations. You might include lessons learned if doing so does not seem too preachy; it all depends on the relationship.

- A statement that "The door is always open" for additional work or for "checkups" or "booster sessions." Indicate that the patient only has to call, and that you will be pleased to see him or her again (if this is true).

- A reminder that you are most pleased to accept referrals from former patients, as these are almost always appropriate and successful.

- Your best wishes.

This note is not the place to indicate any unpaid balances due to you or difficulties with insurance reimbursement.

Premature or Early Terminations

Premature or early terminations are ethically complex. When you feel the therapy is not finished but the patient declines to continue, the decision should be made jointly if at all possible. Handle termination therapeutically, working through the patient's issues; also, document these points, your efforts, and the outcomes.

Here are some suggestions for the last few therapy sessions (or, if the patient cannot be dissuaded, just the last visit):

- Do not argue or defend any perceived attack on your abilities.

- Assert your concern for the patient/family.

- Affirm the patient's right to choose to terminate.

- Express your regret, respect for the patient's decision, and acceptance (not agreement).

- Specify the factual bases for your recommendation to continue therapy at this point. Indicate why you think it may be harmful to stop now, and describe any negative consequences you foresee.

- Encourage the continuation of therapy. You can point out the "honeymoon" or "flight into health" effects and describe how they don't last.

- Offer to resume therapy at any time in the future.

- Offer your assistance in finding another therapist. Perhaps make a referral to an agency. When you do refer or transfer a patient to someone else, ethically you must make sure the professional to whom you are sending the patient is qualified (by training, credentials, experience, licensure status, etc.) or you could be vulnerable.

- Offer your services for emergencies in the interim before the patient finds a new therapist.

- Offer to send your records, with the patient's signed consent, to another therapist.

- Record all this in your notes.

- Send a note in a few days (after waiting to see whether the patient calls to continue, if he or she was uncertain about the decision), with the traditional three referral names and a restatement of some of the points above.

- If you think there is some risk involved in termination at this time, you may prefer to have the patient sign a release indicating that the termination is against your advice. This formality may also encourage the patient to reconsider. If the patient refuses to sign, note this too.

- If you feel the termination poses significant risk to the patient, take the preceding two actions *and* send the letter by certified mail, with an even stronger recommendation to continue treatment somewhere.

Necessary Terminations

In some cases, you may feel that the therapy is not finished, but you are discharging or transferring the client for one or more of the following reasons: Your own needs require it (e.g., you are leaving the area); the client requires services you are not competent to provide (e.g., medications, inpatient admission); financial noncooperation or limitations exist; or the relationship has deteriorated into counterproductivity. Perhaps you or the client have not been able to maintain a schedule or intensity of contacts that would support significant work and change, or the client has not performed or refused his or her responsibilities as specified in the agreed-to treatment plan and its revisions.

When any of these situations exists, one of your concerns is not being negligent. To assure that you are not, do the following:

- Give the client of the reasons for termination, and make a note of the fact that you have done this.

- Give reasonable notice of the end of treatment, and enter this into your notes as well.

- If the client fails to show for his or her last scheduled appointment, make at least one call or send one letter to discover the reasons for the no-show. Record these reasons or your attempts to terminate properly. Offer to meet at least once more to "look at where we were and where we are now," but not to "wrap things up," as this is an invitation to continue in therapy.

It is usually better to discuss the reasons for termination in person, but a call or letter may be your only possibility. Even when there is a face-to-face discussion, it is best to send a letter as well. Keep a copy. A "discharged from treatment" letter can include any of the points above, as well as a number of the following suggestions:

- Indicate that the purpose of the letter is to confirm your final conversations, if you had such.

- Express your regret at the ending of an important relationship.

- List some of the successes and high points, if possible.

- Give the client your reasons for discharging him or her.

- Recommend continuance of therapy, if clinically appropriate: "Since your condition requires treatment . . . " or "I believe you can benefit from continued treatment." Encourage the client to seek services without delay (Simon, 1992).

- Offer recommendations for treatment by someone else. Giving three referral names is traditional but not essential. You have an ethical obligation to know that these care providers are competent to help the client. It may be appropriate to say that you will make a suitable referral if one is desired.

- Indicate that when written consent has been given for doing so, you will send your records or a summary of their treatment to another therapist with whom the client enters treatment.

- Indicate your availability during a specific transitional period. This not only is clinically and ethically appropriate, but will protect you from a charge of abandonment. You can say, "Because your condition requires treatment (or monitoring or follow up) I will continue to be available to you for clinical services until you enter the care of another therapist. You must make such arrangements immediately, because I will only provide care for a period of _____ (1 week, 1 month, etc)." More current opinion suggests that to be safe, you should continue to be available. "Only when another licensed professional has accepted the patient (and vice versa) does the original therapist's responsibility end" (Meyer et al., 1988, p. 50).

- Indicate that the client should now consider "our" treatment over, and that you are not, in any continuing sense, the client's therapist.

- Remind the client that any balance due must be paid. Enclosing the bill makes this clearest, but sending it separately serves to separate the two issues if you want to.

- Offer your "best wishes"—the generic, can't-be-misread closing.

You should make an appropriate effort to follow up with the client, to ensure that you have done all you could to make a transfer go smoothly and cause no harm to the client.

No-Improvement Terminations

When there has been little or no improvement despite appropriate treatment, you must terminate (see APA, 1992a, Section 4.09(b)). After you have done your best, including having reevaluated, reconsidered, and made extra efforts to get things moving forward again, you should do the following:

- Consult a colleague. Be sure, though, that you have honestly prepared the case, recognized and dealt with your ego involvements, and can listen openly. Document this consultation. Modify treatment as suggested by the consultation.

- Try a different approach, with the client's permission.

- If there is still no improvement, you *must* terminate and refer. You must also terminate when the client is being harmed by the relationship, such as in irresolvable transference issues.

- Send a "discharged from treatment" letter as described above.

Reluctant Terminators

When you feel that a client is ready to terminate but the client is apprehensive or resistant, you can encourage termination. If you have discussed progress and options as you went along in therapy, then your pushing for termination will not come as a surprise. Depending on the length and qualities of the therapy, this may take several sessions. Consider the process of termination very carefully and make a plan.

- Expect emotional reactions (relapses, development of "new problems needing immediate treatment," "wanting to be friends/business partners," etc.) and process them. See Section 3.7 on dual relationships.

- Clearly indicate the reasons for termination, so that it cannot be seen as a result of the client's deficiencies. Say that termination is for the client's long-term good, that it is necessary because of managed care requirements, or whatever the truths are.

- When it is appropriate to do so, offer the client the names of up to three other therapists if he or she wishes to continue therapy.

6.4 The Case Closing Summary

It is best to set aside 15 minutes after the last session with a client, to compose a summary while the case is still fresh in your mind. You might try dictating a summary using the headings below, and not having it typed unless you need it, in order to save some costs. A complete narrative on each patient at the end of treatment is better. But just reviewing your notes and adding to them at the end, in the form of a summary, will be valuable.

Outline for Dictation

The following outline assumes that you have *not* been using the forms provided in this book.

A. Client information.

   1. Client's name and some other basic information (e.g., date of birth, Social Security number).

   2. Referral source and reason.

   3. Dates of initial and final contacts, consultations, hospitalizations, referrals.

   4. Presenting problems (e.g., problem list) and severity ratings; levels of functioning.

B. Treatments.

   1. Planned treatments.

   2. Services you actually provided; perhaps a sentence or paragraph about each session by date, specifying:

      a. Problems presented/addressed, homework.

      b. Relationship qualities.

      c. Process, motivations.

C. Narrative summary of therapy including critical incidents, unresolved problems.

D. Status of each problem at discharge/termination and severity ratings; levels of functioning.

E. Information about termination.

   1. Reasons/rationale for termination.

   2. Was treatment prematurely discontinued? (If yes, indicate why.)

   3. Originator of the decision to terminate.

   4. Recommendations and suggestions of continuing care, if any.

   5. Did the patient accept your recommendations at discharge?

F. Optional: Lessons you have learned.

A Termination Summary Form

FORM 41   Form 41 is quite different from but based on a form in Piercy et al. (1989) called "Family Termination Summary," by Larry Constantine, LCSW.

Termination Summary

Client: _____ Date: _____

Therapist(s) signature(s): _____ _____

A. Main reason for termination

❑ The planned treatment was completed. ❑ The client refused to receive or participate in services.

❑ The client was unable to afford continued treatment or did not pay bills on time.

❑ There was little or no progress in treatment. ❑ This is a planned pause in treatment.

❑ The client needs services not available here, and so was referred to: _____

B. Source of termination decision

The decision to terminate was: ❑ Client initiated ❑ Therapist-initiated ❑ A mutual decision

❑ Other (specify): _____

C. Treatment sessions

Referred on date: _____ Date of first contact: _____ Date of last session: _____

Number of sessions: Received: _____ Cancelled: _____ Did not show: _____ Other: _____ Total: _____

D. Kinds of services rendered

❑ Individual psychotherapy, for _____ sessions ❑ Couple/family therapy, for _____ sessions

❑ Group therapy, for _____ sessions ❑ Other: _____

E. Treatment goals and outcomes (code outcomes as follows: N = no change, S = some or slight [about 25% to 35%], M = moderate [about 50%], V = very good [about 75% to 100%], E = exceeded expectation)

Goal	Goal achievement*

Other notable aspects of treatment outcome, change, or progress: _____

_____

_____

This is a strictly confidential patient medical record. Redisclosure or transfer is expressly prohibited by law.

CHAPTER 7

Confidentiality and Releasing Records

7.1 Understanding Confidentiality

Over the course of Chapters 5 and 6, we have considered what client records need to be created from the first contact to the ending of therapy. Now one important issue remains concerning the maintenance of this paperwork: confidentiality.

Confidentiality seems to be crucial for meaningful psychotherapy, and its actual practice is complex. Rubanowitz (1987) found that 80% of patients believe that all information (including financial data for insurers) is confidential. Since this is not true, you must explain what is confidential and what will be released. Yet Baird and Rupert (1987) found that about half of the psychologists they surveyed either said nothing to patients about confidentiality or indicated that everything is confidential—neither of which is realistic. Later studies have confirmed this pattern, although more therapists now discuss confidentiality and get a form signed. The methods of obtaining informed consent in Chapter 4 include detailed explanations of this issue. Because confidentiality is an almost universal concern, you have the responsibility to discuss it, and especially its limits, with every patient.

Basic Definitions

"Confidentiality" is related to the concepts of "privacy" and "privileged communication." It can be seen as lying between the other two concepts in terms of narrowness.

Privacy is frequently considered a basic right granted, by implication, through the Fourth and Ninth Amendments and other sections of the U.S. Constitution. It is understood as the right of an individual to decide how many of his or her thoughts, feelings, or other personal data will be shared with others (Keith-Spiegel & Koocher, 1985, p. 56). This right protects attitudes, beliefs, behaviors, and opinions. The individual can decide to divulge or to withhold, can decide when, how, and under what circumstances to share information; and can do so with regard to which particular others.

Confidentiality is a concept that exists within many professions. "Confidentiality is an ethical concept that prohibits the physician from discussing his patient with anyone except under compelling legal circumstances" (Sadoff, 1988, p. 41). In all states it has legal recognition, but it is not primarily a legal concept. It is an ethic based on a recognition of the sensitive nature of some of the information we therapists collect and record (Wilson, 1980), and on respect of the client's right to privacy.

Privileged communication (or just privilege) is a legal term for a right that belongs to the client, not to the therapist. However, it can be asserted by the therapist to protect the client (as when the therapist's does not want to release the client's records) until the issues are discussed with a client and the client then asserts the privilege. It is granted by state rather than federal laws and by state as well as federal court decisions (*Jaffee v. Redmond et al.*). It restricts a clinician or other person from disclosing, in an open court or in other legal proceedings, information that was given with assumed confidentiality. The restriction can apply to spouses, attorneys, priests, and physicians, as well as to many psychotherapists. The legal bases for privileged communication are extensions of the state statutes concerning attorney–client privilege, which vary from state to state.

In summary, **all privileged communications are confidential, but not all confidential communications are necessarily privileged.** A Venn diagram would show three concentric circles—the largest being privacy, the middle confidentiality, and the smallest, privilege.

The rules protecting confidentiality are confused, confusing, and ambiguous, because they may vary depending on the following circumstances:

- The topics communicated. The abuse of children, and serious threats of harm, are generally not protected; sexual affairs, actions that ended a long time ago, or actions that were situation-specific are generally protected.

- The legal status of those present. Some of these are protected in different situations: spouse, boyfriend or girlfriend, public employee, child, employee, and cotherapist.

- Your credentials, discipline, and licensure. For example, Massachusetts law denies privilege to non-doctoral level-psychologists.

- The state in which you practice. Credentialing laws, case law, legislation, regulations, and legal climate vary with jurisdiction.

- Whether you are doing individual, couple, marital, family, or group therapy.

- A judge's discretion, evolving case law, and court decisions.

- Whether civil or criminal actions will be involved.

- Whether the legal actions are in federal or state courts.

- Other factors unknown at present.

Exceptions to Confidentiality

The common exceptions to the rules of confidentiality, according to Stromberg et al. (1988, p. 371 ff.) and Keith-Spiegel and Koocher (1985, p. 59 ff.), are as follows:

1. **When a patient requests his or her own records.** The law about this may vary from state to state. The main issues are (a) whether the patient would be harmed through too full a disclosure, and (b) the patient's inability to understand the record's wording or ideas. The options include providing a summary rather than the full records, or disclosure to a third party (a mental health professional) agreed upon by the patient and the therapist. Most authorities believe that the therapist should review the records' contents with the patient, explaining and answering questions, and that this will result in increased trust and prevent the misuse of the information. Patient "requests often reflect clinical issues, such as patients wondering 'What is wrong with me?' or, 'What does my therapist think of me?' Usually it is sufficient to deal with these issues directly within psychotherapy without having to show patients their records" (Knapp et al., 1994, p. 19).

2. **The patient may also consent to the release of records.** To truly consent, the patient must have been fully informed of all aspects of what is to be released. This is discussed in Chapter 4, and the client's understanding can be documented by a highly specific release form, such as Form 42 or 43. Problems may arise if the client does not know all of what is in a record. If you suspect that anything you are asked for should not be released, discuss the situation with the client. If the client agrees, he or she can revoke the release and sign a revised version.

   If the request is from a lawyer (e.g., it is a subpoena) and appears inappropriately broad, you can write a letter to both parties (the defense and the prosecution) saying that you need a more specific release or a court order, and let them decide what to do. If you or your clients are involved in a dispute and you are not comfortable with a subpoena you receive, seek a court ruling on the limits of what to disclose. You can ask the court to decide and can discuss it with the judge.

3. **Certain laws require disclosure.** Child abuse or neglect, suspected or proven, is the most common situation legally requiring disclosure. Because you may come to know of child abuse or neglect, you must know exactly what your state law requires of your profession, because you must act immediately (often within 24 hours). Delay or failure is punishable. Similarly, abuse of an elder or handicapped person may require disclosure when a client reports it. As to what to reveal and to whom, the law indicates specifically to whom you must report and what you must tell. You must know your local laws on each of these issues, or you place yourself at real risk. You can usually call the local protective agency and discuss a "hypothetical" case for advice. Many statutes also include a "good-faith" immunity to protect you if a report is harmful or in error.

Laws differ, but these requirements on reporting abuse seem typical:

a. You usually must have seen an allegedly abused child, but many states require you to make a disclosure if you have reason to trust an adult client's report of his or her abusive behaviors. Even where you are not legally required to report this abuse (because the perpetrator, not the child, is your patient), you may have the ethical duty to make a report in order to protect the child or to prevent violence.

b. Even professional students and your assistants may be required to make such reports.

c. Proof of abuse is not needed to make a report; generally, you have no discretion about investigating or do not need to investigate. This is a sticking point for many therapists, because they would prefer to make a decision in what they see as the best interests of the child or family, and do not trust an agency to make good decisions. In the area of child abuse, Taube and Elwork (1990) found that disclosing the mandatory reporting issue to patients led to fewer self-reports of child neglect and punishment behaviors by caregiver clients. Similarly, the legal obligation for psychiatrists to report child sexual abuse in Maryland was counterproductive: The number of self-referrals for child abuse and the self-disclosure rate during therapy both went to zero, and the number of children identified as abused did not increase (Berlin et al., 1991). It appears that we mental health professionals have failed to make our need for options clear to our legislators.

d. You generally must report even abuse that occurred some time ago, if the victim is still under 18 and thus is considered vulnerable.

Some states, such as Pennsylvania, require you to report impaired drivers as well. These may include drivers with epilepsy, hallucinations, disorientation, homicidal tendencies, or a history of accidents or "near-misses" (Knapp & VandeCreek, 1990, p. 62).

4. **When the patient is a litigant and sues you.** Privilege cannot be used as "both a shield and a sword." That is, the client cannot waive privilege and have only some facts supportive of his or her case opened to view (the sword), while protecting himself or herself from the import of other facts (the shield). Once privilege is waived, it is generally waived completely. These situations are, however, negotiated between lawyers and the court, and some material can be excluded if it is of no relevance and is potentially damaging to the client. However, if you have been formally accused of malpractice, you may generally reveal *only* the information necessary to defend yourself—not everything you were told or recorded or received as records from others.

In regard to lawsuits or ethics complaints, be careful about what you reveal to whom. It is natural to want to complain to or seek support from friends, colleagues, or a trusted supervisor. But these are *not* privileged conversations, and these people can be subpoenaed to testify about what you told them. Similarly, although ethics complaints to professional organizations and licensing boards are evaluated in confidence, the information revealed is also not privileged. The amount of material revealed depends on the attorneys and investigators and on the local procedures.

5. **When therapy or evaluations are court-ordered.** In this situation, the results of your evaluation or records of your therapy will be sent to both sides, so you must fully inform the client of this before you perform these services. It would be a good idea to make a note that you have informed the client that anything he or she says during an evaluation may be included in your report (American Psychiatric Association, 1987a). Interestingly, examinations done at the request of a client's attorney may be protected by attorney–client privilege, and so may be suppressed if they are unfavorable to the client.

6. **Any legal proceeding where a client's mental status could be an issue.** Lawsuits over head injuries, custody battles, adoptions, or disability claims can bring the records you created into court. This can include allegations of emotional pain and suffering or having been involuntarily psychiatrically hospitalized.

7. **Other legal proceedings may also require disclosure.** For example, your testimony may be required by a judge.

8. **Parents have rights to information about the diagnosis and treatment of their minor children.**

9. **If your client seriously threatens an identifiable person or persons.** This is future criminal behavior, and you have the "duty to warn or protect" (see Section 3.9 for clarification of this). Note that except in South Dakota, therapists are not required to report past criminal behavior if it is not ongoing.

10. **You must disclose in emergencies.** For example, when a "patient's health is seriously or imminently at stake" (Stromberg et al., 1988, p. 400). Keep the information disclosed to a minimum—that is, what a competent patient would agree would be necessary. In an emergency, a patient's oral consent to disclose is acceptable, but the details should be carefully documented. If the patient is unable (not unwilling) to provide the information or to consent, break confidentiality only if withholding it would endanger the patient and if the local law permits or does not forbid such disclosure.

11. **Nonlicensed therapists do not have privilege.** This includes intern psychologists, most "counselors," and those in training whom you may supervise. In general, students (including psychology interns, trainees, or supervisees) are not specifically covered by statutes granting privilege (Keith-Spiegel & Koocher, 1985, p. 59).

Other Points about Confidentiality and Its Limitations

To obtain reimbursement with Medicare and Medicaid clients, providers are required to disclose more than basic identifying data. Managed care reviewers ask for lots of clinical information. It even appears that workers' compensation insurers routinely expect release of *all* records you create; this may be quite problematic when a client's employer is self-insured, and so the company's benefits staff can see records and may have few safeguards for maintaining their confidentiality. Clients need to know what will be revealed before they use their insurance, and they usually expect to use it from the beginning. Therefore you must inform them of this at the start of treatment. The client information brochure (see Section 4.2) covers this, as does Handout 3.

The sharing of information among members of a treatment team or care providers within an agency is generally acceptable without a release when the client has consented to treatment that he or she understands to involve several persons or departments within the agency (American Psychiatric Association, 1987a). Again, it would be best to include this point in the efforts you make to inform the client. Be especially careful about nonclinical personnel's access to agency records.

When you talk to a consultant about a client, do not add details that might enable the consultant to identify the client (American Psychological Association, 1992a, Section 5.06). This is especially important if the consultant may know the client personally or by reputation, or if a case involves sensitive disorders (e.g., child or drug abuse, sexual difficulties). The consultant rarely needs such knowledge, it cannot be unlearned; and it becomes a burden to the other that he or she does not need to carry. The courts call this "guilty knowledge."

Unless it is very sensitive, you do not need specific permission to share information with a consultant whom the client has approved and from whom you are seeking professional advice. If you want to be careful—perhaps because you do not know the contents of what will be revealed—you might get a consent signed at the first meeting with the client, or document the absence of consent. This does not cover informally discussing a case with several peers, and this kind of consultation is not usually confidential. It is best to share clinical information only when doing so benefits the client, or else you are on thin ice.

In most states, the fact that a person is a client is itself not privileged information (although you should certainly treat it as confidential). Similarly, the dates and number of appointments, as well as billing information, are accessible to the courts (Knapp & VandeCreek, 1990). Moreover, communications, reports, and observations made for purposes other than treatment are not covered by privilege; these include communications for employment or insurance purposes (American Psychiatric Association, 1987a).

Turning a case over to a collection agency or going to small-claims court is not a breach of confidentiality if the client is notified that it may occur. This notification is best included in your client information brochure. However, the information shared with the court should be minimal, given simply to establish the debt's legitimacy (client's identity, dates of service, fees).

Confidentiality rules apply even after the death of the client involved. The privilege passes to the executor or legal representative of the client.

Finally, claims of "that's confidential" cannot be used to protect the therapist, only the client. Such claims cannot be used to conceal harmful practices, protect the autonomy of the therapist, avoid the scrutiny of peers, or defend a need to be "right" (Sweet, 1990, p. 7).

Confidentiality and Children

With a competent adult, the person seeking services and the recipient of those services are the same; however, when the recipient of assessment or treatment services is a child, there are two "clients." In this situation, to whom does the therapist owe the duty of confidentiality? Even when the ethical duty is to the child, the legal duty may be to the parents. The best resolution can be found by looking for the local answers to the following questions suggested by Morris (1993, p. 11):

1. Is a child in psychotherapy accorded legally-protected privileged communication in your state?

2. If yes, what are the exceptions to privileged communications for a child in your state?

3. Is there a common usage lower age limit for children legally granting them privileged communication?

4. Is there legal precedent in your state that has tested the constitutionality of the privileged communication granted to children and adolescents?

The therapist should, of course, inform the child of all the limitations of confidentiality. For example, the child should be told that the therapist will be discussing the contents of each interview (in general ways) with his or her parents, and that nothing can be kept secret. If the therapist will be consulting with school or hospital personnel, the child should be told that as well. Morris (1993) recommends putting these points in writing and obtaining the dated signatures of parents and child. Obviously, the wording of both oral and written statements must suit the child's understanding and reading levels. (See Form 10 of this book for a written statement suitable for an older child or an adolescent.) In general, the approach to an older or "emancipated" adolescent is like that to an adult.

Parental access to information and records varies a great deal. State laws usually do not address this issue, but logic suggests that if you need parental consent to provide treatment, the parents have the right to access the records of that treatment, and vice versa. The most common exceptions to the need for parental consent to treatment are emergencies and cases in which minors have graduated from high school or are married. You could try to discuss the issues of confidentiality in the first session with both adolescent and parent present. Goldberg (1995) suggests, at least, reassuring the parents that you will inform them if their child is in imminent danger.

Confidentiality and HIV-Positive Clients

There are many benefits of confidentiality for HIV-positive clients (including reduced risk of discrimination), but these must be weighed against its possible social costs (such as the infection of third parties). The American Psychological Association's (APA) position as of July 1992 is that no legal duty should be imposed. If it is, however, disclosure should be permitted only "when (a) the provider knows an identifiable third party who the provider has compelling reason to believe is at significant risk of infection; (b) the provider has reasonable belief that the third party has no reason to suspect that he or she is at risk; and (c) the client/patient has been urged to inform the third party, and has either refused or is considered unreliable in his/her willingness to notify the third party" (Fox, 1992, p. 912). Fox goes on to suggest respect for local laws and encouraging (through therapy, teaching, consulting, or referring) HIV-infected persons to reduce the risk of further infection. Some states, such as Pennsylvania, have passed laws specifically prohibiting the warning of potential victims.

A Handout on the Limits of Confidentiality

HANDOUT 8

Issues concerning confidentiality have been incorporated into the client information brochure (see Section 4.2), because the APA ethics code (APA, 1992a, Section 5.01) requires a discussion of confidentiality's limits before therapy begins. The same section requires discussion of limits as new circumstances warrant it. If and when you believe your clients need more specific information, the handout offered below (Handout 8) covers confidentiality issues in greater detail than does the brochure. I recommend offering this handout only to those who raise concerns after reading the more general brochure, or to those whose referral (e.g., by the courts) or history suggests its need. The issues can then be discussed in a a therapy session. Another way to use it is to make it available with other client education materials in a three-ring binder in your waiting room, perhaps entitled "For Your Information."

Like the other forms in this book, Handout 8 can be photocopied and distributed to your clients. It has been written to be generic enough to be applicable to most practices, and addresses issues relevant to adult, child, and family therapy. However, it does not fully address the issue of secrets between spouses in marital therapy. See Margolin (1982) for a discussion of this thorny topic.

Before using this handout, check on alterations you may need to make because of your locality, your profession, or your preferred methods of practice:

- If you treat older children, you might consider amplifying what is said here about what you have to reveal to parents or guardians.

- Weigh what you have to reveal to third-party payers with whom you have contracts in your state. Handout 3 is a more specific informed consent handout for managed care patients. In addition, review the current rules on releasing records of Medicare patients.

- If you do group therapy, consider its confidentiality limitations. (See Form 11.)

- Adapt section 1d to your state's rules about the basis for reporting abuse. States differ in requiring a "suspicion" standard or a "belief" standard. The suspicion standard requires a lower level of certainty to trigger the mandated reporting requirement. Also, states differ in their definitions of elder abuse. Usually elder abuse is defined more broadly than child abuse and includes financial exploitation (Sam Knapp, personal communication, October 2, 1996).

- Section 3a states that anyone you seek consultation from is "required by professional ethics to keep your information confidential." This is an ethical but not perhaps a legal requirement; you, the person seeking consultation, are not the consultant's client.

- Adapt section 3b to your state's rules and preferred practices. This section says, "You have a right to review these records with me"; however, reading them with you may not be possible or may be too costly. The exact means of a client's access to his or her records varies with states and regulations. Sending actual copies allows for misinterpretation and risks revelations to other parties. Sending them to another mental health professional for interpretation may be safest.

- Section 4b says, "I usually give you my bill. . . . " This may not be your policy, so adapt the wording.

- You could expand the policy stated in sections 5d and 5e on your becoming a witness in custody or divorce proceedings. Incorporate some possible alternatives:

  "I will not serve as a witness or provide records for such matters, and I ask you to agree that if such a situation arises, you will accept my policy. If you go to court, you will have to ask another professional to do any evaluations of yourselves, your children, and your relationship."

  "I ask you to agree that my records will not be requested in court by either party, and to keep this in mind during our therapy."

  "I will provide a summary, but not the actual records, to the court. My charge for this summary is $100 per hour of preparation time."

  "I am willing to testify for either party. My fee, which must be paid in advance is $1,000 per day."

- Section 5f covers the question of which family members sign a release-of-records form. The safest method of release for a family's or couple's records is to require the consent of all adults or participants, although this is also the most complex solution.

The general rule is this: **Make certain that the client is informed about all aspects of confidentiality.** A handout like Handout 8, and your detailed notes, should show that you have told the client what he or she needs to know to act in his or her own best interest.

What You Should Know about Confidentiality in Therapy

I will treat what you tell me with great care. My professional ethics (that is, my profession's rules about moral matters) and the laws of this state prevent me from telling anyone else what you tell me unless you give me written permission. These rules and laws are the ways our society recognizes and supports the privacy of what we talk about—in other words, the "confidentiality" of therapy. But I cannot promise that everything you tell me will *never* be revealed to someone else. There are some times when the law requires me to tell things to others. There are also some other limits on our confidentiality. We need to discuss these, because I want you to understand clearly what I can and cannot keep confidential. You need to know about these rules now, so that you don't tell me something as a "secret" that I cannot keep secret. These are very important issues, so please read these pages carefully and keep this copy. At our next meeting, we can discuss any questions you might have.

1. **When you or other persons are in physical danger,** the law requires me to tell others about it. Specifically:

    a. If I come to believe that you are threatening serious harm to another person, I am required to try to protect that person. I may have to tell the person and the police, or perhaps try to have you put in a hospital.

    b. If you seriously threaten or act in a way that is very likely to harm yourself, I may have to seek a hospital for you, or to call on your family members or others who can help protect you. If such a situation does come up, I will fully discuss the situation with you before I do anything, unless there is a very strong reason not to.

    c. In an emergency where your life or health is in danger, and I cannot get your consent, I may give another professional some information to protect your life. I will try to get your permission first, and I will discuss this with you as soon as possible afterwards.

    d. If I believe or suspect that you are abusing a child, an elderly person, or a disabled person I must file a report with a state agency. To "abuse" means to neglect, hurt, or sexually molest another person. I do not have any legal power to investigate the situation to find out all the facts. The state agency will investigate. If this might be your situation, we should discuss the legal aspects in detail before you tell me anything about these topics. You may also want to talk to your lawyer.

    In any of these situations, I would reveal only the information that is needed to protect you or the other person. I would not tell everything you have told me.

2. In general, **if you become involved in a court case or proceeding,** you can prevent me from testifying in court about what you have told me. This is called "privilege," and it is your choice to prevent me from testifying or to allow me to do so. However, there are some situations where a judge or court may require me to testify:

    a. In child custody or adoption proceedings, where your fitness as a parent is questioned or in doubt.

(cont.)

HANDOUT 8. Patient handout on the limits of confidentiality (p. 1 of 3). From *The Paper Office*, pp. 301–303.

b. In cases where your emotional or mental condition is important information for a court's decision.
c. During a malpractice case or an investigation of me or another therapist by a professional group.
d. In a civil commitment hearing to decide if you will be admitted to a psychiatric hospital.
e. When you are seeing me for court-ordered evaluations or treatment. In this case we need to discuss confidentiality fully, because you don't have to tell me what you don't want the court to find out through my report.

3. There are a few other things you must know about confidentiality and your treatment:
   a. I may sometimes consult (talk) with another professional about your treatment. This other person is also required by professional ethics to keep your information confidential. Likewise, when I am out of town or unavailable, another therapist will be available to help my clients. I must give him or her some information about my clients, like you.
   b. I am required to keep records of your treatment, such as the notes I take when we meet. You have a right to review these records with me. If something in the record might seriously upset you, I may leave it out, but I will fully explain my reasons to you.

4. Here is what you need to know about confidentiality **in regard to insurance and money matters:**
   a. If you use your health insurance to pay a part of my fees, insurance companies require some information about our therapy. Insurers such as Blue Cross/Blue Shield or other companies usually want only your diagnosis, my fee, the dates we met, and sometimes a treatment plan. Managed care organizations, however, ask for much more information about you and your symptoms, as well as a detailed treatment plan.
   b. I usually give you my bill with any other forms needed, and ask you to send these to your insurance company to file a claim for your benefits. That way, you can see what the company will know about our therapy. It is against the law for insurers to release information about our office visits to anyone without your written permission. Although I believe the insurance company will act morally and legally, I cannot control who sees this information at the insurer's office. You cannot be required to release more information just to get payments.
   c. If you have been sent to me by your employer or your employer's Employee Assistance Program, either one may require some information. Again, I believe that employers and companies will act morally and legally, but I cannot control who sees this information at their offices. If this is your situation, let us fully discuss my agreement with your employer or the program before we talk further.
   d. If your account with me is unpaid and we have not arranged a payment plan, I can use legal means to get paid. The only information I will give to the court, a collection agency, or a lawyer will be your name and address, the dates we met for professional services, and the amount due to me.

5. **Children and families create some special confidentiality questions.**
   a. When I treat children under the age of about 12, I must tell their parents or guardians whatever they ask me. As children grow more able to understand and choose, they assume legal rights. For those between the ages of 12 and 18, most of the details in things they tell me will be treated as confidential. However, parents or guardians do have the right to *general* information, including how therapy is going. They need to be able to make well-informed decisions about therapy. I may also have to tell parents or guardians some

(cont.)

information about other family members that I am told. This is especially true if these others' actions put them or others in any danger.

b. In cases where I treat several members of a family (parents and children or other relatives), the confidentiality situation can become very complicated. I may have different duties toward different family members. At the start of our treatment, we must all have a clear understanding of our purposes and my role. Then we can be clear about any limits on confidentiality that may exist.

c. If you tell me something your spouse does not know, and not knowing this could harm him or her, I cannot promise to keep it confidential. I will work with you to decide on the best long-term way to handle situations like this.

d. If you and your spouse have a custody dispute, or a court custody hearing is coming up, I will need to know about it. My professional ethics prevent me from doing both therapy and custody evaluations.

e. If you are seeing me for marriage counseling, you must agree at the start of treatment that if you eventually decide to divorce, you will not request my testimony for either side. The court, however, may order me to testify.

f. At the start of family treatment, we must also specify which members of the family must sign a release form for the common record I create in the therapy or therapies. (See point 7b, below.)

6. **Confidentiality in group therapy is also a special situation.**

In group therapy, the other members of the group are not therapists. They do not have the same ethics and laws that I have to work under. You cannot be certain that they will always keep what you say in the group confidential.

7. Finally, here are a few other points:

a. I will not record our therapy sessions on audiotape or videotape without your written permission.

b. If you want me to send information about our therapy to someone else, you must sign a "release-of-records" form. I have copies which you can see so you will know what is involved.

c. Any information that you also share outside of therapy, willingly and publicly, will not be considered protected or confidential by a court.

The laws and rules on confidentiality are complicated. Situations that are not mentioned here come up only rarely in my practice. Please bear in mind that I am not able to give you legal advice. If you have special or unusual concerns, and so need special advice, I strongly suggest that you talk to a lawyer to protect your interests legally.

The signatures here show that we each have read, discussed, understand, and agree to abide by the points presented above.

_____   _____
Signature of client (or person acting for client)   Date

_____
Printed name

_____   _____
Signature of therapist   Date

7.2   Maintaining Confidentiality

Guidelines for Maintaining Confidentiality

- Encourage clients to ask questions about confidentiality concerns when they arise in therapy, and to resolve them before they make any risky revelations. When answering questions, be careful to promise very little specific protection; you cannot know how confidential you can keep a client's specific situation until you are told, and then it may be too late. Clients have rarely formulated their situations within the ethical or legal frameworks you are bound to live by.

- Many clinicians worry that disclosing the limits of confidentiality will inhibit the freedom of discussion necessary for effective therapy. Nowell and Spruill (1993), surveying rather naive college students, found that disclosing exceptions to total confidentiality did result in some inhibition of self-disclosure. However, they also found that offering a complete description of the limitations did not result in more inhibition than a brief, cursory description, which is now seen as essential. Principle 6 of the APA ethics code (APA, 1992a) requires that the limits of confidentiality be communicated explicitly and in advance. The client information brochure (see Section 4.2) incorporates these kinds of notifications.

- If in doubt, consult. By itself, making this effort offers you some malpractice protection and you may learn how to protect your client.

- Avoid giving legal advice on confidentiality, and refer complex questions to the client's attorney.

- Do not gossip or otherwise talk lightly or casually about your patients. Famous patients, fascinating clinical phenomena, bragging, making the irresistible joke—all these are tempting conversational topics. We may try to gain points for ourselves at the expense of our patients, trusting that no one will figure out their identity or use the information. The best rule is *never* to discuss your patients or your work with your spouse, friends, or even other therapists, but only with a consultant or in a carefully prepared presentation. With such a rule, you won't have to keep deciding what to reveal, or feel the anxiety of uncertainty.

- Leave nothing with a client's name on it lying around anywhere—no folders, no letters, no phone notes, no unusable photocopies. Arrange your office and office procedures to prevent the viewing of charts, appointment books, telephone messages, and the like by clients, salespersons, cleaning people, visitors, and other staff members. Lock your door, desk, and cabinet when you are out of the office. If you share an office, each therapist will need a locked record storage area.

- To be safest, develop a rule of never using a client's name in any conversation with anyone outside your consulting room. Never discuss clients, even for consultation or supervision, in any place (whether public or professional) where anyone not bound by your professional code could *possibly* overhear. Certainly do not do so in an elevator or taxi. Make the time for consultation and do it right. Words cannot be unsaid, and lawsuits are depressing.

- Train all members of your staff in all aspects of the maintenance of confidentiality. Make it clear to your staff that client information must not be casually or carelessly discussed (over lunch, in rest rooms, in elevators, etc.), including in the office. If other staff members, employees, or even other clinicians bound by confidentiality are present when you need to communicate, write the client's name down and point to it for your conversation. Similarly, do not allow your staff or office mates to refer to clients who phone or otherwise come up in conversation, except as "this client" or "he" or "she." Finally, make clear your intention to dismiss immediately anyone who breaks any of the rules of the office.

- In some cases, just revealing information in the presence of a third party (such as another therapist, an uninvolved professional, or perhaps even an employee) may void the legal protection of confidentiality. This also applies to your clients, so discourage them from saying private things when others are around. In any situation in which someone other than the patient and therapist is present during the session, determine whether these two essential conditions have been met.

    1. Did the patient intend the session to be confidential? The answer to this question often lies in the original reason for the session. If the patient has a regular, long-term relationship with the therapist (e.g., is being treated for a disorder), then the reason for the sessions are solely for the patient's private benefit, and clearly are intended to be confidential. However, many people contact psychologists in connection with some particular legal rather than psychological problem. Perhaps they are in the process of or contemplating divorce, are being evaluated as parents for custody or adoption purposes, have been raped and are pressing charges, or are fulfilling a condition of probation, and so forth. In these cases, the courts are likely to find that the patient intended immediately or in the future to disclose the fact that he or she was undergoing treatment, in which case there is no evidentiary privilege.

    2. Was the session in fact confidential? There is no privilege if the FBI is lawfully wiretapping the session, or an undercover police officer is actually present in the room. There is also no privilege if the patient tells other people about the session, because that, too, means it is no longer actually confidential.

- Be careful when you replay the answering machine, so that no one else can overhear. Instruct your staff to do the same.

- Assure yourself that your answering service also understands these rules and obeys them. Ask about the staff's training, offer some hypothetical situations, and perhaps call as someone else to test the service.

- Do not use a client's name in the waiting room unless you and the client are alone. It may seem odd, but you can just make eye contact and say, "Won't you please come in?" without mentioning the client's name. If it is a first appointment, saying "I'm Dr. Doe. Are you here to see me?" will serve the same purpose in a busy waiting area. If the office is used by professionals of other disciplines, such as dentists, they are likely to use clients' names freely; do not be swayed.

- *Never* discuss any kind of confidential matter on a portable or cellular phone. Be aware that they are broadcasting devices and do not have the same protections (legal or technical) for confidentiality that wired phones do.

- Make sure you have sufficient sound muffling in your office. You can achieve this with white-noise generators, an air deflector in the air conditioning ductwork, double-studded and double-wallboarded walls, a radio with several speakers (set fairly loud and not under the control of the clients in the waiting room), and heavy weather-stripped or carpeted soundproofed doors.

- Even if a client's spouse is in therapy with the client, it is not appropriate to discuss the client's treatment in detail with the spouse. The law is frequently silent on the issue of the privileged status of what is said to spouses in marriage counseling, or to a therapist's assistants, staff, and employees, so you may not have protection. Court-ordered marriage counseling may be an exception to confidentiality, but check your local rules.

- Make explicit in your client information brochure how you will handle the confidentiality issues of family therapy.

- Keep separate sets of group therapy records. That is, keep a record for each individual in which other members are not identified, and a separate record for the group as a whole. See Form 11, the group therapy contract.

- Develop a clear plan to dispose of your records without breaking confidentiality. See Section 1.6.

Creating Confidential Records

There are three methods of increasing the likelihood of confidentiality of your records:

1. Always abridge as much as possible. This means limiting the client information collected, recorded, retained, and reported. Do not put information of a sensitive nature into a report if it is not *clearly* necessary to the purposes of a report. Simple as this rule is, it is broken frequently. You cannot control the destinies of your reports, and your primary responsibility is to your client. If the information is crucial and very sensitive, consider telling the referral source or other concerned persons orally.

2. Ensure the client's access to his or her records. (The rules about this access should be indicated in your client information brochure.) Access can further protect clients' privacy by (a) informing them of what information has been collected and how it is interpreted and used; (b) allowing them the opportunities to correct errors; and (c) allowing them to make informed decisions before releasing information. All of this is empowering to clients and thus protects them in a larger sense. It is also supported by federal law and perhaps by your local laws.

3. If a client is at risk from the information, write it in a protecting, discreet, thoughtful way.

A Quick Test

1. A physician you know calls to ask: "This is Dr. Jones. Did my patient, Joe Smith, whom I referred to you, come in?" How should you answer?

2. An attorney asks: "Did my client, Joe Smith, come in to see you?" How should you answer?

3. A caller asks: "Did my brother, Joe Smith, get to your office OK?" How should you answer?"

One or more of the following may run through your mind:

- "I don't want to be rude to this caller."

- "My first duty is to conceal the patient's identity."

- "All three of us know Joe was supposed to be here, so where is the risk?"

- "Is there anyone who can overhear this conversation?"

- "Am I certain this is indeed Dr. Jones/Ms. Brown/Joe's sister?"

However mixed your reactions may be, unless you know the caller and are willing to take the risk of breaking confidentiality, the only acceptable answer to all three of these queries is this: "I'm sorry, but I cannot give you that information. If you will have him [don't even use Joe Smith's name, as it could signal that he is known] sign a consent form releasing the information you want, I will check to see if he is known to us, and then I will be able to talk further with you or send you the information you want." Instruct the members of your staff *today* that they are never to take the risk of responding in any other way. As a way to soften the pain of refusal, you should explain the need for privacy, and you can offer to send the caller a copy of your release form.

7.3 Releasing Clients' Records

Note: See also Chapter 4 on informed consent.

The balance of this chapter offers a variety of more specific guidelines to help you answer questions such as these:

- How can you decide whether or not to honor a request for a client's records?

- How can you best protect the client's confidentiality when you do release your records?

- What legal elements must a request for the records of another professional contain?

The first of these questions is addressed here. Later sections include sample forms for requesting records from and releasing records to different requesters. The forms are designed to meet important legal and ethical guidelines.

A Pretest

How sophisticated are you in weighing the relevant issues in releasing records? Pope (1988e) offers the following fictional case history.[1] A 17-year-old married father of a 1-year-old child, living with his parents, comes in complaining of headaches. He is a full-time employee with insurance to pay for your testing. This is an unusual and complicated case, but not entirely unlikely. After you do the evaluation, you receive six requests for your records, from the following:

> (a) the boy's physician, an internist.
>
> (b) the boy's parents, who are concerned about his depression.
>
> (c) the boy's employer, in connection with a worker's compensation claim filed by the boy.
>
> (d) the attorney for the insurance company that is contesting the worker's compensation claim.
>
> (e) the attorney for the boy's wife, who is suing for divorce and for custody of the baby.
>
> (f) the . . . attorney [for the boy], who is considering suing you for malpractice since he doesn't like the results of the tests.
>
> Each of the requests asks for: (a) the full formal report, (b) the original test data, and (c) copies of each of the tests you administered (e.g., instructions and all items for the MMPI).
>
> To which of these people are you legally or ethically obligated to supply all information requested? Partial information? A summary of the report? No information at all? (Pope, 1988e, p. 24)

Again, this is admittedly a complex situation, and Pope does not offer answers. Before reading further, take a pencil and paper and try to indicate which records you would send out and which you wouldn't, and to whom you would send them. My answers can be found at the end of this section (see p. 318).

We still have to act in the real world. Records must often be shared among professionals for the benefit of clients, but breaches of confidentiality can destroy the trust essential for intimate work. The professions have therefore developed procedures for protecting the privacy of records. The following discussion shows how to evaluate a request for your client's records. In general, as in the case above, you need to weigh the needs of the requester against the ethical and legal requirements. These are described next.

Ethical Considerations in Releasing Records

A release that authorizes you to "release and disclose all information and to discuss anything pertaining to this client and the client's progress" appears to be illegally vague and broad.

The basic rule is that consent to release records must be *informed* and *voluntary*, and must be obtained from a *competent* person. These requirements are discussed in Chapter 4. Informed consent to release records requires that the client know and agree to the following:

---

[1]The passage below is reprinted, and the case history is taken, from Pope (1988). Copyright 1988 by Division 42 of the American Psychological Association. Used by permission.

- Which specific person wants the records (name, position, affiliation, function).

- What the records sought contain. Knowledge can come from the client's reading the materials, or from having the materials read and explained to him or her.

- Exactly what information is sought.

- Why this information is sought and exactly how it will be used. What decision will be based on it?

- How the information in the records can be corrected or amended.

- Whether the requester can share this information with anyone else (e.g., consultants, treatment team members).

- What repercussions would follow from granting or withholding permission.

- That the client's consent is time-limited (often 60 days).

- That the client's consent is revocable except for information already released.

- What procedures are available for revoking such consent.

- That the consent and revocation must be given in writing.

Finally, this may seem obvious, but the client must believe that it is in his or her long-term best interest to release the records. For fuller comprehension, your release-of-records form should be available for the client to read; anything the client does not understand must be explained at his or her level of comprehension, and in his or her native language if necessary.

Legal Requirements for a Release of Records

According to the Code of Federal Regulations (42 C.F.R. Part 2, Public Law 93-282, Sections 2.31(a) and 2.33, governing the confidentiality of alcohol and drug abuse patients' records), a valid release form must address all of the following:

- Name of client. Date of birth is also usually sought, as is Social Security number, because names are not unique.

- The name or title of the person or organization requesting disclosure of the record.

- Either the name or general designation of the program from which or person from whom the records are to be released.

- The extent or nature of the information to be disclosed. (A request for "any and all information" should never be made or honored.)

- The purpose of the request, or why these records are needed. (You may receive a request by error which was created in or for another proceeding.)

- The consequences of refusing to release the records (e.g., loss of reimbursement for medical costs or of disability benefits).

- The signature of the client (or his or her representative) and the date signed. (The signature must usually be given within 90 days of the time you receive the form.)

- Verification that the person signing is of legal age, or documentation of his or her "emancipation."

- Verification that the signature belongs to this person, or is validly witnessed.

- A notice that the consent is revocable at any time. (If your suspicions are raised, check—perhaps by calling the client—to see whether the request may have been revoked.)

- When, how, or on what condition upon which the consent will expire if not revoked earlier.

For clarification about how some of these ideas are carried out, see the release forms in Sections 7.4 and 7.5. Additional criteria may be required by your state.

Eight Variations on the Theme of "Please Send Your Records"

Many different people may request your records in many different ways. Each request needs to be considered from an ethical perspective. The following discussion evaluates eight of these variations.

1. A Third Party's Routine Written Request for Records

Consider these usual bases for releasing information to a third party:

- A competent patient has requested release. The disclosure is necessary for the patient's continuing or comprehensive care by another provider or institution, for reimbursement, or for a needed consultation.

- A *surrogate* consent is received for a minor, for someone adjudicated incompetent, or for a dead person.

- A law requires disclosure (e.g., Medicare, mandatory child abuse reporting). See variation 2, below.

Now consider these possible bases against releasing information to a third party:

- The release form sent to you is faulty. It is missing some of the necessary contents of a proper release as listed above. As a courtesy, you could, if you are still in contact with the patient, use one of your releases (perhaps Form 42) to construct a proper release.

- The requester is someone you don't recognize, and you know nothing about the intended uses for this information. "Verify the requester's identity and official capacity" before proceeding, say Stromberg et al. (1988, p. 394).

- The information in your possession is not relevant to the request (e.g., it may not pertain to the request's purposes, the decisions to be made, the time period in question, or even the patient named in the request).

- Confidentiality law or privilege protects against release, and your general duty to protect confidentiality is not overcome by any recognized exception (see Section 7.1 for a list of exceptions).

- In family therapy, the "family" cannot have legal confidentiality; only individual members have this privilege. Thus you will have to clarify and negotiate rules for release with each family members. Ideally, you have specified in your introductory materials that all members must sign a release.

- Is it completely clear that the patient is fully informed about all the information in the record and the effects of passing on all this information? If not, contact the patient directly to clarify the release. In one legal case a patient sued (successfully at first) the psychologist whom she had specifically requested to write a letter to her employer seeking a less stressful job for her, after she had signed a release form. She sued for invasion of privacy and infliction of emotional distress. The psychologist probably would have received a dismissal (before going to the Court of Appeals) if he or she had had the patient see and authorize the release of the exact letter. It is best to have all records released be seen by the patient, or at least to have their release specifically approved by him or her.

- You cannot withhold records that are properly requested and needed for treatment just because you have not been paid (APA, 1992a, Section 5.11). However, ambiguity on this point still remains. You certainly would not withhold records in an emergency with serious consequences, but what if the reqest is being made only for the convenience of the patient (e.g., in support of a school transfer) and he or she is fully capable of paying you? Think it out and decide on the risks.

One last point: Should you type up your notes to make them actually readable? No, just send copies of your records in whatever shape they are in. Typing them up is not what you were asked for, and it would tempt you to make minor revisions (for clarification), which would create doubts about your veracity and integrity.

2. A Patient's Request to See His or Her Own Records

Who actually *owns* a patient's records? Hirsh (1978) says that "records are considered to be the property of the health care provider [who created them] or his or her employing agency [who paid the creator]. Generally, the consumer controls the dissemination of the records, but the right of patients to have direct access to their records varies from state to state."

When a patient asks to see his or her own records, consider these points:

- What disclosure does the applicable state law require? Applicable laws may concern workers' compensation, disabilities acts, dual-diagnosis clients, substance abuse, your specific discipline, relationships with other mental health professions, and so forth.

- Consider why the patient wants these records and work from there. The request may conceal other needs, which can be resolved better through different methods.

- Consider whether there may be errors in the record, which the patient has a right to see, correct, or amend. The client also has the right to add a statement of agreement or disagreement. These rights come from the Privacy Act of 1974 (Public Law 93-579) and, for drug and alcohol clients, the Drug Abuse Office and Treatment Act of 1972 (Public Law 92-255).

- In general, offer to review the records with the patient, or offer a *precis* of the record. The issues are the impact on the patient of the disclosure of a diagnosis (which will require explanation and guidance for the patient to understand productively) and the impact of other information (see variation 3, below).

- What if a couple wants the records of couple therapy? It is best to establish a policy on this and to put it into your client information brochure. Since the records reflect both partners' actions, both must agree to the release.

3. A Patient's Request to See His or Her Own Records, Which Contain Potentially Harmful Information

An example of a patient who could be harmed by information in his or her records is an adult with a history of childhood sexual or physical abuse where the patient may be unaware of or deny the abuse, but it is supported by records released to you.

Your plan in such a case should depend on the circumstances, your understanding of the patient, and the impact of the information. If you think the information will harm the patient, you can withhold it; this is called "therapeutic privilege." You may not have heard of this privilege because it is getting rarer and should be invoked only in extraordinary circumstances (Stromberg & Dellinger, 1993). In such a situation you are asking the patient to understand that some information would be upsetting, and to agree that he or she should be kept ignorant of this information (which seems to go against informed consent). You are also asking that if the information is presented to the patient, he or she will not hold you responsible for any damages (which seems to ask the patient to waive recourse from a harm he or she cannot anticipate—this again seems unfair). If the situation is touchy, go slowly and carefully; give full attention to maintaining the best possible relationship with the patient; document the issues, rationales, and choices made; and get consultation.

The following are some suggestions for proceeding:

- Decide whether it is "advisable and feasible to discuss the records with the patient prior to making them available in order to clarify matters" (Stromberg et al., 1988, p. 422).

- Then decide "which portions of the records should be revealed and which portions (if any) should not be" (Stromberg et al., 1988, p. 422).

- If the patient might be harmed, is there someone else (an advisor or family member) who can then represent the patient for the purpose of reviewing the record?

- If you decide that releasing certain information would not be in the patient's best interest if he or she were to read it, Woody (1988a, p. 210) suggests that you should (1) obtain a release for that specific information, or (2) obtain a waiver from the patient of his or her right to have access to this report. You could also write a letter to the requester justifying your refusal to release damaging information, and base it on your local regulations. Here is an example:

> The regulations of the Pennsylvania Department of Health govern a patient's access to his or her records: "The hospital shall provide the patient, upon request, access to all information contained in his (or her) records, *unless* access is specifically restricted by the attending physician for medical reasons" (Pa. Code 103.22 (b) (15)).
>
> I have discussed the release of these records with my attorney, and in my considered professional opinion, this patient should not have access to the following parts of the records that are attached:
>
> 1.
>
> 2.
>
> 3.
>
> I believe that the patient's coming to know the information contained in these parts will cause him or her to suffer mental anguish and pain without any balancing productive or beneficial effects. It is also, in my opinion, likely that reading this information will interfere with further treatment or cause the patient to lose gains already achieved.
>
> Because of these likely negative effects upon the patient, I strongly recommend that the information contained in these parts of the record not be disclosed to the patient. If a situation arises in which it is absolutely necessary to disclose this information to the patient, I strongly recommend that this be done only by myself or a professional whom I designate, and not by you or any other person, professional, or organization who may obtain these records.

Prepare in advance for this possibility by adding language to your client information brochure. Section 4.2 includes this statement:"I may temporarily remove parts of your records before you see them. This would happen if I believe that the information will be harmful to you, but I will discuss this with you." Ideally, you have avoided using any language in the record that might exacerbate the emotional state of the client.

4. A Parent or Guardian's Request for Records

Parents and guardians have a right to know about minor children's status and progress. This is a right to *information* about the children's treatment, not full access to all their *records*. Remember, you own (or your agency owns) the actual records.

Minors, however, have few rights; so unless your state laws give them privilege, be careful what you write, and be diplomatic and therapeutic with the parents. (See also the forms for consent to treatment of children in Section 4.6.) Young children cannot claim confidentiality, but teens have "rights" to be respected. Be frank in advising children of their lack of these guarantees. You may also be able to negotiate with the parents to accept less information than they desire. Whether a parent is custodial or noncustodial usually makes no legal difference (Stromberg, Lindberg, Mishkin, & Baker, 1993).

If parents or guardians seem to be seeking more information than you think they or others need, try educating them before releasing the data. For example, explain that by their very nature, reports tend to focus on negatives or weaknesses (Sweet, 1990, p. 8). You can also explore the adults' motivations for seeking the records. Take into account parents' legal obligation to know in order to protect their children, as well as their emotional concerns for their children. If there is a difference of opinion about treatment, clarifying this through discussion, or perhaps sending records to another therapist for a "second opinion," may serve the parents' needs.

In custody cases, privilege may be overridden by the "best interests of the child." Try to get permission, at intake, to prevent your notes from being subpoenaed by one party if the other objects. The client information brochure (in Section 4.2) addresses this issue. And see Form 48 for a consent form for releasing information to family members.

5. A Subpoena [2]

If you receive a subpoena, do not release everything (or anything precipitously) just to be done with it. "A subpoena, which is a request for documents, is authorized by a court but actually is filled out and served by the attorney seeking the information" (Tepper et al., 1991). You have to *respond* to a subpoena, but you do not have to *comply* with it. Your options include sending the requested information, challenging the relevance or validity of the subpoena by seeking to "quash" it, or refusing to comply on legal or ethical grounds (e.g., privileged communication or local laws, regulations, or precedents). You may also negotiate sending a summary, or revealing information only in a private meeting with the judge. If you are reluctant to comply immediately, contact the attorney who has requested your records and find out "what type of legal action is pending, and why these materials are being requested. Let the attorney know that you are not attempting merely to avoid complying with the request, but, rather, that you yourself have certain ethical and legal obligations you must satisfy before releasing any patient information" (Tepper et al., 1991). If you are still reluctant, "After obtaining the written consent of your patient, contact [the patient's] attorney, explain the situation, and see if the two attorneys can come to an agreeable resolution" (Tepper et al., 1991).

What happens if you do not comply with a subpeona? Tepper et al. (1991) continue: "Since a subpoena is a court authorized request, non-compliance technically puts you in contempt of court. However, the requesting attorney still must go to a judge to seek further compliance with the subpoena. If you have outlined the grounds for your initial refusal, you later will be able to argue that you acted in a reasonable fashion." If the court orders you to provide the information, you can either comply or appeal to a higher court:

> A court order is a document signed by a judge, requesting that certain materials be provided to a party named in the order. A court order may follow a subpoena or may be issued on its own. By its very

---

[2]Most of the quotations in this subsection are taken from Tepper, Rinella, and Siegel (1991). Copyright 1991 by the Pennsylvania Psychological Association. Reprinted by permission.

nature, a court order indicates that a judge has already authorized the request. You may or may not agree with what you are being requested to do; however, failure to respond to the court order may result in a contempt hearing in which you will be required to explain your behavior before the issuing judge. Nonetheless, if you continue to have questions regarding the court order, such inquiries also may be directed to the requesting attorney, the opposing attorney, or the Court itself. At this stage, a consultation with your own attorney [will] also become necessary. (Tepper et al., 1991)

Woody (1991) suggests placing a specific statement in your client information brochure. Because it is so specialized, it has not been included in the brochure in this book (Section 4.2), but it may suit your practice. Woody's statement is as follows:

> Notice: In the event that a subpoena for records or testimony is received, the policy will be that (1) the client will be notified in writing and provided with a copy of the subpoena; (2) the client must either provide the practitioner with a written waiver of objection to the subpoena (an authorization form for honoring the subpoena will be provided) or indicate that an objection will be filed with the court (with a copy send to the practitioner); and (3) if an objection to that subpoena is to be filed, it is the responsibility of the client to have it filed with the court. (p. 126)

The APA's Committee on Legal Issues (1996) has recently offered guidance on coping with subpoenas and the releasing of client records and test data. Some further suggestions for dealing with a subpoena are as follows:

- Make sure that any request you receive, even a subpoena, is valid and complete (see above). A subpoena is just a request and does not carry the weight of a court order.

- If you release any subpoenaed information, you can charge for it and for your time to prepare it.

- Harry Corsover, PhD, of Evergreen, CO, suggests that when you receive a subpoena, you negotiate with the lawyer and offer him or her some report choices like these: (1) a full mental health treatment report for the whole treatment or a part of it; (2) responses to specific questions; or (3) a detailed, session-by-session summary. The fee for each depends on the time it takes to prepare.

6. A Request to Which the Patient Does Not Consent

If the patient has not given his or her consent to a request for records (e.g., a subpoena from opposing counsel), discuss the issues fully with him or her to lessen any feelings of distrust and lower the risk of a suit for improper disclosure. Discuss the implications of the request and your planned response with the patient; he or she may then decide to give consent. Knapp and VandeCreek (1990) also suggest that you "encourage the patient to consult an attorney for advice" (p. 45). Here are some other suggestions:

- If you do not get consent or a disposition of the request agreed to by the requester, obtain a court ruling on whether the release is proper. Let the judge be your guide.

- In the absence of consent or a court order to release the records, verify that there is a basis for the release.

- Perhaps the patient cannot give consent. He or she may be a minor or may be ruled incompetent because of a variety of factors (significant mental retardation; dementia; intoxication on drugs, alcohol, or medications; etc.). The person seeking your records must seek "substitute consent" from the patient's parent or guardian, or from the court of jurisdiction.

7. A Request for Test Materials, Raw Data, or Protocols of Evaluation

There are few if any laws about the release of records of evaluations (as opposed to the release of treatment records), but it is likely to be treated similarly by the courts (Stromberg, Lindberg, Mishkin, & Baker, 1993). Recently, the APA Committee on Psychological Tests and Assessment (1996) issued guidelines on disclosing test data, accessing records, and providing feedback to the test taker. In these situations, your ethical responsibility is to maintain "test security" for the valid evaluation of future patients. The APA ethics code (APA, 1992a) prohibits the release of raw test results and data to unqualified persons such as judges and attorneys; your local codes of professional conduct may also prevent you from releasing raw data or test materials. Tranel (1994, p. 35) suggests a simple strategy: Advise the attorney or other to hire a psychologist consultant "who is qualified by virtue of licensure, training, and experience, to receive the data" and send the data to this psychologist, with the patient's consent. Tranel also points out that this consultant "must operate under the same rules and standards of ethics and confidentiality" as you do.

8. The Need to Share Records with a Consultant or Referrer

The principle about sharing records with a consultant or referrer is that if the patient has approved of the consultation or has accepted the referral to you or to another professional, you do not need a signed release (American Psychiatric Association, 1987a). However, if you have any doubts because of the kind or amount of material to be discussed or about the patient's understanding, get a signed release. (See APA, 1992a, Section 5.06.)

Guidelines and Considerations in Sending Records

- If you decide to release records, consider the extent of necessary disclosure, and ways to continue to protect confidentiality as much as possible.

- Never copy and send your whole record, because it may contain material irrelevant to the issues at hand.

- Consider the possibility that the patient may read the records, reports, or materials you are sending.

- Weigh the best way to organize and present the necessary information. For example, send written records instead of discussing the contents of the records over the telephone, because this will make it clearer what has and has not been disclosed. If a release must be oral, confirm in writing the contents released as soon as possible. Use fax only when you are sure of confidentiality (see Section 7.6).

- Prepare and retain careful documentation on the following:

    Your discussions with the patient and the patient's responses to the issues involved in the release, such as the content of your records and the nature of confidentiality.

    The information ultimately released, the release date, and the person or agency to whom or which it is provided. Record on the release before making copies (see below) which pages are included; what forms, letters, or notes are enclosed; and so on.

    Either the release signed by the patient (or his or her legal representative), or the response why a duty to disclose without consent seems to exist.

- Both release forms and requests for records to be released by another provider (see Section 7.4) should be prepared in triplicate—an original and two photocopies, each signed in ink (preferably blue so that it is clear that the signature has not been photocopied). These should be distributed as follows: one for the patient or his or her guardian; one for the party releasing the information; and one for the party receiving the information.

- Notifying the recipient that this is sensitive material is important and can be accomplished in several ways. You can use the more specific notices provided in Section 7.7; use your computer's printer to print them as labels on peel-off paper, or have your word processor put the notice in a "header" or "footer" on every page. Some therapists have had a rubber stamp made up with one of the confidentiality notices from Section 7.7, which they then stamp on each page released. But note that a stamp for each page that says simply "Do not copy" or "Confidential" or "Personal and confidential" is probably not legally sufficient notification. In addition, enclose an explanatory, cautioning, and educational cover letter with all records you send. Form 44 can be used for this purpose.

- If you are sending the record to anyone whose credentials you don't know or recognize, you might suggest a specific professional in the requester's location to interpret the records. If your suspicions about the requester's qualifications are raised, write or speak to him or her and suggest that you could send the records directly to the professional for interpretation (with, of course, a new release form).

- Although discretion and sensitivity to the client's wishes in releasing information are appropriate (as in providing selective disclosure), providing false information (e.g., a different diagnosis than in the records) is unethical (Stromberg et al., 1988, p. 392).

- Joseph Rosenfeld, PhD, of Southampton, PA, suggests relabeling releases (especially for parents of school children) as "Sharing of Information."

- You can certainly charge for copying your records and sending them. A charge of $10 to $15 seems to be common, but do charge more if your efforts justify the cost. Make certain to include and clearly mark your federal tax identification number or Social Security number on your bill, or you will waste a lot of time on the phone when requesters want to pay you. It seems fair to charge for nonsubpoenaed records and those requested by non-health-care professionals who will make a profit from the record (e.g., lawyers, insurance companies). I would not charge for a record sent to the patient or his or her face-to-face health care provider (not an agency). If a patient requests that I send copies to several providers, I would send a single copy to the patient and let him or her arrange things.

- In summary, "the overriding rule is '*When in doubt, don't give it out!*' (The next rule, of course, is '*If still in doubt, call your redoubtable lawyer*')" (Stromberg et al., 1988, p. 389; emphasis in original).

Comments on the Pretest

At the beginning of this section (p. 308), I offered a case example from Pope (1988e) that raises many of the issues just examined. Would your answers now be different from your earlier responses? Here is my best understanding of this situation.

First, I would not send the original test data or copies of the tests to anyone, citing in my cover letter both the inability of nonpsychologists (all of the requesters) to interpret the tests' data, and the ethical and professional need to maintain the security of the tests. I would also mention in this letter that if the requesters, after reading my letter or report, believed they had a need for the raw data or for test copies, I would consider releasing these to another sufficiently qualified psychologist who could interpret them for the requesters.

Second, I would contact the young man and tell him of the requests for his records I had received. The issue to be dealt with is the degree to which this man understood the content and implications of my report's contents. If he did not, he could not informedly release the report. I would suggest that he and I meet (at his expense) to discuss the contents, and that he consult his lawyer about the report's consequences in regard to each of the intended recipients, especially his own and the other attorneys.

Third, I would indicate to each requester that I would be willing to create a version of my report that might answer specific questions each might raise, but that since I did not know the requester's needs, I would be very reluctant to release a full report containing a great deal of material that was likely to be irrelevant to the requester's needs, might easily be misunderstood, and could embarrass my client. I would offer to produce these revised reports at my usual per-hour fee, to be paid by the requesters, in advance. As the requesters would probably not initially accept this proposal, I would telephone each one, attempt to clarify his or her needs for information, and discuss (in a general way) whether or not my report might contain information to meet their needs.

7.4 Forms for Requesting and Releasing Information

Both the briefer version (Form 42) and the longer version (Form 43) of the two forms provided in this section give you the option of using them either to have a client release your records, or request records from another provider.

A Briefer Request/Release Form

FORM 42   The following form (Form 42) is a simple and multipurpose one-page document and should meet most of your needs. It can be used for a child or an adult; it can be used either to obtain or to release records; and it leaves spaces to write in some specifics.

Request/Authorization to Release Confidential Records and Information

I hereby authorize:

Person or facility: _____

Address: _____

_____ Phone: _____

to release information from records about _____, born on _____,

and whose Social Security number is_____, for the following purpose(s):

❑ Further mental health evaluation, treatment, or care ❑ Rehabilitation program development or services

❑ Treatment planning ❑ Research ❑ Other:_____

These records concern the time between _____ and _____.

The information to be disclosed is marked by an × in the boxes below, and the items not to be released have a line drawn through them. Page numbers are indicated when appropriate.

❑ Intake and discharge summaries ❑ Medical history and evaluation(s) ❑ Mental health evaluations

❑ Developmental and/or social history ❑ Educational records

❑ Progress notes, and treatment or closing summary ❑ Other:_____

Select only one:

❑ Please forward the records to the address in the letterhead at the top of this form.

❑ Please forward the records to the address written above.

HIV-related information and drug and alcohol information contained in these records will be released under this consent unless indicated here: ❑ Do not release.

I have had explained to me and fully understand this request/authorization to release records and information, including the nature of the records, their contents, and the consequences and implications of their release. This request is entirely voluntary on my part. I understand that I may take back this consent at any time within 90 days, except to the extent that action based on this consent has already been taken. This consent will expire automatically after 90 days from the date on which it is signed, or upon fulfillment of the purposes stated above.

_____   _____   _____
Signature of client   Printed name   Date

_____   _____   _____ _____
Signature of parent/   Printed name   Relationship   Date
guardian/representative

I witnessed that the person understood the nature of this request/authorization and freely gave his or her consent, but was physically unable to provide a signature.

_____   _____   _____
Signature of witness   Printed name   Date

❑ Copy for patient or parent/guardian ❑ Copy for source of records ❑ Copy for recipient of records

FORM 42. Briefer form for requesting/releasing confidential records and information. From *The Paper Office*, p. 319. Copyright 1997 by Edward L. Zuckerman. Permission to photocopy this form is granted to purchasers of *The Paper Office* for personal use only (see copyright page for details).

A More Comprehensive Request/Release Form

FORM 43   I use the following form (Form 43) when I have little confidence in the ethical sophistication of the professional to whom I am sending it. It contains formal and legal language that may impress its recipient, and it cites all the regulations; it may thus educate (or intimidate) the recipient into following ethical practices, such as fully informing the client about what is to be released and what will be done with the information. This longer form has some useful additions and advantages over typical request/release forms:

- It meets the special standards for requesting/releasing drug and alcohol treatment records (see part B).

- It allows telephone contacts (see part C), which is a convenience.

- It includes a release of liability (see part F).

- It adds an authorization to make photocopies for sending multiple records or keeping some copies for later use (see part H).

- It offers your opinion that the signer is competent (see part K).

As always, you can tailor this form to your needs in various ways. You may want to add any other specific records you regularly request to the list in part B.

Other changes you can make to Form 43 include the following:

- If you are not doing treatment, you might want to change the wording at the end of part D to indicate your need and the uses or purposes of the disclosure of the records.

- Releases must have time limits. The one in part G says "90 days," but if that is insufficient, you can replace it with a longer time or this sentence: "It shall be valid no longer than is reasonably necessary to meet the purposes stated above, and not to exceed 1 year."

- You can add one or both of these sentences to part I: "I further understand that I have the right to inspect and copy any of the information I request/authorize for release," and/or "This therapist and I have explored the likely consequences of waiving the privilege of confidentiality."

- In the signatures section (part J), you might want to consider that the older a child is, the more his or her wishes should be considered and honored. So even if your state does not legally give power to an adolescent, you might want to make him or her a participant by having him or her sign the form.

Forms 42 and 43 can even be made interactive by inserting language like that below. (However, I do not know whether this has been tested in a legal setting.)

I, _____, request and authorize the two parties listed below to release to each other all information and records either party may have created (about my history, symptoms, diagnoses, functioning, treatments, prognoses, etc.). These parties are:

_____ and _____

Request/Authorization to Release Confidential Records and Information

Source of information:

Person or facility: _____

Address: _____

_____ Phone: _____

A. Identifying information about me/the patient

Name: _____

Address: _____

_____

Phone: _____ Birthdate: _____ Social Security #: _____

Parent/guardian (if applicable): _____

Address and phone of parent/guardian: _____

_____

B. I hereby authorize the source named above to send, as promptly as possible, the records listed below marked by an X in the boxes below. (The items not to be released have a line drawn through them. Page numbers are indicated where appropriate.)

❑ Inpatient or outpatient treatment records for physical and/or psychological, psychiatric, or emotional illness or drug or alcohol abuse:

Date(s) of inpatient admission: _____ Date(s) of discharge: _____

Start of outpatient treatment: _____ End of treatment: _____ Clinic/patient number: _____

Other identifying information about the service(s) rendered: _____

❑ Psychological evaluation(s) or testing records, and behavioral observations or checklists completed by any staff member or by the patient.

❑ Psychiatric evaluations, reports, or treatment notes and summaries.

❑ Treatment plans, recovery plans, aftercare plans.

❑ Admission and discharge summaries.

❑ Social histories, assessments with diagnoses, prognoses, recommendations, and all similar documents.

❑ Information about how the patient's condition affects or has affected his or her ability to complete tasks, activities of daily living, or ability to work.

❑ Workshop reports and other vocational evaluations and reports.

❑ Billing records.

❑ Academic or educational records.

❑ Report of teachers' observations.

❑ Achievement and other tests' results.

(cont.)

❑ A letter containing dates of treatment(s) and a summary of progress.

❑ HIV-related information and drug and alcohol information contained in these records will be released under this consent unless indicated here: ❑ Do not release.

❑ Other: _____

C. I authorize the source named above to speak by telephone with the therapist identified in part K about the reasons for my/the patient's referral, any relevant history or diagnoses, and other similar information that can assist with my/the patient's receiving treatment or being evaluated or referred elsewhere.

D. I understand that no services will be denied me/the patient solely because I refuse to consent to this release of information, and that I am not in any way obligated to release these records. I do release them because I believe that they are necessary to assist in the development of the best possible treatment plan for me/the patient. The information disclosed may be used in connection with my/the patient's treatment.

E. This request/authorization to release confidential information is being made in compliance with the terms of the Privacy Act of 1974 (Public Law 93-579) and the Freedom of Information Act of 1974 (Public Law 93-502); and pursuant to Federal Rule of Evidence 1158 (Inspection and Copying of Records upon Patient's Written Authorization). This form is to serve as both a general authorization, and a special authorization to release information under the Drug Abuse Office and Treatment Act of 1972 (Public Law 92-255), the Comprehensive Alcohol Abuse and Alcoholism Prevention, Treatment and Rehabilitation Act Amendments of 1974 (Public Law 93-282), the Veterans Omnibus Health Care Act of 1976 (Public Law 94-581), and the Veterans Benefit and Services Act of 1988 (Public Law 100-322). It is also in compliance with 42 C.F.R. Part 2 (Public Law 93-282), which prohibits further disclosure without the express written consent of the person to whom it pertains, or as otherwise permitted by such regulations.

F. In consideration of this consent, I hereby release the source of the records from any and all liability arising therefrom.

G. This request/authorization is valid during the pendency of any claim or demand made by or in behalf of me/the patient, and arising out of an accident, injury, or occurrence to me/the patient. I understand that I may void this request/authorization, except for action already taken, at any time by means of a written letter revoking the authorization and transfer of information, but that this revocation is not retroactive. If I do not void this request/authorization, it will automatically expire in 90 days from the date I signed it.

H. I agree that a photocopy of this form is acceptable, but it must be individually signed by me, the releaser, and a witness if necessary.

I. I affirm that everything in this form that was not clear to me has been explained. I also understand that I have the right to receive a copy of this form upon my request.

J. Signatures

_____ _____ _____
Signature of client Printed name Date

_____ _____ _____
Signature of parent/ Printed name Relationship Date
guardian/representative

I witnessed that the person understood the nature of this request/authorization and freely gave his or her consent, but was physically unable to provide a signature.

_____ _____ _____
Signature of witness Printed name Date

K. I, a mental health professional, have discussed the issues above with the patient and/or his or her parent or guardian. My observations of behavior and responses give me no reason to believe that this person is not fully competent to give informed and willing consent.

_____ _____ _____
Signature of professional Printed name Date

❑ Copy for patient or parent/guardian ❑ Copy for source of records ❑ Copy for recipient of records

7.5 More Specific Forms for Releasing Information

A Release-of-Records Form Letter

It is standard practice to provide a cover letter to accompany any records you send to another professional or organization; this informs the recipient of his or her legal and ethical responsibilities. Or, if for some reason you cannot release a patient's records as requested, you must of course write a letter to explain the reason for the refusal.

FORM 44

The form letter provided below (Form 44) can serve either of these purposes. Its thoroughness can save you effort and impress medical record sophisticates (such as registered record librarians, some physicians, and defense lawyers). However, you may have to modify it to suit your setting, local laws, and practice. For example, if you operate in Pennsylvania, you can add the following protected-information disclosure notices after the one provided for drug and alcohol disclosure. If you work elsewhere, you can substitute your local versions.

> *Psychiatric disclosure—55 Pa. Code Section 5100.34.* This information has been disclosed to you from records whose confidentiality is protected by state law. State regulations prohibit you from making any further disclosure of this information without the prior written consent of the person to whom it pertains.

> *HIV disclosure—the Confidentiality of HIV-Related Information Act (1990).* This information has been disclosed to you from records protected by Pennsylvania law. Pennsylvania law prohibits you from making any further disclosure of this information unless further disclosure is expressly permitted by the written consent of the person to whom it pertains or is authorized by the Confidentiality of HIV-Related Information Act. A general authorization for the release of medical or other information is not sufficient for this purpose.

Also, if you don't keep records for a prolonged period, you could substitute the following for the current first option under "I am unable to comply . . ."

> ❑ My office policy is to retain patients' records for 12 years and then destroy them. In accord with this policy, the records you have asked for no longer exist. I can state only that this person was treated by me between the dates of _____ and _____.

Releasing Psychological Test Results

Note: Forms for permission to test or evaluate a person are provided in Chapter 4 (Forms 16 and 17).

FORM 45

Sometimes you will be specifically requested to send the results of a psychological evaluation to another professional or agency. Form 45 can be used as an authorization form for this purpose. This form is modified from one by Ruth H. Sosis, PhD, of Cincinnati, OH, and is adapted with her kind permission. (Note that, like Forms 42 and 43 but unlike the other forms in this section, Form 45 can also be used to *request* information.)

Re the following patient: _____

Dear Sir or Madam:

Regarding the information you requested in a Request for Information Form or Consent to Release Records Form dated _____:

❑ Please find attached the records or information you requested on the above-named patient. The charge for copying these records is $_____. Please forward this amount with the same courtesy, trust, and dispatch as my staff and I have used in collecting and providing this information to you. Thank you.

Also, please note the following points:

1. *Protected-information disclosure notice: Drug and alcohol disclosure.* This information has been disclosed to you from records whose confidentiality is protected by state and federal law. Federal regulations (42 C.F.R. Part 2, Sections 2.31(a) and 2.33) and state regulations prohibit you from making any further disclosure of it without the specific written consent of the person to whom it pertains, or as otherwise permitted by such regulations. A general authorization for the release of medical or other information is not sufficient for this purpose. These regulations provide for a fine of up to $500 for the first offense and up to $5,000 for each subsequent offense.

2. This is strictly confidential material and is for the information of only the person to whom it is addressed. I can accept no responsibility if it is made available to any other person, *including the patient.* Redisclosure or retransfer of these records is expressly prohibited, and such redisclosure may subject you to civil and criminal liability.

3. Federal and state rules restrict use of this information to criminally investigate or prosecute any alcohol or drug abuse patient.

❑ I have completed the form or forms you sent and have enclosed them.

❑ You have sent a form for me to complete, which will take some of my professional time. If you wish this done, please forward, in the next 10 days, the sum of $_____ to pay for the additional service.

❑ According to my records, this information was sent to you on _____. If you have not received it, please call this office and send another copy of your Request for Information Form.

❑ Enclosed are the remaining records you requested. The other records were sent to you on _____.

❑ I am unable to comply with your request for these records, because:

   ❑ All records are destroyed after 7 years following the date of the last visit. Records of minor patients (14 years and younger) are retained for 7 years after they are no longer minors. Enclosed is the only available information.

   ❑ The records you are seeking are not complete at this time. I will send the records as soon as they are completed.

(cont.)

FORM 44. A release-of-records form letter (p. 1 of 2). From *The Paper Office*, pp. 324–325. Copyright 1997 by Edward L. Zuckerman. Permission to photocopy this form is granted to purchasers of *The Paper Office* for personal use only (see copyright page for details).

❑ No authorization or release was enclosed with your request. I cannot release records without such an authorization or release.

❑ Your request was not sufficiently specific. Please indicate exactly what information is needed.

❑ After a thorough search of the records, my staff and I are unable to locate any record on this person with the information you provided. Please check to see whether he or she may have used another name when treated by me, or provide additional information to help us locate the records, such as date of birth, Social Security number, or dates of service.

❑ I am sure that I have not provided service to this person.

❑ I have not provided service to this person during the time period covered by the release.

❑ I did not originate the records you requested, and so cannot release them.

❑ The information you requested is not available here. You might try contacting: _____.

❑ The authorization enclosed was deficient because it is or was:

    ❑ Not dated, or not dated after treatment ended.

    ❑ Dated more than 6 months prior to the receipt of your request.

    ❑ Not legally adequate.

    ❑ For a minor patient, but had no signed authorization by one or both parents or a guardian. (If the latter is the case, proof of guardianship is also required.)

    ❑ For an emancipated minor, and so a parent's or guardian's signature is not acceptable.

    ❑ Signed by someone other than the patient. Such authorizations must be signed by the patient unless the patient is physically or mentally unable to do so.

    ❑ Signed illegibly, and so I am unable to verify that it is the signature of the patient.

❑ Your Request/Authorization/Consent to Release Records Form does not conform to the requirements of state/federal regulations covering the release of confidential records. Because of the nature of the information contained in this record, a general medical consent form cannot be accepted. Specifically, it _____.

    ❑ I have enclosed a form for you to execute.

❑ The patient is deceased, so an authorization must be signed by the next of kin or the administrator of the estate, and appropriate documentation is required (i.e., death certificate/short form, proof of being the executor of the patient's estate, letters of administration, or power of attorney).

❑ This information is not released directly to patients or families. If you want this information released, please send the name and address of a professional who would understand this information and a suitable Request for Information Form or Consent to Release Records Form.

❑ Other reason: _____.

If you have any questions, please do not hesitate to contact me. If you need additional information, please return this letter with your second request for information or records.

Sincerely yours,

Request/Authorization for Release of Evaluation Information

Name: _____

Address: _____

Phone: _____ Birthdate: _____ Social Security #: _____

Regarding the administration of psychological tests, I give my permission to (select only one):

❑ the professional named in the letterhead at the top of this form, or

❑ _____

of _____

_____

to release the results of the tests taken by me/the patient, in order to:

❑ Assist with treatment planning

❑ Document a need for services

❑ Support an application for _____

❑ Other: _____

and to send these records to (select only one)

❑ the professional named in the letterhead, or to

❑ _____

of _____

_____

I hereby release the person or organization sending these records and results from any liability associated with administering, scoring, interpreting, evaluating, or reporting the results of these tests.

I understand that the records, information, or results will not be given to me by the evaluator.

Signature of client	Printed name	Date

Signature of parent/ guardian/representative	Printed name	Relationship	Date

I witnessed that the person understood the nature of this request/authorization and freely gave his or her consent, but was physically unable to provide a signature.

Signature of witness	Printed name	Date

❑ Copy for client or parent/guardian   ❑ Copy for source of records   ❑ Copy for recipient of records

FORM 45. Request/authorization for release of evaluation information.   Adapted from a form devised by Ruth H. Sosis, PhD, of Cincinnati, OH, and used by permission of Dr. Sosis.—From *The Paper Office*, p. 326. Permission to photocopy this form is granted to purchasers of *The Paper Office* for personal use only (see copyright page for details).

Releasing Information to an Attorney

FORM 46

The sending of records or reports to an attorney should be accompanied by the same consent elements as the sending of records to anyone else. In addition, the release form offered here as Form 46 authorizes your deposition, testimony, and other ways of sharing information. It also adds wording designed to protect you and to assure payment in a legal case where deferring (part of) your payment may be necessary but is not contingent on the outcome of the case.

You should not accept contingency fees, in which you will get paid only if the client wins a judgment. That arrangement could prejudice your professional opinion, make it worthless, and compromise your reputation. You can be certain that opposing counsel will ask you whether your fee is contingent. If so, this will be used as a means of disparaging your findings. The number of similar evaluations and testimonies you have done can also be used to present you either as inexperienced or as a possible "hired gun" if you do a lot of testifying.

The third paragraph of this form waives confidentiality and requires discussion with the client and his or her attorney. The general principle is that confidentiality cannot be waived partially, so once it is waived, all contents of the record are available to both sides. As noted earlier in this chapter, confidentiality cannot be used as "both a shield and a sword"; that is, you cannot release only the evidence that favors your client's side. (However, courts frequently will suppress irrelevant information when asked to do so.) Therefore, all the contents of the record and the implications of those contents should be fully explored before the decision to release is made.

Releasing Records to an Insurance Company or Other Third-Party Payer

FORM 47

You will probably be sending various kind of information to insurance companies, managed care organizations, government agencies, and similar programs to support reimbursement or payments from health insurance policies. In most cases the information is routine and nonthreatening, and usually a release signed by the person insured is attached to or part of the form requesting the information. Form 47 specifically reminds the recipient of the applicable federal confidentiality laws, and so may add some protection for both you and your patient.

Authorization to Release Confidential Information to an Attorney

I do hereby authorize you, the therapist named in the letterhead above, to furnish _____,
my attorney, _____ of _____,
with a full report of your examination, diagnosis, treatments, prognosis, and any other records concerning me/the patient named _____ in regard to the accident/incident/condition for which I/the patient sought your services, which began on _____.

I authorize you, the therapist, to answer any and all questions or other requests for information from my attorney regarding my/this patient's treatment by you, and to appear and to testify regarding my/this patient's treatment and records at depositions or in court or any administrative proceedings.

I completely waive and release any rights of confidentiality I may have concerning these records and information, and agree to hold the therapist harmless and to indemnify him or her from any and all claims made against him or her in connection with the release of these records and information as here authorized.

I understand and accept that I am directly and fully responsible to you, the therapist, for all bills submitted for services you render to me/this patient, and that this agreement is made solely for your additional protection and in consideration of your awaiting payment. I understand that submission of your reports or other written materials may be contingent upon settlement of this account. And I further understand that such payment is not contingent on any settlement, judgment, or verdict by which I/this patient may eventually recover monies, and that I am responsible for this payment.

I hereby authorize and direct my attorney to pay directly to you such sums as may be due and owing to you for mental health/psychological/counseling services rendered to me/this patient, by reason of any other settlement, judgment, or award that may be paid to you, my attorney, or me/the patient as the result of the injuries/incident/condition for which I have/the patient has been treated, or any other litigation on my/the patient's behalf. I hereby state my intention and desire that you be paid at the time you provide services, no matter what is common practice or the legal decisions made.

I affirm that everything in this form that was not clear to me has been explained to my satisfaction.

A photocopy of this release is to be considered as valid as the original.

| _____ | _____ | _____ |
| Signature of client | Printed name | Date |

| _____ | _____ | _____ | _____ |
| Signature of parent/ guardian/representative | Printed name | Relationship | Date |

I witnessed that the person understood the nature of this request/authorization and freely gave his or her consent, but was physically unable to provide a signature.

| _____ | _____ | _____ |
| Signature of witness | Printed name | Date |

For the Attorney:

The undersigned, being attorney of record for the above-named patient, does hereby agree to observe all the terms described above, and also agrees to withhold such sums from any settlement, judgment, or award as may be necessary to adequately protect the above-named therapist or otherwise to guarantee reimbursement.

| _____ | _____ | _____ |
| Signature of attorney | Printed name | Date |

Please date, sign, and return one copy to the therapist's office and keep one copy for your records.

❑ Copy for client or parent/guardian   ❑ Copy for therapist   ❑ 2 copies for attorney

[**FORM 47**—Use the top of this page for your letterhead.]

[The third party's name and address should go here.]

Re: _____

Birthdate: _____

SS #: _____

Authorization to Release Confidential Information
to a Health Insurer or Other Third-Party Payer

A. This form authorizes the provider named in the letterhead above to release information from the patient's/my records maintained while the patient/I was treated by this provider during _____ or from _____ to _____.

B. The information to be disclosed is marked by an × in the boxes below, and the items not to be released have a line drawn through them:

❑ Intake forms, clinical records, summaries, treatment plans, and similar clinical documents

❑ Psychological evaluation(s) or testing records, and behavioral observations or checklists completed by any staff member or by the patient

❑ Psychiatric evaluations, reports, or treatment notes and summaries

❑ Treatment plans, recovery plans, aftercare plans

❑ Admission and discharge summaries

❑ Social histories, assessments, with diagnoses, prognoses, recommendations, and all similar documents

❑ Information about how my condition affects or has affected my ability to complete tasks and activities of daily living, or about how my condition affects or has affected my ability to work

❑ Workshop reports and other vocational evaluations and reports

❑ Billing records

❑ Academic or educational records

❑ Reports of teachers' observations

❑ Achievement and other tests' results

❑ A letter containing dates of treatment(s) and a summary of progress

❑ Other: _____

C. HIV-related information and drug and alcohol information contained in these records will be released under this consent unless indicated here: ❑ Do not release.

D. This information is to be sent to the third-party payer or its agents named above, and is needed for the following purpose(s):

❑ Receiving health insurance benefits, reimbursements, payments for related services, or other similar decisions

❑ Applying for life, disability, or other insurance

❑ Other: _____

(cont.)

FORM 47. Authorization to release confidential information to a health insurer or other third-party payer (p. 1 of 2). From *The Paper Office,* pp. 329–330. Copyright 1997 by Edward L. Zuckerman. Permission to photocopy this form is granted to purchasers of *The Paper Office* for personal use only (see copyright page for details).

E. I understand that, by law, I need not consent to the release of this information. This information is not required for my/the patient's treatment. However, I willingly choose to release it for the purpose(s) specified above. I understand that I may revoke this release at any time within 90 days, except to the extent that action has been taken in reliance on my consent.

F. Also, **please note the following points:**

1. This information has been disclosed to you from **records whose confidentiality is protected by state and federal law.** Federal regulations (42 C.F.R. Part 2, Sections 2.31(a) and 2.33) and state regulations prohibit you from making any further disclosure of it without the specific written consent of the person to whom it pertains, or as otherwise permitted by such regulations.

2. This is **strictly confidential material** and is for the information of only persons who are professionally capable of understanding, appreciating, and acting upon it according to their specific and advanced professional training in the mental health field. Please restrict the availability of these records to those persons in your employ who have the training and experience to interpret and understand the information contained in them. These ethical and legal responsibilities are yours. No responsibility can be accepted by the provider or author of these records if this material is made available to any other person or persons who lack such training, or who would not treat it in a professionally responsible manner, or who otherwise should not have access to it, *including the patient.*

3. Redisclosure or retransfer of these records is expressly prohibited, and such redisclosure may subject you to civil and criminal liability.

4. Federal and state rules restrict any use of the information to criminally investigate or prosecute any alcohol or drug abuse patient.

G. Assignment of health insurance benefits: My signature below authorizes the payment, directly to the above-named provider, of benefits payable under my policy. I understand that such payments will be credited to my account with this provider. I further understand that I am financially responsible to this provider for charges not covered or reimbursed by my policy, up to the fee the provider has agreed to accept.

H. For Medicare patients only: I request that payment of authorized benefits be made to the provider listed above on my behalf. I authorize any holder of medical information about me to release to the Health Care Financing Administration and its agents any information needed to determine those benefits or the benefits payable for related services.

I. I affirm that everything in this form that was not clear to me has been explained to my satisfaction.

J. A photocopy of this release is to be considered as valid as the original.

K. Signatures:

| _____ | _____ | _____ |
| Signature of client | Printed name | Date |

| _____ | _____ | _____ | _____ |
| Signature of parent/ guardian/representative | Printed name | Relationship | Date |

I witnessed that the person understood the nature of this request/authorization and freely gave his or her consent, but was physically unable to provide a signature.

| _____ | _____ | _____ |
| Signature of witness | Printed name | Date |

❏ Copy for client or parent/guardian   ❏ Copy for provider   ❏ Copy for third-party payer

Releasing Information to the Patient's Family

What should a therapist tell the patient's family about the patient? There is always the potential for conflict between a family's legitimate right to information about its members and the therapist's obligation to keep information confidential (Zipple, Landle, Spaniol, & Fisher, 1990). For example, the spouse of a patient may ask a question, or the adult child of an older patient may inquire. Unless the issue of who has a right to know is clarified, staff members may refuse to provide simple and nondisruptive information about a patient to an appropriate family member, because "We do not reveal patient information" (Marsh, 1995). Getting a form such as Form 48 signed early in treatment can lessen problems. If you intend to release significantly different information to different persons/relatives, use several versions of this form.

FORM 48

Form 48, adapted from Marsh (1995), can empower both the patient and family by making the process and content of family communications more explicit and informed. It sets boundaries, specifies contact persons, and then allows you to negotiate the exact information to be supplied with all parties.

7.6 Confidentiality When Faxing Records or Sending E-Mail

If you send clinical information by facsimile machine, you risk compromising its confidentiality. It could be mistakenly sent to the wrong person or department by misdialing; it could be seen by inappropriate people at the receiving end; and/or it could be read by those at your end who should not have access, such as untrained workers. You should make the rules of confidentiality (see Section 7.1) part of the orientation of *all* new hires in your practice. For those whose services you use on a shared or part-time basis, some refresher training should be provided. You, the professional, are the only one who will be held responsible for violations.

Barton Bernstein, an attorney in Dallas, TX, suggests adding a paragraph to your intake forms to let clients know that you may be faxing clinical data to their managed care companies ("Legal Issues," 1992). A warning like this has been included in the client information brochure in this book (see Section 4.2). Many fax machines have ways to send this kind of warning as part of their built-in "cover sheet." Here is a warning in ordinary language that can be added to your fax cover sheet:

> Confidentiality Warning!!
>
> This communication may be **confidential and legally privileged.** If you are not the person to whom it is addressed, do not read, copy or let anyone else besides the addressee see it. Please respect the confidentiality of this personal information and respect the federal and state laws that protect its confidentiality. If this has been transmitted to you by mistake, we ask you to extend the courtesy of calling us back at the voice number listed above and telling us what went wrong.
>
> Thank you very much.

This more legalistic version is based on the article cited above ("Legal Issues," 1992).

[FORM 48—Use the top of this page for your letterhead.]

Authorization to Release Confidential Information to Family Members

Name of patient: _____ Date of birth: _____ Social Security #: _____

I understand that the purpose of this release is to assist with my/this patient's treatment by improving communication between professional service providers or agencies and the important individual(s) in my/the patient's life. To further this goal, I authorize this specific service provider, therapist, case manager, or _____, to release the below-specified information regarding me/the patient to the individual(s) listed below, and to receive information from them.

The information to be disclosed is marked by an × in the boxes below, and the items not to be released have a line drawn through them:

❑ Name of therapist ❑ Name of case manager ❑ Name(s) of treatment program(s)

❑ Admission/discharge information ❑ Treatment Plan ❑ Scheduled appointments ❑ Progress notes

❑ Compliance with treatment ❑ Discharge plans ❑ Treatment summary

❑ Psychological evaluation ❑ Medications ❑ Other: _____

This information is to be disclosed to these persons, who have the indicated relationship to me/the patient:

Name of person	Relationship
Name of person	Relationship
Name of person	Relationship

I understand that I may revoke this release at any time, except to the extent that it has already been acted upon. This release will expire on ❑ I year from this date, ❑ upon my discharge from treatment by this agency or by the person specified above, or ❑ under these circumstances: _____

Signature of client	Printed name	Date

Signature of parent/guardian/representative	Printed name	Relationship	Date

I witnessed that the person understood the nature of this request/authorization and freely gave his or her consent, but was physically unable to provide a signature.

Signature of witness	Printed name	Date

Signature of witness (a second witness is need if person is unable to give oral consent	Printed name	Relationship	Date

❑ Copy for patient or parent/guardian ❑ Copy for provider/therapist/case manager ❑ Copy for family member

FORM 48. Authorization to release confidential information to family members. Adapted from Marsh (1995). Copyright 1995 by the Pennsylvania Psychological Association. Adapted by permission—From *The Paper Office*, p. 332. Permission to photocopy this form is granted to purchasers of *The Paper Office* for personal use only (see copyright page for details).

Confidentiality Warning!!

The information contained in this fax message is intended only for the personal and confidential use of the designated recipient or entity named above. As such, this communication is **privileged, confidential, and exempt from disclosure under applicable law.** If the reader or actual recipient is not the intended recipient or an agent or employee responsible for delivering it to the intended recipient, you are hereby notified that you have received this document in error, and that any review, dissemination, distribution, or copying of this message is strictly prohibited by federal and state laws with civil and criminal penalties. If you have received this communication in error, we apologize for any inconvenience. We would appreciate your notifying us immediately by phone and then return the original to us by the U.S. Postal Service at the address listed above.

Thank you.

The sending of information from or to clients by e-mail will no doubt increase in the future. There have already been errors in such transmissions (e.g., a physician accidentally posted a confidential message in a public area on a large on-line service). Here are some guidelines:

- Until you have fully electronic records, print out all exchanges and place them in the client's chart.

- Ask the clients whether his or her e-mail address is confidential, and ask for permission to use it for confidential messages. Document this permission in the client's chart.

- Indicate which of your e-mail addresses is confidential and which are shared.

7.7 Confidentiality Notifications

I believe that a stamped note on each page of a report warning "Do not make copies," "Do not redistribute," or merely "Confidential" does not provide enough information for the reader to make decisions about what to do with the pages. As a simple and inexpensive alternative, I suggest notices like those given below. These notices include explicit rationales and warnings, so records are less likely to be misused and their confidentiality breached. You can edit one of the notices below or create your own version; you can then place it on the paper in various different ways:

- You can type it onto each page of every document you send out.

- If you use a word processor, it can be printed on every page of reports you create by adding it, from a "glossary" entry, as a "header" or "footer" on each page.

- You can photocopy it onto a sheet of labels, and then stick a label onto each page or onto the first page of records or reports you send out.

- You can make a rubber stamp with the notice's text and use it on each page of records you release.

The sample notices follow. (*Note:* Your state may have additional requirements for the release of HIV information or drug and alcohol information, as Pennsylvania does. If so, you may need to add the exact phrasing or citation of the appropriate laws to your releases.)

This information has been disclosed to you from records whose confidentiality is protected by state and federal laws, which prohibit you from making any further disclosure of it without the specific written consent of the person to whom it pertains, or as otherwise permitted by such regulations.

This is strictly CONFIDENTIAL material and is for the information only of the person to whom it is addressed. No responsibility can be accepted if it is made available to any other person, including the patient. Any duplication, transmittal, redisclosure or retransfer of these records is expressly prohibited. Such redisclosure may subject you to civil or criminal liability.

CONFIDENTIAL PATIENT INFORMATION
Any unauthorized redisclosure is a federal criminal offense (42 C.F.R., Part 2).

Permission to send these records to you has been given, in writing, by the patient they are about. You must not share these records with any other person, agency, or program unless you first obtain written permission to do so from the patient.

Warning: You must protect this document as confidential medical record information. Please handle, store, and dispose of appropriately.

This report may contain sensitive patient information and so should be released only to appropriate professionals.

Appendix: Resources

A.I   Annotated Bibliographies

A.Ia. Independent Practice

Beigel, J. K., & Earle, R. H. (1990). *Successful private practice in the 1990s: A new guide for the mental health professional.* New York: Brunner/Mazel.

Browning, C., & Browning, B. (1986). *Private practice handbook: The tools, tactics, and techniques for successful practice development* (3rd ed.) Los Alamitos, CA: Duncliffs International.

> Nuts and bolts of how to set up and run a private practice. Especially good on marketing. Very comprehensive.

Hendrickson, D. E., & Fraze, J. E. (1986). *How to establish your own independent practice* (5th ed.). Muncie, IN: Accelerated Development.

> The business essentials with some clinical forms.

Hersen, M., Kazdin, A., & Bellack, A. S. (1990). *The clinical psychologist's handbook.* Elmsford, NY: Pergamon Press.

I. C. System. (1992). *Credit and collections manual.* (Available from I. C. System, Inc., 444 East Highway 96, P.O. Box 64639, St. Paul, MN 55164-9971.)

> This simple and clear book can be used for staff training and for reference. It covers the main issues (aging accounts, granting credit, collection measures, laws, etc.).

Innovations in clinical practice: A source book. (yearly volumes). Sarasota, FL: Professional Resources Exchange.

> Useful and up-to-date materials for all aspects of clinical and community practice. A major resource and very highly recommended.

Margenau, E. A. (Ed.). (1990). *The encyclopedic handbook of private practice.* New York: Gardner Press.

> Absolutely comprehensive (1,023 pages). If you intend to stay in private practice, expand your work areas, manage your practice financially, and avoid burnout, this book is essential reading.

Psychotherapy Finances. (Published monthly by Ridgewood Financial Institute, P.O. Box 8979, Jupiter, FL 33468; 800-869-8450.)

Includes a yearly fee survey, many useful ideas on practice and financial planning, and news of developments in the field's financial aspects.

Psychotherapy Finances' *Guide to private practice.* (1995). Jupiter, FL: Ridgewood Financial Institute.

A three-ring binder of about 150 pages of material selected from the monthly newsletter *Psychotherapy Finances.* About half of the binder covers tax, pension, and other financial planning issues for the private practitioner; the other half covers practice issues.

Richards, D. L. (1990). *Building and managing your private practice.* Alexandria, VA: American Association for Counseling and Development.

Addresses every aspect of setting up a private practice (marketing, office choice, etc.).

Rofsky, C. (1991). *How to get paid for what you do.* Columbus, OH: Anadem Publishing.

Tips, forms, and other ways to make your billing practices more effective.

Small, R. F. (1994). *Maximizing third-party reimbursement in your mental health practice* (2nd ed.). Sarasota, FL: Professional Resource Exchange.

An introduction and overview with details and advice on form completion and processing.

Woody, R. H. (1989). *Business success in mental health practice: Modern marketing, management and legal strategies.* San Francisco, CA: Jossey-Bass.

A.Ib. The Law, Ethics, and Malpractice

Except for one videotape, this section includes books only.

American Psychological Association, Committee on Ethics. (1987). *Casebook on ethical principles of psychologists.* Washington, DC: Author.

Austin, K. M., Moline, M. E., & Williams, G. T. (1990). *Confronting malpractice: Legal and ethical dilemmas in psychotherapy.* Newbury Park, CA: Sage.

Examines 15 ethical issues and cites many legal cases in each area.

Bennett, B. E., Bryant, B., VandenBos, G. R., & Greenwood, A. (1990). *Professional liability and risk management.* Washington, DC: American Psychological Association.

This is the essential reading for therapists. It is conservative and comprehensive, and it offers information for all aspects of practice.

Bersoff, D. N. (1995). *Ethical conflicts in psychology.* Washington, DC: American Psychological Association.

Excerpts from more than 100 articles from many sources and perspectives with well-considered commentary. Very instructive.

Besharov, D. J. (1985). *The vulnerable social worker: Liability for serving children and families.* Silver Spring, MD: National Association of Social Workers.

Bongar, B. (1991). *The suicidal patient: Clinical and legal standards of care.* Washington, DC: American Psychological Association.

Realistic standards of care, sophisticated risk management strategies, risk estimators, legal action guidelines, postvention methods, and an up-to-date review of the literature.

Canter, M., Bennett, B. E., Jones, S. E., & Nagy, T. F. (1994). *Ethics for psychologists: A commentary on the APA ethics code.* Washington, DC: American Psychological Press.

Thoughtful commentaries on each section of the 1992 code revision by the authors of the code.

Dickson, D. T. (1995). *Law in the health and human services: A guide for social workers, psychologists, psychiatrists, and related professionals.* New York: Free Press.

   Introductory commentaries on many subjects with reprints of legal decisions.

Ethics in psychiatry [Videotape]. Washington, DC: American Psychiatric Association.

   This is a single videotape of 12 vignettes for discussion groups. It covers many issues, but rather superficially. It is available from the American Psychiatric Association, Office of Education at 202-682-6130 (no loans or rentals). There are other tapes in this series.

Haas, L. J., & Malouf, J. L. (1995). *Keeping up the good work: A practitioner's guide to mental health ethics* (2nd ed.). Sarasota, FL: Professional Resource Exchange.

   Comprehensive, readable, full of practical advice and a usable model for ethical decision making—all in 200 small pages. Very highly recommended.

Herlihy, B., & Golden, L. B. (1989). *Ethical standards casebook* (4th ed.). Alexandria, VA: American Association for Counseling and Development (AACD).

   The codes of AACD (revised in 1988), the 1989 National Board of Certified Counselors, and AACD's divisions, together with essays, guidelines, cases, and a case study section, make this a complete volume.

Hopkins, B. R., & Anderson, B. S. (1990). *The counselor and the law* (3rd ed.). Alexandria, VA: American Association on Counseling and Development.

   Law and practices for counselors. Topics include confidentiality, liabilities in education, community agencies, and duty to warn.

Jacob-Timm, S., & Hartshorne, T. (1994). *Ethics and law for school psychologists* (2nd ed.). Brandon, VT: Clinical Psychology.

   Very thorough coverage of the special areas and considerations of school practice.

Jenkins, P. L. (1989). *Hazards of psychiatric practice: A clinical and legal guide for the therapist.* Chicago: Year Book Medical.

Keith-Spiegel, P., & Koocher, G. P. (1985). *Ethics in psychology: Professional standards and cases.* New York: Random House.

   The standard text, by two psychologists who have been active in ethics committees and teaching courses in ethics for many years. Complete and clear.

Koocher, G. P., & Spiegel, P. C. (1990). *Children, ethics, and the law: Professional issues and cases.* Lincoln: University of Nebraska Press.

Meyer, R. E., Landis, E. R., & Hays, J. R. (1988). *Law for the psychotherapist.* New York: Norton.

   The introduction to the legal system and the concise chapter on malpractice are highly informative and reassuring; highly recommended. Later chapters deal with the courtroom issues (prediction of dangerousness, insanity defense, commitment, personal injury, family law, being an expert witness, etc.). There are also chapters covering diagnoses' effects; reality contact; impulse control; organic brain syndrome; and childhood disorders.

Nurcombe, B., & Partlett, D. F. (1994). *Child mental health and the law.* New York: Free Press.

Pope, K. S., & Vasquez, M. J. T. (1991). *Ethics in psychotherapy and counseling: A practical guide for psychologists.* San Francisco, CA: Jossey-Bass.

   Highly recommended. It is up-to-date, well reasoned and integrated, comprehensive, readable, and practical. Written by experts in the field.

Rave, E. J., & Larsen, C. C. (Eds.). (1995). *Ethical decision making in therapy: Feminist perspectives.* New York: Guilford Press.

Robertson, J. (1988). *Psychiatric malpractice: Liability of mental health professionals.* New York: Wiley.

Rosoff, A. J. (1981). *Informed consent.* Rockville, MD: Aspen Systems Publishing.

Rozovsky, F. A. (1990). *Consent to treatment: A practical guide* (2nd ed.). Boston: Little, Brown.

Simon, R. I. (1987). *Clinical psychiatry and the law.* Washington, DC: American Psychiatric Press.

Stromberg, C. D., Haggerty, D., Mishkin, B. J., Liebenluft, R. F., McMillan, M. H., Rubin, B. L., & Trilling, H. R. (1988). *The psychologist's legal handbook.* Washington, DC: National Register of Health Service Providers in Psychology.

> Seven hundred pages on every possible legal aspect of practice, forensics, and business issues.

Woody, R. H. (1988a). *Fifty ways to avoid malpractice: A guidebook for mental health professionals.* Sarasota, FL: Professional Resource Exchange.

Woody, R. H. (1988b). *Protecting your mental health practice: How to minimize legal and financial risk.* San Francisco: Jossey-Bass.

Zobel, H. B., & Rous, S. N. (1992). *Doctors and the law: Defendants and expert witnesses.* New York: Norton.

> Advice and insights into the processes of malpractice litigation.

A.Ic. Sexual Contact with Clients

This section includes books only.

American Medical Association, Council on Ethical and Judicial Affairs. (1991). Sexual misconduct in the practice of medicine. *Journal of the American Medical Association, 266*(19), 2741–2745.

Bates, C., & Brodsky, A. (1988). *Sex in the therapy hour: A case of professional incest.* New York: Guilford Press.

> The first half documents the abuse of a client and its long-term consequences; the second elaborates on the legal remedies and issues raised by this egregious case of a "psychopathic" therapist who used suing to intimidate professionals into tolerating his abuse for more than 10 years.

Burgess, A. W. & Hartman, C. R. (Eds.). (1986). *Sexual exploitation of patients by health professionals.* New York: Praeger.

> Contains sections from the patient's perspective revealing the methods of manipulation. Includes chapters on malpractice and litigation, professional and legal responses and their effects, and the treatment of offenders.

Edelwich, J., & Brodsky, A. (1991). *Sexual dilemmas for the helping professional* (rev. ed.). New York: Brunner/Mazel.

> Organized by topics (e.g., seduction, power, self-interest, morality, and opportunity). It covers most of the issues.

Gabbard, G. (Ed.).(1989). *Sexual exploitation in professional relations.* Washington, DC: American Psychiatric Press.

Gallagher, H. R. (1990). *By trust betrayed.* New York: Henry Holt.

Peterson, M. R. (1992). *At personal risk: Boundary violations in professional–client relationships.* New York: Norton.

> This wide-ranging and thoughtful book looks at a larger picture than just ethics violations, and so can serve as a preventative program. Peterson examines power differentials, managing them effectively, boundary violations (consisting of role reversal, a secret, a double bind, or an indulgence of professional privilege), the resulting damage, and the healing of each member.

Pope, K. S. (1994). *Sexual involvement with therapists: Patient assessment, subsequent therapy, forensics.* Washington, DC: American Psychological Association.

> This is *the* resource in this area. It integrates issues and offers a sample consent form for

victims, guidelines for treating victims, and issue lists. Its coverage of forensic testimony is very thorough.

Pope, K. S., & Bouhoutsos, J. C. (1986). *Sexual intimacy between therapists and patients.* New York: Praeger.

Public Education Work Group of the Task Force on Sexual Exploitation by Counselors and Therapists. (1990). *It's never O.K.: A handbook for victims and victim advocates on sexual exploitation by counselors and therapists.* St. Paul, MN: Task Force on Sexual Exploitation by Counselors and Therapists. (Available from the Minnesota Department of Corrections, Victim Services Unit, 300 Bigelow Building, 450 North Syndicate St., St. Paul, MN 55104; 612-642-0256.)

Comprehensive, sensitive, informative; very highly recommended.

Rutter, P. (1989). *Sex in the forbidden zone: When men in power—therapists, doctors, clergy, teachers and others—betray women's trust.* Los Angeles, CA: Tarcher.

Sensitive, well researched, and written by an experienced psychiatrist, it speaks directly to us. The last sections, for men and for women, are superb and very highly recommended to therapists and teachers of therapists.

Schoener, R., Milgrom, J. H., Gonsiorek, J. C., Luepker, E. T., & Conroe, R. M. (1989). *Psychotherapists' sexual involvement with clients: Intervention and prevention.* (Available from the Walk-In Counseling Center, 2421 Chicago Ave. S., Minneapolis, MN 55404.)

It justifies its high price by being totally comprehensive (44 chapters and 32 appendices) and authoritative. It is most highly recommended.

Striano, J. (1990). *Can psychotherapists hurt you?* Santa Barbara, CA: Professional Press.

They can—by misdiagnosing medical illnesses, addicting you (i.e., the client) to therapy, inducting you into a therapy cult, and being sexual with you.

These three first-person accounts are also highly recommended:

Freeman, L.. & Freeman, R., H. (1976). *Betrayal.* New York: Stein & Day.
Plaisil, E. (1985). *Therapist.* New York: St. Martin's/Marek.
Walker, E., & Young, T. D. (1986). *A killing cure.* New York: Henry Holt.

Finally, you should be familiar with your state's professional practice law as it applies to you, and with your professional liability insurance contract.

A.Id. Practice Guidelines from Professional Organizations

American Association for Counseling and Development. (1988). *Ethical standards for the American Association for Counseling and Development.* Alexandria, VA: Author.

American Association for Marriage and Family Therapy (AAMFT). (1988). *AAMFT code of ethical principles for marriage and family therapists.* Washington, DC: Author.

American Psychiatric Association. (1985). *Opinion of the Ethics Committee on the principles of medical ethics.* Washington, DC: Author.

American Psychiatric Association. (1986). *The principles of medical ethics with annotations especially applicable to psychiatry.* Washington, DC: Author.

American Psychiatric Association. (1987). Guidelines on confidentiality. *American Journal of Psychiatry, 144,* 1522–1526.

American Psychological Association. (1977). *Standards for providers of psychological services.* Washington, DC: Author.

American Psychological Association. (1981a). Ethical principles of psychologists. *American Psychologist, 36*(6), 633–638.

American Psychological Association. (1981b). Specialty guidelines for the delivery of services by clinical (counseling, industrial/organizational, and school) psychologists. *American Psychologist, 36*(6), 639–681.

American Psychological Association. (1982). *Ethical principles in the conduct of research with human participants.* Washington, DC: Author.

American Psychological Association. (1985). *Standards for educational and psychological tests.* Washington, DC: Author.

American Psychological Association. (1986). *Guidelines for computer-based tests and interpretations.* Washington, DC: Author.

American Psychological Association. (1987). General guidelines for providers of psychological services. *American Psychologist, 42,* 712–723.

American Psychological Association. (1990). Ethical principles of psychologists. *American Psychologist, 45,* 390–395.

American Psychological Association. (1992a). Ethical principles of psychologists and code of conduct. *American Psychologist, 47,* 1598–1611.

American Psychological Association. (1992b). *Consent agreement with the Federal Trade Commission.* Washington, DC: Author.

American Psychological Association. (1993). *Guidelines for ethical conduct in the care and use of animals.* Washington, DC: Author.

American Psychological Association. (1994). Guidelines for child custody evaluations in divorce proceedings. *American Psychologist, 49,* 677–680.

American Psychological Association, Committee on Ethical Guidelines for Forensic Psychologists. (1991). Specialty guidelines for forensic psychologists. *Law and Behavior, 15,* 655–665.

American Psychological Association, Committee on Professional Practice and Standards. (1993). Record keeping guidelines. *American Psychologist, 48,* 984–986.

American Psychological Association, Office of Minority Affairs. (1993). Guidelines for providers of psychological services to ethnic, linguistic, and culturally diverse populations. *American Psychologist, 48,* 45–48.

National Association of School Psychologists. (1992a). *Principles of professional ethics.* Silver Spring, MD: Author.

National Association of School Psychologists. (1992b). *Standards for the provision of school psychological services.* Silver Spring, MD: Author.

National Association of School Psychologists. (1992c). *Professional conduct manual.* Silver Spring, MD: Author.

National Association of Social Workers. (1990). *Code of ethics of the National Association of Social Workers.* Washington, DC: Author.

A.Ie. Clinical Records

Davis, N. M. (1990). *Medical abbreviations: 7000 conveniences at the expense of communications and safety.* (Available from Neil M. Davis, 1143 Wright Dr., Huntington Valley, PA 19006.)

Hersen, M., & Bellack, A. S. (Eds.). (1988). *Behavioral assessment: A practical handbook* (3rd ed.). Elmsford, NY: Pergamon Press.

Jayaratne, S., & Levy, R. (1979). *Empirical clinical practice.* New York: Columbia University Press. Especially useful for social workers.

Kagle, J. D. (1991). *Social work records* (2nd ed.). Belmont, CA: Wadsworth.

Thorough and informative, this book has considered all aspects of recording and the values of each kind of record (narratives, problem-oriented records, time series, goal attainment scaling). Very practical for the busy professional.

Sturm, I. E. (1987). The psychologist and the problem-oriented record (POR). *Professional Psychology Research and Practice, 18,* 155–158.

A good brief summary, tailored to therapy, with several examples.

Weed, L. L. (1969). *Medical records, medical education and patient care.* Cleveland, OH: Case Western Reserve University Press.

Wilson, S. J. (1980). *Recording: Guidelines for social workers.* New York: Free Press.

Comprehensive and practical for learning to record all kinds of therapeutic interactions.

Wilson, S. J. (1984). Privileged communication. In P. Keller & L. G. Ritt (Eds.), *Innovations in clinical practice: A source book* (Vol. 3, pp. 391–405). Sarasota, FL: Professional Resource Exchange.

A.1f. Managed Care

Journals

Behavioral Healthcare Tomorrow. (Published by Institute for Behavioral Healthcare, 1110 Mar West St., Suite E, Tiburon, CA 94920-1879; 415-435-9821; fax, 415-435-9092.)

Although it is rather commercial in content and layout, this journal offers the most solid ideas, treated briefly.

Managed Care Strategies. (Published by Ridgewood Financial Institute, P.O. Box 8979, Jupiter, FL 33468; 800-869-8450.)

Ten pages per monthly issue. Articles in the issue of April 1995: "To Be Accredited or Not—One Group's Experience with the JCAHO," "How One Group Practice Changed Its Payment Scheme to Adjust for High Volume," "An Ohio Medicaid Program May Allow Solos and Small Groups to Get a Foot in The Door," "Medco Is Buying Blocks of Time from Panel Providers," "Brief Notes on Specific Managed Care Organizations," "Employment Opportunities," "Upcoming Meetings."

Open Minds. (Published by Open Minds, 44 South Franklin St., Gettysburg, PA 17325; 717-334-1329; fax 717-334-0538.)

Ten pages per monthly issue. Articles in the issue of June 1993: "Industry Profile: College Health Enterprises," "Industry Profile: Corphealth, Inc.," "Pro and Con: A Look at Harvard's New Mental Health and Chemical Dependency Benefit Plan," "Industry Analysis: Do Insurance Companies Discriminate against Recovering Alcoholics?", "Professional Opportunities," "Industry News," "Industry Statistics," "Patient Functional Improvement Correlated with Satisfaction Level," and other small sections.

Practice Strategies. (Published by American Association for Marriage and Family Therapy, P.O. Box 79445, Baltimore, MD 21279-0455; 919-553-0637; fax, 410-223-2329.)

Ten pages per monthly issue. Articles in the issue of April 1995: "Provider Memberships, Standard Credentialling Top AMMBHA Agenda," "Outcomes Can Mean a Yes or No for Network Providers," "Competition, Managed Care Credited for Holding Down Healthcare Costs," "Capitation Bottom Line: Focus on Costs," "Large Groups Share Secrets for Success," "Providers Should Measure Outcomes Now, Advise Groups, Companies and Consultants," "Multi-Discipline Group Pursues Linkages—Finds a Niche with Pain Management,"several two- or three-paragraph notes on specific managed care organizations; "Employment Opportunities."

Psychotherapy Finances. (Published by Ridgewood Financial Institute, P.O. Box 8979, Jupiter, FL 33468; 800-869-8450.)

Books

Austad, C. S., & Berman, W. H. (Eds.). (1991). *Psychotherapy in managed health care: The optimal use of time and resources.* Washington, DC: American Psychological Association.

    Chapters of this edited book focus on applying different theoretical models to various clinical populations.

Browning, C. H., & Browning, B. J. (1994). *How to partner with managed care: A ''do-it-yourself kit'' for building working relationships and getting steady referrals.* Los Alamitos, CA: Duncliffs International.

    This book focuses, in great detail, on the "brass tacks" of working with managed care. Valuable if you need this; depressing to those whose values managed care mangles.

Corcoran, K., & Vandiver, V. (1996). *Maneuvering the maze of managed care: Skills for mental health practitioners.* New York: Free Press.

    This is the best book of the lot for the practitioner. Heavily researched and clearly written, it offers background and direction, as well as forms and procedures.

Goodman, M., Brown, J., & Deitz, P. (1992). *Managing managed care: A mental health practitioner's survival guide.* Washington, DC: American Psychiatric Press.

    After a brief introduction to managed care, this book offers to the general psychological practitioner interventions aimed at lessening patient impairment—a unifying concept and language across disciplines and settings. The construction of behavioral treatment plans based on this model is fully illustrated.

Lowman, R. L., & Resnick, R. J. (Eds.). (1994). *The mental health professional's guide to managed care.* Washington, DC: American Psychological Association.

    This is not a book on "how to do it in managed care." In great detail and richness, it reviews mental health policy from many perspectives.

MacKenzie, K. R. (Ed.). (1995). *Effective use of group therapy in managed care.* Washington, DC: American Psychiatric Press.

    Just what the title says.

Poynter, W. L. (1994). *The preferred provider's handbook: Building a successful private therapy practice in the managed care marketplace.* New York: Brunner/Mazel.

    This book mainly concerns how to market your private practice to managed care organizations.

Reiss, B. F. (Ed.). (1994). Psychoanalysis and dynamic psychotherapy: The mental health provider and managed care [Special issue]. *Psychoanalysis and Psychotherapy, 11*(2).

    This special issue of a journal focuses on psychodynamics and managed care. It can be purchased from International Universities Press (800-835-3487).

Shueman, S. A., Troy W. G., & Mayhugh, S. L. (Eds.). (1994). *Managed behavioral health care: An industry perspective.* Springfield, IL: Charles C Thomas.

    The authors are all top administrators in managed care practices or organizations and are still clinicians, so their perspectives are intriguing.

Stout, C. E., Theis, G. E., & Oher, J. M. (Eds.). (1996). *The complete guide to managed behavioral healthcare.* New York: Wiley.

Todd, T. (1994). *Surviving and prospering in the managed mental health care marketplace.* Sarasota, FL: Professional Resource Exchange.

    A small book (100 pages) on what managed care is and how to work within it; can serve as an introduction to the topic.

Winegar, N., & Bistline, J. L. (1994). *Marketing mental health services to managed care*. New York: Haworth Press.

> The authors offer many examples of how to formulate cases in ways that enhance communication with managed care reviewers.

Yenny, S. L., & American Psychological Association Practice Directorate. (1994). *Business strategies for a caring profession: A practitioner's guidebook*. Washington, DC: American Psychological Association.

> A good overview of the current status of the professional field supports the selection of a model of practice. More than half of this small (120-page) book is then devoted to quick notes on administrative systems, personnel, claims processing, computers, marketing, and consultants.

A.2 Resources for Therapy with Minorities

This list was complied by Mark Leach, PhD, of Hattiesburg, MS.

Atkinson, D. R., Morten, G., & Sue, D. W. (1993). *Counseling American minorities: A cross-cultural perspective* (4th ed.). Madison, WI: Brown & Benchmark.

Comas-Díaz, L., & Griffith, E. E. H. (1988). *Clinical guidelines in cross-cultural mental health*. New York: Wiley.

Dana, R. H. (1993). *Multicultural assessment perspectives for professional psychology*. Boston: Allyn & Bacon.

Ho, M. K. (1987). *Family therapy with ethnic minorities*. Beverly Hills, CA: Sage.

Ho, M. K. (1992). *Minority children and adolescents in therapy*. Newbury Park, CA: Sage.

Katz, J. (1985). The sociopolitical nature of counseling. *The Counseling Psychologist, 13*, 615–624.

Locke, D. D. (1992). *Increasing multicultural understanding: A comprehensive model*. Newbury Park, CA: Sage.

McFadden J. (Ed.). (1993). *Transcultural counseling: Bilateral and international perspectives*. Alexandria, VA: American Association for Counseling and Development (now called the American Counseling Association).

Paniagua, F. A. (1994). *Assessing and treating culturally diverse clients: A practical guide*. Thousand Oaks, CA: Sage.

Pedersen, P. B. (1991). Multiculturalism as a generic approach to counseling. *Journal of Counseling and Development, 70*, 6–12.

Ponterotto, J. G., Casas, J. M., Suzuki, L. A., & Alexander, C. M. (Eds.). (1995). *Handbook of multicultural counseling*. Thousand Oaks, CA: Sage.

Ponterotto, J. G., & Pedersen, P. B. (1993). *Preventing prejudice*. Thousand Oaks, CA: Sage.

Ridley, C. (1994). *Overcoming unintentional racism in counseling and therapy*. Thousand Oaks, CA: Sage.

Sue, D. W., & Sue, D. (1990). *Counseling the culturally different: Theory and practice* (2nd ed.). New York: Wiley.

A.3 Suppliers

A.3a. Mail-Order Suppliers of Office Equipment

Discounters: The following companies have large catalogs of computers, and all types of office equipment, video and audio equipment, telephones, appliances, and so on, at the current best overall discounts. Their phone salespeople are generally well informed, reliable, and efficient, although they can be pushy. In New York: 47th Street Photo, 800-234-4747; Executive Photo, 800-223-7323; J & R Music World, 800-221-8180.

Hello Direct, 5884 Eden Park Place, San Jose, CA 95138-1859; 800-520-3311 or 408-972-1990; fax, 408-972-8155.
   A 50-page informative catalog of everything you could use with a telephone (headsets, faxes, answering machines, telephones, etc.). A little more expensive than the discounters, but very well informed and excellent service.

Quill Corporation, P.O. Box 94080, Palatine, IL 60094-4080; 800-789-1331; fax, 800-789-8955.
   Quill publishes a 375-page semi-annual catalog offering all office supplies and most equipment. It offers free shipping on most orders of $45 or more, phone ordering, and all the popular assets of modern distribution. Reliable, cheap, courteous, honorable.

A.3b. Mail-Order Suppliers of Office Forms and Stationery

American Medical Association (AMA), P.O. Box 7046, Dover, DE 19903; 800-621-8335.
   The source for HCFA insurance forms. Charge card orders for these forms can be placed by calling the 800 number.

Business Envelope Manufacturers, P.O. Box 517, Thorofare, NJ 08086; 800-275-4400.
   A good-sized catalog of fairly low-cost imprinted stationery and office supplies.

Colwell Systems, 201 Kenyon Rd., Champaign, IL 61820; 217-351-5400.
   Especially good for billing and "one-write" checking forms.

Graftek Communications, P.O. Box 3487, Boca Raton, FL 33427-3487; 800-848-2992.
   Graftex offers imprinted HCFA-1500 forms and other supplies for billing Medicare.

Histacount, 301 Grove Rd., Thorofare, NJ 09086; 800-645-5220.
   A large catalog of imprinted stationery, forms for health care professionals, and some paper office supplies.

Medical Arts Press, 8500 Wyoming Ave. N, Minneapolis, MN 55445; orders, 800-328-2179.
   A large (120-page) catalog of quality stationery and office management materials, mainly for medical offices.

New England Business Service, 500 Main St., Groton, MA 01471; 800-225-6380, fax, 800-234-4324.
   A good-sized catalog of every kind of paperwork (forms, computer checks, etc.). Good selection of stationery.

The Overheadshrinkers, P.O. Box 3677, South Pasadena, CA 91031-6677; 818-799-6882.
   Suppliers of a "SuperΨbill" for therapy and one for testing, a release, and a simple evaluation summary. These forms are expensive, but are well designed and will save time and confusion.

Quill Corporation, P.O. Box 94080, Palatine, IL 60094-4080; 800-789-1331; fax, 800-789-8955.
   A very large catalog of low-cost mail-order office supplies of every imaginable kind.

Reliable Office Supply, P.O. Box 1502, Ottawa, IL 61350; 800-735-4000, fax, 800-326-3233.
   About equal to Quill in the size of its catalog; cheaper on some items; different shipping costs. Compare on what *you* buy.

SYCOM, 1801 West Highway 66, Flagstaff, AZ 86001; 800-356-8141.
   A good-sized catalog of imprinted stationery and forms for health care professionals. There is also a 56-page catalog called "Business Solutions for Psychotherapists" with some useful forms (although most are for large practices), and the general catalog contains more options. Especially good on stationery designs and papers and collection forms.

UAL Medical Products, 650 Columbia St., Brea, CA 92821; 800-992-5755; fax, 800-998-7706.

    A large assortment of labels for collection and general office needs.

U.S. Government Printing Office, Superintendent of Documents, P.O. Box 371954, Pittsburgh, PA 15250-7954; 202-512-1800; fax, 202-512-2250.

    The primary source for HCFA-1500 billing forms.

Visible, 1750 Wallace Ave., St. Charles, IL 60174; 800-323-0628.

    A good-sized catalog of low-cost mail-order office supplies.

A.3c. Miscellaneous

Credit cards: Professional Services Account, c/o Maryland Bank, N.A., P.O. Box 15464, Wilmington, DE 19885-9440; 800-526-8286 (Monday through Friday 8 A.M. to 8 P.M., Saturday 8 A.M. to 5 P.M.).

Billing services: ABS, Inc., Willow Lawn Drive, Richmond, VA 23230; 800-296-4089; fax, 800-296-0331.

Collection agency: I. C. System, Inc., 444 East Highway 96, P.O. Box 64639, St. Paul, MN 55164-9971.

A.4   Publishers and Distributors of Tests, Clinical Forms, and Other Materials for Practitioners

All of the sources listed here have catalogs.

Accelerated Development, C/O Taylor & Francis, 1900 Frost Rd., Suite 101, Bristol, PA 19007-1598; 800-222-1166.

    A small catalog of "psychologically based books written by professionals."

ADD Warehouse, 300 Northwest 70th Ave., Suite 102, Plantation, FL 33317; 954-792-8944.

    As its name suggests, this company specializes in products for Attention-Deficit/Hyperactivity Disorder (ADHD).

American Counseling Association (formerly American Association for Counseling and Development), 5999 Stevenson Ave., Alexandria, VA 22304-3300; 800-347-6647; fax, 800-473-2329.

American Psychiatric Press, Order Department, 1400 K St., NW, Washington, DC 20005; 800-368-5777.

American Psychological Association, Order Department, P.O. Box 2710, Hyattsville, MD 20784; 800-374-2721.

Behavioral Science Book Service, Newbridge Communications, 3000 Cindel Dr., Delran, NJ 08370-0001; 800-363-4815.

    A mail-order distributor of about 100 books a year at about 25% discount from list prices. The company screens books, and you receive very useful reviews and a postcard to be returned 13 times a year. Selections are well balanced among professions and interests. An excellent way to keep yourself and your (deductible) professional library up to date.

Brunner/Mazel, 19 Union Square West, New York, NY 10003; 800-825-3089.

    A large catalog of current and high-quality older books in all areas. Especially strong in all kinds of family therapy and psychoanalysis.

Bureau for At-Risk Youth, 135 Dupont, Planview, IL 11804.

    All kinds of printed materials about children and adolescents: posters, self-esteem-building programs and books, materials on disorders, and so forth. Useful for parents, kids, and professionals.

Channing L. Bete Company, 200 State Rd., S. Deerfield, MA 01372; 413-665-7611.

Publisher of hundreds of "Scriptographic" booklets for patient education on all diagnoses and conditions, treatments, family dynamics, and so on. If you want to introduce concepts with a simple, visual format and brief text, one or more of these books will do it.

Childswork/Childsplay, P.O. Box 61586, King of Prussia, PA 19406; 800-962-1141.

"A catalog addressing the mental health needs of children and their families through play."

Consulting Psychologists Press, P.O. Box 10096, Palo Alto, CA 94303; 415-969-8901.

"Testing, teaching and training materials."

The Guilford Press, 72 Spring St., New York, NY 10012; 800-365-7006.

A large catalog of high-quality books, videotapes, audiotapes, and software for all aspects of psychology, not to mention the publisher of this book and the *Clinician's Thesaurus* (Zuckerman, 1995).

Human Services, 4205 Herschel Ave., Dallas, TX, 75219; 800-873-2834; fax, 214-522-0460.

Human Services offers the following: poster-size educational cards called "Headlines," which can be personalized; a client education quarterly newsletter, *Update on Human Behavior*, which can also be personalized; an annotated bibliography called "Building a Successful Private Practice"; and an 8½" × 11" appointment calendar for mental health professionals, with long days (7 A.M. to 9 P.M.), DSM and CPT codes, pages for referral tracking and sources, a list of drugs and their side effects, a list of conferences and associations, and other features.

Impact Publishers, P.O. Box 1094, San Luis Obispo, CA 93406; 805-543-5911.

Very useful and high-quality books on assertiveness, relationships, families, and personal growth written by professionals for clients and professionals. You will not regret assigning or lending them to clients.

Institute for Personality and Ability Testing, P.O. Box 1188, Champaign, IL 61824; 800-225-4728.

A catalog "of psychological assessment instruments, computer interpretative services, and books."

Institute for Rational–Emotive Therapy, 45 East 65th St., New York, NY 10021-6593; 800-323-IRET.

A catalog of workshops and training programs, and about 100 books, posters, and tapes about cognitive therapy.

Jastak Associates, P.O. Box 3410, Wilmington, DE 19804-0250; 800-221-WRAT.

Jastak offers "simple and precise tools for the testing professional." About 30 tests of academic and cognitive skills (mainly for children), and 12 monographs on test development.

Metritech, P.O. Box 6479, Champaign, IL 61826-6479; 800-747-4868.

A small and interesting catalog of tests for personality, extroversion, stress tolerance, work motivation, ADHD, organizational culture, school leadership, adolescents' social skills, etc.

Multi-Health Systems, 908 Niagara Falls Blvd., North Tonawanda, NY 14120-2060; 800-456-3003.

"Assessment material and computer software for mental health, education, industry, organizations, and research." A leader in the field.

National Computer Systems, Professional Assessment Services, 5605 Circle Dr., Minnetonka, MN 55343; 800-NCS-7271.

A great variety of tests and scoring systems.

New Harbinger Publications, 5674 Shattuck Ave., Oakland, CA 94609; 800-748-6273 or 510-652-0215; fax, 510-652-5472.

A large number of professionally written self-help materials (which are quite useful in therapy), as well as some excellent ones for professionals. Highly recommended.

Ohio Psychological Publishing Company, 6100 Channingway Blvd., Suite 303, Columbus, OH 43209; 614-224-3288 or 800-486-1985.

High quality and informative "Questions and Answers about . . . " brochures for the public, *your office, and other professionals. This company also publishes the National Psychologist,* a monthly newspaper of use to clinicians because of its national and unaligned political information, and a very functional datebook.

Professional Resource Exchange, P.O. Box 15560, Sarasota, FL 34277-1560; 800-443-3364.

This company publishes the extraordinarily useful and fully current yearly series *Innovations in Clinical Practice;* it also publishes and distributes a line of books of great relevance to the practicing clinician.

Psychological and Educational Publications, 1477 Rolins Rd., Burlingame, CA 94010-2316; 800-523-5775; fax, 415-340-7287.

A medium-sized catalog of hard-to-find tests in academic skills, development, psychological difficulties, and intellect.

Psychological Assessment Resources, P.O. Box 998, Odessa, FL 33556; 800-331-TEST.

A comprehensive and selective collection of "testing resources for the professional," especially in computerized versions. The standard source for this field.

Psychological Corporation, P.O. Box 839954, San Antonio, TX 78283-3954; 800-211-8378.

A very large catalog of "tests, products, and services for psychological assessment."

PRO-ED, 8700 Shoal Creek Blvd., Austin, TX 78757-6897; 512-451-3246.

A large catalog specializing in special education materials.

Research Press, P.O. Box 9177, Champaign, IL 61826; 800-519-2707.

High-quality, behavior-therapy-oriented training and clinical materials (print, video) in mental health, and especially in developmental disabilities and special education.

Sigma Assessment Systems, P.O. Box 610984, Port Huron, MI 48061-0984; 800-265-1285; fax, 800-361-9411; e-mail, 70363.3413@compuserve.com.

A medium-sized collection of tests and books, especially strong in the personality and vocational areas. Many classics.

Slosson Educational Publications, P.O. Box 280, East Aurora, NY 14052; 800-828-4800.

Test products for all educational settings.

Western Psychological Services, 12031 Wilshire Blvd., Los Angeles, CA 90025; 800-222-2670.

A large catalog of evaluation materials for all practice areas of psychology and counseling.

John Wiley & Sons, 1 Wiley Dr., Somerset, NJ 08875; 800-433-8234.

A fully informative catalog of tests, books, and journals.

In addition, many useful books and materials can be found advertised in the classified and display advertising sections of the following publications:

APA Monitor—monthly newspaper of the American Psychological Association.

Communique—newsletter of the National Association of School Psychologists.

NASW News—newsletter of the National Association of Social Workers.

Guidepost—newsletter of the American Counseling Association.

National Psychologist—published by Ohio Psychological Publishing.

References

Ackley, D. C. (1997). *Breaking free of managed care: A step-by-step guide to regaining control of your practice.* New York: Guilford Press.

Adams, S., & Orgel, M. (1975). *Through the mental health maze.* Washington, DC: Health Research Group.

Adler, W. N. (1988). The sexualization of psychiatric practice. *MPS News* (Maryland Psychiatric Society), pp. 3–4.

Affleck, D. C., & Garfield, S. L. (1961). Predictive judgements of therapists and duration of stay in psychotherapy. *Journal of Clinical Psychology. 17,* 134–137.

Alabama Psychological Association. (n.d.). *Client–therapist intimacy: Appropriate and inappropriate conduct.* Montgomery: Author.

Allen, J. P., & Columbus, M. (Eds.). (1995). *Assessing alcohol problems: A guide for clinicians and researchers.* (NIAAA Treatment Handbook Series 4). Bethesda, MD: National Institute on Alcohol Abuse and Alcoholism.

Allen, M. H., Serper, M. R., & Elfenbein, C. (1994). Psychiatric principles. In L. R. Goldfrank, N. E. Flomenbaum, N. A. Lewin, et al. (Eds.), *Goldfrank's toxicologic emergencies.* Norwalk, CT: Appleton & Lange.

American Medical Association. (1995). *Physicians' current procedural terminology* (4th ed.). Washington, DC: Author.

American Medical Association, Office of General Counsel. (1973). *Medicolegal forms with legal analysis.* Washington, DC: American Medical Association.

American Professional Agency. (1992). *Important information concerning your professional liability claim.* Amityville, NY: Author.

American Psychiatric Association. (1987a). APA guidelines on confidentiality. *American Journal of Psychiatry, 144,* 1522–1526.

American Psychiatric Association. (1987b). *Diagnostic and statistical manual of mental disorders* (3rd ed., rev.). Washington, DC: Author.

American Psychiatric Association. (1994). *Diagnostic and statistical manual of mental disorders* (4th ed.). Washington, DC: Author.

American Psychiatric Association. (1996). *American Psychiatric Association practice guidelines.* Washington, DC: Author.

American Psychological Association (APA). (1981). Specialty guidelines for the delivery of services by clinical (counseling, industrial/organizational, and school) psychologists. *American Psychologist, 36*(6), 639–681.

American Psychological Association (APA). (1992a). Ethical principles of psychologists and code of conduct. *American Psychologist, 47,* 1598–1611.

American Psychological Association (APA). (1992b). *Consent agreement with the Federal Trade Commission.* Washington, DC: Author.

American Psychological Association (APA), Committee on Ethics. (1988). Trends in ethics cases, common pitfalls and published resources. *American Psychologist, 43,* 564–572.

American Psychological Association (APA), Committee on Legal Issues. (1996). Strategies for private practitioners coping with subpoenas or compelled testimony for client records or test data. *Professional Psychology: Research and Practice, 27*(3), 245–251.

American Psychological Association (APA), Committee on Professional Practice and Standards. (1993). Record keeping guidelines. *American Psychologist, 48,* 308–310, 984–986.

American Psychological Association (APA), Committee on Professional Practice and Standards. (1996). Twenty-four questions (and answers) about professional practice in the area of child abuse. *Professional Psychology: Research and Practice, 26*(4), 377–385.

American Psychological Association (APA), Committee on Psychological Tests and Assessment. (1996). Statement on the disclosure of test data. *American Psychologist, 51*(6), 644–648.

American Psychological Association (APA), Committee on Women in Psychology. (1989). If sex enters the psychotherapy relationship. *Professional Psychology: Research and Practice, 20,* 112–115.

American Psychological Association (APA), Office of Minority Affairs. (1993). *Guidelines for providers of psychological services to ethnic, linguistic, and culturally diverse populations.* Washington, DC: Author.

Anderten, P., Staulcup, V., & Grisso, T. (1980). On being ethical in legal places. *Professional Psychology: Research and Practice, 11,* 764–773.

Appelbaum, P. S. (1993). Legal liability and managed care. *American Psychologist, 48*(3), 251–257.

Appelbaum, P. S. (1996). Suits against clinicians for warning of patients' violence. *Psychiatric Services, 47*(7), 683–684.

Association for Advancement of Behavior Therapy. (1977, May 22). *Professional consultation and peer review* [Pamphlet]. New York: Author.

Baird, K. A., & Rupert, P. A. (1987). Clinical management of confidentiality: A survey of psychologists in seven states. *Professional Psychology Research and Practice, 18*(4), 347–352.

Baker, E. K. (1988). Use of journal writing for psychologists. In P. A. Keller & S. R. Heyman (Eds.), *Innovations in clinical practice: A sourcebook* (Vol. 7, pp. 269–282). Sarasota, FL: Professional Resource Press.

Barge, B. N., & Fenalason, K. J. (1989). *Dealing effectively with malpractice litigation.* (Available from Human Factors Department, Risk Management Services Division, St. Paul Companies, 385 Washington St., St. Paul, MN 55102)

Barnett, J. E., & Yutrzenka, B. A. (1994). Nonsexual dual relationships in professional practice, with special applications to rural and military communities. *Independent Practitioner, 14*(5), 243–248.

Beck, A. T. (1986). Hopelessness as a predictor of eventual suicide. *Annals of the New York Academy of Sciences, 487,* 90–96.

Beck, A. T., Kovacs, M., & Weissman, A. (1979). Assessment of suicidal intention: The Scale for Suicide Ideation. *Journal of Consulting and Clinical Psychology, 47,* 343–352.

Beck, A. T., Schuyler, D., & Herman, I. (1974). Development of suicide intent scales. In A. T. Beck, H. L. P. Resnik, & A. J. Lettieri (Eds.), *The prediction of suicide.* Bowie, MD: Charles Press.

Beck, J. C. (1982). When the patient threatens violence: An empirical study of clinical practice after Tarasoff. *Bulletin of the Academy of Psychiatry and the Law, 10,* 189–201.

Beck, J. C. (Ed.). (1985). *The potentially violent patient and the* Tarasoff *decision in psychiatric practice.* Washington, DC: American Psychiatric Press.

Beck, J. C. (1990). The potentially violent patient: Clinical, legal, and ethical implications. In E. A. Margenau (Ed.), *The encyclopedic handbook of private practice* (pp. 697–709). New York: Gardner Press.

Beckham, E. E. (1992). Predicting patient dropout in psychotherapy. *Psychotherapy, 29,* 177–182.

Beeman, D. G., & Scott, N. A. (1991). Therapists' attitudes toward psychotherapy informed consent with adolescents. *Professional Psychology Research and Practice, 22*(3), 230–234.

Bennett, B. E., Bryant, B., VandenBos, G. R., & Greenwood, A. (1990). *Professional liability and risk management.* Washington, DC: American Psychological Association.

Berk, M., Rubin, R., & Peck, S. (1994). *Super-pak practice builders: Forty forms for psychotherapists.* Island Park, NY: Private Practitioners Group.

Berkowitz, S. (1995). Common questions and answers regarding process notes. *Massachusetts Psychologist Quarterly, 39*(2), 4–12.

Berlin, F. S., Malin, H. M., & Dean, S. (1991). Effects of statutes requiring psychiatrists to report suspected sexual abuse of children. *American Journal of Psychiatry, 148*(4), 449–453.

Bindrim, P. (1980, July). Group therapy: Protecting privacy. *Psychology Today,* pp. 24–28.

Blumenthal, S. J., & Kupfer, D. J. (Eds.). (1990). *Suicide over the life cycle: Risk factors, assessment and treatment of suicidal patients.* Washington, DC: American Psychiatric Press.

Boedecker, A. L. (1995). Practicing with integrity: Responding to a malpractice suit. *Networker: Newsletter of the New Hampshire Psychological Association, 7*(7), 2–3.

Bongar, B. (1991). *The suicidal patient: Clinical and legal standards of care.* Washington, DC: American Psychological Association.

Bongar, B. (1992). Effective risk management and the suicidal patient. *Register Report, 18*(6), 1–26.

Branscomb, L. (1996, Winter). Clinical advantages of the extended psychotherapy disclosure form: A feminist ethical perspective. *Georgia Psychologist,* p. 46–49.

Bratten, E. B., Otto, S., & Handelsman, M. M. (1993). What do people want to know about psychotherapy? *Psychotherapy, 30*(4), 565–570.

Bouhoutsos, J., Holroyd, J., Lerman, H., Forer, B. R., & Greenberg, M. (1983). Sexual intimacy between psychotherapists and patients. *Professional Psychology: Research and Practice, 14,* 185–196.

Broadman, K., Erdmann, A. J., Jr., & Wolff, H. G. (1949). *Manual: Cornell Medical Index Health Questionnaire.* New York: Cornell University Medical College.

Brock, G. W., & Barnard, C. P. (1988). *Procedures in marriage and family therapy* (2nd ed.). Boston: Allyn & Bacon.

Brodsky, S. L., & Schumacher, J. E. (1990). The impact of litigation on psychotherapy practice: Litigation fears and litigaphobia. In E. A. Margenau (Ed.), *The encyclopedic handbook of private practice* (pp. 664–676). New York: Gardner Press.

Caldwell, C. B., & Gottesman, I. I. (1990). Schizophrenics kill themselves too: A review of the risk factors for suicide. *Schizophrenia Bulletin, 16*(4), 571–584.

Cannella, M. (1995, Summer). Resident's column. *New Jersey Psychiatric News.*

Canter, M., Bennett, B. E., Jones, S. E., & Nagy, T. F. (1994). *Ethics for psychologists: A commentary on the APA ethics code.* Washington, DC: American Psychological Press.

Cervantes, N. (1992). Ethical responsibility of therapists: Spousal abuse cases. *Psychotherapy Bulletin, 26*(4), 12–15.

Charles, S. C. (1985). Doctors and the litigation process: Going against the grain. *Child and Adolescent Psychotherapy, 3,* 219–222.

Charles, S. C., Warnecke, R. B., Nelson, A., & Pyskoty, C. E. (1988). Appraisal of the event as a factor in coping with malpractice litigation. *Behavioral Medicine, 14*(4), 148–155.

Charles, S. C., Wilbert, J. R., & Franke, K. J. (1985). Sued and non-sued physicians' reactions to malpractice litigation. *American Journal of Psychiatry, 142*(4), 437–440.

Ciarlo, J. A. (1979). Awareness, use, and consequences of evaluative data in a community mental health center. *Community Mental Health Journal, 15*(1), 7–16.

Claiborne, C. D., Berberoglu, L. S., Nerison, R. M., & Somberg, D. R. (1994). The client's perspective: Ethical judgements and perceptions of therapist practices. *Professional Psychology: Research and Practice, 25*(3), 268–274.

Cohen, R. J. (1979). *Malpractice: A guide for mental health professionals.* New York: Free Press.

Cohen, R. J. (1990). The professional liability of behavioral scientists. In E. A. Margenau (Ed.), *The encyclopedic handbook of private practice* (pp. 651–663). New York: Gardner Press. (Original work published 1983)

Confidentiality of HIV-Related Information Act, 35 P.C.S.A. 7601 et seq. (1990).

Corey, G. (1984). Ethical issues in group therapy. In P. Keller & L. G. Ritt (Eds.), *Innovations in clinical practice: A source book* (Vol. 3, pp. 406–418). Sarasota, FL: Professional Resource Exchange.

Cross, H., & Deardorff, W. M. (1987). Malpractice in psychotherapy and psychological evaluation. In J. R. McNamara & M. Appel (Eds.), *Critical issues, developments, and trends in professional psychology* (Vol. 3, pp. 55–79). New York: Praeger.

Cull, J. G., & Gill, W. S. (1988). *Suicide Probability Scale.* Los Angeles: Western Psychological Services.

Dauser, P. J., Hedstrom, S. M., & Croteau, J. M. (1995). Effects of disclosure of comprehensive pretherapy information on clients at a university counseling center. *Professional Psychology: Research and Practice, 26*(2), 190–195.

Eichelman, B. S., & Hartwig, A. C. (1995). *Patient violence and the clinician.* Washington, DC: American Psychiatric Press.

Eidetics. (1988). *The malpractice suit: A survival guide for physicians and their families* [Videotape]. Boston: Author.

Eimer, B. (1988). A patient's guide to psychotherapy. In P. Keller & S. Heyman (Eds.), *Innovations in clinical practice: A source book* (Vol. 7, pp. 499–501). Sarasota, FL: Professional Resource Exchange.

Elwork, A. (1993, April). Adolescents and informed consent: Facts and fictions. *Pennsylvania Psychologist Update,* pp. 1–3.

Epstein, R. S., & Simon, R. I. (1990). The Exploitation Index: An early warning indicator of boundary violations in psychotherapy. *Bulletin of the Menninger Clinic, 54*(4), 450–465.

Eskenazi, A. (1990). An orientation letter for new clients. In L. G. Ritt & S. R. Heyman (Eds.), *Innovations in clinical practice: A source book* (Vol. 9, p. 423) Sarasota, FL: Professional Resource Exchange.

Everstine, L., Everstine, D. H., Heyman, G. M., True, R. H., Frey, D. H., Johnson, H. G., & Seiden, R. H. (1980). Privacy and confidentiality in psychotherapy. *American Psychologist, 35*(9), 828–840.

Ewing, C. P. (1983). Ethical issues in clinical practice. In P. Keller & L. G. Ritt (Eds.), *Innovations in clinical practice: A source book* (Vol. 2, pp. 399–410). Sarasota, FL: Professional Resource Exchange.

Ewing, C. P. (1990). Legal issues in terminating treatment. In E. A. Margenau (Ed.), *The encyclopedic handbook of private practice* (pp. 720–236). New York: Gardner Press.

Ewing, J. A. (1984). Detecting alcoholism: The CAGE questionnaire. *Journal of the American Medical Association, 252,* 1905–1907.

Fine, M. A., & Kurdek, L. A. (1993). Reflections on determining authorship credit and authorship order on faculty–student collaborations. *American Psychologist, 48*(11), 1141–1147.

Folman, R. (1990). *Legislative action on therapist misconduct: Implications for clinical training and treatment.* Address presented at the annual convention of the American Psychological Association, Boston.

Folstein, M. F., Folstein, S. E., & McHugh, P. R. (1975). Mini-Mental State: A practical method for grading the cognitive state of patients for the clinician. *Journal of Psychiatric Research, 12,* 189–198.

Forman, B. (1983). Marketing concepts for psychotherapists. *Psychotherapy in Private Practice, 1*(4), 39–49.

Foster, S. (1996, January). The consequences of violating the "forbidden zone." *Counseling Today,* pp. 25–53.

Fox, R. E. (1992). Proceedings of the American Psychological Association, Incorporated, for the year 1991. *American Psychologist, 47*(7), 912–913.

Freud, S. (1958). Further recommendations on the technique of psychoanalysis: On beginning the treatment. In J. Strachey (Ed. and Trans.), *The standard edition of the complete psychological works of Sigmund Freud* (Vol. 12, pp. 121–144). London: Hogarth Press. (Original work published 1913)

Fulero, S. M. (1988). *Tarasoff:* Ten years later. *Professional Psychology: Research and Practice, 19*(2), 184–190.

Fulero, S. M., & Wilbert, J. R. (1988). Record-keeping practices of clinical and counseling psychologists: A survey of practitioners. *Professional Psychology Research and Practice, 19*(6), 658–660.

Garber, B. D. (1994). Practical limitations in considering psychotherapy with children of separation and divorce. *Psychotherapy, 31*(2), 254–261.

Garfield, S. L. (1986). Research on client variables in psychotherapy. In S. L. Garfield & A. E. Bergin (Eds.), *Handbook of psychotherapy and behavior change* (3rd ed., pp. 213–256). New York: Wiley.

Garfield, S. L., & Wolpin, M. (1963). Expectations regarding psychotherapy. *Journal of Nervous and Mental Disease, 137,* 353–362.

Gartrell, N. (1992, August 7). *Western Journal of Medicine.*

Goldberg, R. (1995, October). Ethical dilemmas in working with children and adolescents. *Pennsylvania Psychologist Update,* pp. 7–9.

Gonsiorek, J., & Brown, L. (1989). Post-therapy sexual relationships with clients. In G. Schoener, J. Milgrom, J. Gonsiorek, E. Luepker, & R. Conroe (Eds.), *Psychotherapists' sexual involvement with clients* (pp. 289–301). Minneapolis: Walk-In Counseling Center.

Goodman, M., Brown, J., & Deitz, P. (1992). *Managing managed care: A mental health practitioner's survival guide.* Washington, DC: American Psychiatric Press.

Gorlin, R. A. (1990). *Codes of professional responsibility* (2nd ed.). Washington, DC: Bureau of National Affairs.

Gottlieb, M. C. (1993). Avoiding exploitative dual relationships: A decision-making model. *Psychotherapy, 30*(1), 41–48.

Gottschalk, L. A., Mayerson, P., & Gottlieb, A. A. (1967). Prediction and evaluation of outcome in an emergency brief psychotherapy clinic. *Journal of Nervous and Mental Disease, 144,* 77–96.

Grant, R. L., & Maletzky, B. M. (1973). Application of the Weed system to psychiatric records. *Psychiatry in Medicine, 3,* 119–129.

Graziano, A. M., & Fink, R. S. (1973). Second order effects in mental health treatment. *Journal of Consulting and Clinical Psychology, 40,* 356–364.

Group for the Advancement of Psychiatry (GAP). (1990). *Casebook in psychiatric ethics.* New York: Brunner/Mazel.

Grunder, T. M. (1980). On the readability of surgical consent forms. *New England Journal of Medicine, 302,* 900–902.

Gustafson, K. E., & McNamara, J. R. (1987). Confidentiality with minor clients: Issues and guidelines for therapists. *Professional Psychology Research and Practice, 18,* 503–515.

Gustafson, K. E., McNamara, J. R., & Jensen, J. A. (1994). Parents' informed consent decisions regarding psychotherapy for their children: Consideration of therapeutic risks and benefits. *Professional Psychology: Research and Practice, 25*(1), 16–22.

Gutheil, T. G. (1980). Paranoia and progress notes: A guide to forensically informed psychiatric recordkeeping. *Hospital and Community Psychiatry, 31,* 479–482.

Gutheil, T. G. (1992). Approaches to forensic assessment of false claims of sexual misconduct by therapist. *Bulletin of the American Academy of Psychiatry and the Law, 20,* 289–296.

Gutheil, T. G. (1993) Letter to the editor. *Hospital and Community Psychiatry, 44*(10), 1005.

Gutheil, T. G., & Appelbaum, P. S. (1982). *The clinical handbook of psychiatry and the law.* New York: McGraw-Hill.

Gutheil, T. G, & Gabbard, G. O. (1993). The concept of boundaries in clinical practice: Theoretical and risk management dimensions. *American Journal of Psychiatry, 150,* 188–196.

Guy, J. K., Brown, C. K., & Poelstra, P. L. (1992). Safety concerns and protective measures used by psychotherapists. *Professional Psychology Research and Practice, 23*(5), 421–423.

Haas, L. J., & Malouf, J. L. (1989). *Keeping up the good work: A practitioner's guide to mental health ethics.* Sarasota, FL: Professional Resource Exchange.

Haas, L. J., Malouf, J. L., & Mayerson, N. H. (1986). Ethical dilemmas in psychological practice: Results of a national survey. *Professional Psychology Research and Practice, 17,* 317–321.

Hall, J. E. (1988). Records for psychologists. In P. A. Keller & S. R. Heyman (Eds.), *Innovations in clinical practice: A source book* (Vol. 7, pp. 243–246). Sarasota, FL: Professional Resource Exchange. (Original work published 1987)

Handelsman, M. M. (1990). Do written consent forms influence clients' first impressions of therapists? *Professional Psychology Research and Practice, 21*(6), 451–454.

Handelsman, M. M., & Galvin, M. D. (1988). Facilitating informed consent for outpatient psychotherapy: A suggested written format. *Professional Psychology: Research and Practice, 19*(2), 223–225.

Handelsman, M. M., Kemper, M. B., Kesson-Craig, P., McLain, J., & Johnsrud, C. (1986). Use, content, and readability of written informed consent forms for treatment. *Professional Psychology: Research and Practice, 17,* 514–518.

Hansen, J. C., Green, S., & Kutner, K. B. (1989). Ethical issues facing school psychologists working with families. *Professional School Psychology, 4,* 245–255.

Hare-Mustin, R. T., Marecek, J., Kaplan, A. G., & Liss-Levinson, N. (1979). Rights of clients, responsibilities of therapists. *American Psychologist, 34,* 3–16.

Hawkins, I. L., & Bullock, S. L. (1995). Informed consent and religious values: A neglected area of diversity. *Psychotherapy, 32*(2), 293–300.

Herron, W. G., & Sitkowski, S. (1986). Effect of fees on psychotherapy: What is the evidence? *Professional Psychology: Research and Practice, 17*(4), 347–351.

Higuchi, S. A. (1994). Recent managed care legislative and legal issues. In R. L. Lowman & R. J. Resnick (Eds.), *The mental health professional's guide to managed care* (pp. 83–118). Washington, DC: American Psychological Association.

Hillard, J. R. (1995). Predicting suicide. *Psychiatric Services, 46*(3), 223–225.

Hines, P., & Hare-Mustin, R. (1978). Ethical concerns in family therapy. *Professional Psychology, 9,* 165–171.

Hirsh, H. L. (1978). Will your medical records get you into trouble? *Legal Aspects of Medical Practice, 6,* 46–51.

Hirshfeld, R., & Davidson, L. (1988). Risk factors for suicide. In A. J. Frances & R. E. Hales (Eds.), *American Psychiatric Press review of psychiatry* (Vol. 7, pp. 307–333). Washington, DC: American Psychiatric Press.

Hodges, W. F. (1991). *Interventions for children of divorce: Custody, access, and psychotherapy.* New York: Wiley.

Hoffman, R. S. (1980). The itemized statement in clinical psychiatry: A new concept in billing. *Journal of Irreproducible Results, 26*(3), 7.

Hulteng, R. J., & Goldman, E. B. (1986). Potential liability in outpatient practice: A primer for psychotherapists. In L. G. Ritt & S. R. Heyman (Eds.), *Innovations in clinical practice: A source book* (Vol. 5, pp. 233–242). Sarasota, FL: Professional Resource Exchange.

Hussey, W. R. (1986). How to use small claims court for collections. In L. G. Ritt & S. R. Heyman (Eds.), *Innovations in clinical practice: A source book* (Vol. 5, pp. 245–256). Sarasota, FL: Professional Resource Exchange.

Hurvitz, N. (1976). Marital problems following psychotherapy with one spouse. *Journal of Consulting Psychology, 31,* 38–47.

Interstate Insurance Group. (1994, October). *Psychologists professional liability claims-made insurance policy* [Form No. PLJ-2008]. (Available from Chicago Insurance Company, 55 E. Monroe St., Chicago, IL 60603)

Jaffee v. Redmond et al., 51 F.3d 1346, WL 149366 (7th Cir. 1995).

Jensen, J. A., McNamara, J. R., & Gustafson, K. E. (1991). Parents' and clinicians' attitudes toward the risks and benefits of child psychotherapy: A study of informed-consent content. *Professional Psychology Research and Practice, 22*(2), 161–170.

Jobes, D. A., & Berman, A. L. (1993). Suicide and malpractice liability: Assessing and revising policies, procedures, and practice in outpatient settings. *Professional Psychology: Research and Practice. 24*(1), 91–99.

Kachorek, J. (1990). Record keeping. In E. A. Margenau (Ed.), *The encyclopedic handbook of private practice* (pp. 96–112). New York: Gardner Press.

Kagle, J. D. (1991). *Social work records* (2nd ed.). Belmont, CA: Wadsworth.

Kaplan, A. I. (1990). Nonsexual dual relationships: Protecting the psychologist. *Illinois Psychologist, 28*(3), 25, 30.

Keith-Spiegel, P. (1977, September). *Sex with clients: Ten reasons why it is a very stupid thing to do.* Paper presented at the annual convention of the American Psychological Association Washington, DC.

Keith-Spiegel, P., & Koocher, G. (1985). *Ethics in psychology: Professional standards and cases.* New York: Random House.

Keller, P. A., & Ritt, L. G. (1982). Introduction to office forms, In P. A. Keller & L. G. Ritt (Eds.), *Innovations in clinical practice: A source book* (Vol. 1, pp. 213–226). Sarasota, FL: Professional Resource Exchange.

Kennedy, J. A. (1992). *Fundamentals of psychiatric treatment planning.* Washington, DC: American Psychiatric Press.

Kertay, L. & Reviere, S. (1993). The use of touch in psychotherapy:Theoretical and ethical considerations. *Psychotherapy, 30*(1), 32–40.

King, J. H. Jr. (1977). *The law of medical malpractice.* St. Paul, MN: West.

Kiresuk, T. & Sherman, R. (1968). Goal attainment scaling: A general method for evaluating comprehensive mental health programs. *Community Mental Health Journal, 4,* 443–453.

Kiresuk, T. , Smith, A., & Cardillo, J. E. (Eds.). (1994). *Goal attainment scaling: Applications, theory, and measurement.* Hillsdale, NJ: Erlbaum.

Klein, J., Macbeth, J., & Onek, J. (1984). *Legal issues in the private practice of psychiatry.* Washington, DC: American Psychiatric Press.

Knapp, S. (1980). A primer on malpractice for psychologists. *Professional Psychology: Research and Practice, 11,* 606–611.

Knapp, S. (1992a, April 16). *Record keeping.* Handout presented at workshop, Practicing Safely and Ethically in the 1990s, Pittsburgh, PA.

Knapp, S. (1992b, April). Medicare update. *Pennsylvania Psychologist Update,* p. 7.

Knapp, S., & Tepper, A. M. (1992, May). Caught in the middle: The parent, child and psychologist triangle. *Pennsylvania Psychologist Quarterly,* p. 16.

Knapp, S., & VandeCreek, L. (1981b). Behavioral medicine: Its malpractice risks for psychologists. *Professional Psychology: Research and Practice, 12,* 677–683.

Knapp, S. & VandeCreek, L. (1983). Malpractice risks with suicidal patients. *Psychotherapy: Theory, Research, and Practice, 20,* 274–280.

Knapp, S., & VandeCreek, L. (1990). *Pennsylvania law and psychology.* Harrisburg: Pennsylvania Psychological Association.

Knapp, S., VandeCreek, L., & Tepper, A. (1994, May). Patient access to records: What should the practicing psychologist do? *Pennsylvania Psychologist Quarterly,* pp. 18–19.

Koss, M.P. (1979). Length of psychotherapy for clients seen in private practice. *Journal of Consulting and Clinical Psychology, 47,* 210–212.

Kovacs, A. L. (1987). Insurance billing: The growing risk of lawsuits against psychologists. *Independent Practitioner, 7,* 21–24.

Kramer, S. A. (1990). *Positive endings in psychotherapy: Bringing meaningful closure to therapeutic relationships.* San Francisco: Jossey-Bass.

Lamb, D. H., Clark, C., Drumheller, P., Frizzell, K., & Surrey, L. (1989). Applying *Tarasoff* to AIDS-related psychotherapy issues. *Professional Psychology, 20*(1), 37–43.

Lazarus, A. A. (1976). *Multi-modal behavior therapy.* New York: Springer.

Legal issues: How to avoid problems with cellular phones and fax machines. (1992). *Psychotherapy Finances, 18*(2), 3.

Levenstein, J. (1994a). Treatment documentation in private practice: I. The PIC treatment plan. *Independent Practitioner, 14*(4), 181–185

Levenstein, J. (1994b). Treatment documentation in private practice: II. PIRC progress notes. *Independent Practitioner, 14*(5), 233–237.

Ley, P. (1982). Studies in recall in medical settings. *Human Learning, 1,* 223–233.

Liberman, B. (1990). Letter to the editor. *Independent Psychologist, 10*(4), 5.

Lidz, C. W., Meisel, A., Zerubavel, E., Carter, M., Sestak, R. M., & Roth, L. H. (1984). *Informed consent: A study of decision-making in psychiatry.* New York: Guilford Press.

Lipman, A. J. (1995). Treating borderline personality disorder. *Contemporary Psychology, 40*(10) 996–997.

Littrell, J., & Ashford, J. B. (1995). Is it proper for psychologists to discuss medications with clients? *Professional Psychology: Research and Practice, 26*(3), 238–244.

LoVerde, M. E., Prochazka, A. V., & Byyny, R. L. (1989). Research consent forms: Continued unreadability and increasing length. *Journal of General Internal Medicine, 4*(5), 410–412.

Mallory, S. D., Gert, B., & Culver, C. M. (1986). Family coercion and valid consent. *Theoretical Medicine, 7,* 123–126.

Maltsberger, J. T. (1986). *Suicide risk: The formation of clinical judgement.* New York: New York University Press.

Margolin, G. (1982). Ethical and legal considerations in marital and family therapy. *American Psychologist, 37*(7), 788–801.

Marine, E. C., & Caudill, O. B. (1996, Winter). What have we learned about false memory cases? *New Mexico Psychologist,* pp. 11–12.

Marsh, D. T. (1995, January). Confidentiality and the rights of families: Resolving possible conflicts. *Pennsylvania Psychologist Update,* pp. 1–3.

Meek, C. (1986b). Guidelines for using an answering machine in your practice. In L. G. Ritt & S. R. Heyman (Eds.), *Innovations in clinical practice: A source book* (Vol. 5, pp. 271–275). Sarasota, FL: Professional Resource Exchange.

Meek, C. (1987). Suggestions on the collection of fees. In P. A. Keller & S. R. Heyman (Eds.), *Innovations in clinical practice: A source book* (Vol. 6, pp. 271–276). Sarasota, FL: Professional Resource Exchange.

Meek, C. (1990). Parent/guardian responsibility for a child in treatment. In L. G. Ritt & S. R. Heyman (Eds.), *Innovations in clinical practice: A source book* (Vol. 9, pp. 265–270). Sarasota, FL: Professional Resource Exchange.

Meek, C., Keller, P. A., & Ritt, L. G. (1985). A collection of office forms. In P. A. Keller & L. G. Ritt (Eds.), *Innovations in clinical practice: A source book* (Vol. 4, pp. 345–360). Sarasota, FL: Professional Resource Exchange.

Meisel, A., Roth, L. H., & Lidz, C. W. (1977). Toward a model of the legal doctrine of informed consent. *American Journal of Psychiatry, 134,* 285–289.

Meiselman, K. C. (1990). *Resolving the trauma of incest.* San Francisco: Jossey-Bass.

Meyer, J. D., & Fink, C. (1989). Psychiatric symptoms from prescription medications. *Professional Psychology: Research and Practice, 20*(2), 90–96.

Meyer, R. G., Landis, E. R., & Hays, J. R. (1988). *Law for the psychotherapist.* New York: Norton.

Monahan, J. (1981). *The clinical prediction of violent behavior.* Washington, DC: U.S. Government Printing Office.

Monahan, J. (1993). Limiting therapist exposure to *Tarasoff* liability: Guidelines for risk containment. *American Psychologist, 48*(3), 242–250.

Monahan, J., & Stedman, H. J. (Eds.), (1994). *Violence and mental disorder: Developments in risk assessment.* Chicago: University of Chicago Press.

Moreland, K. L., Eyde, L. D., Robertson, G. J., Primoff, E. S., & Most, R. B. (1995). Assessment of test user qualifications: A research-based measurement procedure. *American Psychologist, 50*(1), 14–23.

Morris, R. J. (1993). Ethical issues in the assessment and treatment of children and adolescents. *Register Report, 19*(1), 4–12.

Morrison, J. K., Fredrico, M., & Rosenthal, H. J. (1975). Contracting confidentiality in group psychotherapy. *Journal of Forensic Psychology, 7,* 1–6.

Nagy, T. F. (1994, July–August). Guidelines and direction when treating clients with repressed memories. *National Psychologist,* pp. 8–9.

National Center for Health Statistics. (1988). *Vital statistics mortality data: Multliple cause-of-death detail.* Hyattsville, MD: U.S. Department of Health and Human Services.

Negley, E. T. (1985). Malpractice prevention and risk management for clinicians. In P. A. Keller & L. G. Ritt (Eds.), *Innovations in clinical practice: A source book* (Vol. 4, pp. 243–251). Sarasota, FL: Professional Resource Exchange.

Nowell, D., & Spruill, J. (1993). If it's not absolutely confidential, will information be disclosed? *Professional Psychology: Research and Practice, 24*(3), 367–369.

Parsons, J. P., & Wincze, J. P. (1995). A survey of client–therapist sexual involvement in Rhode Island as reported by subsequent treating therapists. *Professional Psychology: Research and Practice, 26*(2), 171–175.

Patten, C., Barnett, T., & Houlihan, D. (1991). Ethics in marital and family therapy: A review of the literature. *Professional Psychology: Research and Practice, 22,* 171–175.

Pekarik, G. (1985). Coping with dropouts. *Professional Psychology: Research and Practice, 16*(1), 114–123.

Perry, S., France, A., & Clarkin, J. (1990). *A DSM-III R casebook of treatment selection.* New York: Brunner/Mazel.

Philadelphia Society of Clinical Psychologists, Committee on Ethics. (1988, January–February). Ethical issues in psychotherapy termination. *Pennsylvania Psychologist,* p. 10.

Piercy, F., Lasswell, M., & Brock, G. (1989). *AAMFT forms book.* Washington, DC: American Association for Marriage and Family Therapy.

Polythress, N. G. (1992). Expert testimony on violence and dangerousness: Roles for mental health professionals. *Forensic Reports, 5*(1), 135–150.

Pope, K. S. (1987). Preventing therapist–patient sexual intimacy: Therapy for a therapist at risk. *Professional Psychology Research and Practice, 18*(6), 624–628.

Pope, K. S. (1988a). Dual relationships: A source of ethical, legal and clinical problems. *Independent Practitioner, 8*(4), 17–25.

Pope, K. S. (1988b). How clients are harmed by sexual contact with mental health professionals: The syndrome and its prevalence. *Journal of Counseling and Development, 67,* 222–226.

Pope, K. S. (1988c). Fee policies and procedures: Causes of malpractice suits and ethics complaints. *Independent Practitioner, 8*(4), 24–29.

Pope, K. (1988d). Avoid malpractice in the area of diagnosis, assessment, and testing. *Independent Practitioner, 8*(3), 18–25.

Pope , K. (1988e). More on avoiding malpractice in the area of diagnosis, assessment, and testing. *Independent Practitioner, 8*(4), 23–24.

Pope, K. S. (1989a). Malpractice suits, licensing disciplinary actions and ethics cases: Frequencies, causes, and costs. *Independent Practitioner, 9*(1), 22–26.

Pope, K. S. (1989b). Therapists who become sexually intimate with a patient: Classification, dynamics, recidivism and rehabilitation. *Independent Practitioner, 9*(3), 28–34.

Pope, K. S. (1990). Therapist–patient sex as sex abuse: Six scientific, professional, and practical dilemmas in addressing victimization and rehabilitation. *Professional Psychology: Research and Practice, 21,* 227–239.

Pope, K. S., & Bouhoutsos, J. (1986). *Sexual intimacy between therapists and patients.* New York: Praeger.

Presser, N. R., & Pfost, K. S. (1985). A format for individual psychotherapy session notes. *Professional Psychology: Research and Practice, 16*(1), 11–16.

Pressman, R. M., & Siegler, R. (1983). *The independent practitioner: Practice management for the allied health professional.* Homewood, IL: Dow Jones-Irwin.

Psychiatrists' Risk Retention Group. (1996). *Description of coverage.* Arlington, VA: Author.

Quinn, V. (n.d.). *Professional therapy never includes sex.* (Available from California Department of Consumer Affairs, 1020 N Street, Sacramento, CA 95814; single copies available at no charge)

Redlich, F. C., & Pope, K. S. (1980). Ethics of mental health training. *Journal of Nervous and Mental Disease, 168,* 709–714.

Repressed memory claims expected to soar. (1996, May–June). *National Psychologist,* p. 7.

Reynolds, W. M. (1991). *Adult Suicidal Ideation Questionnaire.* Odessa, FL: Psychological Assessment Resources.

Rosenthal, V. A. (1976, Spring). A bare branch with buds. *Voices,* pp. 2–10.

Roth, L. (Ed.). (1987). *Clinical treatment of the violent person.* New York: Guilford Press.

Rubanowitz, D. (1987). Public attitudes toward psychotherapist–client confidentiality. *Professional Psychology: Research and Practice, 18,* 613–618.

Rudd, M. D., Dahm, P. F., & Rajab, M. H. (1993). Diagnostic comorbidity in persons with suicidal ideation and behavior. *American Journal of Psychiatry, 150,* 928–934.

Sadoff, R. L. (1988). Record keeping in private practice. In F. Flach (Ed.), *Psychiatric risk management.* New York: Directions in Psychiatry.

Satler, J. M. (1977). The effects of therapist–client racial similarity. In A. S. Gurman & A. M. Razin (Eds.), *Effective psychotherapy: A handbook of research* (pp. 250–288). Elmsford, NY: Pergamon Press.

Saunders, T. R. (1993). Some ethical and legal features of child custody disputes: A case illustration an applications. *Psychotherapy, 30*(1), 49–58.

Schinka, J. (1984). *Personal Problems Checklist.* Odessa, FL: Psychological Assessment Resources.

Schinka, J. (1989). *Health Problems Checklist.* Odessa, FL: Psychological Assessment Resources.

Schlosser, B., & Tower, R. B. (1991). Office policies for assessment services. In P. A. Keller & S. R. Heyman (Eds.), *Innovations in clinical practice: A source book* (Vol. 10, pp. 393–405). Sarasota, FL: Professional Resource Exchange.

Schwitzgebel, R., L. & Schwitzgebel, R. K. (1980). *Law and psychological practice.* New York: Wiley.

Sederer, L. I., & Libby, M. (1995). False allegations of sexual misconduct: Clinical and institutional considerations. *Psychiatric Services, 46*(2), 160–163.

Simon, R. I. (1992). *Clinical psychiatry and the law* (2nd ed.). Washington, DC: American Psychiatric Press.

Skinner, H. A. (1982). The Drug Abuse Screening Test (DAST). *Addictive Behaviors, 7,* 363–371.

Slovenko, R. (1973). *Psychiatry and law.* Boston: Little, Brown.

Small, R. (1994). *Maximizing third-party reimbursement in your mental health practice* (2nd ed.). Sarasoa, FL: Professional Resource Exchange.

Smith, D., & Fitzpatrick, M. (1995). Patient–therapist boundary issues An integrative review of theory and research. *Professional Psychology: Research and Practice, 26*(5), 499–506.

Smith, M. L., & Glass, G. V. (1977). Meta-analysis of psychotherapy outcome studies. *American Psychologist, 32,* 752–760.

Soisson, E., VandeCreek, L., & Knapp, S. (1987). Thorough record keeping: A good defense in a litigious era. *Professional Psychology: Research and Practice, 18,* 498–502.

Sommers-Flanagan, J., & Sommers-Flanagan, R. (1995). Intake interviewing with suicidal patients: A systematic approach. *Professional Psychology: Research and Practice, 26*(1), 41–47.

Sonne, J. L. (1994). Multiple relationships: Does the new ethics code answer the right questions? *Professional Psychology: Research and Practice , 25*(4), 336–343.

Soreff, S. M., & McDuffee, M. A. (1993). *Documentation survival handbook for psychiatrists and other mental health professionals: A clinician's guide to charting for better care, certification, reimbursement, and risk management.* Seattle, WA: Hogrefe & Huber.

Sperry, L., Gudeman, J. E., Blackwell, B., & Faulkner, L. R. (1992). *Psychiatric case formulations.* Washington, DC: American Psychiatric Press.

Stadler, H. A. (1985). *Confidentiality: The counselor's dilemma* [Videotape]. Alexandria, VA: American Association for Counseling and Development.

Stromberg, C. D., & Dellinger, A. (1993, December). Malpractice and other professional liability. In *The psychologist's legal update, 3.* Washington, DC: National Register of Health Service Providers in Psychology.

Stromberg, C. D., Haggarty, D. J., Mishkin, B., Liebenluft, R. F., McMillan, M. H., Rubin, B. L., & Trilling, H. R. (1988). *The psychologist's legal handbook.* Washington, DC: National Register of Health Service Providers in Psychology.

Stromberg, C. D., Lindberg, D., Mishkin, B., & Baker, M. (1993, April). Privacy, confidentiality, and privilege. In *The psychologist's legal update, 1* (p. 8). Washington, DC: National Register of Health Service Providers in Psychology.

Stromberg, C. D., Schneider, J., & Joondeph, B. (1993, August). Dealing with potentially dangerous patients. In *The psychologist's legal update, 2* (p. 10). Washington, DC: National Register of Health Service Providers in Psychology.

Stuart, R. B. (1975). *Treatment contract*. Champaign, IL: Research Press.

Sturm, I. E. (1987). The psychologist and the problem-oriented record (POR). *Professional Psychology: Research and Practice, 18,* 155–158.

Sullivan, T., Martin, W. L., & Handelsman, M. M. (1993). Practical benefits of an informed-consent procedure: An empirical investigation. *Professional Psychology: Research and Practice, 24*(2), 160–163.

Sweet, J. J. (1990). Further considerations of ethics in psychological testing: A broader perspective on releasing records. *Illinois Psychologist, 28*(4), p. 5–9.

Tarasoff v. Regents of the University of California, 131 Cal. Rptr. 14, 551 P.2d 334 (1976).

Taube, D. O., & Elwork, A. (1990). Researching the effects of confidentiality law on patients' self-disclosures. *Professional Psychology Research and Practice, 22*(1), 72–75.

Taylor, L., & Adelman, H. S. (1989). Reframing the confidentiality dilemma to work in children's best interests. *Professional Psychology: Research and Practice, 20,* 79–83.

Teisman, M. (1980). Convening strategies in family therapy. *Family Process, 19,* 393–400.

Ten steps to create a successful treatment plan. (1993, August). *Managed Care Strategies, 1*(6), 5–6.

Tepper, A. M., Rinella, V. J., Jr., & Siegel, A. M. (1991, November). Subpoenas and court orders in the everyday practice of psychology. *Pennsylvania Psychologist Quarterly,* pp. 14–15.

Thorn, B. E., Shealy, R. C., & Briggs, S.D. (1993). Sexual misconduct in psychotherapy: Reactions to a consumer-oriented brochure. *Professional Psychology: Research and Practice, 24*(1), 75–82.

Tranel, D. (1994). The release of psychological data to nonexperts: Ethical and legal considerations. *Psychotherapy: Theory, Research,and Practice, 25*(1), 33–38.

Truscott, D., Evans, J., & Mansell, S. (1995). Outpatient psychotherapy with dangerous clients: A model of clinical decision making. *Professional Psychology: Research and Practice, 26*(5), 484–490.

United Nations. (1971, December 20). *Declaration of the rights of mentally retarded persons* (General Assembly Resolution No. 2856 [XXV]). New York: Author.

Vaccarino, J. M. (1978). Consent, informed consent, and consent forms. *New England Journal of Medicine, 298,* 455.

Vinson, J. S. (1987). Use of complaint procedures in cases of therapist–patient sexual contact. *Professional Psychology: Research and Practice, 18*(2), 159–164.

Walters, G. C., Solomon, G. S., & Walden, V. R. (1982). Use of the MMPI in predicting persistence of male and female patients. *Journal of Clinical Psychology, 38,* 80–83.

Weed, L. L. (1971). *Medical records, medical education and patient care: The problem-oriented record as a basic tool.* Chicago: Yearbook Medical.

Weiner, B. A., & Wettstein, R. M. (1993). *Legal issues in mental health care.* New York: Plenum Press.

Weiner, I. (1989). On competence and ethicality in psychodiagnostic assessment. *Journal of Personality Assessment, 53,* 827–831.

Wendorf, D., & Wendorf, R. (1985). A systemic view of family therapy ethics. *Family Process, 24,* 443–353.

Werth, J. L., & Carney, J. (1994). Incorporating HIV-related issues into graduate student training. *Professional Psychology: Research and Practice, 25*(4), 458–465.

Werth, J. L., & Liddle, B. J. (1994). Psychotherapists' attitudes toward suicide. *Psychotherapy: Theory, Research, and Practice, 31*(3), 440–448.

Whiston, S. C., & Sexton, T. L. (1993). An overview of psychotherapy outcome research: Implications for practice. *Professional Psychology: Research and Practice, 24,* 43–51.

Widiger, T. A., & Rorer, L. G. (1984). The responsible psychotherapist. *American Psychologist, 39,* 503–515.

Wilbert, J. R., Charles, S. C., Warnecke, R. B., & Lichtenbert, R. (1987). Coping with the stress of malpractice litigation. *Illinois Medical Journal, 17*(1), pp. 23–27.

Wilcoxon, A., & Fenell, D. (1983). Engaging the non-attending spouse in marital therapy through the use of therapist-initiated written communication. *Journal of Marital and Family Therapy, 9,* 199–203.

Wilkinson, A. P. (1982). Psychiatric malpractice: Identifying areas of liability. *Trial, 18*(10), 73–77, 89–90.

Willbach, D. (1989). Ethics and family therapy: The case management of family violence. *Journal of Marital and Family Therapy, 1,* 43–52.

Williams, M. (1992). Exploitation and inference: Mapping the damage from therapist-patient sexual involvement. *American Psychologist, 47*(3), 412–421.

Wilson, S. J. (1980). *Recording guidelines for social workers.* New York: Free Press.

Wollersheim, J. P. (1974). The assessment of suicide potential via interview methods. *Psychotherapy, 11,* 222–225.

Woody, R. H. (1983). Avoiding malpractice in psychotherapy. In P. A. Keller & L. G. Ritt (Eds.), *Innovations in clinical practice: A sourcebook* (Vol. 2, pp. 205–216). Sarasota, FL: Professional Resource Exchange.

Woody, R. H. (1988a). *Fifty ways to avoid malpractice: A guidebook for mental health professionals.* Sarasota, FL Professional Resource Exchange.

Woody, R. H. (1991). *Quality care in mental health: Assuring the best clinical services.* San Francisco: Jossey-Bass.

Wright, R. H. (1981a). Psychologists and professional liability (malpractice) insurance. *American Psychologist, 36,* 1485–1493.

Wright, R. H. (1981b). What to do until the malpractice lawyer comes: A survivor's manual. *American Psychologist, 36,* 1535–1541.

Wyatt, R. J. (1994). *Practical psychiatric practice: Forms and protocols for clinical use.* Washington, DC: American Psychiatric Press.

Wyatt v. Stickney, 325 F. Supp. 781 (M.D. Ala. 1971).

Younggren, J. N. (1993). Ethical issues in religious psychotherapy. *Register Report, 19*(4), pp. 1–8.

Younggren, J. N. (1995). Informed consent: Simply a reminder. *Register Report, 21*(2), 6–7.

Zipple, A. M., Landle, S., Spaniol, L., & Fisher, H. (1990). Client confidentiality and the family's need to know: Strategies for resolving the conflict. *Community Mental Health Journal, 26,* 553–545.

Zhu, S., & Pierce, J. P. (1995). A new scheduling method for time-limited counseling. *Professional Psychology: Research and Practice, 26*(6), 624–625.

Zuckerman, E. L. (1995). *Clinician's thesaurus* (4th ed.): *The guidebook for writing psychological reports.* New York: Guilford Press.

Zung, B. J. (1979). Psychometric properties of the MAST and two briefer versions. *Journal of Studies on Alcohol, 40,* 845–859.

Index

Note: The titles of figures, forms, and handouts are shown in **boldface**.